T0351494

NEMESIS
THE FIRST IRON WARSHIP
AND HER WORLD

HEIC Steam Vessel Nemesis
By the river Eurotas Zeus as a swan took Leda, and from the egg she laid came forth Helen of Troy. And so Leda became a god, Nemesis, the divine anger, the keeper of order. Thereafter, if man displeased the gods either by angering them through immorality or inciting their jealousy by excessive success or happiness, the imprudent mortal was pursued by Nemesis bearing both a wheel and a sword, a scourge hanging at her girdle.

NEMESIS
THE FIRST IRON WARSHIP
AND HER WORLD

ADRIAN G. MARSHALL

RIDGE BOOKS
SINGAPORE

© Adrian Marshall

Published under the Ridge Books imprint by:

NUS Press
National University of Singapore
AS3-01-02, 3 Arts Link
Singapore 117569
Fax: (65) 6774-0652
E-mail: nusbooks@nus.edu.sg
Website: http://nuspress.nus.edu.sg

ISBN: 978-9971-69-822-5 (Paper)

First edition 2016
Reprint 2017

All rights reserved. This book, or parts thereof, may not be reproduced in any form or by any means, electronic or mechanical, including photocopying, recording or any information storage and retrieval system now known or to be invented, without written permission from the Publisher.

National Library Board, Singapore Cataloguing-in-Publication Data

Marshall, Adrian G., author.
   Nemesis : the first iron warship and her world /
   Adrian G. Marshall. – Singapore : NUS Press, National
   University of Singapore, [2016]

      pages cm
      Includes bibliographical references and index.
      ISBN : 978-9971-69-822-5 (paperback)

      1. Nemesis (Warship) - History. 2. Warships – Great
   Britain – History – 19th century. 3. Sea-power – Great
   Britain – History – 19th century. 4. Great Britain – History,
   Naval – 19th century. 5. Great Britain – Colonies – Asia –
   History – 19th century. 6. Navy-yard and naval stations,
   British – Singapore – History – 19th century. I. Title.

   VA454
   359.0094109034 -- dc23
   OCN908412980

Cover Image: 'Nemesis, with other boats, destroying the Chinese War Junks in Anson's Bay, 7 January 1841.' Original watercolour by W. A. Knell, from which the etching was taken. © National Maritime Museum, Greenwich, London.

Designed by: Nelani Jinadasa

Printed by: Mainland Press Pte Ltd

for Tuck-Chee

CONTENTS

LIST OF ILLUSTRATIONS

LIST OF MAPS

LIST OF TABLES
(in Appendix 1, p. 251)

PREFACE

"In this history I know that you will find all the entertainment you can desire; and if any good quality is missing, I am certain that it is the fault of its dog of an author rather than any default in the subject."

—Cervantes, Don Quixote, part 1, chapter 9

This is the story of the world's first iron warship – the first ship with truly watertight transverse bulkheads, the first iron steamer to enter the Southern Hemisphere, to round the Cape of Good Hope and steam into East Asian waters – and her role in the expansion of Britain's power in the East, and in the introduction of iron construction to the most powerful of nineteenth century navies, the Royal Navy. The Nemesis, built in England at the end of the period later known as the Industrial Revolution, epitomised the very essence of that revolution – iron, coal and steam in the service of mankind, particularly in the service of transportation and, here I should add, of empire. And a study of her life provides a fascinating glimpse of the eastern extremities of that empire at the start of Queen Victoria's long reign, and of the men (very rarely women) who served there. Indeed, as Bernard said in his preface to the first edition of his book on the early years of the ship, "In addition, therefore, to her own interesting tale, the Nemesis supplied a valuable foundation upon which to build up a more enlarged history."

Of course that enlarged history is essentially anglo-centric, but then the *Nemesis* served a government who viewed the world anglo-centrically and virtually all that we know of her derives from that imperial world. More sadly, almost all that we know of her derives from the rulers of that world, the captains and admirals and newspaper editors. What life was like for most of those who served in her, those sailors and soldiers, British and Indian, African and Chinese, often crammed below or upon her single deck, can only be guessed at.

Likewise it is difficult to get any true picture of how the indigenous people of the places she visited, rulers or ruled, viewed her or her role – the people of China, the Malay Archipelago, Siam, Burma and India. The *Nemesis* served British imperialism and the British, like others before them, came to Asia primarily to take what they desired. Of course such rapaciousness needed justification, and these justifications were by the height of empire codified into a high moral purpose: to bring security, religion, education, health, and, through free trade, wealth. Or as Queen Victoria herself put it: "to protect the poor native and to advance civilisation." Some communities did indeed come to recognise these as benefits, for example in Rajah Brooke's Sarawak; to others, such as the Chinese, contact with the British brought little but misery.

The British in their imperial territories were always greatly outnumbered and, seeking greater security, created barriers to protect themselves, many social and cultural rather than physical. These barriers were built upon an underlying belief in their own superiority, a belief essential to any successful imperial enterprise. And such a belief, though incorrect, allowed ordinary people to achieve extraordinary things. If one of the challenges of history is to attempt to see people and events as their contemporaries saw them, then one of its joys is to marvel at things achieved under what seem from today's perspective the most trying of circumstances. I have found the story of this ship full of such marvels.

As a biologist who came across the *Nemesis* through my interest in the visit in the 1850s of the great naturalist Alfred Russel Wallace to Rajah Sir James Brooke in Sarawak, Borneo, I had much to learn about ships and about empire. The main sources of information for each chapter are outlined at the end. A number are contemporary, many are secondary. Only two major primary sources have been examined. Firstly, the British Library in London houses the India Office Records, a vast collection of documents (covering apparently 14 km of shelving), and amongst these are a most valuable handful pertaining to this ship. These yielded data on both the origins of the *Nemesis* and her fate, previously unknown. Secondly, the fine new National Library of Singapore contains copies of contemporary Singapore newspapers which of course reported much on maritime and imperial matters. Two other libraries have proved particularly useful: that of the National Maritime Museum, Greenwich, which contains an unsurpassed collection of books on ships and the sea, and the Sarawak Museum Library in Kuching, Malaysia, which houses a fine collection of early books on Borneo and Southeast Asia. I am greatly indebted to the staff of these institutions for their assistance over many happy days.

Concerning place names, I have generally used modern versions, following Philip's *Atlas of the World, Comprehensive Edition* (London, 2003), giving the nineteenth-century equivalents in brackets at the first mention.

I am most grateful to Peter Schoppert, Director, and Christine Chong Ping Yew, Editor, at NUS Press for the care they have taken over both text and illustrations and for their many wise suggestions; and three anonymous reviewers who, viewing the text as experts in their fields, made significant contributions to the structure of the book. My friend Adrian Foote and my sister Hazel Marshall read the book as non-specialists and provided many valuable comments. Lord and Lady Wilson of Tillyorn provided unsurpassed accommodation in London during some of my researches there. And finally I pay tribute, always and forever, to my partner Tuck-Chee Phung for his unfailing love and support for what has been for me an enormously enjoyable project.

"THE NEMESIS"

"In this splendid vessel, commanded by Captain W. H. Hall, we have the pleasing task of welcoming to our shores the first Iron Steamer that ever rounded the Cape of Good Hope. She is the largest of her class built, being 168 ft long, 29 ft beam, and 630 tons burthen. The engines are 120 horse power, by the celebrated makers Messrs. Forester and Co. of Liverpool, and, of course, upon the best construction. Twenty days coal can on an emergency be stowed in her. She carries two medium 32 pound pivot guns, one aft the other forward, and 10 swivels; and is manned by 50 seamen ... Altogether this beautiful vessel does great credit to her scientific builder John Laird Esq., Birkinghead, Liverpool."

—*The Colombo Observer*, Saturday 10 October 1840
[from the *Singapore Free Press*, 5 November 1840]

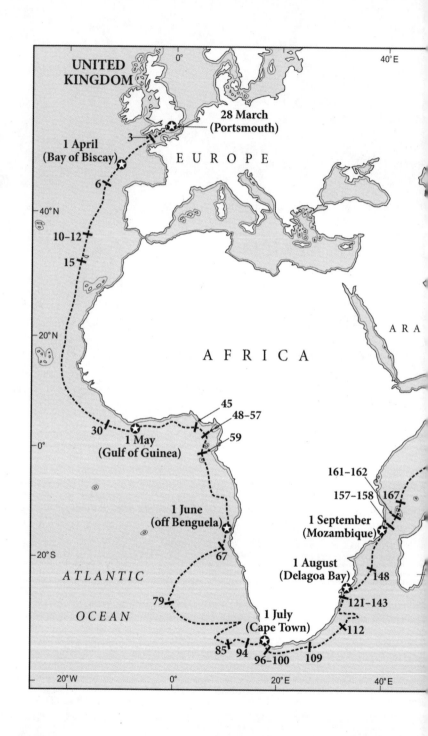

UNITED
KINGDOM

28 March
(Portsmouth)

3

1 April
(Bay of Biscay)

6

E U R O P E

40°E

40°N

10–12

15

20°N

A F R I C A

A R A

0°

30

45

48–57

1 May
(Gulf of Guinea)

59

161–162

157–158 167

1 June
(off Benguela)

1 September
(Mozambique)

20°S

67

1 August
(Delagoa Bay)

148

ATLANTIC

79

121–143

OCEAN

1 July
(Cape Town)

112

85 94

96–100 109

20°W

0°

20°E

40°E

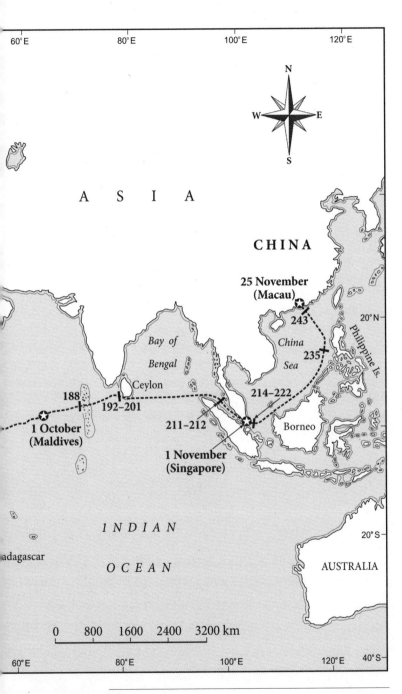

N
W   E
S

A S I A

CHINA

25 November
(Macau)

243

20°N

Bay of
Bengal

China
Sea

235

Philippine Is.

Ceylon

214–222

188

192–201

211–212

1 October
(Maldives)

Borneo

1 November
(Singapore)

I N D I A N

20°S

adagascar

O C E A N

AUSTRALIA

0   800   1600   2400   3200 km

40°S

The voyage to China, 1840 (produced by Lee Li Kheng)

{ 1 }

THE STONES OF ST IVES

It was a clear morning when she sailed, a fine early spring day. If the partings on the quay seemed somewhat subdued, it was perhaps because almost no one there, neither those setting out nor those left behind, knew where she was bound nor the length of her voyage. By mid-morning steam was up and all the crew were on board, together with the few passengers she was to carry to Southampton. From the bridge Captain Hall ordered her cast off, and as the paddles started turning and the low black ship drew away from the quay, muted cheers and last farewells rang out amidst a flutter of scarves and handkerchiefs.[1]

And so the *Nemesis* steamed north down the Mersey as her sails were set, only the two gaffs and the jibs for the wind was light and from the north-east. Passing Perch Rock she turned west, those still watching from Birkenhead seeing the smudge of black smoke from her tall funnel growing fainter and fainter. With little wind and plenty of fuel, Hall kept the engines going and by the time the sun set dead ahead Anglesey lay close to port. In the early evening she turned south-west and dawn of the second day, Sunday 8 March of the year 1840, saw the ship steaming down Cardigan Bay in hazy weather. Hall called those available to Divine Service immediately after breakfast so that he and his most important passenger, her builder John Laird, would have most of the daylight hours free to continue their testing and training. About midday just south of St David's Head the engines were slowed and the crew turned to the guns, both the big 32-pounders as well as some of the

1

long-sixes being test-fired, giving Laird the chance to see how his iron ship acted as if at war.

Throughout the afternoon the weather continued to thicken so that when night fell it was particularly dark. Running under full sail as well as steam at about her maximum speed of 9 knots, Hall set a course which took her well clear of Land's End. None the less he took the precaution of placing a leadsman at the bow before going below for dinner. It had been a long day and the captain and his guests retired early to bed.

At about two o'clock in the morning, the crew mostly asleep and the ship still going full speed, the leadsman suddenly sensed that all was not well, that land lay much too close ahead. He cried out a warning, and First Officer Pedder immediately ordered the course altered to starboard and the sails taken in, but it was too late. With a sickening crash, the Nemesis struck, the bows rising as she ground to a halt, her paddles uselessly churning the water. In the darkness below those asleep were violently woken and now as the engines were stopped officers, sailors and passengers staggered up the steep companionways to the deck, a number nursing bruises but none seriously injured. When some order had been restored Hall saw that his ship was not ashore but rather held fast on submerged rocks, but fortunately on a rising tide. Assessing the damage, it was reported that she had been holed towards the bows in front of the first bulkhead, the first compartment now flooded. Hearing this, Hall and Laird went below again, forward to the bulkhead; it was holding fast, no water seeping through. Doubtless, the two men viewed this with the greatest satisfaction – the value of truly watertight bulkheads, never before found in a ship, so emphatically proved. Without them the Nemesis would certainly have sunk, now no more than a name on the list of the 600 British ships lost at sea that year. But if the bulkheads had proved their worth surely something must be seriously amiss with her compass, a problem bedevilling iron ships at the time, for as dawn broke it was found that she lay on the Stones, a shoal at the entrance to St Ives' Bay on the north coast of Cornwall fully 12 miles east of her intended route.

As the tide rose the deck grew more level, and at about 7 am the engines were started and, floating free, she was backed from the shoal. As St Ives itself provided little shelter, Hall decided to move on to Mount's Bay on the south Cornish coast where temporary repairs could more easily be made, and so they limped anxiously around Land's

End, anchoring off St Michael's Mount just after midday. Although each compartment was provided with a hand-pump this proved too small to be useful, so Hall bought a larger pump from a vessel anchored nearby to empty the flooded compartment, the hole being stopped from the outside with a tarpaulin. Only then could the full extent of the damage be seen: an outer iron plate on the starboard side cut right through, the wooden sleepers of the lower deck forced up and the large bolts holding them sheared off, and the lower plates of the bulkhead severely bent. But although some plates had been indented by as much as 3 inches, Hall and Laird were comforted to see how well the rivets had held. Now the hole was stopped from the inside too, and as dusk fell they were ready to continue eastwards to Southampton, anchoring the following evening in the sheltered waters of the Solent. The next morning, Wednesday, they steamed up Southampton Water to the docks to drop their passengers, though not Mr Laird who wished to oversee repairs, and then back down again to the Royal Naval Dockyard at Portsmouth.

The visit to Portsmouth had not been planned for the *Nemesis* was not a Royal Navy ship. But with her lying safely amongst such ships, it would be useful to consider some facts about that navy with whom she worked closely throughout her life. On 1 May 1840 the Royal Navy, by far the most powerful navy in the world,[2] had 202 ships in commission (Table 1) of which 28 were Line of Battle ships rated First to Third, 31 were Below the Line rated Fourth to Sixth, and 143 were unrated, including 28 steamships. These vessels could be commanded by officers of various ranks – master, lieutenant, commander or captain. To complicate matters, those below the level of captain who were in command of non-rated ships were addressed as Captain, such officers seeking eventually to be posted, becoming a post-captain in command of a rated ship – though still addressed as Captain! And to add further confusion, the ship's type could alter depending upon who was in command; for example, a Sixth Rate was known as a 'frigate' if commanded by a post-captain but as a 'sloop' if by a commander. So in this story it seems simplest when mentioning a naval ship to indicate her approximate size not by her rating or her type but by the number of her guns.[3]

The Royal Navy powerfully reflected a central feature of British society at that time: the importance of patronage to promotion.[4] In the parlance of the period 'the strength of a man's interest' – his family, his social, naval and political connections – was paramount; this was the norm and certainly not perceived as corrupt. But it was debilitating:

"Of course it is disagreeable to be ordered about like a dog by a man much younger than yourself who has been promoted not for any merit of his own but merely because he is Sir Somebody Something..."[5] The overriding aim of any ambitious officer was to be posted, to become a Post-Captain, for thereafter advancement was automatic as those above him died, a process that could neither be stopped nor accelerated, a process independent of his interest. So provided he lived long enough he was bound to become an admiral. Hence the old naval toast "To a bloody war or a sickly season."[6]

But William Hutcheon Hall was not well connected – although, thanks to the *Nemesis* and a long life, he did eventually become an admiral.[7] When appointed to the ship he had already served in the Navy for 28 years but still ranked only as master. Born in Berwick in Northeast England in 1797 he entered the Navy at the age of 14, by no means a particularly tender age at that time. In October 1811 he was appointed First-Class Volunteer and then Midshipman on HMS *Warrior* (74 guns), serving under Captain the Honourable George Byng for the rest of the French wars in the North Sea and the Baltic. Upon the defeat of Napoleon in 1815 he transferred to HMS *Lyra* (10 guns), Captain Basil Hall, and on her sailed in 1816 for the first time to China, the *Lyra* accompanying HMS *Alceste* (38) carrying Lord Amherst's embassy to the Chinese court.[a] Returning to England in November 1817, sailing via St Helena where the ship's officers paid their respects to Napoleon, he was shortly after appointed first to HMS *Falmouth* (20 guns), then *Dwarf* (10) and *Iphigenia* (42), in the latter undertaking anti-slavery patrols off the west coast of Africa. His first command came in 1822 when he was appointed Acting Master of HMS *Morgiana* (18 guns), again off West Africa. In May 1823 he was officially promoted to master, soon transferring to HMS *Parthian* (10 guns) the following year "nearly losing his life by intrepidly jumping overboard to the rescue of Mr Price, Captain's Clerk." This was an act

---

[a] "The *Lyra* in the short space of 20 months, viz. from 9 February 1816 to 14 October 1817, visited Madeira, the Cape, Java, Macao, the Yellow Sea, the West Coast of Corea, the Great Loo-choo Island (Okinawa), Canton, Manila, Prince of Wales's Island (Penang), Calcutta, Madras, the Mauritius, and St. Helena; having run, in direct courses, a distance of 11,940 nautic leagues, or 41,490 statute miles." (Hall 1818). In February 1817 on the voyage home the *Alceste* was wrecked off the coast of Sumatra.

of bravery Hall repeated on 17 January 1840 from the *Nemesis* when he "jumped into Clarence Dock, Liverpool, and saved the life of Robert Kelly, engineer."[8]

Over the next 12 years Hall saw service on various ships in the West Indian, Mediterranean and home stations but, approaching 40 years old, was still no more than a master. But he was lucky to have a job at all: at one point in the 1820s there were 5,339 commissioned officers in the Royal Navy of which only 550 were working, a mere ten per cent.[9] So promotion was bound to be painfully slow, at least for those not well connected. In nice contrast to Hall's predicament is the career of Henry Keppel (1809–1904) whom we will meet a number of times in this story.[10] The twelfth child of the fourth Earl of Albemarle and his wife Elizabeth, Keppel entered the Navy at the age of 12, was promoted to lieutenant at 19, to commander at 23 and post-captain aged only 28. But this was slow compared with Thomas, Lord Cochrane, the tenth Earl of Dundonald (1775–1860), who appeared on the crew list of HMS *Vesuvius*, captained by his uncle, at the tender age of five, an age when, with another relative well placed in the Horse Guards, he was also listed as an officer of His Majesty's 104th Regiment. This practice of 'false muster' was quite common, and allowed Cochrane when he first actually went to sea at the age of 17 to claim 12 years sea-time. Certainly one of the most notable sailors of his time, Cochrane spent only 18 months as a midshipman, was promoted from lieutenant to commander aged only 24 and to post-captain at 25.[11] And what for a man who was *really* well connected? Lord Adolphus Fitz-Clarence (1802–56), the seventh of ten illegitimate children of William, Duke of Clarence, later King William IV, with the comic actress Dorothy Jordan, entered the Navy aged 12, was lieutenant at 19, commander at 21 and post-captain at 22.[12]

Hall, like a number of the more far-sighted but less well-connected officers, came to believe that steamships were the vessels of the future and that a knowledge of their workings would enhance his prospects. Paid off in late 1836 from HMS *St Vincent* (120 guns) in which he had served for over two years, he set out for Glasgow to learn more about steam, probably at Napier's works on the Clyde which was a favourite place for such studies, their hospitality to Naval officers being proverbial. Thereafter he gained further experience on steamers trading to Ireland, and in 1839 crossed the Atlantic on the steamer *British Queen*, arriving in New York on 30 July and from there examining steamships on the Hudson and Delaware rivers.

Back in England within three months, Hall, still only a master of the Royal Navy, was offered the command of the *Nemesis* in November 1839, just prior to her launch at Birkenhead, his appointment officially dating from 26 December and her first river trials.[13] Exactly why or by whom Hall was chosen is unknown. But he was clearly an officer of wide experience, including a visit to China, and must certainly have been well regarded to have obtained what was to prove to be a most significant assignment.

At Portsmouth with his stricken ship Hall first made what he called "the usual visits", visits to present his card incumbent upon an officer of the Royal Navy at a Royal Naval port, and then sent word about his predicament to London, to Mr Thomas Peacock at the offices of the Honourable East India Company in Leadenhall Street. Immediately Peacock wrote to Sir John Barrow, secretary to the Lords Commissioners of the Admiralty, requesting that the port admiral at Portsmouth be authorised to dock the *Nemesis* and order her repair. Sir John replied the same day, Thursday 12th, saying that the admiral had now been so authorised, adding "I am directed at the same time to send you herewith a Memorandum addressed to all Her Majesty's officers connected with this Department, directing them to afford the 'Nemesis' every assistance which my Lords request may be delivered to the Master in charge of that vessel", a memorandum that Hall subsequently found of much value.[14]

Within a day or two Mr Peacock himself came hurrying down to Portsmouth, a man of whom Hall later wrote that "no one stood more conspicuous" in providing help. Now with the *Nemesis* safely docked Laird set about the task of organising repairs, also sensibly taking advantage of the fact that his revolutionary iron ship was lying in the middle of a Royal Naval dockyard. Writing to the Admiralty he suggested that one of their surveyors might like to examine her, and the Admiralty obliged, asking Mr Augustin Creuze to make a detailed survey of the ship he later called "a private armed steamer bound from Liverpool to Odessa."[15]

Two weeks passed, partly waiting, partly working. Repairs necessitated the replacement of two iron plates from the bottom and one from the bulkhead, the removal, flattening and return of a few bent plates, and the replacement of a little angle-iron. As the Navy was unused to iron ships, material had to be sent down from Birkenhead so that the total cost of repairs, materials and labour, rose to about £30, distressing Laird for he could have done the work for £20 at his own shipyard. But finally she was sound again, her hull as good as new, every spare inch packed with fuel and provisions. Now she carried coal for 12 days steaming, about 145 tons, water and provisions for a crew of 60 men for four months, and ships' stores including duplicate machinery and additional armaments for two years. Thus fully laden she drew 6 ft of water, compared with perhaps 13 ft for a comparable wooden ship or 23 ft for some of the fine 74s lying beside her, her bulwarks no more than five ft above the water, her paddles deeply immersed.

Saturday 28 March 1840 dawned damp and grey as the ship began to stir. Hall had that night put up outside the dockyard at the same comfortable inn that had accommodated Peacock, but he had arranged to be woken before dawn and was on board soon after first light. He immediately ordered the boilers fired so that steam was well up when the last of those who had spent the night ashore straggled back to the ship. By mid morning all was ready and again the *Nemesis* headed out to sea, great clouds of the blackest smoke billowing from her funnel, the cheers of farewell from the shore quickly drowned out by the thrashing of her paddles. As she passed Naval ships at anchor there, the 'wooden walls' towering over her low iron hull, many of their crews came to the sides to cheer and wave, so that the captain considered that his ship had indeed been given a fitting farewell.[16]

Throughout Sunday they steamed back from whence they'd come, westwards along the south coast of England to Lizard Point. There they turned south and at daylight on Monday saw the Lizard slip below the horizon, for the *Nemesis* and for many of her crew the last of England that they would ever see.

{ 2 }

THE HONOURABLE COMPANY

And so the *Nemesis*, "a private armed steamer bound from Liverpool to Odessa", steamed south across the Bay of Biscay into the teeth of a moderate gale, the ship moving gracefully at about 8 knots through a heavy swell, "floating like a duck" according to her captain. Passing Cape Finisterre on 2 April, virtually all aboard must have assumed that the next day they would turn east towards Gibraltar and the Mediterranean. But as the 3rd and 4th passed and the ship continued south all must have realised that the rumours of Odessa were without foundation.[1]

So where was she bound and under whose direction? The answer lies in the visit to Portsmouth of Mr Peacock. Thomas Love Peacock (1785–1866), 'a kind-hearted, genial and friendly man', is best known today as a novelist and poet who satirised the politics and culture of his time, but he mainly earned his keep from the Honourable East India Company.[2] He entered their service in 1819 as an assistant in the Examiners' Office, the office dealing with the vast amount of paperwork received from India, rising to be chief examiner between 1836 and 1856. Early on Peacock became fascinated with steam navigation and, although no sailor, realised its potential for the Company for whom he worked. He became deeply involved in their 'Select Committee on Steam Navigation to India' which reported in 1834, and that year was instrumental in getting four small iron paddle ships sent in parts to India for assembly there – 'Peacock's Iron

Chicks' (see Table 8). But he hurried down to Portsmouth that March day as clerk to the Secret Committee of the Court of Directors, the Secret Department dealing with the foreign affairs of the Company, its name derived from that of the cabal which in the seventeenth century actually controlled the Company. Clearly, his interest in the *Nemesis* expressed the Company's interest.

That Company for whom the *Nemesis* was built was a commercial concern unique in British history, indeed in world history, a company that in 250 years grew from a handful of enterprising London merchants into the foundation stone of the world's largest empire.[3]

From well before the time of Christ eager merchants in dhows and prahus and junks had been scouring the islands of the Malay Archipelago for spices – for cloves and pepper, nutmeg and mace, rare products light to ship to China or Arabia and there enormously profitable to sell.[4] And it was in good part this spice trade which, around 1500, tempted Europeans to undertake ever more adventurous voyages from the ports of Spain and Portugal. Whereas the Spanish tended to look west, the Portuguese looked east and it was they who first rounded the Cape of Good Hope and reached the Spice Islands. First to arrive, the Portuguese dominated the trade in spices to Europe throughout the sixteenth century but were largely driven out by the Dutch in the first half of the seventeenth, the Dutch themselves relinquishing their dominance to the British in the second half of the eighteenth century.

On 31 December 1600 a Royal Charter was granted to a group of English merchants founding what was later to be called 'the Honourable East India Company', even 'the Grandest Society of Merchants in the Universe' but then more properly known as 'The Company of Merchants of London trading into the East Indies'. What united these merchant-adventurers were two powerful beliefs: a patriotism derived in part from the defeat of the Invincible Armada 12 years before that gave them enormous confidence in their country, its rights and power; and an almost religious zeal for freedom of trade, so that they in no way considered that Spain had any monopoly on the treasures of the Americas or Portugal on the riches of the Indies.

The Company's first fleet sailed from London in February 1601, reaching Aceh in northern Sumatra in June 1602. These early voyages were one-off affairs, the ships, the crews, the finances being found for a single voyage, the profits, if any, being enjoyed by the investors upon the ships' return. But inevitably, as profits began to roll in a more permanent arrangement was desired. Of course the arrival of aggressive British merchants into a market already heaving with islanders and Indians, Chinese and Arabs, not to mention Portuguese and Dutch, meant that conflict was inevitable. And the vagaries of climate meant that both the supply of produce for shipment and the availability of ships to carry it were anything but regular. So places for storage and safe harbours for loading were necessary, and these trading posts or 'factories' necessitated treaties and alliances with local rulers or, failing these, the seizure of the necessary land. And then all this paraphernalia needed to be defended from competitors, and administered.

And so grew, more by chance than design, what came to be the largest company the world had ever seen, a merchant company ruling a diverse collection of towns and territories with a vast administration and powerful military establishment. The base was India, the Company acquiring Surat in 1629, and then Madras in 1639, Bombay in 1668 and Calcutta in 1690, the last three the centres of the three Presidencies that were to form British India, but its tentacles reached from Arabia throughout the Indian Ocean and the Malay Archipelago to China (their first ship reached Canton (Guangzhou) in 1637), a private imperialist enterprise of remarkable scope.

As long as the Company was seen to consist merely of a fleet of ships, some scattered ports in distant lands and a London office, only those with a financial interest might wish to interfere. But in 1757, through Robert Clive's victory at Plassey, the Company gained its first substantial landholding, and so when the mother country emerged from the Seven Years War of 1756–63 with a global empire, a good chunk of this was seen to be ruled by the Company. Now, a private enterprise which presumed to govern vast territories and wage wars, collect taxes and vastly enrich selected citizens, indeed to act in many ways as a sovereign government and yet be supported by the British Crown, was clearly in need of regulation by that Crown. From the 1760s onwards, the affairs of the Company and of the British Government became increasingly intertwined, each calling upon the other to support its various adventures, each blaming the other for its failures, and unsurprisingly as the years went by, one, a private company, slowly losing its independence to the other, the government of an increasingly powerful and self-confident nation.

From its earliest days the Company, *Jan Kampani* or the Valiant Company to Indians and thus popularly 'John Company', maintained a monopoly over the carriage of goods between Britain and the East, but trade within the East had been open to others. Initially this 'country trade' had been carried out by indigenous traders, gathering goods from scattered settlements to the factories. But as the factories grew so did those settled there become increasingly involved until the 'country trade' dominated their lives, be they Company servants or independent merchants.

Although at the time many in the British Government saw that a commercial company governing much of India was indeed absurd, few in that Government, already confronting a colonial revolt in North America, wished to be saddled with the administrative and financial responsibilities of Company commitments in distant Asia. Many others no doubt considered that to transfer a potential cornucopia of riches from a Company well known to be often venal and corrupt to a Government whose frequently revolving Ministries were no less venal and corrupt would be a madness that would perhaps destroy both Company and constitution. And then in 1770 a hideous famine struck Bengal, killing perhaps a third to a half of the population and playing havoc with Company finances. Meanwhile the line of erstwhile Company servants returning to England with ever larger fortunes looted from India lengthened, and as these 'Nabobs' attempted to buy influence wherever they could, be it the Court of Directors or Whitehall or Bengal, so the clamour for reform became irresistible.

And thus followed Parliamentary legislation, always controversial, often bitterly fought. First, the Regulating Act of 1773 which initiated Government participation in the administration of India, including the appointment of a Governor-General and Council. Next, the India Act of 1784 which made the Governor-General a royal appointment and set up a Board of Control in London controlling the Company's Court of Directors – indeed, converted the Company into something not unlike a government department, with the president of the Board of Control a member of the Cabinet. Then the Charter Act of 1813 which gave the Crown sovereignty over all the Company's possessions, and broke the Company's trading monopoly. That year the trade to India was opened to competition, the same fate befalling the China trade in 1833.

The president of the Board of Control in Lord Melbourne's Cabinet of 1835–41 was Sir John Hobhouse (1786–1869),[5] a friend and supporter of the Foreign Secretary, the forceful and interventionist Henry Temple, Lord Palmerston (1784–1865). Sometime in 1838 the Board of Control decided with the Court of Directors on a major expansion of the Company's steam fleet. Three new wooden paddle steamers were ordered from builders on the Thames, the *Cleopatra*, *Queen* and *Sesostris*, and a two-year-old Irish cargo steamer, the *Kilkenny*, was bought in January 1839 and renamed *Zenobia*, all four sailing in 1839 for Bombay (*see* Table 8). Throughout 1839 scores of letters were sent and received by the Court of Directors' Finance and Home Committee concerning all aspects of these four ships: their building, naming, manning and costs.[6] Nowhere was the *Nemesis* mentioned.

Unknown to the Court of Directors, Hobhouse in 1838 also ordered the Secret Committee to arrange for the building of four other warships, these to be of iron, for both river and sea service, their ownership and destination to be kept a closely guarded secret. Unfortunately, the remaining records of the Secret Committee contain all too little information about these vessels, and nowhere explain exactly why they were ordered nor why secrecy was so important. None the less something of the ships' history can be pieced together. Their first mention comes in a memorandum from Hobhouse dated 7 September 1839. "The Secret Committee is authorised and requested to provide all the armament, furniture and stores of every description, not included in the Contracts, which are necessary to complete the sliding-keel vessels for sea."[7] These 'sliding-keel vessels' were being built at two yards, the ships later named *Phlegethon* (530 tons, 90 hp) and *Nemesis* (660 tons, 120 hp) at Lairds of Birkenhead, yard numbers 27 and 28,[8] *Pluto* (450 tons, 100 hp) and *Proserpine* (400 tons, 90 hp) at Messrs Fairbairn & Company on the Thames.[a] All four were to travel to India under their own power.

Also under construction at Lairds at this time were two other iron vessels for the Company, the *Ariadne* and *Medusa* (both 432 tons, 70

---

[a] Pluto (sometimes Hades) ruled the Underworld with his wife Proserpina (Persephone). When men died their souls went below to the Underworld to be examined before the Tribunal of Hades and his three assessors. When judgement was announced those that had committed no crimes were conducted to the Elysian Fields or to the Isles of the Blessed, whereas those that had sinned were cast into Tartarus, a sombre jail whose triple walls were bathed by the river Phlegethon.

hp), yard numbers 25 and 26, these to be sent in parts to Bombay.[b] Completed at Birkenhead in December 1839, the largest prefabricated steamers yet built, both were assembled and launched at Bombay the following year. From the yard numbers it would appear that the *Nemesis* was the last of the four Laird's ships to be started, her keel laid in August 1839. Yet the first apparent mention of the *Ariadne* and *Medusa* comes in a memorandum dated 27 November 1839 from Peacock of the Secret Committee to Hobhouse: "in obedience to your directions, we shall take measures for the provision of two additional steam vessels suited for both river and sea service."

From the fragmentary information available on the origins of the six iron steamers one suspects that much of the correspondence was merely formalising decisions already made by powerful people, the secrecy perhaps desired in order to bypass controversy. For by 1839 Melbourne's government was extremely weak and its finances dire.

But the desire for a greatly expanded steam fleet at this time is understandable. In the late 1830s threats to Britain's Indian empire were perceived from both west and east, from Afghanistan and from Burma (*see* chapters 19 and 27). In a letter from India dated 9 February 1838 the Secret Committee was warned about disturbances in British Burma; the *Indus* steamer had been sent from Calcutta to Moulmein, reinforced by HMS *Rattlesnake* (28 guns) then in the Bay of Bengal.[9] So it is likely that these new ships were ordered to meet these concerns, iron vessels with their shallow draft being thought particularly suitable for action on the Indus and Irrawaddy. From the timing of expenditure (Table 5) and the vessels' completion, it is probable that these orders date from the second half of 1838. But by the time the first ships reached Asia in 1840 these threats had largely dissipated and a new one had arisen further east. So it was in Chinese waters that all six first saw action.

And the secrecy was presumably due to costs. The four new wooden vessels were pretty expensive, and now to ask the Court of Directors for a considerable additional sum (Table 5) for vessels of controversial construction would no doubt have delayed things – so the money was allocated to the Secret Committee. But, unsurprisingly, rumours arose.

---

[b] Ariadne, the daughter of King Minos, fell in love with Theseus when he went to Crete to slay the Minotaur. Medusa, with hair of serpents, was one of three monsters who dwelt at the ends of the earth whom to look upon meant death.

On 17 October 1839 three members of his staff wrote to Hobhouse "... regarding the expenditure already incurred ... most erroneous opinions have, as you are aware, been expressed, and which have given rise to a motion for discussion by the General Court in December next." So they suggest that the Secret Committee "informs the Court, in general terms, that the large Secret expenditure in the past and in the current year, has been principally in the purchase and equipment of steam vessels, the details of which cannot yet be conveniently stated."[10]

The first of the six iron vessels to be completed was the *Pluto*. On 16 September 1839 the Secret Committee "ordered that the steam-vessel *Pluto* be taken on a trial voyage round the Isle of Wight, in charge of Captain I. P. Campbell and a Channel Pilot." And then on 25 September Peacock wrote a flurry of letters to government departments. To the Admiralty he wrote "requesting that Commander Richard Francis Cleaveland RN be appointed Commander of *Pluto*, and that Lt James Johnstone McCleverty RN be second in command." In a second letter to the Admiralty he stated "...it is essential that ... an order be addressed by the Lords Commissioners of the Admiralty to the respective Flag Officers, Captains, and Commanding Officers of Her Majesty's ships and vessels, stating that the vessel is employed on a particular service and not interrupt her in her progress. ... that in order to maintain the secrecy which from the start has been considered so important to observe respecting the destination of these vessels, the Committee are of opinion that the *Pluto* should be entered outward for Gibraltar, and should proceed to her destination under secret instructions." Thus was the *Nemesis* entered for Odessa. Writing to the Treasury concerning ship's stores, Peacock asked that Customs should also be kept in the dark, "...the *Pluto*, a steam vessel in the service of the East India Company, the destination of which as well as the authority to which it belongs, it is considered important to keep secret at present." And finally to the Foreign Office, this time from Hobhouse himself to Palmerston: "My Lord, An iron steam vessel, called the *Pluto*, which has been provided by the Secret Committee of the East India Company, under the authority of the Commissioners for the affairs of India, is about to proceed to Calcutta under the command of Mr Richard Francis Cleaveland, a commander in the Royal Navy: and I have to request that your Lordship will give directions that this vessel may be furnished with an order commanding Her Majesty's Consular officers to give to the commander any assistance that he may require. It is desirable that the destination of the *Pluto*, and the authority to which she belongs, should not be mentioned."

On 10 February 1840 the nation enjoyed the spectacle of a royal wedding, the 20-year-old Queen Victoria marrying her first cousin Prince Albert. The festivities over, between the 14th and 27th Peacock dispatched a similar flurry of letters concerning the *Nemesis*, the first requesting "that William Hutcheon Hall, Master of the Royal Navy, be appointed Commander of the *Nemesis*, Lt William Pedder RN to be First Officer, Mr Edward Ludlow Strangways, Mate of the RN, to be Second Officer." As in fact Hall had been appointed Commander the previous December, again it hints at formalising decisions already taken. Then between 8 and 10 April there was the same flurry of correspondence concerning the *Proserpine*, and on 11 August concerning the *Phlegethon*. In the second half of September the *Proserpine*, Captain John James Hough RN, left England for the east in company with the *Phlegethon*, Captain Richard Francis Cleaveland RN and First Officer Lieutenant James Johnstone McCleverty RN, the same two men appointed to the *Pluto* 12 months before.

So what had happened to the *Pluto*? It appears that something had gone horribly wrong with her although we do not know what. Perhaps there is a hint in a statement by Gibson-Hill that the *Pluto* was "the first boat to be fitted with the new oscillating engines by Maudslay, Sons & Field,[c] and it is said that they had stood in the shop for several years, as possible purchasers considered them dangerous".[11] On 27 July 1841, Peacock was again writing to the Admiralty: "... *Pluto* ... which from defects in her construction was brought home for repairs, and is again nearly ready for sea ... it is desirable as in the case of the *Pluto* originally, and in the cases subsequently of the *Nemesis*, *Proserpine* and *Phlegethon*, the *Pluto* should be provided with the following papers..." And there followed a similar series of requests to those sent 22 months before, the last dated 15 October. The *Pluto*, Lieutenant John Tudor RN and First Officer Lieutenant George Taylor Airey RN, finally sailed for the east on 28 October 1841, two years behind schedule, the last of the Secret Committee's six iron steamers to leave the shores of England.

So it was by chance that the *Nemesis*, the largest of the six and the last to have her keel laid down, was the first to reach the east and the first to prove her prowess as a warship. When she steamed out of Birkenhead that March morning in 1840 the Company that owned her was certainly not 'the Grandest Society of Merchants in the Universe'. Rather, it was an institution in the throes of a remarkable metamorphosis, so that when the Company was finally dissolved in 1858, there stood in its place, fully formed, the Indian branch of a worldwide imperial government. Throughout her life it was this that the Nemesis served: the government of British India.

{ 3 }

THE PECULIAR ART

"... there are only two or three individuals who understand the peculiar art of iron ship-building, and Messrs Laird of Liverpool are the most eminent and experienced in this line..."

—Captain Sir Edward Parry,
Controller of Steam at the Admiralty, November 1839[1]

The great estuary of the Clyde on the west coast of Scotland has for centuries been the commercial heart of that country, the banks, as the river narrows, lined with the businesses of the sea. There in the 1730s an enterprising young man, Alexander Laird, set about establishing a rope and sailcloth factory in his home town of Greenock near Glasgow. The sound business sense and hard work of himself, and later of his son John, assured its success, and by the time John's 18-year-old son William became a partner in 1798 Lairds was one of the largest factories of its kind in the country.[2]

In 1804 William married Agnes Macgregor and a few years later the couple with their three children, John, Mary and Macgregor, decided to move south, to the booming English port of Liverpool on the Mersey, second only to the Thames at London, to establish another branch of the family business. Like his father and grandfather before him, William was an intelligent and progressive businessman, and soon came to realize that for ships the future lay not in the power of wind but of steam. In 1822 he, with some friends, set up the St George's Steam Packet Company to provide a steamer service between Liverpool and Glasgow, and two years later bought some land across the river from crowded Liverpool at Birkenhead, a hamlet of a dozen houses near an ancient priory. Joined in 1828 by his eldest son John, then 23, 'William Laird & Son' there set up the Birkenhead Iron Works initially to build boilers, but soon turning their attention to building complete iron ships, launching their first in October 1829, the little *Wye*, a lighter of 50 tons.[a]

Within a few years Lairds were seen to be the most enterprising of all companies involved in building iron ships, taking advantage of the fact that these were both particularly suitable for steam propulsion and could be prefabricated. Their first major iron steamship, the 148-ton *Lady Lansdowne*, was built at Birkenhead in 1833 and shipped in parts to Ireland for service on the Shannon River, and the following year the 249-ton *John Randolph* was similarly shipped across the Atlantic to the Savannah River in Georgia, the first iron steamer in America. By 1835 they had built nine steamships, two of these, *Euphrates* (186 tons) and *Tigris* (109 tons) for the Honourable Company (*see* Table 8).[3]

The Industrial Revolution, the name given to the period from perhaps 1760 to 1840, was indeed truly revolutionary and the country that led these changes, Great Britain, saw in those 80 years almost all aspects of her society transformed. Central to this were the remarkable changes in the transportation of man and his goods, changes wrought largely by the power of steam and the strength of iron.

The use of steam power in the service of mankind can be said to date from 1712 when Thomas Newcomen, a blacksmith from Devon in southwest England, built an engine to draw water from a tin mine in the neighbouring county of Cornwall. Over the next 50 years the Newcomen engine spread first throughout Britain and then Europe and, in 1753, to the New World. In the hands of the great pioneers of steam power, James Watt of Glasgow and Matthew Boulton of Birmingham, this basic engine was much improved, the most significant development being the conversion of vertical motion into rotary, allowing steam to power cotton mills. But neither of these men was interested in ships, and it was in France in the summer of 1783 that the story of steamships begins.[4]

On 15 July that year a strange vessel cast off from the bank of the River Saône by Lyon belching smoke from a tall black funnel. On either side of her long narrow hull two paddle wheels churned the waters, and with her bows pointing upstream she moved into the centre of the river and for 15 minutes slowly made progress against the flow. Thus the designer of the *Pyroscaphe*, le Marquis Claude de Jouffroy d'Abbans,

---

[a]   Ships' dimensions. See note in chapter 4.

can justly be called the creator of the world's first successful steam-powered vessel.

The interest in steam navigation grew rapidly, both in Europe and in the United States. On 12 October 1788 in the US a small steam-powered vessel built by John Fitch made a successful ascent of the Delaware River for 20 miles, and two days later a little vessel belonging to William Symington steamed out onto Loch Dalswinton in Scotland with the poet Robert Burns on board. Symington is generally credited with building the first practical steamer when in 1801 he fitted an engine to the *Charlotte Dundas* which was then put to work towing barges along the Forth & Clyde Canal.

But the prospect of steam navigation particularly excited the Americans with their long rivers and great distances between settlements, and it was there that it was first commercially exploited. In 1807 Robert Fulton's *North River Steam Boat of Clermont*, powered by an engine built in England, carried fare-paying passengers down the Hudson River to New York. To Fulton also belongs the honour of the world's first steam warship, *Demologos*, launched in 1814 but never commissioned, a catamaran with a paddle wheel between the hulls designed as a mobile battery for the defence of New York harbour. By 1820 there were over 100 steamers plying the rivers and coastal waters of the US, Fulton's *Chancellor Livingstone* steaming regularly from Albany to New York in 18 hours with berths for 120 people and room for many more on deck.

Not until 1812 did Europe see a steamship in regular service when Henry Bell's *Comet* started a passenger service on the River Clyde, the same vessel inaugurating the first ocean service in 1819, between Glasgow and the Western Isles. By 1820 there were only 43 steamships in the whole of the British Empire, but thereafter growth was rapid; by 1827 there were 225 steamers registered at British ports, one of them, the *United Kingdom*, at 1,000 tons and with engines of 200 hp, the largest steamship in the world. By 1840, the year that the *Nemesis* left England, that number had grown to 1,325, and lying on the stocks in Bristol was Isambard Kingdom Brunel's revolutionary *Great Britain*, iron hulled and screw driven with engines developing 1,800 hp, with both transverse and longitudinal bulkheads, and at 322 ft overall and 3,443 tons by far the largest ship ever built.[5]

The revolution in inland transport started on water too. Of course inland waterways had been navigated for centuries, but the opening of the Bridgewater Canal close to Liverpool and Manchester in 1761, the first canal to be built in Britain that did not follow an existing watercourse, heralded huge changes.[6] Roads were almost uniformly appalling and canals could transport much greater loads more safely with much less horsepower; whereas a team could perhaps pull a 1 ton wagon along a rutted road, a single horse could tow a 50-ton barge. Within 60 years over 2,200 miles of canals had been built, giving Britain the remarkable total of over 4,000 miles of navigable inland waterways. By the 1820s many steam-powered vessels plied the canals, but it was the application of steam power to wheeled vehicles, 20 years behind the use of steam on water, that altered inland communications most profoundly.[7] If we remember, firstly, that in the 1840s no more than 100,000 people out of a population of 18 million owned a carriage or riding horse, and secondly that until the advent of the train the mail coach was the fastest form of land travel known, averaging about 11 mph, a speed similar to that enjoyed in the Roman Empire, then 'revolution' is no exaggeration.

The world's first steam-powered railway locomotive was tested successfully by Richard Trevithick in South Wales in February 1804, but it would be another 21 years before something that we would recognise as a proper railway first saw the light of day. The opening of the Stockton & Darlington Railway in Northeast England in September 1825 is often considered as the beginning of the 'Railway Age', but as with the 'Canal Age' it was again near Liverpool that that age truly began. In October 1829, the same month that Laird's *Wye* was launched at Birkenhead, the Rainhill railway trials took place across the river, Robert Stephenson's locomotive *Rocket* easily winning, averaging over 24 mph on its final run. Thus it was the *Rocket* that had the honour, in September of the following year, of opening the world's first true railway, the 31-mile double-tracked Liverpool & Manchester Railway. Thereafter the speed of development was explosive. By 1838, with about 250 miles of line in the country, London's first terminus, Euston, was completed, allowing direct communication between the capital and the industrial heartland at Birmingham.[b] By 1840, the year the *Nemesis* left for the east, a line first reached her birthplace Birkenhead from Chester. By 1845 about

---

[b]   The electric telegraph, another revolution in communications, was first demonstrated to the public in 1837, a mile-long wire being constructed beside the new London & Birmingham Railway. But it was in the USA that it was rapidly developed, Samuel Morse sending the first telegram in 1844 (Crump 2007).

2,400 miles of track crisscrossed the country, by 1850 over 5,000 miles and by 1855 7,200 miles. As the Duke of Wellington feared, the railways did indeed encourage the lower orders to "move about": in 1855 they carried 111 million passengers.

Early steamships were essentially confined to the calm waters of inland lakes and rivers, but as early as 1809 a steamship had ventured to sea, the *Phoenix* in the US running south from New York to Delaware Bay. But the first true sea voyages were undertaken in 1815 off the British Isles when the *Marjory*, and soon after the *Duke of Argyle*, steamed from the Clyde to the Thames. Only four years later the *Savannah* crossed the Atlantic from west to east, although she did so very largely under sail. Not until 1838 did a true trans-Atlantic steamer service begin: on 23 April the *Sirius* arrived in New York from Cork, Ireland, after a voyage of 19 days carrying 40 passengers, followed later that same day by Brunel's *Great Western* just 15 days out from Bristol, half the time of the fastest crossing by sail. The *Great Western*, launched in 1837 specifically for the Atlantic crossing, was at 1,320 tons and 450 hp both larger and more powerful than the largest naval steamer launched that year, HMS *Gorgon*. Built to carry up to 240 passengers in three classes and with a crew of 60, the *Great Western* heralded the birth of the great Atlantic liners, a revolution in comfort and reliability.

As soon as steamships went to sea the disadvantages of paddle wheels as a means of propulsion became all too apparent.[8] Firstly, the wheels worked best when the float at the bottom had perhaps one foot of water above it, but this varied greatly with the variable weight of the ship and the calmness of the water. As fuel was burnt the ship rode higher; in rough seas one paddle could be deeply immersed when the other was almost out of the water; and in strong winds she tended to turn upwind as the leeward wheel had greater power. Secondly, only the float at the bottom was actually perpendicular and thus truly efficient, although by the early 1840s this deficiency was partly overcome by the capacity to feather the floats. And finally the vessel needed to be long and narrow so that the wave profile at the paddles was relatively flat, an unprofitable shape for a merchantman.

Thus for the merchant fleet sail still had its advantages. The fine clippers of the 1860s, with no need to stop for coal, no machinery to repair and overhaul, and thus with smaller crews and no fuel bills, remained highly profitable. But that decade saw the development of the marine compound engine and with this it became clear that steam would replace sail for the merchant fleet also. Whereas the percentage of steam vessels by tonnage in the world's leading merchant fleets was 3 per cent in 1840 and only 13 per cent 30 years later, parity between sail and steam was reached by the early 1890s. Even so, at the start of the Great War of 1914–18, a hundred years after the first true sea voyage by a steamship, a fifth of the world's mercantile tonnage was still powered by the wind.

From early days there had been interest in a terminal screw or propeller which would not only be always totally immersed but would, if positioned in front of the rudder, provide a slipstream that would make the rudder much more effective at slow speeds. But wooden hulls were not well suited for screw propulsion; they were too flexible to fully withstand the vibrations and stresses of shaft rotation, changing shape if the ship grounded, as they often did at berth, and with age tending to 'hog', the bow and stern dropping compared with amidships. So screw propulsion came into its own only with the development of iron hulls.

Although the screw-driven *Little Juliana* had been successfully tested in New Jersey in 1804, it was not until 1836 that functional patents were taken out on a screw, in May by Francis Pettit Smith and in July by John Ericsson, both in England. The following year saw the launch of Lairds' 14th ship, the *Rainbow*, at 581 tons the largest iron vessel yet built. And in 1838 they launched their first screw vessel, Ericsson's little 33-ton *Robert F. Stockton* destined to ply the rivers of New Jersey for over 30 years. That same year Smith's wooden *Archimedes* was launched in London, the world's first sea-going screw ship, and it was the promotional voyages of both the *Rainbow* and the *Archimedes* that persuaded the Directors of the Great Western Steamship Company to allow Brunel to make their *Great Britain* truly revolutionary, iron hulled and screw driven.

Lairds recognised early on the many advantages of iron ships: they were cheaper to build, easier to maintain and repair, more durable, less likely to leak, with more space for cargo and more salubrious as living quarters for the crew.[9] Great advances in the production of iron had been made in the second half of the eighteenth century; by 1800 Britain was producing about 150,000 tons and by 1840 ten times that amount. And as iron became more readily available and therefore cheaper, so wood suitable for ship-building became increasingly scarce and thus expensive. To build a ship of oak required about one 100-year-old tree for every ton of ship, so a new First Rate could consume over 3,500 trees, the timber of 900 acres (365 ha) of forest.[10] Thus by 1840 a large wooden hull was costing one third more than an equivalent iron one. In evidence before the 1834 Parliamentary Select Committee appointed to examine 'The Means of Promoting Communication with India by Steam', the committee in which Mr Peacock played an active role, Macgregor Laird had made two important points. Firstly that a strong iron vessel did not weigh half as much as a wooden one, and would therefore draw considerably less water and be faster. And secondly that her cargo capacity would be much greater, her sides including framing being only 4 inches thick compared with 12 inches for a wooden ship, giving about 20 per cent more usable space.

In 1822 the *Aaron Manby,* starting a regular London to Paris steamer service, became the first sea-going iron vessel, but it would be another ten years before an iron ship undertook a true ocean voyage. In June 1832 the little *Alburkah,* launched the previous year at Lairds though not actually built by them, only 55 tons with engines of 15 hp and draft of only 6 ft, set out from Liverpool with the sailing brig *Columbine* and the wooden paddle ship *Quorra* bound for West Africa with Macgregor Laird on board. John Lander's expedition to the River Niger proved the value of shallow-draught iron steamers for river travel but was disastrous in human terms. Of the 48 men who left England on the two steamers only seven, including Macgregor, returned safely.[11]

But there were difficulties with iron.[12] To start with there were problems obtaining iron plates of even thickness and riveting them together to form a watertight seal. Then there were fears of lightning strikes and of the rivets popping in a storm but these proved unfounded. However the problems of fouling by marine organisms remained daunting. The bottoms of naval ships had first been sheathed in 'copper' (yellow metal) in 1761 and the whole fleet coppered by 1782, making the ships faster, easier to maintain and longer lived, but coppering could not be used on iron hulls as electrolysis caused rapid corrosion. And could the magnetic compass ever be made to work accurately in an environment of iron? Unsurprisingly, Lairds were pioneers in solving this problem too, realizing in the early 1830s that it must be overcome if iron ships were to be capable not just of river work but of prolonged sea voyages. In October 1835 they initiated trials on the Shannon with the 263-ton *Garryowen,* and three years later these were extended with the much larger *Rainbow,* conducted on the Thames by the Astronomer

Royal, Sir George Airy.[13] It was Airy's compass correctors, a system of magnets and soft iron placed around the binnacle, that had been fitted to the *Nemesis* in Liverpool but fitted incorrectly, an error that nearly brought her to an untimely end on the Stones of St Ives.

{ 4 }

THIS SPLENDID VESSEL

"In this splendid vessel, commanded by Captain W. H. Hall, we have the pleasing task of welcoming to our shores the *first Iron Steamer* that ever rounded the Cape of Good Hope. She is the largest of her class built, being 168 ft long, 29 ft beam, and 630 tons burthen. The engines are 120 horse power, by the celebrated makers Messrs. Forester and Co. of Liverpool, and, of course, upon the best construction."

—*The Colombo Observer,* Saturday 10 October 1840[1]

The year 1839 was certainly the busiest that Laird's shipyard had yet enjoyed. In the ten years since they started building ships 20 vessels had been constructed, but this year alone was to see a further 12 added to their list, all but three for the Honourable Company, seven of these prefabricated at Birkenhead to be shipped in parts to the East.[2] In January the iron paddle steamers, *Comet* (205 tons) and *Meteor* (150 tons), had been completed, to be assembled in Bombay for service on the Indus. In June three more were ready for shipment, the 153-ton steamers *Nimrod, Nitocris* and *Assyria*, this time to the Middle East for use in surveying a possible route to India via the Tigris and Euphrates rivers. And in December a further pair, the Secret Committee's *Ariadne* and *Medusa*, each of 432 tons and bound again for Bombay.[a]

---

[a] Ships' dimensions.
Tonnage. In the 1840s there was some confusion between tonnage as a measure of volume and as a measure of weight (displacement). The 'Builders' Measurement' (bm) used until 1854, derived tonnage from length and breadth, not a true weight but more a volume for cargo purposes and tax. Generally I have

In August John Laird proudly officiated at the keel-laying of the shipyard's most ambitious vessel to date, the 660-ton *Nemesis*, a vessel destined also for the East but not in parts, rather to voyage there under her own power. The long keel plate lying between the stocks was only 1 ft wide, slightly curved in section, the concave side uppermost.[3] To this as the days went by were riveted the frames, each of 3″ wide angle-iron, placed 18″ apart amidships increasing to 3 ft apart fore and aft. These ran up either side to end on the angle-iron gunwale, being joined from one side to the other by the deck-beams, two bars of angle-iron placed back to back with an iron bar 9″ deep and 1/4″ thick sandwiched between them. To these frames the 'planking' was then riveted, a total of about 240 iron plates each 8 ft long and 2 ft 6″ wide. And here the experience and sheer expertise of Lairds becomes apparent in the detail. The plates attached to the keel were 7/16″ thick, the next five rows or 'strakes' forming the bottom of the vessel on either side were 6/16″, the strake at the turn of the bilge and the five forming the sides reducing from 5/16″ to 4/16″. The six strakes from the keel to the turn of the bilge were clinker-built, slightly overlapping, and the remainder carvel-built, without overlap, the carvel plates being riveted to a strip of iron plate on the inside. Clinker plates required less care at the edge and fewer rivets, and were easier to replace; carvel plates were considered stronger for the vertical sides.[4] The riveters worked from the inside using 3/4″ iron rivets at 3″ intervals, these being applied at almost welding heat so that when they cooled and contracted the fitting was very tight. As the outer part of the hole to take each rivet was counter-sunk, the outer surface of her hull was perfectly smooth.

Soon the shape of the new ship could be discerned, a low flat-bottomed vessel, long and narrow with a square stern, 173 ft from stem

---

followed the usual contemporary practice and given bm.
Length. This is measured in various ways. For example, the *Nemesis* was 184 ft overall, 173 ft from stem to taffrail, and 165 ft between perpendiculars. Where possible I have followed the usual practice and given length between perpendiculars. (1 foot (ft) = 12 inches (″) = 0.305 m).
Horsepower. This proved difficult to measure in early steamships. Usually I have given 'nominal horsepower' (nhp) which is a measure of the geometry of the engine, useful as an indicator of size and probable cost but with little relation to the real power. 'Indicated horsepower' (ihp) is two or three times larger than nhp.
Speed. This is given in nautical miles per hour, knots. 1 knot = 1.15 mph or 1.85 km/h.

to taffrail but only 29 ft wide and 11 ft deep, as long as a large Fourth Rate frigate but much narrower and lower. In cross-section she was oblong, her bottom curved down only 6" in 15 ft, the corners rounded off to an arc of a circle of about 3 ft diameter, and her sides curved slightly outwards, giving a circumference from gunwale to keel to gunwale of only 47 ft. As riveters and iron-smiths completed her planking so carpenters came on board to lay along her bottom five stout 'keelsons', 12" square sleepers of red pine, bolted to angle-iron brackets attached to the frames; here and elsewhere every connection between wood and iron had felt sandwiched in-between. Upon the keelsons and upon the deck-beams the floor and deck were bolted, each of planks of fir 3" thick, the heads of the 1" bolts being sunk about 1/2" and covered with lead so that they were hardly visible. This wooden deck, typical of early iron vessels, made her notably weak at deck level; as waves passed below her the deck would first be compressed and then, the wave amidships, stretched.[5] This weakness would soon nearly prove her undoing.

While her flat bottom and shallow draught would certainly make her ideal for river work, they would pose serious problems on the open sea where she could all too easily be blown to leeward. So she was fitted with two sliding-keels, each of oak, 7 ft by 7 ft and 4.5" thick which could be lowered to a depth of 5 ft by a small windlass and endless chain, each housed in a watertight iron trunk measuring 7 ft 6" by 1 ft running from base to deck. These trunks were attached to two of the six iron bulkheads, probably the third and fifth from the bows, which divided the *Nemesis* into seven watertight compartments, the wooden floor sleepers passing through but with watertight joints. Although Lairds had been fitting bulkheads to their vessels since building the *Garryowen* in 1834, the *Nemesis* was the first ship with truly watertight divisions, an innovation that proved vital outside St Ives.

The engine-room occupied the large central compartment which was subdivided by a partial bulkhead, with large coal bunkers against both end bulkheads, these insulating both the officers' quarters behind and the sailors' berths ahead from the heat of the fires. Bunkers were also placed along the sides, and somewhere were tanks holding at least 1,000 gallons of fresh water. Above the engine-room ran the two large oak paddle-beams, each 12" square, which passed through the sides in sockets about 80 ft behind the bows carrying the shaft to the paddle wheels. The paddle boxes reared well above the deck, and between them ran a bridge raised 8 ft above the deck, with no shelter provided although an awning could be raised in calm weather. Neither was any shelter provided for the helmsman, the wheel being in the traditional position aft, just in front of the rudder. Nearby the compass was suspended; probably two were carried, both fitted with Airy's compass correctors. The rudder itself was of wood but to it was attached a false rudder, two iron plates pivoted on the lower part of the wooden rudder with a chain up to the taffrail with which it could be let down to the same depth as the sliding-keels. Hawseholes for anchor-chains were provided both fore and aft, those at the stern useful if she was to be run ashore to land troops and then winched off again using her anchors.

The urgency with which the Company must have viewed her construction is indicated by the fact that within three months her hull was completed, the outside given several coats of red-lead before being varnished, and on Saturday 23 November 1839 she was launched. Why her sister ship *Phlegethon* (530 tons) took a full year to construct is not known, her keel laid in the yard the previous spring but not launched until April 1840. Now the *Nemesis*, 'a low black craft' drawing at this time only 2 ft 4″, was towed across the Mersey from Birkenhead to the Trafalgar Dock at Liverpool, to the yard of Messrs George F. Forrester & Company, engine-builders. There she was fitted with her two 60-horsepower side-lever engines (which today would be called a single two-cylinder engine of 120 hp), her two wrought-iron box boilers each with three furnaces, and her masts, spars and rigging. Foresters were not such experienced engine builders as Napiers on the Clyde or Maudslays on the Thames, but they were close at hand and well known to Lairds.

Side-lever engines (*see* Appendix 2) were ideal for a flat-bottomed ship built to serve in distant waters for they had a low centre of gravity and were comparatively reliable and simple to maintain. The two lowered that December into the central compartment of the *Nemesis* were bolted down to a wooden platform set in 'mastic cement', a mixture meant to absorb some of the vibration. Each had wrought-iron supports, stronger than the more usual cast-iron and also smaller and lighter, and a single vertical cylinder 44″ in diameter with a stroke of 4 ft, this driving the paddle-shaft held between the paddle-beams. The paddle wheels were 17 ft 6″ in diameter to the inner edge of the rim, each weighing about two tons and with a balance weight fitted to ensure that the crank-pins did not 'stick at the bottom'. They turned usually at about 18 rpm although the remaining logs of the *Nemesis* record speeds of 16–22 rpm.[6]

The wheels were protected by paddle boxes, these supported fore and aft by flat platforms, the sponsons. To each wheel were bolted 16 pine-wood floats measuring 6 ft 9" by 1 ft 3", those at sea-level needing to be laboriously removed when under sail. Apparently the *Nemesis* was fitted with an early form of 'disconnecting apparatus' to disconnect the shaft when sailing, something only recently developed, a more sophisticated form being fitted to her sister ship *Phlegethon*.[7]

The engines of the *Nemesis* developed only 120 nominal horsepower, and whilst adequate for inland waters she was greatly underpowered at sea. Foresters could certainly build larger engines; those fitted the previous year to the *Liverpool*, a wooden paddle steamer of 1,150 tons, were almost four times the power at 468 hp, and later in the century engines of similar power would have been fitted to a ship the size of the *Nemesis*. But it is likely that this lack of power was deliberate, in order to economise on fuel. With both engines under full pressure of steam the *Nemesis* consumed prodigious amounts of fuel, about 8 tons a day at 5 knots in fine weather to 14 tons at 8 knots in heavy weather.[8] The average was about 12 tons of fuel per day, whether coal or wood, half a ton an hour, this producing about 8 gallons of ash every hour which the poor stokers had to dispose of. When fully laden with coal her coal-holds and bunkers carried about 140 tons, but for longer sea voyages with coal also stacked in sacks on the deck she could carry about 175 tons, but this still only 15 days supply. Add to this the weight of her engines, boilers and paddle wheels, perhaps 120 tons as it is usual to allow one ton per unit of horsepower, then her steam apparatus would weigh at least 260 tons. But of course she did not rely solely upon steam power.

The *Nemesis*, like all steamships of her time, was built as much to sail as to steam; not until the launch of HMS *Devastation* in 1871 did the Royal Navy have a mastless battleship that relied solely upon engines.[9] She carried two masts, the fore-mast 66 ft tall set 46 ft in front of the paddle-shaft and the main-mast 75 ft tall set 34 ft behind. Each was built up from huge wooden poles, these supported by standing rigging and carrying running rigging to raise, lower and adjust the sails. The upper poles and the yards could be 'sent down' in stormy weather. Between them stood the funnel, not hinged for lowering when sailing, over 30' high to create a good draught, the top unornamented, the stays of both funnel and masts formed of chain at the top and rope below. Although mainly square-rigged, effectively a two-masted schooner, she could also carry fore-and-aft sails, a gaff sail on each mast and jibs rigged from fore-mast to bowsprit and jib-boom. Typically for sail-assisted steamers the positioning of her masts and rigging, dictated by her engines, was far from ideal for sailing, but none the less under full sail in a fair wind, with the paddle-floats removed, she could run as fast under sail as under steam, up to 10 knots. A contemporary Fifth Rate frigate could reach 13 knots (15 mph), the fastest sustainable speed known to man until the advent of the steam train.

Built for war, the *Nemesis* was well armed. Three of Lairds' iron ships completed in Bombay in 1839 later had guns mounted upon them, river steamers for the Indus Flotilla, the *Indus*, *Comet* and *Meteor* (from 149 to 308 tons).[10] So although the *Nemesis* was their first true warship Lairds clearly understood the problems of guns on iron hulls; throughout her life those on the *Nemesis* appear never to have caused any problems. Her main armament was two 32-pound guns, the standard British shot gun, 'medium guns' according to the Royal Navy. These were mounted fore and aft on pivot-carriages, capable of firing in all directions – though the abundance of rigging must have somewhat limited their scope. These were almost certainly made at the Ordinance Factory at Woolwich on the Thames and supplied through Mr George Armstrong, a merchant of Liverpool who was employed by the Royal Navy to export guns overseas.[11] During her sea trials in January 1840 the guns were well tested, John Laird requiring them to be fired double shotted and with an extra charge of gunpowder – that is with two 32-pound iron balls and two canvas or paper cartridges each containing 11 pounds of 'black powder', all kept in place with a rope wad – and he was delighted to see that this caused no damage at all.[12]

The 32-pounders, made of cast iron, muzzle-loading and smooth bored, were each about 6 ft long and weighed 25 cwt (1.3 tonnes).[13] Served by a gun-crew of perhaps seven men they could be fired on average up to once a minute, throwing five types of projectile: round shot (the standard iron cannon-ball) or explosive shells; grape-shot (small iron or lead balls sewn into a canvas container) or canister (a number of 3-pound balls in a metal container), both used against human targets; and carcasses, incendiary bombs.[14] They were certainly formidable weapons; at the extreme range of perhaps one mile (1.6 km), shot could still penetrate 2 ft of solid oak.

In addition the *Nemesis* carried five long brass 6-pounders, 'long-sixes' or 'chasers', two on each side, and one on the bridge used to test the range; there were also ten small iron swivels along the bulwarks, and a variety of boat guns and small arms. Throughout her life the armaments were of course altered to suit her circumstances, sometimes supplemented by field guns and howitzers when carrying troops into action. She also carried Congreve rockets, with perhaps six tubes for both 12- and 24-pounder rockets placed at the bows and on the bridge. War rockets, first encountered by the British in India in 1799, were developed at the Woolwich Arsenal by William Congreve (1772–1828) who created the world's first effective rocket weapons system, the main tactical purpose initially being to scare the enemy and their war animals.[15] There is no record that she ever had carronades, a popular short-range gun that lobbed heavy shot, descriptively called a 'smasher'.

She also carried a number of ship's boats, these not 'lifeboats' but rather boats essential for her inshore activities. Exactly how many she had initially is not known, but she certainly carried a jolly-boat in davits at the stern, perhaps one or more cutters stowed on deck and some gigs and dinghies.[b] Not until 1848 was she fitted with paddle-box boats, large boats carried upside down forming the top of each paddle box; such boats were trialled in 1839 but were perhaps too new to be considered then.

Sadly we know very little about the *Nemesis* below her deck, not even how her seven compartments were accessed. Headroom was clearly limited but then in contemporary naval ships this was sometimes as little as 5 ft, 6 ft being thought of as very generous. She had no portholes, deck housings providing the only natural light and ventilation. The crews' quarters were in front of the engines, an open mess-deck providing extremely crowded conditions with perhaps canvas partitions offering a little privacy to warrant officers. Behind the engines was comparatively spacious accommodation for Captain Hall, with both a sleeping and a dining cabin, with small cabins for the other officers, and probably a wardroom and chart room. Here would be kept the vital charts and instruments for navigation, including at least two valuable chronometers (Table 5).

---

[b]   The largest boat carried on board a warship was the *longboat*, carvel-built, for the carriage of heavy goods, often kept provisioned as a lifeboat. Smaller boats were clinker-built, the *cutter* 24 to 32 ft long for sailing or pulling by up to 14 oars, the broader *jolly-boat* and narrower, faster *gig* by 6 oars, the open *dinghy* by a pair of oars.

The galley in other steamers of the period was on deck or sometimes on the sponsons. Although its location on the *Nemesis* is never given, it was almost certainly, at least in good weather, below the bridge against one of the paddle boxes: later a cook was killed on the *Phlegethon* when a 32-pound shot passed through a paddle box and entered the galley.[16] About lavatories and washing facilities there is also no news. In sailing ships 'the heads', forward of the forecastle and floored with gratings, were used by the crew as their lavatory. Again, some contemporary steamers had lavatories on deck, sometimes little hutches on the after-sponsons, but for the *Nemesis* it was probably canvas screened buckets and chamber pots just as it would have been ashore in house or hotel.

Concerning her building costs there is, by chance, a record of her 'initial cost', presumably her total construction, running and testing costs until the Company took over payment of her crew on 1 April 1840, three days after she left Portsmouth.[17] Later in her life when she was hired by the Royal Navy the fee per year was ten per cent of her 'initial cost' and this is precisely stated as 289,427 rupees or £28,943 (about £1,592,000 today).[c] Her sister ship *Phlegethon* cost £24,288 and the *Pluto* £40,315 (Table 4). Unfortunately no record exists for the *Proserpine* as she was never hired by the Navy, but the high cost of the *Pluto* compared with Lairds' two ships and the great delay in sending her east indicates that her rebuilding must have been extensive.

For many contemporary Royal Navy ships we know their 'first cost',[18] presumably equivalent to 'initial cost'. Typically, steamships cost twice as much as sailing ships of similar size due to the high cost of

---

[c] *Monetary values.* In contemporary accounts from the Honourable Company these are given in three currencies: pounds sterling, Spanish dollars and rupees. The pound sterling (£) was divided into shillings and pence until decimalised in 1971. Reals were exported by Spain from Mexico and Peru to the east where they became the standard currency, called *pieces of eight* in the 17th century and then Spanish dollars ($). In the 1840s there were two rupees (rp) minted, the Sicca Rupee in Bengal at about 10 per £, the Company's rupee (Bombay and Madras) being slightly less valuable, 100 of the former equalling about 107 of the latter. For simplicity I have converted most values into pounds sterling using the decimal system. Exchange rates were somewhat variable; those I have used are £1 = 10 rp = $4.
The pound equivalent to 2007 for the 16 years 1839–1854 averaged £55.77, ranging from £48.15 in 1840 to £64.44 in 1851 (data from Bank of England Museum).
Generally I have used an equivalence of £1 then equals £55 today, though this may be irrelevant as the UK economy may have grown 2,000-fold.

their machinery. HMS *Dover*, the first iron ship ordered for the Royal Navy and launched from Lairds yard in 1841 cost £10,153, including machinery at £5,300 but she was notably smaller than the *Nemesis*, only 110 ft long, 224 tons and with engines of 90 hp. HMS *Alecto*, a wooden paddle steamer launched in 1839 of similar size to the *Nemesis* (164 ft, 800 tons, 200 hp) cost £27,268, including machinery at £10,700. And the initial cost of the *Tenasserim*, a wooden paddle steamer of 769 tons and 220 hp launched at Moulmein, Burma, in 1841 for the Bengal Marine, was £39,885. So it appears that the cost of the *Nemesis* was fairly typical for a steam vessel of her size, whether of iron or wood.

The year the *Nemesis* sailed east, 1840, marked a turning point for steam at sea. The first generation of steamers, from Henry Bell's *Comet* of 1812 to Brunel's *Great Western* of 1837 were wooden ships with paddle wheels housed in boxes amidships whose single-expansion engines exhausted steam into jet-condensers. The second generation, from perhaps 1840 to 1870 saw a movement to iron hulls, screw propellers and compound engines with surface condensers. Although without doubt the *Nemesis* was a pioneering vessel – the first iron sea-going warship, the first with truly watertight bulkheads – and played a significant role in promoting iron hulls for fighting ships, she was in many ways a typical paddle ship of her time. Considering this, it is salutary to remember that on 19 July 1839, a month before the keel of the *Nemesis* was laid at Birkenhead, at Paterson's Yard in Bristol 130 miles to the south, the keel of Brunel's *Great Britain* had been laid, a ship destined at her launch four years later to be a true landmark in maritime history.[19] In fact the *Nemesis* lacked a number of innovations coming into use in paddle ships of the late 1830s. This is certainly not because Lairds did not know of them, and probably not because of cost; rather, as she was to serve in distant waters she needed to be as simple to maintain as possible. Her paddle wheels could not be feathered so that each float entered the water vertically; rather, being fixed radially they entered and left the water at an angle, this slapping generating useless energy. But feathering wheels, though ten per cent more efficient in suitable waters, were at the time unreliable. Nor was she fitted with paddle-box boats. There is no mention of any form of ventilating system driven from the engines, although Lairds did fit 'Dr Reid's ventilating apparatus' (and paddle-box boats) on HMS *Albert*, launched in 1840 for the 1841 anti-slavery expedition to the Niger.[20] And finally there is no record of any form of engine-room telegraph from the bridge, something that had been fitted to ferry boats on the Tay in Scotland as early as 1821, and which would surely have been of value for a warship manoeuvring in narrow waters.

The *Nemesis* undertook river trials in late December and, soon ready for sea, was registered at the Port of Liverpool on 13 January 1840, 'the sole property of John Laird of Birkenhead, shipbuilder'. This registration, approved by the Secret Committee, has given rise to the belief that she was in fact owned by Lairds, a speculative venture to advertise the advantages of iron hulled steamers, and only later bought by the Company.[21] But Lairds had no need thus to speculate. The *Nemesis*, although given the yard number 28, was the 31st vessel built in their yard since the first was launched in 1829, and 12 of these had been specifically for the Company. As she herself was taking shape in 1839, at 660 tons the largest vessel they had yet built, four other iron paddle ships were growing beside her, three for the Company and one for the Royal Navy: the *Phlegethon*, *Ariadne* and *Medusa*, and the packet HMS *Dover* (224 tons), the Royal Navy's very first iron ship. And the following year saw the launching at the yard of three more Navy ships, these for the 1841 Niger expedition. Clearly, neither the Navy nor the Company needed to be persuaded of the excellence of Laird's ships.

1.

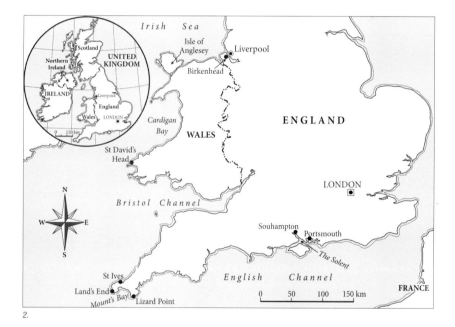

2.

1. Captain W. H. Hall (a woodcut from a daguerreotype; reprinted from Illustrated London News, 23 December 1854)

2. Map: Birkenhead to Portsmouth, March 1840 (produced by Lee Li Kheng)

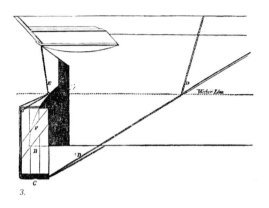

3.

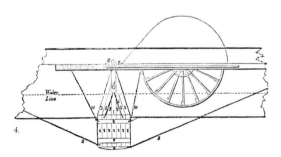

4.

3. Nemesis – *the temporary rudder (reprinted from Bernard (1844)*

4. Nemesis – *the temporary lee-board (reprinted from Bernard (1844)*

5. *HMS* Albert, *built by Lairds in 1840, and fitted with both paddle-box boats and ventilating apparatus (from a daguerreotype; © National Maritime Museum, Greenwich, London)*

FROM A DAGUERREOTYPE PICTURE BY THE POLYTECHNIC INSTITUTION

A View of Her Majesty's Iron Steam Vessel Albert, Cap.ⁿ H.D. Trotter as She appeared in Deptford Dock Yard previous to her sailing for the Niger, fitted with Cap.ⁿ G. Smith's Paddle Box Safety Boats & D.ʳ Reids Ventilating Apparatus

5.

A3

A5

8.

A7

9.

10.

6. Nemesis *scudding before a heavy gale off the cape of Good Hope on her passage from England to China'* (© National Maritime Museum, Greenwich, London).

7. 'View of Point de Galle, from the sea', Ceylon, 1843 (reprinted from Cunynghame, 1844)

8. 'The Fighting Temeraire tugged to her last berth to be broken up, 1838', Joseph Mallord William Turner . (The Fighting Temeraire © The National Gallery, London. The Turner Bequest, 1856)

9. The capture of Rangoon, May 1824; Diana *in the foreground (reprinted from Moore, 1825)*

10. Captain Charles Elliot, 1855 (reprinted from Blake, 1960)

{ 5 }

AT THE DEVOTION
OF THE WIND AND SEAS

"But I cannot tell where you should look for me if you send out any pinnace to meete me. I live at the devotion of the wind and seas."

—James Lancaster, the commander of the Company's First Fleet, drifting rudderless off southern Africa, 1603[1]

On Monday 6 April 1840, ten days out from Portsmouth, the *Nemesis* steamed into the lovely port of Funchal on Madeira.[2] Anchoring off the Loo Rock to the west of the town, Captain Hall and some of the officers immediately went ashore to pay their respects to the Governor who in turn eagerly accepted an invitation to view their remarkable ship. Hall knew Madeira well and liked it, finding the town lively, the country lovely and the people, from Governor to muleteers, hospitable. The following day, with coaling well under way, Hall treated himself to a visit to the estate of an old Portuguese nobleman high in the hills about seven miles from the town. The last of the coal, and the crates of madeira, were brought on board on Wednesday morning and so that evening they sailed, watched by a crowd gathered on the surrounding hills.

With the north-east trade winds blowing nicely, the next 12 days were spent entirely under sail, the *Nemesis* passing through the Canary Isles between Palma and Tenerife on the 11th and later midway between the Cape Verde islands and the coast of Africa. Sailing vessels bound for the Cape of Good Hope usually voyaged via the South American coast and Rio de Janeiro, at about 30°S turning east to cross the southern Atlantic, but the *Nemesis* was to take the eastern passage. About the 20th, off

Sierra Leone, the wind dropped and the engines were started and she proceeded under steam eastwards along the African coast, passing 200 miles off Cape Palmas on the 26th. Here the wind picked up again and so the engines were stopped and, travelling closer to shore, she continued eastwards for the next two weeks, making fitful progress in often stormy weather against unusual southerly winds and a lee current.

Although sometimes within sight of the shore, Hall nowhere attempted to land which must have been of considerable comfort to the crew. Rumour had been rife in Madeira that the purpose of their voyage was further exploration of the Niger, and many would have known of the harrowing experiences of the younger Laird brother, Macgregor, on that river with John Lander's expedition eight years before (*see* chapter 3).

> Beware and take care
> Of the Bight of Benin.
> For one that comes out
> There are forty go in.[3]

By Monday 11 May the *Nemesis*, now off Cape Formosa at the Niger delta, turned south, steaming for the next three days against headwinds and a pitching sea to the shelter of Prince's Island, Principe. West Bay was an excellent anchorage in all seasons, used often by ships of the Royal Navy's West African Squadron on anti-slavery patrol from their base at Freetown. Two of these were now lying there, HMS *Wolverene* (16 guns) and *Viper* (6 guns) and beside them the *Nemesis* anchored.

Three weeks later, on Monday 1 June, a huge anti-slavery meeting was held in London, attended by the Queen's new German consort, Prince Albert, who made there his first public speech in English. In a letter the previous December to the Lords Commissioners of the Treasury Lord John Russell, Secretary of State for the Colonies, had written: "In whatever light this traffic is viewed, it must be regarded as an evil of incalculable magnitude ... I find it impossible to avoid the conclusion that the average number of slaves introduced into Foreign States or the colonies in America and the West Indies, from the western coast of Africa, annually exceeds 100,000 ... The number of slaves actually landed in importing countries affords but a very imperfect indication of the real extent of the calamities which this traffic inflicts upon its victims."[4]

For nine days the *Nemesis* lay in West Bay, refitting and refuelling. The problem for steamers taking the eastern passage to the Cape was fuel. No coal was available from Africa – the small stock from Europe kept at West Bay was extremely expensive at £6 a ton (in England it ranged from 55p to £2 a ton, and even in Singapore averaged less than £2)[5] – and good wood could be obtained only from Fernando Po and Prince's Island. Of course all ships, both steamers and sailing vessels, required fuel wood, and Mr Carnaero, a merchant in Port St Antonio, could supply 100 logs for a Spanish dollar, about 9 tons for £1. But Royal Naval ships stationed off West Africa preferred to employ men, usually from the Kroo country, present-day Sierra Leone and Liberia, to live on the island to cut wood. These worked in teams, cutting the logs inland, hauling them to the harbour and stacking them there, each pile with a ship's name upon it. A single man could cut about 50 logs a day, somewhat over a ton, and the *Nemesis* needed 70 tons, Hall knowing, from his time on anti-slavery patrol, that he had to take on sufficient fuel here to reach the Cape. So now he used his Memorandum from the Admiralty authorising him to obtain assistance from Royal Navy ships, and ordered that wood waiting for other ships be loaded on the *Nemesis*. Captain Tucker of the *Wolverene* was certainly helpful, actually giving up the wood he had already loaded. As the wood was new, it had to be burnt with a little coal, but luckily enough remained from England so that none had to be bought at that inflated price.

Hall thought highly of the kroomen, finding them strong, hardworking and intelligent. He enjoyed watching them as they removed barnacles from the hull of his ship, "great, muscular, black, curly-headed fellows, bobbing down under the water, some with broom sticks, some with scrapers, and others with bits of iron bar." So impressed in fact that he hired three to join his crew, Tom Liverpool, Thomas Benaly and Jack Wilson, initially at £1.80 a month but soon rising to the able-seaman's pay of £3.00. They proved to be well disciplined and courageous sailors; Tom died in China, but the other two were still with the *Nemesis* when she reached Calcutta in 1843. And there, honouring their original agreement, Hall arranged for them to be sent back at company expense to Africa, to Prince's Island.

On the morning of Saturday 23 May the last of the provisions for the long voyage to the Cape were brought on board, the goats, pigs and poultry, some bartered for rather than paid for: "1 white frock and 12 shirts for fruit and vegetables; 24 blankets for 2 bullocks". The ship was now stacked with about 3,000 logs, many piled on the decks, and there were good supplies of fresh fruit and vegetables – yams, maize, coffee, bananas, pineapples, limes – and plenty of water of excellent quality from a nearby spring. So that evening the boats were hoisted in, the anchor weighed and the ship steamed out to sea again passed the *Wolverene* and *Viper* and their cheering crews.

A single day saw them cover the 120 miles to St Thomas Island, São Tomé, and on Sunday afternoon they entered the Bay of Chaves. Anchoring, Hall and some of his officers went ashore at St Anne de Chaves to pay their respects to the Governor at his fine house. Hall could speak no Portuguese so it was fortunate that the island's commandant, a very large and very finely dressed African, knew enough English to act as translator. Seeing that the island was heavily wooded, Hall suggested that it might make a most suitable fuelling depot for steamers, and to this the Governor agreed, reminiscing about the visit of the steamer *Enterprize* some 15 years before (*see* chapter 8).

On Monday 25 May, 59 days out from England, the *Nemesis* crossed the Line. Ploughing on southwards, she was making only about 5 knots against an adverse wind in a heavy swell when she came within hailing distance of HMS *Waterwitch* (10 guns) who confirmed that no suitable fuel-wood was available on the African coast to the south, either at Loango or Cabinda. Knowing the great distance to the Cape, Hall decided to see if he could save fuel by using only a single boiler and paddle wheel. With 'sail-assist', the ship heeled to leeward and the leeward wheel was more deeply immersed so tending to make the ship head into the wind, a tendency which sails on the foremast nicely counteracted. So now Hall ordered the weather-wheel disconnected, all sail put on and the course altered to 5 1/2 degrees to the wind. This proved successful; with the wheel revolving at 12–15 revolutions per minute the speed increased to 7 knots and the ship made much less leeway. Further experiment showed that both engines could not be powered by a single boiler, nor could both wheels be powered by a single engine, and that, if running with the wind or in heavy weather, both engines and both wheels must be used. Hall concluded that his ship was certainly much under-powered for ocean travel.

As they sailed south so they sailed into winter weather. And now the disadvantages of paddle steamers at sea became all too apparent to the crew. As the ship pitched both wheels came out of the water at once and the engine raced and then both plunged deep and the engines almost stopped; and as she rolled one wheel was too shallow and the other too deep and she went on her way like a corkscrew. And all the time the thud of the engines, now racing now slowing, reverberated through the iron hull. But it was not the engines that caused the first emergency.

On the morning of 2 June, moving against a strong southerly wind, the helmsman suddenly lost control of the ship. A rapid examination showed that the drop rudder had been lost, a serious situation because in choppy seas the true rudder was often out of the water. Hall ordered his carpenters to make a new drop rudder from wood, believing this would be stronger than the original iron one. As the true rudder could not be 'choked', prevented from moving, the fitting of the new drop-rudder proved a hazardous affair but it was completed safely by nightfall.

Over the next few days the weather continued to deteriorate, becoming more foul than Hall had ever witnessed in all his years off the coast of Africa. By now much of the 70 tons of fuel wood they had carried from Principe only two weeks before had been used, and, with just 32 tons of coal remaining, Hall ordered the engines stopped, some floats removed and all sails set. But in this weather it was immediately apparent that the sliding-keels were insufficient to prevent the *Nemesis* falling so much to leeward as to make little progress. Hall, discussing their predicament with his officers, remembered the lee-boards found on flat-bottomed Dutch barges, and it was decided to construct wooden ones for the *Nemesis*. Again the carpenters did a fine job and these were soon fitted just aft of the paddle boxes and proved most successful, reducing leeway by fully one half.

On 14 June, at 26° 16'S, 0° 41'E and still over 1,000 miles from the Cape, a sudden calm descended and the boilers were fired, but after a single day's steaming a breeze sprang up and the engines were again shut down. Over the next few days the wind steadily increased until by the 18th the *Nemesis* was bowling along at 9 knots in a decent gale. In this weather the lee-boards proved their worth, but they needed repairing and strengthening several times. And then on the 20th the wind veered south and she now found herself going into the teeth of a gale and with a current dead against her of about 40 miles a day. At 36° 54'S, 11° 20'E she was only 350 miles from the Cape, but Hall realised that if he aimed for the Cape but was driven north he would have to make for St Helena for more fuel. As this island lay about 1,700 miles in the opposite direction, to the north-west, this was, to put it mildly, undesirable. And so on the 21st she stood away to the west, moving further from her destination with the aim of getting south of it. By the 29th the Cape was still 230 miles away but now in a north-easterly direction, so, with the last of her coal, steam was got up. On 1 July Table Mountain was finally sighted and that evening the *Nemesis* steamed into Table Bay to the relief of the crew and the amazement of those on shore. It had proved an anxious voyage.

Hall when later writing about the voyage was clearly writing about a ship he loved. But the past 95 days had certainly shown up the weaknesses of the *Nemesis* as a sea boat. With her shallow draught – 6 ft on leaving England but only 4 1/2 ft at the Cape when all her fuel, water and provisions had been used – she may have 'sailed like a duck' and never shipped a sea in even the roughest weather, but she was difficult to control and made much too much leeway under sail. Later Hall recommended that such vessels built for coastal work should, if sent to sea, be fitted with a proper fixed keel which could later be removed. Certainly, her engines were under-powered and her appetite for fuel prodigious, and she surely must have been unusually uncomfortable in heavy seas. But winter was no time for any ship in the South Atlantic and she had arrived safely and with no major injury.

Table Bay, exposed to fierce winter gales from May to August, held few ships, most having anchored in Simon's Bay ('False Bay') to the east, but the *Nemesis* with her shallow draught found a sheltered cove in which to lie. Europeans had first settled here in the seventeenth century when the Dutch 'United East India Company', the VOC, had built some warehouses, a modest shipyard and a fort to act as a supply base for ships sailing between the Dutch Republic and their eastern possessions.[6] Now the crew could again relax ashore, the captain and officers paying their courtesies to the Governor, the men enjoying the facilities of the picturesque little port. On the 3rd the Governor himself came aboard with his party, and Hall entertained them by steaming around the bay, firing the forward gun with different charges of powder to show them its power and range. By then the ship's fame had spread, and the sound of the gun brought a crowd of thousands down to the shore, Africans, Malays and Europeans, and all were astonished to watch her run alongside the old wooden pier, astonished both that iron could float and that her draught was so shallow. After the Governor's party had disembarked other Europeans were allowed on board; they came in their hundreds, and there was much speculation about her final destination, a secret still known only to her captain.

After two days' rest it was time to start the necessary repairs and restocking. The new wooden drop rudder was strengthened as were the lower masts, the new lee-boards repaired, the decks caulked, and a number of other minor tasks carried out. As she could lie alongside the pier, coaling proved very simple, a crowd of coolies carrying 100 tons on board in only three hours. And re-victualling with good stocks of fresh water and food was equally easy. Hall later was to write to Mr Peacock "I beg to mention that I drew on you from the Cape for £1,192.19.5 our expenses for coal etc.", admitting also that although he had paid for 200 tons of coal only 170 tons had actually been loaded.[7] And so on Saturday 11 July the *Nemesis* left Table Bay, low in the water now fully stocked again with coal, water and provisions, steaming south then east, rounding the Cape of Good Hope and on the following day passing six or seven miles south of Cape Agulhas, the most southerly point of Africa, the first iron steamship ever to pass that way.

{ 6 }

THE CREW OF THE CAPTAIN'S GIG

> Oh, I am a cook and a captain bold,
> And the mate of the Nancy brig,
> And a bo'sun tight, and a midshipmite
> And the crew of the captain's gig.
>
> —"The Yarn of the 'Nancy Bell'", W. S. Gilbert

Although the voyage to Cape Town had had its fair share of dangers and difficulties, the crew would well have known that the times ahead were likely to prove just as challenging. For now the *Nemesis* entered the most treacherous part of any voyage between Britain and her Indian possessions, the seas off southeast Africa where the warm, fast moving Agulhas Current meets the low pressure systems from the Antarctic. And she entered them in what was generally considered the worst month of the year, July.

So who were the men who were to meet these challenges and take her further east? The crew on departure from England numbered 56 (Table 7): seven Commissioned Officers of which three were from the Royal Navy, three Engineers, three Warrant Officers, 12 Petty Officers and 31 'private men', experienced Able Seamen with perhaps seven years sea-time, inexperienced Ordinary Seamen, Stokers and Boys.[a] Due to the nature of her voyage this is likely to have been the fewest

---

[a] In the Royal Navy 'commissioned officers' were appointed by Queen's Commission, 'warrant officers' by warrant from an authority such as the Navy Board. 'Petty officers' were also warrant officers but in a supporting role (e.g., Gunner's mate supporting the Gunner). Forming the third tier were the 'private men', able and ordinary seamen, and servants.

possible for the safe running of the ship; subsequently, crew numbers varied from 75 to 93 men.[1]

For a ship of this size a total of about seven Commissioned Officers was typical.[2] The Captain was in complete charge of the ship and all men on board and his pay reflected this, Hall at £40 per month[b] earning almost three times as much as his First Officer. If he had been a Post-Captain on one of Her Majesty's ships he would have received more than double this amount. The First Officer was in charge of the daily running of the ship, the Second to Fourth Officers each commanding one of the three watches. As they oversaw the vital task of navigation, they had to be both literate and numerate, skilled in the use of the necessary instruments and in the interpretation of charts which, at that time, were all too often inaccurate.[c] The Surgeon, almost certainly having learned his trade by apprenticeship (whereas physicians were university graduates), acted as both surgeon and physician for all on board and tried to ensure the ship and the men were kept clean; lousiness was a particular problem, lice carrying typhus, 'ships' fever'. The Purser was responsible for stocking the ship and managing all her stores. At the bottom of the officers' scale, although the *Nemesis* carried none on this first voyage, was the Midshipman, often a boy as young as 12 who would earn no more than £5 per month, with a supplementary allowance from parents or guardian obligatory in the Royal Navy but not in the Company.[d]
[3] All these men would probably have been considered 'gentlemen' by education or family though it is unlikely that any had a strong 'interest'. But they could read and write, skills few 'private men' possessed, these therefore being able to rise no further than Warrant Officer.

The working day for all on board was divided into six four-hour watches starting at 8 pm, each man working two watches. The last watch, the 'dog watch' from 4–8 pm, was divided into two so that men did not work at the same time each day. The passing of the watch was

---

[b]   Payments were made per lunar month, Hall thus earning £520 per year (about £28,600 today).

[c]   And these inaccuracies were not minor: the charts on the troopship *Belleisle* on her voyage to China in 1841/42, carrying 1300 souls, placed both the Cape Verde Islands and Java Head in the Sunda Straits 45 miles to the west of their real positions (Cunynghame 1844).

[d]   If the age of 12 seems young, it should be remembered that at the time boys of 14 (and girls of 12) could legally marry without parental consent. And children of 9 could be employed down coal mines or in mills, working 9 hours a day and up to 48 hours a week (Pool 1993).

marked by half-hourly bells, 'eight bells' signalling the changing of the watch. For the laborious task of working the engines there were only three Engineers and seven Stokers, so for each watch the engines were managed by only three men, a single Engineer to manage the controls and two Stokers to feed the six voracious furnaces. At least twice this number was really needed, two Engineers and four Stokers per watch, and this was indeed the number subsequently employed.

Engineers had in 1837 been designated Warrant Officers, on a par with the Gunner, Carpenter and Boatswain (the 'bosun' supervised all above-deck activities and was in charge of basic discipline) but as they were scarce they were much better paid. The First Engineer earned £20 per month, exactly half Captain Hall's pay but more than anyone else on the ship. Indeed the Second Engineer was the third highest paid man on board at £16 per month,[e] the First Officer and the Surgeon receiving only £15. Other Warrant Officers were paid £5 per month, Petty Officers £3 or £4, Able Seamen £3 and the most junior Boy £1, typical wages for seamen of that time. Ashore in England a skilled worker might work six ten-hour days a week for about £4 per month, daily meal breaks and any holidays unpaid. An unskilled worker might take home £2.50 a month, a farm labourer, if he had a job at all, perhaps £1.50, and a house-maid working day and night in some country mansion, £1. For comparison, the income of a lower middle-class family might be £8 a month, and for an upper middle-class one over £12.[4] So the senior men on board were without doubt well paid, and the most junior, with free board and lodging, not ill-paid.

But his wages were only a part, and with luck a small part, of what a man could earn on a warship. For those serving in the Indian forces the most important allowance was *batta*, originally an amount intended to defray expenses when serving overseas but now seen as a rightful part of basic pay.[5] And it could be substantial. Hall noted in his diary that for service at Canton in 1842 the *batta* for officers of the *Nemesis*, not the whole crew, amounted to £1,204.30: for the Captain £547.00, an amount greater than his annual pay; and, divided between them, the four Officers £219.15, the Purser and Surgeon £219.00, the Engineers £109.57, the Boatswain, Gunner and Carpenter £109.58.[6] And then, as we shall see, there was prize money and 'head money'.

---

[e]   An engine-driver on the railways, an elite occupation, would have been paid half this amount, £8 per month (Wolmar 2007).

Crews of naval ships were recruited by the Captain and his officers for a single commission, usually about three years, drawing upon a pool of craftsmen and labourers who saw themselves primarily as seafarers, not as members of any naval service. Ships at that time required a crew with a formidable range of skills and Hall, taking a pioneer vessel on a voyage of unknown length to a secret destination, must have faced a daunting task in Liverpool that winter trying to find men of both suitable expertise and character. Certainly, he was not always successful; the first crew member to leave the ship did so only 11 days out, at Madeira, and three men deserted at Cape Town. Indeed, shore leave was rare in good part to prevent desertion; a generous Captain sailing on distant seas might, in a year, allow his men three 'long leaves' of three days each.[7] So why did men join? For the seaman there was the lure of adventure, of seeing far-off lands and, as the *Nemesis* was a warship, of possible riches from *batta* and prize money and from plunder. If these were the carrots, the sticks were the appalling poverty at home; disastrous harvest failures in both 1838 and 1839, coinciding with a trade recession, heralded the start of the worst economic depression the nation had yet experienced, the 'Hungry Forties'. To a poor man a secure wage and regular meals would have been a considerable attraction.

On her voyage to the east the *Nemesis* was, unsurprisingly, crewed only by Europeans, but thereafter in Asian waters many local men were employed (Table 7). Officers and Engineers were always European or perhaps 'East Indians', Caucasians born in India, or 'Eurasians', those of mixed race. Of the remainder of the crew, many and sometimes all were Asian, mostly Indians ('lascars'), but also Filipinos ('Manila men'), Chinese ('Chinamen') and 'Malays'. Of the latter many probably came from Java for the Javanese were the preeminent sailors of the Archipelago. These men were paid the same wages as the equivalent Europeans, an Asian Able Seaman thus earning £3 a month compared with perhaps £1 on a local trading vessel.[8] Whether this mix of races and religions – Christian, Hindu, Buddhist, Moslem – lived and worked smoothly together we are never told.

Sadly, Bernard's book on the early days of the *Nemesis* and subsequent accounts tell us virtually nothing about the crew, neither officers nor men nor the nature of their daily lives. And in the twenty-first century it needs a powerful imagination to form any impression of what that life must have been like. Not only is it difficult to visualise the ship itself, but those on board came from a society which by our standards was extremely harsh – with poverty endemic, malnourishment rife, ill-health and early death all too common, and education all too rare – and then served from perhaps 12 years old in a world that was almost uniquely secluded, the world of the ocean-going ship.[9]

Living aft of the engines were the six officers, Hall with a cabin of his own, the others probably with canvas cots screened off with curtains. Perhaps the three engineers and three warrant officers also shared this space, 12 men altogether. Forward of the engines, 'before the mast', all the other crew members lived, at least 43 men and at times as many as 80 – and that is not counting any passengers carried, these sometimes on later voyages lasting many days numbering well over 200. And separation would have been *de rigueur*: men from women passengers, officers from men, perhaps one race or religion from another. The living quarters were lit and ventilated only from above and must in a tropical noon have been insufferably hot, and at night, lit only with candles and the occasional lamp, depressingly dark.

At any one time two-thirds of the crew would not be working, instead eating, amusing themselves or sleeping, their hammocks slung virtually touching. In the Royal Navy the official allocation for each 6 x 3 foot canvas hammock was 14 inches for a seamen and 28 inches for a petty officer, although luckily not everyone was trying to get some sleep at the same time. Each man would have his hammock, blankets, sheets and pillow, and, slung from a hook, his ditty bag. Here he kept his personal possessions – his clothes and caps, a mug, plate and cutlery, a comb, soap and mirror, a box with pipes and tobacco (although tobacco was often chewed), checkers or chess, and if he was literate perhaps a Bible or navigation manual, pens, paper and ink. He might also have packed in some extra provisions such as treacle, cheese and ham to supplement what was otherwise a pretty dull diet; Hall, living much more spaciously, certainly had a supply of smoked salmon, pickles and champagne. And then some would have carried a flute or fiddle, a wise captain knowing the importance of having some musicians on board.

With the vagaries of wind and sea it was of course necessary to take on considerable quantities of drinking water and of food, much of it dried and packed in casks. Hall at 43 was probably twice the age of the average seaman on board and he would have understood the importance of giving these young and energetic men a diet that was both nourishing and satisfying. All would eat three times a day, the captain usually eating alone and the officers separately from the men.

Breakfast, taken at about 8 am, might be grits (a coarse oatmeal) in butter, perhaps with prunes 'to keep the body open' and tea or coffee sweetened with brown sugar. Dinner at noon, the main meal of the day and an important social event, might have offered cheese with duff (a dough pudding) and some vegetables and, at least four times a week, a little meat – "salt beef, saur kraut and a pint of black-strap" (cheap red wine, diluted).[10] Whenever possible, live animals would be brought on board and these needed feeding and watering until they in their turn were eaten, a welcome change from the standard 'salt junk', salted beef or pork. As would be any fish that the men caught. Supper during the dog watch would be similar to breakfast. Each day a man would be allowed about a pound of unleavened bread (the famous 'ships biscuits', too often fortified with weevils) with butter and cheese, and to wash it all down generous amounts of beer, black-strap or 'grog', diluted rum. On ships of the Royal Navy a gallon of beer was allowed each man each day – but this was 'small beer', with very little alcohol. For the water carried on board soon became virtually undrinkable – indeed, if a sailor had to partake he was advised to hold the tankard in one hand, pinch his nose with the other, and suck the water through clenched teeth to filter out the worms; presumably those who had lost teeth through accident or scurvy just had to swallow the wildlife. So alcoholic drinks or hot tea or coffee were a necessity and, unsurprisingly, drunkenness a nasty problem.

Apart from the crew's necessities – possessions, food, drink – a vast array of materials was needed to care for the ship, most prominently coal. In the officers' quarters were kept the vital navigation instruments – the charts and chronometers (valuable items as Table 5 shows), instruments for estimating latitude, telescopes; and on deck the compasses, hand logs and hour-glasses for estimating speed and plumb-lines for depth. Then there were the weapons, gunpowder and ammunition, the wood, iron and tools necessary for repairs to hull and engines, sails, sail-cloth and mending materials, paint, caulking and pitch, ropes and spare anchors, tallow, cotton and oil for lanterns – the list is endless.

Cleanliness was certainly known to be desirable and a good captain ran a clean ship with a well-scrubbed crew. The men would wash themselves on deck, usually from a bucket, sometimes in a bathing tub. Clothes would be washed twice a week, with perhaps a designated 'make & mend day', sailors of necessity being skilled with needle and thread. But none the less the smell from active sweating men, from the livestock, from the engines, the galley, the 'heads', must have been powerful, the heat and noise often intense, and all in the most crowded of conditions and with absolutely no privacy. And then the boredom which at times, even in that slow-paced world, must have been debilitating interspersed with periods of intense activity and danger such as that now about to befall them. Anarcharsis writing in 600 BCE seems to have got the measure of it, seeing three kinds of people, "the living, the dead and those that sail in ships."[11]

{ 7 }

THE NATURE OF IRON

> "You may smile Captain, but you don't know the nature of iron. How should you? When once it begins to work and crack as our sides do now, it is sure to go further; nothing can stop it."
>
> —The boilermaker to Captain Hall, 24 July 1840[1]

Captain Hall's instructions from Cape Town were to take the Inner Passage, the Mozambique Channel, passing between Africa and Madagascar and then eastwards to Ceylon, a route used during the south-west monsoon, although the more popular route for Company ships was the Middle Passage, passing east of Madagascar.[2] On Tuesday 14 July, sailing in an ever freshening NNW wind, Algoa Bay (now Port Elizabeth) was sighted from the masthead. On the next day the officers watched with consternation as the barometer fell precipitously to 28 inches and the wind strengthened to a powerful gale. As the seas rose so every second float board was removed from the paddle wheels, and the canvas reduced. By nightfall the seas were huge. Dawn broke on the 16th with no sign of a lessening of the storm. As Hall later wrote to Peacock, "The breeze soon freshened to a gale, with high seas, much lightning to the west, and the ship going at nine or ten knots obliging me to carry all sail to keep her before the seas, now increasing with the gale, and threatening to overwhelm our long low barky ... Now was to be seen the extraordinary fact of the main rudder *out* of the water and the jibboom *under*."[3] Throughout that day the crew's sole aim was to keep the flat-bottomed ship's head to the wind. Those not directly

49

employed in this struggle could do nothing to help, they and their ship being truly at the mercy of the sea.

By nightfall everyone was exhausted from both worry and the wild motion of the ship, those not on duty seeking what rest they could below. Hall was asleep in his cabin when, at 3 am on Friday the 17th, he was awoken by a tremendous crash. Rushing up on deck he saw that the ship had broached, lying side-on to wind and waves and in imminent danger, but before long she was again got before the wind. The helmsman told him that an enormous wave had struck her squarely on the port beam, but those on the bridge felt that that tremendous noise must herald more than a wave strike. Soon word came from below that water was seeping through the coal bunkers into the engine-room and it appeared as if some plates might have cracked amidships. But it was not until first light that the full extent of the damage could be seen.

The jolly-boat had been torn from the stern davits and was lost, and the starboard paddle wheel had been snapped in two and now one piece, almost severed from the rest, dragged through the water. Using a large boat-anchor like a fish-hook, the piece was with some difficulty secured to the ship. But much worse was what they found beside the wheels: on both sides, just in front of the after paddle or sponson beam, there was a large perpendicular crack about 2 1/2 ft long. This lay between two of the angle iron ribs, here 18 inches apart, and extended almost entirely through the second iron plate from the top and partly through the upper one, these having split with such violence that the edges projected out about 2 inches, leaving a large gap in the sides. With the storm still raging there was every possibility that the crack would lengthen. The ship had begun to split apart.

It was fortunate that William Hall was an effective captain, both just and decisive, for the predicament in which he found himself that Friday morning was truly dire. Under his command were 54 men in a fearsome storm and far from land on a ship of untried construction that was breaking apart beneath their feet. If the ship went down all would certainly die for the remaining ship's boats were totally inadequate as lifeboats. Swimming was a rare accomplishment amongst Victorian sailors, so even if near shore the best a man could hope for if thrown into the sea was to find a spar to cling to until rescued – but rescued here they would never be. As Hall wrote later in a private letter to Peacock, "few on board ever expected to reach port again. I feel utterly at a loss to express my feelings on the occasion – suffice it to say that *they were severe.*"[4]

It was extremely lucky that the broken section of the paddle wheel had been made secure as quickly as possible for it almost immediately came entirely adrift – and to have lost fully two-fifths of the entire wheel, carrying 6 of the 16 paddle boards, would have been disastrous. Using a stout block and tackle it was now hauled on board, and over the next week was repaired and, with immense difficulty, reattached. Hall realised that removing half the paddle boards, the usual practice when a paddle steamer was under sail, had weakened the wheel and he now ordered iron bars to be screwed on below each second board – and never again ordered the boards' removal except on the quietest of seas.

By the 18th the weather was calmer and the *Nemesis* was making 4 knots with a single engine turning a single wheel. On the 20th she passed within 40 miles of Cape Natal but as there was nowhere there where she could be beached for repairs, Hall decided to continue north to Delagoa Bay (now Maputo Bay) on the African coast at 26°S. But the next day the seas began to rise again under a north-east wind, an unusual quarter for the time of year, and again the crew began to fear for their lives. These winds, meeting a strong current which was running at more than 50 miles per day, caused the sea to roll heavily behind the vessel so that at times her rudder was entirely out of the water and her bowsprit submerged. As these great waves passed beneath her they tested one of her major weaknesses, the flexibility of her wooden deck. Suddenly the cracks began to lengthen in a most alarming manner, both sides being equally bad, and she began to ship even more water. And just as pumping became still more essential, the furnaces of the port boiler were damaged and could scarcely be used. Everyone was now employed night and day trying to save the ship. As the following seas threatened to break over her at any instant, some were employed to heighten the bulwarks, fixing four breadths of stout planking over the stern and along the quarters to help break the force of the water. Others attempted to reduce the top weight fore and aft, dragging the bow anchors aft and laboriously dismantling the heavy stern gun and placing it in the coal-bunkers amidships. As the seas were now so high the single usable engine was repeatedly unable to turn the single usable paddle wheel over the centre, and engineers had to stand by continuously to assist. By the 22nd the cracks had lengthened to 3 1/2 ft on both sides, and so two or three rivets were cut out on each side of the crack and a new iron plate placed outside and bolted through to a stout oak plank on the inside. And all this in very heavy weather.

On the evening of Thursday 23rd the ship stood off from land but she was taking in so much water that Hall ordered the engine stopped and she lay-to under sail all night. This night, exactly a week since she had first broached, was one of great danger for the *Nemesis*. The seas were still extremely rough, the ship only just controllable. But dawn brought some relief, the north-east gale moderating and by afternoon the wind had shifted to the south-east. With the paddle wheel and boiler now repaired steam was got up and she again sailed north. Over the past eight days she had moved no more than 150 miles closer to her destination, and Delagoa Bay still lay 200 miles away. But then the winds again strengthened, shredding the single sail she was carrying with its force, and the cracks began to lengthen still further. In one 2 1/2 hour period they increased by 18 inches, now extending from the deck to below the waterline. As the vessel pitched and rolled they opened sometimes to an inch and slid laterally past each other by as much as 5 inches, this causing the deck planking to begin to start. The ship was now taking in a lot of water; luckily the pumps coped well with this, but as the cracks led directly to the engine room there was the awful danger that if they choked the water would rise and douse the boilers.

Hall received little comfort from the boilermaker. "You may smile Captain, but you don't know the nature of iron. How should you? When once it begins to work and crack as our sides do now, it is sure to go further; nothing can stop it." The solution was to try to prevent the cracked plates both separating and overlapping. Firstly, thick planks were placed on the deck over the cracked area and bolted to the paddle-beams. Then bolts were passed through the two angle-iron ribs on either side of the crack and tightened, aiming to prevent separation, and blocks of wood in the form of a letter X were placed between the ribs to prevent overlapping.

It must have been with enormous relief to all on board when on 26 July the morning mists lifted and they saw land to the west, the Peninsula de Santa Maria by Delagoa Bay. Running past the peninsula they entered the bay and dropped anchor close inside. That day, the first safe one they had enjoyed for almost two weeks, was a Sunday and Hall, a devout man, called the crew to a service of thanksgiving for their deliverance. And then, at last – a time to again eat properly, to wash themselves and their clothes, and to sleep.

Far to the south the dreadful weather of that July proved nearly disastrous to another British ship, the *Erebus*. The British Antarctic Expedition under Captain James Clark Ross had left England the previous September in HMS *Erebus* and *Terror*. Now fierce storms separated the two ships, the boatswain of the *Erebus* was swept overboard and the whole crew of the rescue boat very nearly lost.[5]

On the 27th the *Nemesis* steamed the 20 miles across the great bay to the Portuguese settlement of Delagoa (now Maputo) on the western shore, Hall wishing to pay his complements to the Governor of the fort before he started to repair his ship. Knowing that his was the first steamship ever to have entered the bay, he decided to impress by steaming up the estuary below the fort, the English River, there firing a salute and raising the Portuguese flag. To see a ship as large as his steaming into such shallow waters would, he knew, greatly surprise those watching. The only problem was that although the salute was successfully fired the flag would not unfurl and, fearing a nasty misunderstanding, Hall had to order a sailor to quickly shin up the mast and unfurl it by hand. Having finally found safety after such a fearful ordeal, it would have been ironic then to have been fired upon by the fort of a friendly power.

Anchoring in English River they soon welcomed on board the aide-de-camp of the Governor in all his finery, but as none of the crew could speak Portuguese and the aide had no English, they merely stood around smiling, downing large glasses of wine. Later, Hall and some of his officers called upon the Governor at his fine bungalow and were courteously received, this time communicating through a Bombay merchant who could speak both Portuguese and Hindustani, and a member of the *Nemesis'* crew who could understand the latter language.

Delagoa itself did not impress the British, being small and dilapidated with few Europeans, and apparently almost wholly reliant upon the slave trade. This trade, supposedly illegal in Portuguese settlements, was certainly thriving. The main market on the Mozambique coast was not here but at Quelimane, over 600 miles to the north. From there the Portuguese, buying slaves for as little as $1.50 a man, had been shipping as many as 5,000 a year to Rio de Janeiro where they could fetch perhaps ten times that amount. But Delagoa was an active slave port too. When some of the officers of the *Nemesis* were invited on board a brig flying the Portuguese flag anchored below the fort, they saw she was well fitted out as a slaver, with planks stacked ready to build a slave deck, boilers for their food, and piles of shackles and chains. But Hall decided that it would be prudent not to raise this matter with the Governor, having no power to intervene and requiring a welcoming place in which to repair his severely damaged ship. Thus on the evening of the 28th he invited the Governor and his family to dinner on the *Nemesis*, his guests bringing gifts of fresh vegetables and ivory.

An area of sandy shore close to the fort was chosen as the place to beach the *Nemesis*, and at Hall's request this was patrolled by Portuguese soldiers, with neither local people being allowed to enter nor British sailors to leave. Hall spoke to his crew about the great amount of work that needed to be done, promising them double pay upon good behaviour. Then on the 31st, with her fuel removed to the shore and guns put into boats, the *Nemesis* was hauled ashore. No sooner was she truly beached than the sky suddenly darkened and with a tremendous drumming of wings an enormous swarm of locusts descended upon them. To the superstitious amongst them this must have seemed an ominous sign – the Seventh Plague of Egypt – and many were indeed alarmed and all greatly inconvenienced. The 30th had been a windless day but on the 31st a north-east wind had sprung up and it was this that had brought the locusts, but overnight it veered to the south-west and the following day increased to a strong gale which carried all the insects away. To the Englishmen's amazement the local people saw the plague as a gift from heaven, collecting the insects enthusiastically, and for the next few days they feasted upon them, stripping off their legs and wings and lightly roasting them with much singing and dancing.

With the ship high and dry the crew rapidly gathered to stare in amazement at the full extent of the damage. On both sides the split amidships now extended 7 ft down from the deck, half of it below the waterline, thus severing almost one third of the hull! Without doubt, if repairs had not been made at sea she would have split in half and been lost with all hands, only the briefest of footnotes in the history of steamships. But now, in this desolate place, and with virtually nothing other than the skills and materials she carried with her, work began to make the ship strong and seaworthy again. The top two plates on either side which had fractured were replaced, and over the third, which was only partly broken, a new plate was riveted. By good fortune they had found by the fort a pile of excellent timbers, well seasoned, probably from a wreck and, after some hard bargaining, acquired them. Two of these newly bought beams were now placed below the deck, across the angle-iron ribs against either side of the vessel. The upper one, 23 ft long, 1 ft wide and 6" thick, was positioned 2 ft below the deck and secured there by large bolts run through the side plates in the centre of the space between each rib. Then the gap between beam and plate was filled with well-seasoned red pine. The lower beam was somewhat shorter than the upper but otherwise identical, and, when the *Nemesis* reached Mozambique, a third beam identical to this was also fitted. Although only a couple of the deck angle-irons, between the gunwale and the deck, had given way a beam 25 ft long was placed along the deck beside each paddle box and bolted to the sponson beams.

And so by Wednesday 12 August, with other minor repairs completed, the bottom cleaned of barnacles and the whole hull painted, the *Nemesis* was again ready to face the sea. Hall was certainly anxious to leave, only he knowing just how much they were behind schedule and how far they still had to go. But he also realised that the crew needed to be thoroughly rested, the voyage ahead certainly long and possibly perilous. So he decided to wait a few days before sailing, sending word to the Governor that he did not expect to depart until the beginning of the following week. On hearing this, one of the Portuguese merchants arranged a hunting trip for some of the officers up-river where they took potshots at a wide variety of game – buffalo, zebra, hippopotamus – but none were killed. Others were entertained by a local tribe who, coming from a settlement about 30 miles inland, were paying their annual visit to the Governor. The 700 warriors made a most impressive sight, dressed in skins decorated with ostrich feathers, each carrying spears, a club and a shield, their heads shaved and faces notched with fierce tattoos. In the evening the Governor provided a tubful of rum and a merry time was had by all, with much dancing and singing. Although the chief failed to impress, Hall describing him as an old man arrayed in a loose dressing gown and bright red night-cap with a wife of unsurpassed ugliness, he invited him and his party on board, presenting him with a musket and bayonet and receiving the next day a spear and shield in return.

If the English sometimes viewed the Africans with considerable condescension, they viewed the Portuguese too as often little more than savages, Hall recalling a terrible story he had heard about at incident some 18 years ago at Delagoa. Apparently, a dozen poor natives living close to the fort, seeking there protection from the depredations of another tribe, were accused of stealing from the governor's garden. With no pretence at justice, they were summarily taken out and flogged to death with bullock-hide whips, the watching soldiers prodding them awake with thorny bushes each time they fainted.

On Sunday evening the Governor invited Hall and his officers to a fine meal at his bungalow, enlivened by local dancers, while on the ship the crew enjoyed a special dinner of roast beef and plum pudding with an extra glass of grog as a reward for work well done. The next morning, Monday 17 August, steam was got up and the Governor and his family taken on an excursion around the bay. Upon landing, the Governor fired a salute of seven guns, but Hall did not reply as he had three men on board sick with fever. And so they sailed again for the open sea.

Finding the winds strong and the seas high as she turned north, the *Nemesis* initially kept close to the shore but as the winds moderated she took the most direct route for Mozambique which she reached on the 31st, the whole journey except the final mile or two under sail. Throughout this time Hall was particularly exercised by the inaccuracies of both compasses. The settings made in Portsmouth seemed little better than those made in Liverpool which had so nearly proved disastrous, and so now whenever near the coast he stationed a leadsman on each paddle-box and another in the bow. He had decided long before not to try to move the fixed compass nor the large magnets, and had found that a compass suspended from a cross-spar about 12 ft above the head of the helmsman was best – but with the days often stormy and the nights always dark, this was far from satisfactory. Thus on any clear night an officer could always be seen on the bridge, anxiously trying to get accurate sightings on the stars.

In the harbour of Mozambique Hall was surprised to see at anchor what he initially supposed to be three slavers, for he knew the governor there to be opposed to the trade. But it soon became apparent that one was in fact HMS *Acorn* (16 guns) which, flying a decoy flag, had just brought two slavers into port, and Hall immediately went to pay his respects. Fascinated by the travails of the *Nemesis*, Captain Adams offered what assistance he could, and thus with the help of the *Acorn's* carpenters her third and final lateral beam was fitted. The *Acorn* also provided another useful service, as Hall later told Peacock. "I was compelled to leave Barnard Owen, fireman, on board HM Brig *Acorn*, Captain Adams, for a passage to the Cape – his conduct has at all times been too notorious to allow him remaining on the ship."[6]

The Governor proved a generous host. Brigadier-General Joachim Pereira Morinho, a friend of Britain who had served with the Duke of Wellington in the Peninsular War, presented the ship with a fat ox, four sheep, a large pig, stacks of fruit and vegetables, and 8,000 pieces of fuel wood. And he allowed her to take on all the water she needed at no charge. For this generosity Hall could send only the gesture of some smoked salmon and English pickles. But there were other ways in which the Nemesis could repay such kindness. On the morning of 1 September the Governor, seeing that the presence of two British ships, one the first steamer ever to visit, provided a good opportunity to impress the citizens with the determination both of his administration and the Royal Navy to suppress the slave trade, started the day with the ostentatious auction of the two slavers, both fine ships. Then, in full dress uniform, he crossed to the Nemesis in the state barge under salute from the fort's batteries watched, as he had no doubt hoped, by a great crowd on the shore. The Nemesis, decked out with flags, was crowded and colourful and, after inspecting the ship, the Portuguese party were invited to a splendid buffet lunch, complete with champagne toasts to the health of the Queens of Britain and of Portugal. There followed the necessary excursion around the harbour, a large inlet about 6 miles in diameter, the Governor duly impressed and the crowd no doubt amazed by the long low ship, not a sail unfurled, black smoke belching from the tall funnel and paddles thrashing the water. Then, with the Governor returned to the town under a 21-gun salute and the sun low in the sky, the ship turned again to the sea after what Hall thought had been a very successful and certainly enjoyable 24 hours.

Over the next three days the ship moved slowly north-east, sailing against a strong south-westerly current, and it was not until the 4th that she reached the Comoros, less than 250 miles distant from Mozambique. Sailing east of wooded Moheli Island it was dark when she entered the large bay on the north of Johanna (Anjouan) and, using flares to announce her arrival, was guided to an anchorage by a fire on the beach. Despite the late hour Hall, knowing that his visit must again be very brief, went ashore immediately with First Officer Pedder to call upon the sultan. Met by an uncle of the sultan and the prime minister they were led to the palace where Sultan Alloué, together with local worthies, awaited them. The visitors were clearly charmed by the handsome young man, finding him both friendly and well educated, and were surprised by the excellence of the English he and his officers spoke, and to be asked about the health of Queen Victoria and Prince Albert and whether the Thames Tunnel[a] was yet finished.

Early the next morning the Nemesis, surrounded by a flotilla of boats filled with the curious, was again decked out with flags, and Hall and many of the men went ashore, firstly to enjoy an excursion arranged by the sultan around the old Moorish town, with its white flat-roofed houses and turreted walls, and to attend a fine breakfast. The sultan then took the officers to a party to celebrate the eighth day after the birth of one of his nephews, each officer being attended by a serving girl whose job was to elegantly fan them, much to their pleasure.

Leaving the party for a secluded room, the sultan sent for Hall to join him and there, alone, he told him a disturbing tale. The sultan's father had four years before been murdered because of his opposition to slavery, and now he himself, still trying to suppress the trade, was also threatened by rebellion. Although he had requested assistance from the Indian Government none had been forthcoming, and he now asked the captain if he could provide some help. Hall had neither the time nor the authority to assist but, touched by the young man's predicament, he agreed to give him some powder and shot, provide a British flag to be flown over the palace, and write a letter to the rebel leader saying that the sultan was now under British protection. With the letter written and the flag raised to a 21-gun salute, the sultan was invited on board the Nemesis and given the requisite tour of the bay.

As night fell on the 5th the Nemesis again weighed anchor. With only 25 tons of Cape coal remaining, a mere two days' supply, and an ocean to cross, sails were set and she turned north. For the next five days she struggled against a very strong current running to the south-west at about 60 miles a day, not losing sight of Comoro Island, a mere hundred miles from Johanna, until the 10th. A week later, on the morning of Thursday 17 September, she crossed the Line at about 54° east, and with a current running eastwards made better progress. For the next two weeks they sailed without sight of land, using steam only for a few hours on the 21st. Then on the last day of the month in squally weather the Maldives were

---

[a] The Thames Tunnel, the first tunnel under a major river, started in 1825 but discontinued between 1828 and 1836, was in fact not completed until 1843. It was designed by Marc Brunel, his son I. K. Brunel of Great Britain fame working on its construction.

sighted, and, passing through the centre of the archipelago under steam, she anchored the next morning, Thursday 1 October, off Feawar, one of the most easterly islands. There the inhabitants appeared frightened by this strange ship and although boats gathered around no one would come aboard, but when some of the officers landed to stretch their legs the village people proved friendly enough, inviting them to their houses and to view the little mosque. Remaining only a few hours, they set off eastwards again before nightfall, and on the afternoon of 5 October entered the harbour of Point de Galle in Ceylon under steam, only 13 tons of coal remaining.

In England Hall had been told to take the *Nemesis* to Galle, and this he had achieved though not without great danger and well behind schedule, and there await further instructions. "Scarcely had she fairly reached her moorings, when a dispatch was delivered to the Captain from the Government of India containing orders from the Governor-General in Council, to complete the necessary repairs, and take in coal and provisions with all possible expedition, and then to proceed to join the fleet off the mouth of the Canton River, placing himself under the orders of the naval Commander-in-Chief. Great was now the rejoicing of both officers and men. ... The road to distinction was now made known to them; they were at once to be engaged in active operations, in conjunction with Her Majesty's forces."[7]

Hall in his turn wrote immediately to Mr Peacock – "The engines, I am glad to say, are in splendid order ... We are well on board; no death, no accident has occurred since leaving England"[8] – and then on the evening of his arrival set off by coach for Colombo 70 miles to the north. Not until 1844 was Galle made a proper victualling and refuelling station, and so all arrangements had to be made in Colombo where Hall also met Governor Mackenzie. Returning a few days later, he found the necessary work on the *Nemesis* well under way. Local men had been employed to help – men who to those sailors new to the east appeared somewhat strange for they were slight of build and beardless, wearing their hair long, tied in a knot at the top adorned with a large tortoise-shell comb, so that it was rumoured that of an evening one or two sailors had found themselves making an embarrassing mistake. It took a full eight days to get the ship ready for sea again, the decks caulked, sundry repairs carried out and a great variety and volume of stores brought on board. Now there was no mystery about her destination, and on the 14th the governor's son, Lieutenant Keith Mackenzie, bound for China as Military

Secretary to the Commander-in-Chief, came on board and that evening she sailed, her departure watched by crowds on the shore, a few signal rockets adding gaiety to the occasion.

From Galle their course lay due east over calm seas and they covered the 1,600 miles to Penang in ten days, the journey slower than expected due partly to the poor quality of the coal which required the furnaces to be cleaned out twice a day instead of once, and partly due to the mass of barnacles now sticking to her hull. At Penang she was run on shore on fine firm sand and her bottom scraped and painted, and on the 27th was again on her way, south down the Straits of Malacca. There she passed the Company's steamer *Diana* heading north, the first steamship she had seen since leaving England, and on Friday 30 October turned east towards a port that she would later get to know very well, anchoring that afternoon in the roads, the anchorage, of Singapore.

{ 8 }

THE NAVIES OF THE EAST

"The Lion of the Week has been the new iron steamer *Nemesis* which anchored in our roads on the afternoon of Friday last." Thus was the ship welcomed by the editor of the *Singapore Free Press*, one of many to visit her and be entertained by Captain Hall and the crew. Although no more than a small village 21 years earlier when Stamford Raffles landed, Singapore was now a vibrant settlement of perhaps 40,000 people, largely Chinese.[1] Europeans numbered some 400 to 500, about half of whom had settled there, the others passing through on the many ships that crowded the roads. Along Boat Quay half a dozen ships' chandlers were gathered, and here everything necessary for a ship could be readily acquired. For the officers, cramped for many months on board, M. Dutronquoy's London Hotel provided both spacious rooms and a fine dinner: "pork chops, curried fowl, roast duck, ham, cheese and potatoes for a dollar each, and [they] gave us good beer, madeira and claret." And for the sailor as night fell, in the alleys of the Chinese quarter all that he might wish for was eagerly sold. Of course not all were enamoured; Surgeon Cree of HMS *Rattlesnake* considered "the people are as ugly as they are made with their flat yellow faces, small piggy eyes and long pigtails."[2] And then there was the distressing sight of the smoke-filled opium dens. "Here the unfortunate victims of this degrading vice may be seen undergoing all the different stages consequent upon the use of this pernicious drug. Some, totally bereft of their senses, wallow, like beasts of the field, in filth; whilst others, not yet arrived at that stage of listless inactivity, are throwing their emaciated bodies into the contortions of maniacs, revelling with each other."[3]

Hall had hoped to arrive in Singapore at least a couple of months earlier. But now in late October the north-east monsoon had set in and the Nemesis faced a more difficult voyage through the South China Sea than had been expected. Over the next few days she was thoroughly overhauled and fully provisioned.[4] Her crew too needed replenishment. Three seamen whose wages had been paid by John Laird to Singapore were discharged, and four had 'run', so a number of new men – notably stokers – were engaged, Indians ('lascars'), Chinese ('Chinamen') and Filipinos ('Manila-men'), all paid at the same rate as Europeans; indeed from now on her stokers were nearly always Asians. The ship was also loaded with the maximum amount of coal that she could carry, 175 tons, enough for 15 days steaming. This took 20 coolies working all night and all day, paid a dollar (25p) for the night shift and half a dollar for the day, somewhat more than an Able Seaman was paid.[5]

On the evening of Wednesday 4 November, the Nemesis weighed anchor and again turned east, towards Borneo. On that very day up a shallow and winding river on that great island an historic confrontation had taken place between a British adventurer and the local ruler. James Brooke, in whose life the Nemesis was to play a significant role, had finally presented Rajah Muda Hassim of Sarawak with an ultimatum: without greater personal authority he could no longer assist the Rajah in putting down a rebellion. He would leave and not return unless promised the government of the territory.

The journey to the Canton (Pearl) River through the South China Sea proved uneventful, the Nemesis due to the monsoons following an eastern route along the north-west coast of Borneo to Luzon in the Philippines. She passed Manila Bay on the morning of the 17th having covered 1,600 miles in 12 days, and continued northwards to Cape Bolinao and then north-west to the coast of China. The islands south of Hong Kong were first sighted on Tuesday 24 November and at daylight on the 25th the Nemesis steamed through the Taypa roads and anchored in shallow water just off Macau, at last safe in Chinese waters. It had been a long journey and a slow one, covering about 20,600 miles in 243 days of which 181 were spent at sea.

No sooner had the Nemesis anchored than a boat came off to meet her bearing a message from the Portuguese Governor warning of the shallows. Indeed, word of this strange ship so close in shore soon spread and it was not long before the Praya Grande, the esplanade, was filled with a crowd of curious people. Hall went ashore to pay his respects and to thank the Governor for his concern, and then, after firing a salute, sailed on to join the British fleet anchored across the estuary of the Canton River north of Lantao Island. Eight ships were lying there, three Ships-of-the-Line, all Third Rate, one Fifth Rate, one Sixth Rate, two sloops and the troopship *Rattlesnake*.[a] The *Rattlesnake*, a converted Sixth Rate, had arrived from England in June taking as many days as the *Nemesis* but only 164 at sea.

For Hall it was clearly a somewhat emotional arrival. Not only had he brought the *Nemesis* safely to China, completing the longest voyage ever undertaken by a steamship, but here he was again in a place he had visited in his youth, a 19-year-old midshipman on HMS *Lyra* accompanying Lord Amherst's embassy to China. Saluting Admiral the Honourable George Elliot's flagship, HMS *Wellesley* (74 guns), Hall was delighted when this was "immediately returned by the *Wellesley*, precisely as if the *Nemesis* had been a regular man-of-war." And there she lay, "her *iron* frame swinging, side by side, with the famed 'wooden walls' of England's glory."[6]

With the *Nemesis* again anchored amongst ships of Her Majesty's navy, all wooden sailing vessels, it is interesting to consider how that navy viewed the intruder, steam powered and iron hulled. It has often been said that the Royal Navy embraced steam and iron slowly and reluctantly, but this is not so.[7] Indeed at that time, of 202 naval ships in commission 28 were already powered by steam (Table 1). With responsibility for by far the largest navy in the world, and with a vast empire to defend, the Admiralty was naturally cautious about introducing radical new developments. Of course they kept abreast of all new ideas but were interest only in those of proven practicality. None the less, in the 40 years between the Napoleonic and Crimean wars, 1815 to 1854, the Royal Navy saw the biggest transition in its history, and, considering its responsibilities, it is difficult to imagine that steam or iron could have been more swiftly adopted.

---

[a]   The *Rattlesnake* was the vessel later made famous by its surveying voyage to the Australian seas between 1846 and 1850 under the command of Captain Owen Stanley carrying the naturalist Thomas Henry Huxley, later to become Charles Darwin's greatest supporter (Goodman 2005).

The Navy's first steamship, *Comet*, was launched at Deptford on the Thames as early as 1822.[8] This little ship of 238 tons, with side-lever engines of 80 hp, was designed for use as a tug- or tow-ship on that river, and famously was employed that very year to tow the royal yacht *Royal George* (330 tons) down-river at the start of King George IV's first visit to Scotland. The following year came *Lightning* (296 tons) also a tug but for use at Plymouth, and destined in 1824 to be the first Royal Navy steamer to take part in hostile operations, though not in action, accompanying bomb vessels[b] to Algiers. By 1831 the steamship could be considered a regular part of the Royal Navy, 14 vessels supplying a tug and packet-boat service. By 1837 the Navy List showed 27 steam vessels, that year seeing the launch of HMS *Gorgon* (1,109 tons), the first naval steamer of more than 1,000 tons and the first with real fighting capacity. In September of the following year HMS *Temeraire*, one of the last remaining First Rates that had fought at Trafalgar in 1805, was towed up the Thames by a steam tug to be broken up at Rotherhithe. J. M. W. Turner's great painting of that scene, exhibited at the Royal Academy in 1839, can now be seen as heralding the end of the sailing navy. A decade earlier, in 1827, the Battle of Navarino proved to be the last great battle fought amongst purely sailing warships. A decade later, in 1848, the Royal Navy ordered its last new vessel powered solely by the wind.

Those who attended the launching of the *Nemesis* that November day in 1839 would have passed on the stocks in Laird's yard the frame of the Navy's very first iron ship, the packet HMS *Dover* (224 tons), 110 ft long with a draught of only five ft, her paddles powered by engines of 90hp. Screw vessels followed soon after. In June 1843 the Navy purchased its first screw vessel, the iron hulled *Dwarf* (164 tons), launched the previous year as a merchantman, and in late October the wooden hulled screw steamer HMS *Rattler* (867 tons) put to sea for her first propeller trials. On 3 April 1845 the famous tug-of-war between the *Rattler* and her sister ship, the paddle steamer HMS *Alecto*, which the *Rattler* won, provided useful data on screw development to an Admiralty already well aware of the potential of screw warships. By 1846 the Navy had 16 iron vessels and a further nine were being built; of these 25, seven were powered by screws. That same year the wooden hulled HMS *Terrible*

---

[b]   Ships armed with one, or occasionally two, heavy mortars for shore bombardment.

was commissioned, the largest and most powerful paddle warship ever built for the Royal Navy. *Terrible* was certainly a most formidable fighting vessel, at 1,847 tons larger than a contemporary Third Rate and armed with 19 large guns. But at her launch she was already obsolete; not only did she prove extremely expensive to run and maintain, but the Navy needed steamships that could fire a full broadside, something only a screw ship could do.

Although the Royal Navy played a major role in the defence of India, the Indian Government also had its very own navy – or, to be accurate, two navies: the Bombay Marine, called the Indian Navy from 1830 and under martial law, and the Bengal Marine of Calcutta to which the *Nemesis* belonged, a local service not under martial law.[9] Since 1827 officers of these navies had had their ranks accepted by the Royal Navy, but Royal Naval officers of the same rank always took precedence. Furthermore, Royal Navy ships could claim prize money unavailable to Company naval ships. As the Governor-General of Bengal supervised the two smaller presidencies of Bombay and Madras, but as Bombay had both the finer harbour and the larger navy, it comes as little surprise that not only was there friction between the Royal and Company navies but also between the Calcutta and Bombay branches of the latter.

If the Royal Navy embraced both steam and iron with some trepidation, then the Company's navies, enjoying a very different role, embraced them with alacrity. Of primary interest to the Company's servants in India was rapid and reliable communication with their presidencies from Bombay to Singapore and with their masters back in England. Early in the century the Governor-General, Lord Wellesley, had complained that he had waited 'about seven months without receiving one line of authentic intelligence from England.'[10] [c] Secondly, the Company's military concerns were primarily in shallow waters, securing ships against pirate attacks and ensuring their dominance over coastal and river communities. Steam propulsion and iron construction could greatly enhance both interests.

When the *Nemesis* joined the fleet in Hong Kong in November 1840 the two Indian navies employed a total of 26 steamships, all of which

---

[c]   Communications by sail between Europe and Asia were certainly slow: the average time a VOC ship took for the 15,000 mile outward journey from Holland to Batavia was eight months, and for the 13,400 mile return journey seven and a half months (Jacobs 1991).

were armed (Table 8). The Indian Navy owned 35 vessels of which 20 were steamers, twelve iron hulled of 40–432 tons and 10–70 hp, and eight wooden steamers of 160–876 tons and 160–280 hp. Of the twelve iron ships eight formed the 'Indus Flotilla' and four were employed surveying the Tigris and Euphrates rivers. The Bengal Marine had six steamers, all wooden, from the little *Diana (ii)*, 133 tons and 32 hp, currently stationed in Singapore waters where the *Nemesis* had met her, to their latest and largest ship *Queen*, 766 tons and 220 hp. The *Nemesis* was their first iron vessel.[11]

In 1823, just a year after the launch of the Navy's *Comet*, steam power arrived in eastern seas. On 12 July that year at Kyd's yard near Calcutta a small teak paddle ship of 133 tons rolled down the slipway into the Hooghly River. The *Diana (i)* was 100 ft long, 17 ft wide and of 132 tons, her 12 foot diameter wheels powered by engines of 32 hp brought from England giving her a maximum speed of about 8 knots. Built for use as a tug on the Hooghly, she joined there an even smaller vessel, the *Pluto*, a dredger launched the previous year, not herself steam-powered but with a steam-driven bucket chain. With the outbreak of hostilities in Burma in early 1824 (*see* chapter 28), Commander Frederick Marryat, later of *Mr Midshipman Easy* fame, suggested to the Bengal Government that both these vessels be bought. The *Diana*, bought for 80,000 rupees, was immediately fitted with Congreve rockets, and leaving Calcutta on 13 April 1824 arrived on the Irrawaddy in May. There she became the first steamship ever employed in war, a few months before *Lightning* was present at, but not involved in, hostile action in Algiers. Later that year the *Pluto* was converted to steam power, her bucket-chain replaced by a paddle wheel, and she joined the *Diana* in Burma in January 1825 for use as a floating battery and troop carrier.

In London in 1822 and in Calcutta at the end of the following year meetings were held to consider the possibilities of steam navigation between Britain and India. These recommended the introduction of a steamship mail service either via the Cape or via Suez, the Indian Government and merchants offering a prize of 100,000 rupees, about £10,000, for the first steamship to make two round trips between England and Calcutta before the end of 1826, each passage taking no longer than 70 days. The challenge was accepted by a group of merchants in Calcutta who in 1824 placed an order for a suitable vessel with Gordon & Company's yard at Deptford on the Thames. This ship, sensibly called the *Enterprize*, was launched on 23 February 1825, a wooden paddle steamer of 464 tons, 142 ft long with cabins for 20 passengers. She carried three masts and was square rigged, her 15-foot paddle wheels being turned by two engines each of 60 hp.[12]

The *Enterprize*, Captain James Johnston, left Falmouth on 16 August 1825 with 17 passengers, 380 tons of coal and a small amount of cargo bound for India, the first steamer ever to attempt the journey. Travelling via Cape Town on the 13 October, she reached Calcutta on the 7 December, a voyage of over 14,000 miles completed in a total of 114 days, with 103 days at sea of which 64 were steam-powered. For the past century the average sailing time for the 13,500 miles to Bombay had in fact been 114 days, the fastest 90 days, so this was hardly an improvement. Although too slow to win the prize, she was immediately bought by the Bengal Government, the owners accepting £40,000 although she had cost £43,000 to build. The *Diana* had already proved that steamships could play a valuable role in the war then being conducted in Burma, and in January 1826 the *Enterprize* was sent to join her, not as a warship but rather as a packet to carry dispatches between Calcutta and Rangoon.

But Calcutta was not the only eastern port where merchants intent on developing steam were to be found. The arrival of the *Enterprize* in Calcutta coincided with the launch in Surabaya, Java, in November 1825 of the paddle steamer *Vander Capellen*, built there in Kerr's Yard for British merchants but tactfully named after the Governor-General of Java, Baron G. A. G. P. van der Capellen. On 17 April 1827 this vessel anchored in the roads at Singapore, the first steamship to visit the young settlement, then only eight years old. It would be another two years before a second steamer visited, the *Enterprize* carrying down from Calcutta the Governor-General of India, Lord William Bentinck, on a tour of the Straits Settlements – Penang, Malacca and Singapore.

That same year, 1829 (incidentally the year that the steam engine *Rocket* proved her worth at the Rainhill railway trials in England – *see* chapter 3), saw the launch of the first steamer built in Bombay, the *Hugh Lindsay*, designed to run between Bombay and Suez, a journey she undertook once a year from 1830. Unfortunately her overall design left much to be desired. Although she could not hope to reach her first port, Aden, in less than ten days she was provided with bunker space for only half the amount of coal required; thus the accommodation for fare-paying passengers was reduced, but even then she could not hope to make the journey at all against the monsoon winds of June to September. 1830 also saw the first steamer in Chinese waters, the steam tug *Forbes* sailing from Calcutta via Singapore to Macau, and the following year the *Sarah Jane* arrived in Sydney from England, the first steamship to visit Australia.

Lord Bentinck had been appointed Governor-General in 1827. A devout moderniser, he clearly saw the potential of steam for improving communication between the ever-growing eastern empire and the home country. Speaking to Parliament some years later Bentinck could say "Steam navigation is the great engine of working [India's] moral improvement. In proportion as the communication between the two countries shall be facilitated and shortened, so will civilized Europe be approximated, as it were, to these benighted regions; as in no other way can improvement in any large stream be expected to flow in."[13] But of course it was not only to and from India that better communications were needed but also within India, where, as in the United States, the great rivers, here the Ganges and Indus, were the major trunk routes.

In 1831 the Governor-General sent Captain Johnston of *Enterprize* fame back to London to meet Mr Peacock, already an acknowledged expert on steam navigation. The result was the construction between 1832 and 1835 of 'Peacock's Iron Chicks', four river steamers of 275 tons and 60 hp designed to pull barges carrying passengers and freight on the Ganges.[14] Encouraged by Bentinck, the London Parliament in 1834 appointed a committee to examine the 'Means of promoting communication with India by steam'. Two routes through the Middle East were considered; that via the Euphrates was examined by an expedition in 1835–37 under Captain Francis Chesney using two Lairds-built iron steamers, the *Tigris* and *Euphrates*;[15] the other was via Suez and the Red Sea.

The year 1837 was a milestone in the development of communications between Britain and India. For the first time a regular service was initiated, the 'Overland Route', mail and passengers going by steamship to Alexandria in Egypt, then overland by river-boat and camel train to Suez, there to be met by a steamer that took them to Bombay. Such a service demanded reliable all-weather steamers and for this the *Hugh Lindsay* was quite inadequate, so the Bombay government ordered three new wooden paddle vessels from England, the *Atalanta*, *Semiramis* and *Berenice*.

The voyage of the *Atalanta*, leaving England on 29 December 1836 for Bombay via the Cape, took a total of 106 days of which 68 were spent at sea (not to mention 989 tons of coal, over a ton for every 12 miles travelled). The Overland Route could halve that time. In 1839 Commander Henry Giffard, ordered to join his new command, HMS *Cruiser*, in Singapore left England on 10 June and by steam and sail reached Alexandria on 2 July. Crossing Egypt by horse-drawn canal boat, Nile sailing vessel and horse-drawn carriage, on 7 July he embarked at Suez on the *Atalanta*, reaching Aden on the 15th and then continued in a small Company sailing ship to Bombay on the 27th. The journey had taken just 47 days.[16]

In December 1841 Major-General Lord Saltoun and his aide-de-camp Captain Arthur Cunynghame sailed from England for China via the Cape on HMS *Belleisle*, a Third Rate converted to a troopship now packed with 1,300 people, the voyage as far as Singapore taking 161 days. On their return from India in 1844 they travelled via the Overland Route, leaving Calcutta for Suez on the 15 March "on board the gigantic steam-ship *Bentinck*" with 130 passengers, and reaching England from Alexandria on the steamer *Great Liverpool* with 172 passengers on 10 May, 56 days from Calcutta. As Cunynghame wrote: "How much, then, ought we to feel ourselves indebted to steam! Now, home can be reached in two short months from any one of the presidencies, and although some little difficulties or discomforts are to be met with in the transit, yet what wonderful changes are the consequence, what incalculable advantages to be enjoyed from this astonishing power."[17]

{ 9 }

EMPIRES AND ADDICTS

The origins of the Anglo-Chinese war of 1839–42, the first 'Opium War', can be traced to an addiction, not that of the Chinese to opium but rather that of the British to tea.[1] Tea, drunk in China from before the time of Christ, was first brought to Europe by the Portuguese early in the seventeenth century.[2] While certainly available in London by the 1650s, the marriage in 1662 of King Charles II to the tea-addicted daughter of the King of Portugal, Catherine of Braganza, gave it royal approval. And this mild stimulant took Britain by storm. By 1721 over 1.2 million pounds were being legally imported into Britain, and by 1770 about 4 to 5 million with probably as much smuggled in, all from China: tea was not imported from India until 1858. With the tea tax rising to 112 per cent in the early 1780s smuggling was immensely profitable, but then in 1784, the year that the India Act converted the Company into something resembling a government department, the tax was slashed to 12.5 per cent and smuggling virtually ceased. By 1800 the Company was importing 23 million pounds, all from a country largely uninterested in British exports, draining Britain of silver, the only form of payment acceptable to the Chinese. But the British government remained as attracted to the beverage as the drinkers themselves for the import tax remained immensely profitable, providing annually 10 per cent of state revenue. So what was to be done? Could something be found that the Chinese craved for as much as the British craved for tea, and would be willing to pay for in silver?

The use of opium in China, largely for medicinal purposes, dates back at least to the Tang dynasty in the seventh century CE, when Arabs traded it from Asia Minor. In 1517 the first European ship, from Portugal, reached China followed later by those from Spain, the Netherlands, France and Britain, and these began carrying the drug from its main source, India. In about 1620 the Spaniards first brought tobacco from their American empire to the Philippines and from there it entered China where, unfortunately, a taste arose for mixing it with opium, a predilection which turned opium from a medicine to an addictive drug. Seeing this, the Emperor Tzu Tung (r. 1628–44) tried to ban tobacco, but banning imports into China proved then and subsequently quite impossible. But for a hundred years opium imports remained modest, about 200 chests by 1727 (a chest being 140 pounds) and 1,000 by 1767. In 1773 the Company took over both Bengal and Bihar, inheriting the state monopoly on opium to add to their monopoly on trade with China, but that year the drug earned the Company only £39,000.

In 1796 both the sale and smoking of opium were made illegal in China, leading the governor in Bombay to direct the commanders of all ships sailing there: "You must take most particular care that no opium is laden on board your ship by yourself, officers or any other person, as the importation of that article at China is positively forbid and very serious consequences may attend your neglect of this Injunction."[3] But there is no doubt that the injunction was indeed neglected, though largely by country ships. By the early nineteenth century opium exports from India to China averaged about 4,500 chests a year, a highly profitable if illicit trade readily conducted along the coasts between Canton and Shanghai. This amount kept the price high and provided a rough trade balance without greatly antagonising the Chinese authorities. But as the century advanced, the Company's control over the China trade grew increasingly weak. By 1825 British imports into China amounted to about £5 million but fully three quarters was on private account, £2.75 million being opium, and of British exports worth about £4.5 million only half was the Company's share, virtually all tea.

As the Company's monopoly weakened so also did its own trade balance with the mother country. Steam power in Britain allowed the mechanised weaving of cotton and, now comparatively cheap, cotton goods found a huge and profitable market in India. Clearly India had to increase its export trade. And what more profitable than to allow, or certainly not hinder, the flow of opium to China?

And this endeavour was, unwittingly, forwarded by a reform-minded British parliament that in 1833 abolished the Company's monopoly on trade with China. The resulting free-for-all saw tea imports from China grow within a year to 30 million pounds and opium exports to China rise from 11,100 chests in 1827/28 to 40,200 in 1838/39.[4] By then opium provided one seventh of the income of the Company, and tea one tenth of the British budget. And so if people in Britain did inveigh against the trade, and inveigh they did, there was simply too much money involved for the government to act against it.

And opium was exported to Britain too, 196,200 pounds (about 1,400 chests) entering the country in 1840.[5] There the drug was entirely legal, widely available and openly used. Indeed, it would have been unthinkable to practice medicine in the Europe of the 1830s without it. Of particular value was laudanum, a camphorated tincture of opium dissolved in alcohol, widely used as a pain-killer and general curative and for relaxation, and generally considered no more harmful than alcohol itself; indeed, it was given to babies to calm them – *Mother Bailey's Quietening Syrup*. As the *Singapore Free Press* reported in May 1839 (interestingly in an issue that also reported an 'extraordinary chemical and optical discovery' by a certain M. Daguerre):[a] "Notwithstanding all that has been said against opium, it is now well ascertained that when taken in moderate quantities, it is not only not injurious but, in certain constitutions, highly beneficial." That might have been true of laudanum but was certainly not true when the drug was smoked as it was in China. There, it had initially been popular amongst the ruling classes and the military, but as the supply increased and the price fell so it moved inland from the coasts and down the social ladder to the poor, with devastating consequences. By 1840 it has been estimated that perhaps one percent of the population were addicted, 4 million people. Others suggest a figure three times as high.

Since 1703 all legal trade with China had had to be conducted solely through Canton, the one entrepôt allowed European traders, and there only though a cartel of merchants, the Co-hong, who had purchased the monopoly to conduct business with these foreigners. The Act of 1833 liberalising the British side of this trade had established the post

---

[a]   The 'daguerreotype', the first commercially viable photographic process, was announced in France that January. Although photographs were being taken in the East in the 1840s, sadly there seem to be none of the *Nemesis* or her sister ships.

of 'Chief Superintendent of Trade' in Canton, and to this position Lord William Napier (1786–1834) was appointed. Arriving in China in July 1834 Napier presented his credentials to the Viceroy of Canton, Lu Kun, who promptly rejected them. A few years earlier, in 1828, two Scotsmen trading in Canton, Dr William Jardine and James Matheson, both strong advocates of free trade who correctly foresaw the ending of the Company's monopoly, had joined forces to form Jardine, Matheson & Co., a company that soon became pre-eminent in the China trade.[6] When Lu Kun roundly rebuffed Napier's overtures Jardine was delighted; like many merchants, British, French and American, he wished to see free trade imposed on the Chinese by force: a people whom his partner described as possessing "a marvellous degree of imbecility and avarice, conceit and obstinacy."[7] And this Napier proceeded to do. In September 1834 he ordered two frigates and a cutter to sail up to Canton. At the entrance to the Canton River – the Hu Men or Tiger's Gate to the Chinese and Bocca Tigris or Bogue to Europeans – they were fired upon from the forts. But the 60 Chinese guns, all fixed in masonry, proved quite useless against the ships and were quickly silenced, the British sailing on to anchor at Whampoa below Canton.

Here in this early military encounter were all the ingredients of the clash of cultures which gave rise to the first Opium War: the mutual disdain of each for the other, the aggressive determination by the British to enforce their will and the overwhelming strength to do so, and the complete ignorance of the Chinese of their own weaknesses and of the capacities of their opponent. In 1793 Lord Macartney had undertaken the first British embassy to the Imperial Court in Peking attempting, and failing, to ameliorate the terms of trade between the two nations. Upon his departure the Qianlong Emperor (r. 1735–96) had written bluntly to King George III: "Our ways have no resemblance to yours, and even were your envoy competent to acquire some rudiments of them, he could not transplant them to your barbarous land ... Strange and costly objects do not interest me. As your ambassador can see for himself, we possess all things. I set no value on strange objects and ingenious, and have no use for your country's manufactures."[8]

Whereas at the end of Qianlong's long reign the Qing Dynasty was at the zenith of its powers, 40 years later internal tensions had caused it to become ever more insular and conservative just as Britain and its military forces, transformed by the Industrial Revolution, had grown ever stronger and more assertive.[9]

Within three months of his arrival Lord Napier fell ill with fever and died in October 1834, the post then taken in quick succession by two others, John Francis Davis and Sir George Robinson, who proved as ineffective as Napier, caught between the xenophobia of the Chinese and the aggressiveness of the merchant community, and without the energy to tackle either. Then in late 1836 Captain Charles Elliot was appointed the fourth Chief Superintendent by Lord Palmerston who, as Foreign Secretary in the Whig Government of 1835 to 1841, played a critical role in events in China.

Charles Elliot (1801–75) in many ways exemplifies the British rulers of the East.[10] Typically, he was both a Scot and with a strong 'interest' – his father Sir Hugh Elliot had been Governor of Madras (1814–20), one of the three Indian Presidencies, his uncle, the First Earl of Minto, had been Governor-General of India (1807–13), his cousin, the Second Earl, was currently First Lord of the Admiralty (1835–41), and another cousin, Lord Auckland, had been the previous First Lord and was now Governor-General (1836–41). Entering the Navy in 1815, Charles served widely, from the Indian Ocean to the Caribbean, becoming a lieutenant at the age of 21 and obtaining his first command at 24. Promoted post-captain at 27 he then virtually retired from the Navy, serving instead the Colonial and Foreign Offices. Appointed 'Protector of Slaves in British Guiana' in 1830, he returned to Britain to play a useful role in the Abolition of Slavery Act of 1833. In December of that year he was appointed Master Attendant under Napier in Canton, becoming Chief Superintendent exactly three years later. A Whig grandee – indeed, a 'mandarin' – well informed, clear-minded and self-confident, disliking bloodshed and despising the avarice of merchants, Elliot, believing the opium trade to be "a traffic which every friend to humanity must deplore,"[11] strongly favoured a conciliatory approach in which the benefits to both Britain and China of any agreement were clearly apparent.

Soon after Elliot's appointment the Daoguang Emperor (r. 1820–50), increasingly concerned about the devastation caused by opium, again announced a ban on its importation and use, but Western merchants took no notice and imports continued unabated. The Emperor, his authority denied in his own country, then decided to enforce his ban, on the 31 December 1838 appointing Lin Ze-xu (1785–1850) as Imperial Commissioner to Canton to carry out his wishes. Lin was an able, thoughtful and scholarly man, a good diplomat and comparatively broad-minded but ignorant of the West. Although only 53 years old, he had already held the post of Governor-General of Hubei and Hunan, proving to be an honest ruler and an effective enforcer of the opium ban, and now determined to make the British stick to their legitimate trade in tea and silk – and rhubarb which he believed vital for foreigners to avoid constipation.[12]

Lin, travelling south by sedan chair and river boat, reached Canton on Sunday 10 March 1839, covering the 1,200 miles from Peking in 60 days.[b] There he immediately ordered the seizure of 3,000 chests of opium, perhaps acting on a precept of Sun Tzu's *Art of War*: "It may be asked, when a large, well-organised opponent is about to come to you, how do you deal with it? The answer is that you first take away what they like, and then they will listen to you."[13] Or perhaps he was encouraged by the fact that the only British warship in Chinese waters at the time was the sloop HMS *Larne* (18 guns). On the 18th he summoned 12 Co-hong merchants and ordered them to seize all opium currently in the region, a task that was clearly beyond their powers, but it stimulated them to relay clearly the Imperial Commissioner's intent to the British Chamber of Commerce. So when Elliot arrived in Canton from Macau on the 24th to meet the British, American, Indian and Co-hong merchants, he was left in little doubt as to Lin's resolve. He therefore ordered a retreat to Macau, but Lin would not allow this, no doubt realising that the opium trade would continue from there unabated. So on the 26th he ordered his troops to seal off the factories, and the following day Elliot told the merchants to surrender their opium. Promised by Elliot, without any authority, that they would be reimbursed for all their losses, the merchants surrendered 20,283 chests, over £2 million worth, and Lin had it transported to Chuanbi, an island 35 miles south of Canton, and there destroyed. The merchants thought the amount unnecessarily large but were not unduly concerned as before there had been something of an opium glut and now prices would rise nicely. The siege was not lifted until 5 May, Lin expelling all foreigners from Canton on the 24th of that month. When news of 'The Siege of the Factories', greatly embroidered, reached Britain there was much indignation at the horrors perpetrated upon the poor British merchants by the cruel Chinese.

---

[b]   This was a rapid journey for such a man, 20 miles a day. Messages sent by horse relay would usually cover no more than 25 miles a day, although express messages to and from the Imperial Court could travel ten times as fast, a remarkable average of 10 mph.

Arriving in Macau at the end of May, Elliot sent a report to India via the *Larne*, and to London via a merchant ship and the overland route, requesting that warships and troops from India be sent to China. The merchants, immediately resuming the opium trade from Macau, also contacted the British government to request military assistance, believing that Palmerston was their man – someone who would pursue a vigorous policy in China. Later that year, in December, Jardine in London wrote to his partner Matheson in Hong Kong about the advice he had given Palmerston. "My advice is to send a naval force to blockade the China coast from the Tartar Wall (the Great Wall) to Tienpack, or from 40 to 20 degrees north; the force to consist of two ships of the line, two frigates and two flat-bottomed steamers for the river service with sufficient number of transports to carry ... six or seven thousand men."[14] That Lin's actions caused no more than a temporary lull in trade can be gauged from their company's accounts: in 1832/33 profits were £309,000 but fell to £53,000 in 1838/39, rising to £235,000 the following year.

With the departure of the *Larne* on 30 May there were no Royal Navy ships in Chinese waters so it was with some pleasure that a week later the British community welcomed the arrival of the armed merchantman *Cambridge* (1,080 tons), owned and captained by Joseph Douglas. She had sailed from Bombay in February bound for Whampoa, the port 13 miles below Canton, with a cargo of opium, cotton and other produce. But, hearing of the plight of the English at Canton, Douglas had sold his opium at Singapore and refitted the *Cambridge* as an auxiliary man-of-war, adding a further 30 guns to the six 18-pound carronades he already had on board. Elliot immediately said that he would hire the ship for £14,000 for eight months and appointed Douglas Commodore of the non-existent fleet.

On 7 July 1839 on the Kowloon peninsula opposite Hong Kong island a party of British and American sailors in a drunken brawl killed a fisherman, Lin Wei-Xi. Commissioner Lin immediately asked for the culprits to be handed over for punishment, but this Elliot refused to do, saying he did not know who had struck the fatal blow. Instead, five British sailors were tried before Elliot, two found guilty of manslaughter and sentenced to be transported to England for imprisonment where in fact they were immediately released by orders of the government. To increase pressure on the British Lin on the 17 August ordered that supplies to Macau be cut, this forcing the merchant community to move to ships anchored off Kowloon where they could be readily supplied by local villagers.

With their position so precarious, the British were delighted by the arrival on 30 August of HMS *Volage* (28 guns), the ship that on 19 January that year had added Aden to the British Empire, a vital acquisition as a coaling station for the success of the Overland Route.[15] A few days later, on 4 September, Elliot in his cutter *Louisa* supported by a hired opium brigantine and boats from the *Volage* and *Cambridge* attacked three Chinese junks which were harassing the merchant fleet and their suppliers, eventually driving them back at the cost of four British men injured. This, the Battle of Kowloon, marks the opening of the Opium War.

About 26 September the *Volage* was joined by HMS *Hyacinth* (18 guns), and in early November these two, with Elliot on board the *Volage*, sailed up to the Bogue where Admiral Guan Tian-pei (1779–1841) had gathered a fleet of 15 warships and 14 fireships. After some half-hearted negotiations, at noon on 3 November the British opened fire and within an hour had sunk four junks and damaged most of the rest before Elliot ordered action to cease. The Battle of Chuenpi, in which one Sixth Rate and a sloop saw off the finest fleet the Chinese could assemble, represented a resounding defeat for the Chinese but typically the messages to Peking gave no indication of this; as both promotions and rewards derived from victories there was little incentive to tell of defeats. So when Lin later asked the Emperor for more resources to defend Canton, the Emperor was unconvinced, writing in the margin "A pack of nonsense!"

Commissioner Lin did however express himself very directly in a letter addressed to Queen Victoria in January 1840: "The Way of Heaven is fairness to all; it does not suffer us to harm others in order to benefit ourselves ... But there is a class of evil foreigner that makes opium and brings it for sale, tempting foolish people to destroy themselves, merely in order to reap profits. Formerly the number of opium smugglers was small; but now the vice has spread far and wide, and the poison penetrated deeper and deeper ... What is here forbidden to consume, your dependencies must be forbidden to manufacture, and what has already been manufactured Your Majesty must immediately search out and throw into the bottom of the sea, and never again allow such poison to exist in Heaven or on earth." And he concluded: "On receiving this, Your Majesty will be so good as to report to me immediately on the steps you have taken at each of your ports."[16] Sadly, although the letter left Canton, it apparently never reached the young Queen. How fascinating to have seen her reply.

{ 10 }

A WAR MORE UNJUST

> "...a war more unjust in its origin, a war calculated in its progress to cover this country with a permanent disgrace, I do not know and have not read of."
>
> —William Gladstone MP to Parliament, 8 April 1840[1]

Making moral judgements about actions taken and attitudes displayed by people in previous centuries is fraught with difficulties. Today current Chinese histories report that the war was solely to enforce the illegal trade in opium, unscrupulous merchants supported by an immoral government.[2] Yet this under-estimates the almost religious belief of the British at that time in 'free trade'. And if it struck the Chinese mandarins then as almost incomprehensible that the British state should by force support mere commerce, the work of the despised merchant class, such support was seen by the British as the very essence of good government. Yet freedom to trade was not absolute; the most important single task for the Royal Navy in those years was the suppression of the trade in slaves (*see* Table 1). But without doubt, the strength of their belief in free trade, a trade which cynics may say always favours the most powerful societies, allowed many good British people to support the war and yet in all sincerity decry the trade in opium.

Certainly, distress about the opium trade and the consequent hostilities between Britain and China was not confined to China. In London a meeting was called for for 13 February 1840. "A number of philanthropic individuals having directed their attention to the contraband trade in opium carried on between British India and China, an association has now been formed for the purpose of endeavouring to suppress the traffic, under the conviction that it is discreditable to this country, prejudicial to its commercial interests, and injurious to the cause of Christianity, as well as productive of an enormous amount of vice and misery among the inhabitants of China."[3] And in India the newspaper *Friend of India* spoke out: "In demanding indemnity for the twenty thousand chests of contraband Opium, which the Chinese Government has confiscated, we cast a stain upon our national honour which will not easily be obliterated ... In Europe we are advocates of freedom, justice, equity. In Asia, the abettors of the most gigantic system of smuggling that the world has ever seen."[4]

On 25 March 1840, three days before the *Nemesis* left Portsmouth, a letter was published in the United Services Journal from someone calling himself 'An Observer' and titled 'War with China'. "... I cannot yet believe there will be a war; for the declaration of such will move every spark of true British feeling of bravery, of justice, and of religion, there is left in the country to oppose it; and for this reason, that it is nothing more, and can be looked upon as nothing less, than an opium war ... As things are, Russia or France – with their navies – may insult the [British] flag with impunity; while the poor Chinese – with their painted pasteboard boats – must submit to be poisoned, or must be massacred by the thousand, for supporting their own laws in their own land."[5]

To the British government this was not a war about opium. If the defence of free trade was the primary cause, it was the 'insult' to the British flag at Canton and the confinement of British men, women and children which was the final straw.[6] Certainly, by the time of the arrival of the *Volage* and *Hyacinth* in Chinese waters in September 1839 – when the *Nemesis* was growing on the stocks at Birkenhead – a decision had been taken to send troops to China. Palmerston wrote to Elliot on 18 October saying as much, and on the 24th the troopship *Rattlesnake* left England for the east.[7] On 14 February 1840 Palmerston again wrote to Elliot promising both land and naval forces, and on the 20th to Lord Auckland, Governor-General of India, instructing him to send a suitable force to China to seize Zhoushan (Chusan) and open northern ports to trade; and then to extract from the Chinese an indemnity to cover both the losses suffered by British merchants and the Co-hong and the costs of the expedition itself.[8] But it would be another seven weeks before the matter was raised in Parliament. There on 8 April, the day that the *Nemesis* left Madeira, the 30-year-old William Gladstone rose in the

Commons to reply to the government. "They [the Chinese government] gave you notice to abandon your contraband trade. When they found you would not do so they had the right to drive you from their coasts on account of your obstinacy in persisting with this infamous and atrocious traffic ... justice, in my opinion, is with them; and whilst they, the Pagans, the semi-civilised barbarians have it on their side, we, the enlightened and civilised Christians, are pursuing objects at variance both with justice and religion ... a war more unjust in its origins, a war calculated in its progress to cover this country with a permanent disgrace, I do not know and have not read of. Now, under the auspices of the noble Lord, that flag has become a pirate flag, to protect an infamous traffic."[9] Yet such was the reach of opium that Gladstone himself took laudanum when preparing for major Parliamentary debates.[10]

During April, May and June a formidable fleet, 'the China Expedition', arrived in Singapore on its way to China, warships of the Royal Navy, transports, and wooden steamships of the Company's navies.[11] Of the four steamers, the *Madagascar* on Saturday 10 May was the first to arrive, carrying the Naval Commander, Commodore Sir Gordon Bremer (1785–1850) from Calcutta on 18 April, followed by the *Atalanta* on the 14th from Bombay, and the *Queen* on the 23rd and *Enterprize* (the second of that name) on 11 June both from Calcutta.[12] This was a good season for sailing north as the southern monsoon was about to set in, and Singapore harbour was also crowded with 20 to 30 junks awaiting the winds to blow them back to Siam (Thailand) and Cochin-China (Vietnam).

Bremer had in fact left England over two years before, in February 1838, captain of HMS *Alligator* (28 guns), in company with HMS *Britomart* (10 guns), Captain Owen Stanley, bound for Australia to found a colony which could act as a place of refuge for ships passing through the Torres Straits.[13] There that October they sailed into a bleak and open bay, Port Essington, in the very north of the country, north-east of present-day Darwin, landing a small garrison and erecting a number of wooden buildings. But the place proved a disaster from the beginning, its harbour too shallow and exposed, the local people unwelcoming, the place extremely unhealthy, and the termites voracious. In September 1849 HMS *Maeander* (46 guns), captained by Henry Keppel, sailed from Singapore bound for England by way of Australia and Cape Horn, a circumnavigation that would take her until July 1851. Her first task was to evacuate Port Essington, "about the most useless, miserable, ill-managed hole in Her Majesty's dominions" as Thomas Henry Huxley put it.[14] Embarking the remainder of the garrison she sailed for Sydney on 1 December, leaving behind only feral cattle, ruined buildings and numerous graves to mark 11 years of struggle. If few settlements proved as successful as Singapore, few proved as hopeless as Port Essington.

Amongst the first ships to reach China in June 1840 was the *Madagascar* with Commodore Bremer, her passage up the Canton River on the 16th causing considerable excitement to those Chinese who witnessed it. Lin himself was duly impressed by 'cart-wheel ships that can put their axles in motion by means of fire, and can move rather fast'.[15] Bremer now hoisted his pennant on the *Wellesley* (74 guns) where he immediately held discussions with Elliot. The main body of the fleet arrived on 21 June and, seeing this formidable armada, the Chinese naturally assumed that it was going to attack Canton, so there was much relief when on the 24th and 25th they sailed out to sea again and turned east, leaving only HMS *Druid* (36 guns) and *Volage*, *Hyacinth* and *Larne* to blockade Canton.

By the end of the month the ships were approaching the island of Zhoushan south of the mouth of the Yangtse River. The first arrivals were met with pleasure by the Chinese, believing them to be merchant ships that had been denied Canton. Some merchants were welcomed on board the *Rattlesnake* with rum and snuff, bringing tea as a present, and they proved jolly company.[16] But they had misread the situation. On 5 July the fleet opened fire on the town, within nine minutes reducing much of it to rubble, whereupon it was occupied and comprehensively looted. With typical sensitivity the British on finding a huge and finely constructed tumulus of coffins tumbled some carelessly into the sea and set fire to the rest.[17] So those perusing the *Canton Press* that October should have expressed little surprise when they read: "Our readers are aware that soon after the occupation of Chusan became known, many enterprising British merchants took up to that port cargoes of British manufactures, with the view of opening there a market for them. We are sorry to say that this spirited enterprise has been totally unsuccessful, and that ships and cargoes are returning, without having effected any sales whatever."[18]

In August two more 74s, the *Blenheim* and the *Melville*, joined the ships off Zhoushan. Now, a year after the arrival of the *Volage* at Macau, the British fleet in Chinese waters had grown to a total of 48 ships. Of these, 28 were transports carrying 4,000 troops from India under the temporary command of Major George Burrell; Indian sepoys from Bengal and Madras, a corps of Madras sappers and miners, and men from three regiments nicely representing the United Kingdom – the Royal Irish, Cameronians and Hertfordshire. At this time there were about 200,000 Indian and 30,000 British troops in India and its dependencies, the British forces containing no less than 29 British regiments of foot, almost a quarter of the entire British infantry.[19] In India such a force would have been vastly swollen by a whole variety of servants, family members and non-combatants. In the Bengal army where the sepoys (private soldiers in an Indian regiment) were mostly high-caste Hindus each fighting man required five camp-followers, and for the lower caste Bombay force, three. But how many such hangers-on accompanied the force to China is uncertain.

Of the 20 warships in Chinese waters three were Line of Battle, all Third Rates; five Below the Line, Fifth and Sixth Rates; eight unrated; and the four armed wooden steamers belonging to the Company. The Royal Naval ships alone carried 538 guns between them. By the end of hostilities 24 months later the China squadron had more than doubled: 36 Royal Navy ships of which two were wooden steamers, and 12 Company steamers of which five were iron hulled (*see* Table 9).

To oppose this colossal force, in fact a mere ten per cent of the Royal Navy, there was at the time really no such thing as a 'Chinese Navy'. Throughout the Manchu dynasty the Chinese had paid scant attention to naval matters. As they themselves had come from the land to the north and west, it was from there that they believed all threats would hail. Learning nothing from the Macartney and Amherst embassies of 1793 and 1817 about British naval prowess, they left the command of seas off their immense coasts to a series of local squadrons raised by and acting under the orders of local mandarins, the crews untrained for warfare. At the Battle of Chuenpi the previous November the largest naval force that the Chinese could handle as a unit had been roundly defeated by just two quite modest vessels.

Chinese warships, war-junks (*dabing chuan*), were very different vessels from those of the Royal Navy. They could be very large, some over 1,000 tons, but their structure and armaments were totally different. Derived from cargo-junks, fine trading vessels, seaworthy and easy to handle, they had not been fundamentally modified, still consisting largely of cargo space, with small bed-spaces for the crew forward and the captain's house aft. The poop aft could be as high as that of a 74, and the mast or masts could be huge, 11 ft in circumference, carrying great square mat sails though smaller vessels often also had oars, up to 20 per side.

Most significantly, even the largest was vastly outgunned by a mere Sixth Rate, even by the *Nemesis*, let alone a great floating fortress such as the *Wellesley*. They were usually armed with from 4 to 14 large guns, but these were generally fixed and often poorly made, the powder for them being brought on deck in large red barrels, a nice target for the accurate British guns. Equally important, the captain and crew, usually 80 to 100 men, were not military people but civilians, sometimes accompanied by their families. The fighting men, 'water-braves', were soldiers with no special naval training[a] and armed with spears, swords and matchlocks and sometimes large 'jingals', similar to duck-guns. With large eyes painted on either side of the bows, many flags and streamers flying from the masts, and the crew's shields, saucers of rattan or cane up to 3 ft in diameter brightly painted, green or yellow, hanging over the bulwarks, they presented to the highly trained British seaman a colourful but hardly daunting spectacle.

The *Melville* had brought from England the new naval Commander-in-Chief, Rear-Admiral George Elliot (1784–1863), appointed also to act as co-plenipotentiary with his cousin Charles. The admiral carried with him a letter to the Court at Peking from Lord Palmerston, which, as it was not a 'petition', he had unsurprisingly failed to get forwarded first from Xiamen (Amoy) and now from Ningbo nearby on the mainland. The two Elliots, transferring to the *Wellesley* as the *Melville* had been seriously damaged when entering the harbour at Zhoushan, sailed on north for Peking accompanied by three other warships, three transports and the steamer *Madagascar*,[b] arriving off the Bei He (Peiho) River on 5 August. After much coming and going a mandarin of suitable rank, Qi-shan (Kishen), finally accepted the letter through an intermediary and it was delivered to the Emperor on the 20th. The British then waited for a reply, and waited in vain, the Chinese kindly supplying their impatient visitors with "a liberal supply of bullocks, sheep, and poultry, an offering of no

---

[a]   This situation pertained in the British navy until the seventeenth century. The Royal Navy as the Victorians knew it dated from about 1660, the restoration of Charles II.

[b]   Although of only 350 tons but of wood, her draught was 11.5 ft compared with 6 ft for the 660 ton *Nemesis*.

trifling value to men in such circumstances."[20] So, as it was impossible with the force available to further press their demands, they set off back to Zhoushan on 15 September. But their endeavours had in fact some effect; dismayed at the impunity with which the British had approached the capital, the Emperor summarily dismissed Commissioner Lin, replacing him with Qi-shan.

At Zhoushan fevers and dysentery were playing havoc with the troops, something which was to become all too familiar in Chinese waters. After a further fruitless month the fleet set off back to Macau which they reached on 20 November, leaving six sailing vessels and the *Atalanta* in the north. Between 13 July and the end of the year 448 men of the expedition had died of disease; the Cameronians, sailing north with 930 officers and men, had by December lost 240 dead through sickness with only 110 men still fit enough for active service.[21] It is nice to know that amongst the 5,329 admissions to the British field hospital at Zhoushan there had been 1,600 Chinese, surely not only from the consequences of bombardment and looting.[c]

If the failure of the expedition to the north was of some embarrassment to the military, the merchants apparently viewed it with equanimity. In late 1840 James Matheson could write: "But as they [the Elliots] have no mode of raising money for the expenses of the war unless from drug sales in China, we think they cannot avoid giving it some toleration."[22]

---

[c]   And sad to know that in Great Britain at that time there were no more than 7,500 hospital beds for a population of 18 million (Pool 1993).

{ 11 }

THE NEVERMISS

The arrival of the *Nemesis* at Macau on Wednesday 25 November 1840 coincided with changes amongst the leadership on both sides of the conflict. Four days later Qi-shan, the new Imperial Commissioner, arrived at Canton from Peking and the British learnt that Admiral Elliott, now ill, was to return to England on the *Volage*. Thus only four months after relinquishing it, command of the naval forces passed back to Commodore Sir Gordon Bremer, with Charles Elliot the sole plenipotentiary.

By early December most of the fleet was back below the Bogue, and it was here on board the *Wellesley* that Elliot first met the new Imperial Commissioner. Elliot was well aware of what Palmerston wanted: freedom to trade at five ports (Canton, Xiamen (Amoy), Fuzhou (Foochow), Ningbo (Ningpo) and Shanghai), and money to cover the total cost of the war as well as the opium destroyed by Lin. And he also knew that he would almost certainly not be able to obtain all this. As negotiations dragged on throughout December Elliot shuttled back and forth between the fleet and his home in Macau on the *Nemesis*, valuing the speed and reliability of the new ship.

Although Elliot was a man who kept his own counsel it became obvious to Captain Hall that hostilities would soon be resumed and so he urgently set about preparing his ship.[1] Most importantly, the serious damage sustained off Africa had to be properly repaired. Then he arranged for a much broader bridge, perhaps 15 ft wide, to be built between the paddle boxes. Mounted on this was a 6-pound brass swivel gun, useful for trying the range, and also a rocket tube and supply of Congreve rockets, the whole being covered by an awning in hot weather. Besides the two 32-pounders mounted fore and aft there were now four brass 6-pounders and an 8-inch howitzer. With the crew increased from 60 to 90 men more boats were required and the *Nemesis* now carried two cutters, a pinnace, gig, jolly-boat and dinghy as well as what was called 'a large Chinese boat'. As Hall hoped to be able to take advantage of the strength and shallow draught of his ship when landing troops by running her straight on shore, he had a prefabricated gangway constructed which could be put over the bows. And as a final touch, in deference to the practice on Chinese war-junks, he had two huge eyes painted on either side of the bows. But his notes give no indication that he knew what other features of his ship, not decorative but central to her success, stemmed from the culture he was now about to engage: it was the Chinese whose ships first had paddle wheels to power them, watertight compartments, sliding-keels and stern-post rudders, the Chinese who first used coal as a fuel, the Chinese who invented gunpowder and the magnetic compass.

In early January 1841 Elliot ordered Bremer to prepare for an assault on the fortifications at the Bogue. At 8 am on Thursday 7 January the *Nemesis* drew alongside the troopships and embarked about 500 of the 600 sepoys of the 37th Regiment, the remainder with others embarking on the steamers *Enterprize* and *Madagascar*.[2] As the ships approached the entrance to the Canton River the men would have seen ahead two promontories, to the left the hill of Big Taikok, and to the right Chuenpi with its two small hills, the river about 3 miles wide between them. Steaming on, both banks receded, to the east around Anson's Bay, and then the water narrowed again with Little Taikok to the west and the high headland of Anunghoi to the east about 5 miles above Chuenpi. Here, with the river only about a mile wide and the current strong, lay the islands of South and North Wangtong and beyond the hilly Tiger Island and the Tiger's Gate from which the Bocca Tigris or Bogue took its name. Each of these places had been fortified, the forts in the shape of a D, the flat side to the river, all poorly designed and hopelessly armed compared with the forces now ranged against them.

By 9 am the three steamers had landed almost 1,500 troops on Chuenpi – soldiers, two-thirds being sepoys, marines and seamen, together with a company of Royal Artillery with one 24-pounder and two 6-pounders. The *Nemesis* and the steamer *Queen* then moved on to bombard a watchtower, while the *Madagascar* and *Enterprize* supported the *Calliope, Larne* and *Hyacinth* against the main fort. Within 25 minutes, the accurate shelling of the *Nemesis'* two 32-pounders and the *Queen's* single 68-pounder had silenced the watchtower and the British flag was soon seen flying over it to the cheers of the steamers' crews. At the fort the Chinese were soon hemmed in. "A frightful scene of slaughter ensued despite the best efforts of the officers to restrain their men." Lieutenant John Ouchterlony of the Madras Engineers watched as bodies rolled down the slope from the fort until piled three or four deep below, "a ghastly pile".[3] The slaughter was perhaps partly because the Chinese had been told to fear capture by these fierce foreigners, but also because the foreign officers failed to restrain their troops, those fleeing also being shot. From the *Nemesis* Third Officer John Galbraith saw "At a rocky point the Chinese were lying where they had been shot down, like sparrows, in heaps, while the whole surface of the hill was chequered with bodies, many more than half consumed by fire, and all smouldering; for when shot, many had fallen forward on their matchlocks and their cotton clothing, like tinder, had ignited."[4] Such slaughter seems to have been common throughout the war. Years later a staff officer, Armine Mountain, provided a justification for such behaviour: "The slaughter of fugitives is unpleasant but we are such a handful in the face of so wide a country and so large a force that we should be swept away if we did not read the enemy a sharp lesson whenever we came into contact."[5]

Meanwhile across the river HMS *Druid* (46 guns), *Samarang* (26), *Columbine* (18) and *Modeste* (18) bombarded the Big Taikok fort and within an hour this too had been silenced and taken. By about 11 o'clock Hall saw that the lower fort on Chuenpi was about to fall and he turned the *Nemesis* towards Anson's Bay where a fleet of 15 war-junks lay. But in his enthusiasm he rounded Chuenpi too close and struck a rock, breaking the outer paddle ring and two spokes. As Galbraith reported, this "gave the old barky a terrible list to port, but fortunately did not stop us; ranged up almost within a biscuit throw of the walls, and poured in a round of grape and canister from both guns, which must have killed a considerable number of them for we observed them falling dead or wounded out of their ports. ... Our guns were beautifully served, pumping the shot into them nearly the whole time; in fact it was the admiration of the whole fleet (which had nothing to do but look on) ... I repeatedly saw our 32-pound shot go slap through one junk into another."[6] For the first time Hall ordered the use of Congreve rockets and the very first, fired from the bridge, entered a large junk and presumably hit the gunpowder barrels for she instantly blew up, a huge explosion stunning all who saw it. "... she appeared to lift out of the water, her masts being launched right over her bows, a bright flash succeeded by a cloud of thick, white smoke, and then a deadening report, and all was over with the junk and her unfortunate crew."[7] By 11.30 am the Chinese had hauled down their colours and the sailors were seen escaping ashore, and Hall sent in his boats and those supporting him from other ships. Of the 15 junks only four escaped, the rest being either blown up or captured and burnt. Turning up a river two more junks were found abandoned and, as the tide was falling, one was destroyed but the other taken in tow, the *Nemesis* rejoining the squadron with her prize by 5 pm, her only damage a single shot hole in a paddle-box, her nickname now 'the Nevermiss'.

The actions of the *Nemesis* that January day, the very first engagement of an iron warship, demonstrated to many present the utility of such shallow-draught vessels in coastal waters. Indeed, Elliot considered that her 'services had been equal to those of two line-of-battle ships'.[8] Hall certainly made the most of it on behalf of his ship: the *Canton Register* carried a full account of the ship's role just 12 days later, and an article on "the far-famed *Nemesis*" on 20 March.[9] The engagement that day also demonstrated conclusively the enormous gap between the military might of the two adversaries. Certainly the British were impressed by the great bravery of many Chinese, from Admiral Guan Tian-pei to individual soldiers and sailors. But their equipment and their tactics were lamentable: guns on both forts and junks mounted immovably so that they could fire only over the attacking ships; gunpowder of the poorest quality; soldiers armed with guns last seen in British forces in the previous century, matchlocks requiring three men to fire them. The result was a slaughter of Chinese, at least 400 being killed and about 150 captured, many seriously wounded; amongst the British forces a total of 38 were wounded and none killed. The British captured 173 guns of which 82 were removed from junks including 10 handsome brass ones of Portuguese manufacture. One of these was later that month presented to Hall by his officers and crew with a letter requesting him to accept it as "a mark of their remembrance of the coolness and judgement which he had shown throughout that day."[10] In contrast, poor Admiral Guan faced a mutiny, the ships' crews threatening to disband unless paid a gratuity, and the Admiral actually had to pawn some of his own clothes in order to scrape together enough to give each man $2, less than £1.[11] But the Emperor in distant Peking was not to learn of this; to him this devastating defeat was represented as a draw.

At dawn the following day, the 8th, Bremer ordered his three 74s, as yet unused, up-river to attack Anunghoi, the strongest of the Bogue forts. The *Nemesis*, already there, had just started firing on the fort when the *Wellesley* hoisted a signal to cease engagement, much to the crew's disgust. The Chinese had apparently sent envoys to Elliot on the *Wellesley* seeking a truce and Elliot, much more concerned with salvaging the seasonal trade, getting the tea out and the cotton in, than humiliating the Chinese, ordered Bremer to desist. At 4 pm that afternoon the *Nemesis* carried the truce agreement from the *Wellesley* to Anunghoi. For the next 12 days negotiations continued, the *Nemesis* now a useful packet, shuttling Elliot back and forth between Macau and the fleet at Chuenpi, until on the 20 January he announced to the fleet the results of his negotiations.

The Convention of Chuenpi had four main clauses: the island of Hong Kong was ceded outright to Britain; an indemnity of $6 m was to be paid over 6 years; official communications between Britain and China were to be direct and on the basis of equality; and trade was to reopen on the Canton River immediately after the celebrations of the new Year of the Ox. On New Year's Day, the 23rd, the *Enterprize* was dispatched to Calcutta with details of the Convention, and the *Columbine* sent up the coast to Zhoushan to recall the ships and troops there. Beating up the China Sea against the monsoon, she did not arrive there until 8 February, her arrival doubly welcome to Surgeon Cree on the troopship *Rattlesnake* as it brought him his first letters from home since leaving England more than 15 months before.[12]

Although the Convention required ratification from both Peking and London, Elliot and Bremer had no intention of waiting for this. On the 26th Bremer landed on Hong Kong island and formally took possession while Elliot travelled up-river on the *Nemesis* to meet Qi-shan. Joined by the *Madagascar* at Chuenpi carrying an honour guard of marines and two ships' bands, the little flotilla arrived just four miles below Whampoa that evening. There the following morning, at the Pagoda at the Second Bar, Elliot finally met the Commissioner with due ceremony and on comparatively equal terms, finding him very formal but gentlemanly. Whether the two felt any satisfaction at the outcome of their talks we do not know; but we do know that many British merchants were furious with Elliot for not securing enough money and many Chinese equally angry with Qi-shan for ceding land. And later this displeasure was also strongly expressed by each man's superior, Lord Palmerston in London and the emperor in Peking. Indeed Palmerston in one of his less perspicacious moments informed Elliot "It seems obvious that Hong Kong will not be a mart of trade". But the Queen was pleased, confiding to her uncle Leopold that "Albert is much amused by my having Hong Kong."[13]

So that day the bands played, the food and drink were plentiful, and the celebrations concluded with a spectacular display of fireworks from the *Nemesis*. The following morning Galbraith "and two or three others walked up to the pagoda above the Second Bar. They brought seats for us, and would make us eat a lot of sweetmeats and drink tea, an old attendant hovering around us with a large pot of hot water, ready to fill our cup whenever he could, it was no use to say no."[14] And this just three weeks from the slaughter at Chuenpi. Later a further party of mandarins accompanied by merchants of the Co-hong were entertained on board before she dropped down-river, steaming on to Hong Kong on the 29th. That day the *Nemesis* carried both Elliot and Bremer right round their new island possession before returning the commodore to the *Wellesley* and the captain to Macau.

{ 12 }

THE DEVIL'S IMPS AT CANTON

> "On the second day at 10 o'clock the devil's imps embarked on
> board a fireship and sailed up to Neisheng where they made use of
> fire-arrows and great guns with which they attacked and smashed
> Neisheng and burned several tens of carrying vessels…"
>
> —A public poster in Canton, from the Canton Register, 15 June 1841[1]

By early February the British were already hard at work setting up shop in Hong Kong, the *Nemesis* spending much of her time shuttling people between Macau and the island.[2] But Elliot knew that to ensure that the other clauses of the Convention were observed, most critically that concerning the indemnity, it was necessary to get a proper treaty signed with the Chinese. To try to hurry this along he again met Qi-shan on the river above Anunghoi on 11 and 12 February, setting a deadline of the 22nd for ratification. But Hall, sent up the river on the 14th to learn what was happening, saw that the Bogue forts were being repaired and hurried back to Macau.

On hearing Hall's report Elliot realised that another show of force was necessary, and for this Bremer decided to use most of the ships available to him. On Friday 19th a formidable armada moved up-river towards the Bogue: three Third Rates, a Fifth Rate, four Sixth Rates, a sloop and a survey ship, together with the Company steamers *Nemesis, Madagascar* and *Queen*, a troop-ship and four transports. The following day word was received that the Chinese had rejected the treaty, and hostilities re-opened on the 23rd when the *Nemesis* accompanied by troops in four ships' boats destroyed a fort being built on South Wangtung. On the

25th Hall embarked 130 men of the Madras Native Infantry whose job would be to build a battery on South Wantung that could bombard two Chinese forts about half a mile away on North Wangtung. To land them he chose a muddy beach and, dropping an anchor behind to help get her off again, ran his ship hard ashore, the bows raised high on the mud, the deck at the stern almost awash, as the soldiers safely disembarked using the new prefabricated gangway. Overnight the battery was built and armed with two howitzers, and at dawn opened up on the forts to the north with shells and rockets, weapons new to the Chinese. The exchange of fire continued for five hours with not a single casualty amongst the British forces.

The day was beautiful but windless and it was some hours before the 74s *Blenheim* and *Melville* accompanied by the *Queen* and rocket boats came abreast of the Anunghoi forts, anchoring out of range of the Chinese guns. Meanwhile the flagship *Wellesley* accompanied by the seven other naval ships anchored across the river opposite North Wangtung. Soon after 10 o'clock both sections of the fleet opened up with broadsides. The scene can only be vaguely imagined: some hundreds of large guns in the hands of some of the world's finest gunners playing upon forts crowded with ill-trained and virtually defenceless soldiers, the incredible noise of firing and the explosion of shells and rockets, curling white smoke – the fog of war – hanging thick over the river in the still air. As calmly viewed from the *Nemesis* by Hall "the scene on all sides at this moment was extremely imposing."[3] By 1 pm the bombardment had done its worst and the *Nemesis* and *Madagascar* carried troops to North Wangtung where further slaughter was accomplished. As Captain Edward Belcher with the troops reported: "Opposition there was none. The unfortunate Chinese simply crammed the trenches, begging for mercy. I wish I could add that it was granted."[4] By 4 pm the action was over, all the forts on both sides of the river taken, the guns spiked or removed, the buildings destroyed, and by dusk the troops were back on their respective ships.

During that day at least 500 Chinese were killed. "Among these, the most distinguished and most lamented was poor Admiral Kwan (Guan), whose death excited much sympathy throughout the force … He was altogether a fine specimen of a gallant soldier …"[5] When the next day his body was claimed by his family the *Blenheim* raised the Chinese flag to half-mast and fired a salute of minute guns in his honour. In contrast, the British forces suffered only eight wounded and one accidentally killed. Over 1,300 Chinese were taken prisoner and, to their apparent astonishment, quickly transported to the mainland and set free. And the amount of ordinance captured was also prodigious: 460 pieces of cannon, including four very large brass guns made by the Portuguese in 1627, which says something about the state of gun-making in China.

To take advantage of the shock of defeat, Bremer immediately dispatched the 'light squadron', seven of his smaller ships, up the river towards Canton, led by the *Nemesis* carrying Elliot. Sometime in the early afternoon of the 27th below Whampoa the *Nemesis* came upon a prize that was worth the taking, Captain Douglas's *Cambridge*. With the arrival of the *Volage* and the *Hyacinth* in September 1839 the *Cambridge* had, to her captain's disappointment, become redundant and in November he sold her to the American firm Delano. In early 1840 Delano had stripped out her guns and sold her on to Commissioner Lin who believed she would be useful for training and as a model for Chinese ship-builders. Now seeing her lying near a fort surrounded by war-junks, Hall immediately opened fire with shot, shell and rockets, this returned enthusiastically by the Chinese. The *Nemesis* was hit several times, one ball nearly piercing a steam-chest which would have been disastrous. At 3.30 pm Elliot and Hall led a landing party ashore, Hall avoiding injury when a brave Chinese officer fired four arrows at him: "had they been musket-balls, however, he could scarcely have escaped."[6] Within half an hour the fort was taken and soon after the *Cambridge* was theirs too, the crew disappearing over one side as the British climbed up the other. As she was seen to be in the poorest condition it was decided to burn her and, after searching carefully for anyone remaining on board, she was set on fire. Soon after dark the fire reached her magazine and she blew up spectacularly, the explosion, it was said, being heard in Canton.

On Tuesday 2 March the 'light squadron' anchored above Whampoa only 12 miles below Canton, causing considerable panic, the Prefect there asking Elliot for an immediate three-day truce which was granted. Down-river much was happening that day too; from Zhoushan came the squadron earlier ordered back to Macau, and from Madras HMS *Cruiser* (18 guns) carrying Major-General Sir Hugh Gough (1779–1869) to assume command of all land forces.[7] Gough, at 61 still wiry and energetic, had in 1837, after many years on half-pay, been sent to India as second-in-command of the Madras Army. Charming and brave and loved by his troops, he was no tactician, always preferring the bold frontal assault to more subtle strategies. Now with Elliott and Bremer he set about assessing the situation, the three steaming on the *Nemesis* to visit the squadron above Whampoa, a squadron which incidentally had not a single person present who could speak Chinese. There a plan was hatched to see if the *Nemesis* with her shallow draught could find a completely new river passage direct to Canton west of the main river.

By now it was clear to Bremer and others that this iron ship was unusually strong, much less liable to damage than an equivalent wooden ship and, with her watertight compartments, could more readily be risked. On Saturday 13 March at 3 in the morning the *Nemesis* quietly left the Macau roads towing two boats, carrying Elliot and Captain James Scott of HMS *Samarang* as senior officer with a local pilot and two British interpreters, Messrs Morrison and Thom. Over the next two and a half days she achieved all that was wished of her, finding her way to the Canton River through enemy territory in dangerously constricted and shallow rivers, destroying three military stations, six batteries, nine war-junks and 115 guns. As Bremer later told the Governor-General Lord Auckland, the ship had demonstrated that "the British flag can be displayed throughout these inner waters wherever and whenever it is thought proper by us."[8]

On the morning of 18 March the British attacked Canton, destroying seven forts and batteries, scattering a vast variety of local boats and meeting no serious resistance. At 1.30 pm Captain Hall and the interpreter Robert Morrison landed at the British Factory, abandoned in May 1839, Hall soon displaying the Union Jack from an upper window to cheering sailors below. "The handsome hall of the British factory, with its beautiful decorations of pier glasses, pictures, marble flooring, chandeliers, &c, was literally gutted, as also the hall used as a chapel."[9] With the factories now recovered it was expected that Elliott would press the Chinese hard, particularly over the question of the indemnity, but this he failed to do, soon agreeing to open trade under the old terms much to the annoyance of both Gough and Bremer, and indeed of most of the military. Charles Elliot's motives are somewhat hard to fathom; unlike so many on imperial service, he left no justifying autobiography, not even any diaries. Self-confident and private, he divulged little to his companions. Hall, who spent much time in his company in the first half of 1841, clearly had little idea of what was going through his mind. Although no admirer of merchants Elliot was indeed the 'Superintendent of Trade' and it seems that his greatest determination was to see business restored. And in this he was initially successful; before the end of the month the season's tea was smoothly moving westwards and the first chests of opium were being safely delivered to Jardine Matheson's floating warehouse, the *General Wood*. By mid-April trade was virtually back to normal.

On Wednesday 31 March the *Queen* carrying Sir Gordon Bremer, accompanied by the *Madagascar*, left for Calcutta, Bremer wishing to confer in person with Lord Auckland; but he was not in good health and was away longer than expected, not returning to China until 18 June, again on the *Queen*. In his absence Captain Sir Humphrey Le Fleming Senhouse (1781–1841) of the *Blenheim* assumed command of naval forces, somewhat depleted by the return of the Third Rate *Melville* to Britain for urgently needed repairs. Whereas April saw increasingly frenetic trading activity, diplomatic activity appeared to have died a death. Despite the arrival in Canton on the 14th of two more imperial commissioners negotiations were going nowhere, and by the end of the month it was apparent that the Chinese were rearming and rebuilding. So on 10 May Elliot, this time accompanied by his wife, again embarked on the *Nemesis* for Canton. But negotiations the following day decided nothing and Elliot returned post-haste to the *Blenheim* to confer with Gough and Senhouse about yet another attack on Canton, much to their displeasure. As Hall put it, "At length even Captain Elliot himself began to catch a glimmering of the truth, which seemed to steal but slowly upon his unwilling eyes."[10]

By this time the British military leaders had come to realise that limiting the war to Canton would never lead to success. Whatever defeats they inflicted on the Chinese would reach the emperor's ears in distant Peking as victories or at best as draws, and nothing could be finally resolved without the emperor's agreement. The war must be carried much nearer to the seat of empire. But with the indemnity as yet unpaid plans to again head north were shelved, and after five days of hectic activity the whole fleet once more sailed for the Canton River, only the *Druid* remaining to protect Hong Kong.

The *Nemesis* carrying Elliot reached Canton on the evening of Thursday 20 May to find the city in a state of great excitement, citizens pouring out and soldiers pouring in. On the morning of the 21st Elliot ordered all foreigners to leave the factories by sunset. That afternoon the *Blenheim*, towed by the *Atalanta* (for towing, steamers were always lashed alongside their charges), dropped anchor just six miles below the city, by far the largest ship ever to have come so close. By now the atmosphere was extremely tense, so Hall kept the boilers alight, he himself sleeping on the bridge. At about 11 pm the *Modeste* (18 guns) lying upstream saw fire-rafts being prepared and raised the alarm, and Hall proudly noted that the *Nemesis* was under way and under command of the helm within nine minutes, a feat an equivalent sailing ship could never have accomplished.

Fire-rafts, a favourite Chinese weapon, consisted of two or three small boats chained together, their contents set alight and then allowed to drift down on the enemy in the hope that they might hang across the bows of a ship and set it alight. In the event only a few rafts were lit and set free, some were towed clear by ships' boats and others went ashore, setting the suburbs alight and providing the watching British with 'a grand spectacle'.[11] Meanwhile the *Nemesis* engaged the Shaming battery in the dark, but the bow gun jammed and the rudder got fouled so that the stern gun could not be brought to bear. So Hall ordered that Congreve rockets be fired, but the first placed in the tube and ignited was not projected. Hall put his arm in the tube and successfully freed it but his hand was severely burnt; if it had not been released and had exploded in the tube it would almost certainly have killed a number of people on the bridge, including Captain Elliot. Now the marines were ordered to fire into the embrasures, these distinguished in the dark by the flash of the Chinese guns, and this they did with such effect that the battery was soon silenced, allowing the *Nemesis* to be got in order again. At dawn it was seen that her funnel and paddle boxes were riddled with bullet holes.

The following morning with Hall confined to his cabin Captain Thomas Herbert of HMS *Calliope* (26 guns) took temporary command of the *Nemesis*. The *Canton Register* of the 29 May takes up the tale: "Meanwhile a number of war-junks were seen issuing from a creek opposite to Fa-tee, and the steamer *Nemesis* went to meet them; but they, unwilling to have anything to say to so formidable an antagonist, retreated again to the creek, and the steamer again gave her assistance at Shaming; which was no sooner perceived by the junks than they came out a second time. This time however the steamer was not content with merely driving them back, but followed them into the creek; what passed there was from the position of our informant hid from his view, but loud reports and immense volumes of white and black smoke rising into the air at short intervals, but too plainly told that the work of destruction was going on there. In less than three hours upwards of 40 war-junks were set fire to and blown up, a sight which can have been anything but pleasing to Yihshan (I-shan), the rebel quelling general. The return of the *Nemesis* from this successful expedition followed by the *Herald* and her own boats can be described as affording a sight in the highest degree cheering and comical at the same time. The steamer was covered all over with the flags and pennants captured from the junks; the boats' crews were all arranged in handsome mandarin dresses and caps; and the crew of one boat in order to be perfect in their new costume, had each man of them, a tail dangling from under their caps, which we hope were spoils from the living Chinese, who saved themselves by leaving their tails behind. The loss of life in this exploit is said not to have been great, the Chinese having ample time to save themselves by flight before the vessels blew up. We are sorry to have to record one casualty aboard the steamer; her gallant commander Captain Hall was severely wounded in the hand by the bursting of a rocket."[12]

A contemporary Chinese perspective of any aspect in this war is hard to come by, but the same newspaper on the 15 June provided such a version of the events of the 22nd translated from a public poster in Canton: "On the second day at 10 o'clock the devil's imps embarked on board a fire-ship and sailed up to Neisheng where they made use of fire-arrows and great guns with which they attacked and smashed Neisheng and burned several tens of carrying vessels... On the third day the devils were off the Fa-tee creek where they seized and carried off several passage boats [troop carriers]. They then commenced a simultaneous attack on the Leipaoutoy or Shaming fort – the Hoychupaoutoy or Dutch folly – and all along the side of the river. They used their fire-arrows, with which they burnt several hundreds of houses, shops, and sheds belonging to the inhabitants of the banks of the river... The fire lasted uninterrupted for two days."[13]

By noon on Monday 24 May the British forces, numbering about 3,500 men in total, were finally prepared for the assault on Canton. After a 21-gun salute to celebrate Queen Victoria's 22nd birthday, disembarkation began. Surgeon Cree watched the soldiers leave the troopship *Rattlesnake* moored only 4 miles below the city, each man with a haversack containing two days' rations and his ammunition.[14] Those landing were divided into two groups, one of 300 to 400 men to retake the factories, their boats towed up by the *Atalanta*, the second and main party towed by the *Nemesis*. On board that ship were Gough, Senhouse and Elliot as well as 300 men of the 49th Regiment, whilst behind were a string of perhaps 70 boats carrying 1,700 men, marines and armed seamen, sepoys, sappers and miners, artillery, storemen and camp followers, an extraordinary and colourful scene. By dusk nearly 2,400 men were safely ashore, and overnight their guns and supplies were landed. The artillery alone consisted of four 12-pound howitzers, four 9-pound field guns, two 6-pound field guns, three 5 1/2 inch mortars and 152 32-pound rockets – hot work throughout a dark and sultry night with the prospect of battle looming, the first land battle of the China campaign.

The British army in India at this time consisted of a diverse body of soldiers.[15] The Company army had a few 'European' regiments, perhaps 20 per cent of its strength, and a growing number of 'native' regiments, the sepoys a mix of Hindus, Sikhs and Muslims. All regiments were commanded by British officers, and even the most experienced Indian non-commissioned officer was unable to give an order to the freshest-faced and most ignorant of English ensigns. In Bengal regiments where about two-thirds of the sepoys were high-caste Hindus, but apparently not in those of the Madras and Bombay presidencies, caste interfered with duty, Hindu sepoys refusing certain duties such as entrenching and even being loath to travel over water. The Company also hired regular regiments of the British Army, these perhaps serving in India for 20 years or more, men of 'the Queen's regiments' viewing themselves as distinctly superior to mere Company men.

The British soldier, whether Queen's or Company's, came mostly from the Celtic fringes, Ireland and Scotland, and from the bottom of the social spectrum, "the scum of the earth"[a] as the Duke of Wellington so unkindly described them.[16] In contrast the officers were very largely drawn from the ruling classes, the aristocracy, landed gentry and the richer middle classes, this structure perpetuated by the purchase system whereby commissions were bought at a fixed price – and could later be sold. With an initial commission costing a minimum of £450 (about £25,000 today), and low pay and the cost of maintaining appearances necessitating a private income, clearly the poor were not welcomed. As Lieutenant William Laurie of the Madras Artillery put it: "There is so

---

[a]   The 1841 census of Great Britain (excluding Ireland) gave a total population of 18.6 million: English 15.0, Scotland 2.6, Wales 0.9, others 0.1 million.

broad a line of demarcation between the commissioned officer and the soldier in the East India Company's service, that no hope exists for the latter to rise to a higher grade."[17]

The regimental structure (theoretically a Regiment consisted of eight Companies of 100 men each) was fundamental to the success of British forces. If in China and elsewhere in the world British land forces often triumphed against considerable odds, this was due in good part to the better organisation, discipline and cohesion derived from a regimental structure. Soldiers of the Queen's regiments did not kill or die primarily for their country but rather for the honour of their regiment. And the sepoys could equally be imbued with love of regiment, whereas love of Empire or of Company would have been much harder to instil. And of course where poverty abounded, whether in Ireland or India, men fought for those who paid them (the sepoy was paid seven rupees a month, 70 pence) and preferably for those who led them to victory and to plunder.

At this time a fully dressed, fully laden British infantryman carried a remarkable 70-pounds burden into battle, dressed uniformly whether in a British winter or a tropic summer.[18] As Garnet Wolseley (1833–1913) wrote as a fiercely ambitious young ensign, "The Queen's Army took an idiotic pride in dressing in India as nearly as possible in the same clothing they wore at home ... Could any costume short of steel armour be more absurd in such a latitude?"[19] Little wonder that often in eastern campaigns more were felled by *coup de soleil*, sunstroke, than by enemy bullets. The soldier's main weapon was his musket, the Brown Bess in service for the past 100 years and weighing with the bayonet an additional 12 pounds, slow to use but simple and durable. His officers were more exotically but equally unsuitably dressed but also unsuitably armed, carrying a sword and a single-shot pistol, inaccurate and unreliable.

And what of the Chinese land forces opposing this British invasion, a mixed bag of more than 45,000 men? Here there was no single 'army' but rather three types of men-at-arms, only one of whom the British learned to truly respect.[20] The Manchu, conquerors of China in 1644, still lived largely in their own quarters in any city of note, keeping separate "in person, habits, modes of life, and privileges..." Amongst them, hereditary soldiers formed an army in eight divisions or banners, the Manchu Bannermen, impressively tall and pale, fearless and honourable in battle but numbering perhaps no more than a quarter of a million, their task to keep order throughout an empire with a population of about 400 million. The Army of the Green Standards, raised by the provincial governor from the local Han people, was in reality little more than a conglomeration of constabularies. And finally there were village militias. And, as Indian sepoys did not fight for a British empire, so the men of the Green Standards and the militias did not fight for China or for the Manchu Emperor but rather for their village and their local chief. Between the groups there was a certain animosity borne of the distaste of the Han for their erstwhile conquerors, but what they had in common, in a decaying empire of increasing poverty and lawlessness, were soldiers often unpaid, underfed and ill-led, and always ill-trained and hopelessly armed.

Chinese soldiers were particularly proud of their bows and arrows, though they also carried swords and spears. About one in ten were armed with matchlocks, a smooth-bore gun rarely effective above 200 yards, using no wadding or ramming, the powder ignited by a length of slow-burning cord, these redundant amongst British forces for over 100 years. Instead, the British carried flintlocks, the powder in a flashpan ignited by the spark of flint against steel; percussion muskets were available from 1839 but as yet were uncommon in the east. Most significantly, the guns of the British forces were tipped with bayonets. If in European wars the bayonet charge had become a rare event, in India it was still common and much of the slaughter in China was accomplished with the bayonet, though Indian sepoys often preferred the swords that they carried unofficially. The Chinese had no field artillery though gingals were used, heavy things requiring two or three men and a tripod, firing metal scraps or a ball of up to one pound in weight. Protected by helmets of iron or brass and sometimes chain-mail, and carrying shields of rattan painted with fierce animals, the soldiers, perhaps steeped in Sun Tzu's Art of War – "So in night battles you use many fires and drums, in daytime battles you use many banners and flags, so as to manipulate people's ears and eyes"[21] – appeared to hope that their fierce demeanour, somersaults and loud shouts, would protect them against the muskets and howitzers of their enemies.

By nine o'clock on the morning of 25 May the invaders' advanced party had reached the walls of Canton, the view of this great city from the heights deeply impressing the British. For Hall, "the two most wonderful things he ever witnessed in his travels were the falls of Niagara and the city of Canton."[22] By midday under torrential rain the first of the heavy guns had arrived but Gough estimated that it would need at least a day to plan the attack and so scheduled it for 7 am on Thursday 27th. But unknown to either him or Senhouse, Elliot was again negotiating with the Imperial Commissioners, this time on board the *Calliope*, and early on Thursday they received a note suspending operations. Both men were furious, Gough calling Elliot "as whimsical as a shuttle-cock".[23] When news of the truce circulated in Canton, soldiers of the Greens started to leave the city for their homes. On Saturday 29th, another very hot and wet day, some regrouped and started to harass the British, incensed by word of the invaders' desecration of graves and the rape of women by black (Indian) troops. In the wet and misty conditions a company of the 37th Madras Native Infantry, 60 sepoys with three British officers, became lost and, their flintlocks useless in the rain, were surrounded by the Greens. Two companies of marines were quickly dispatched to search for them, armed with the new rain-proof Brunswick percussion muskets, successfully rescuing them but not before a private had been killed and 15 men injured. This skirmish was of so little consequence to the British that it was not even mentioned in dispatches, but with little else to celebrate 'The Battle of San-yuan-li' grew in the Chinese mind into a great popular victory, and to this day it is still sometimes so considered.[24]

On 1 June orders were given to withdraw from Canton to Hong Kong. The total British casualties in this, the first land operation in China, were two officers and 14 other ranks killed and 112 wounded. Chinese casualties were reported as 1,500 killed and 4,500 wounded but this must be a considerable exaggeration. What is doubtlessly true is that Elliot's decision to accept the truce so urgently desired by the Chinese saved many lives on both sides. Later he said that he felt that Gough's plans to take only the forts would have been insufficient, and that troops would have had to enter the city itself, a city with half a million inhabitants within the walls and another half million without. Such an assault would have led to massacre and rape by the invaders, something the discipline of the British forces seemed unable to control, accompanied by the flight of the authorities and respectable citizens, leaving the rabble to sack the place and the British to inherit a smoking ruin.

The fear of looting by the local mob was very real to the British as they themselves wished to plunder any town captured. Looting, from the Hindi word *lut*, the plundering of private property, was officially frowned upon but seldom foregone. But the taking of prizes, the plundering of government property, was seen as a legitimate way for both officers and men to profit from their military efforts, and a prize court had already been arranged in Singapore. And such profits could be huge: after the Sind campaign of 1843 the Governor, Sir Charles Napier, 'mad Charlie', was awarded over £68,000 (about £4 million today), an eighth of the entire booty; and Commander Nott of the steamer *Comet* received £8,000, perhaps 15 times his annual salary.[25]

If the conflict to date had resulted in remarkably few casualties for the invaders, mosquitoes and dirty water continued to play havoc with them. By the time the fleet re-assembled in Hong Kong no less than 1,100 troops were on the sick list, largely from malaria and dysentery. The wounded too were dying in droves, unsurprisingly as the conditions under which naval surgeons and their assistants had to operate are horrible to contemplate. The sick and wounded were placed wherever room could be found, and surgery carried out amongst them, operations performed without anaesthetics, except possible laudanum and a strong drink, and with only the most cursory cleanliness. Certainly, most amputees soon died, not usually from shock or loss of blood but from gangrene.

The most senior casualty of this epidemic of sickness was Sir Humphrey Le Fleming Senhouse who on 13 June aged 60 finally succumbed to malaria on his flagship *Blenheim*. On the 17th the *Nemesis* had the honour of carrying his body to Macau where he was buried with due ceremony. That same day surgeon Cree, himself suffering from malaria together with half the crew of the *Rattlesnake*, watched his friend Captain William Brodie die of the same disease.[26] By chance, within a day of Senhouse's burial the steamer *Queen* returned to Hong Kong from Calcutta with Sir Gordon Bremer who immediately resumed naval command.

Whatever Elliot's colleagues thought of his behaviour – and some in the military such as Lieutenant Ouchterlony supported him[27] – he had in fact made some progress. Although there was no mention of opium, of Hong Kong, of trading arrangements for Canton let alone of opening other ports for trade, it was agreed that the $6 million demanded should be paid in six days rather than six years and that compensation should also be received for the damage sustained by the British factory. As Elliot well knew that his masters in both London and Calcutta were particularly concerned with the costs of this distant war, perhaps £30,000 every month, he must have watched with some pleasure as, early in June, HMS

Conway (28 guns) and the *Calliope* sailed from Hong Kong, the former loaded with $2.5 million, 65 tons of silver, bound for London and the latter with $3 million for Calcutta.[b] But this ransom for Canton, although raised from the Co-hong and not directly from the people, was viewed very differently by the Cantonese. As those who had arranged it were largely Manchu, a myth arose that the Cantonese had been on the point of expelling the foreigners when betrayed by the Manchu. Subsequently this fable proved powerful in raising anti-foreign sentiment, a central feature of the calamitous Taiping Rebellion of 1850–64.[28]

---

[b]   Over £600,000 and about £750,000 respectively.

1. *Macau (reprinted from Ouchterlony, 1844)*

2.

3.

2. European factories at Canton (reprinted from Ouchterlony, 1844)

3. A Chinese junk (reprinted from Keppel, 1899)

4. Map: The coast of China: Hong Kong to Shanghai (produced by Lee Li Kheng)

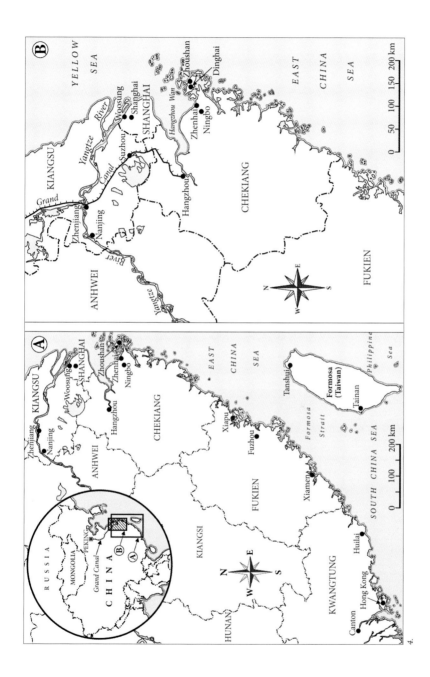

5.

5. 'Nemesis, with other boats, destroying the Chinese War Junks in Anson's Bay, 7 January 1841' (Original watercolour by W. A. Knell, from which the etching was taken. © National Maritime Museum, Greenwich, London)

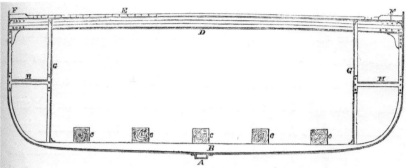

A Keel.
B Floorings.
C Keelsons.
D Deck beams (iron.)
E Deck.

F Covering board, 18 ft. by 4 in.
G Longitudinal iron bulkheads, built into the vessel, forming the sides of the coal-boxes.
H Angle-iron stay-beam between.
I *Side frame* and coal-box bulkhead.

6.

7.

6. Phlegethon – *cross-section through the engine-room showing the built-in coal-box bulkheads to provide additional strength (reprinted from Bernard, 1844)*

7. *Model of the* Nemesis *from the Hong Kong Museum of Coastal Defence*

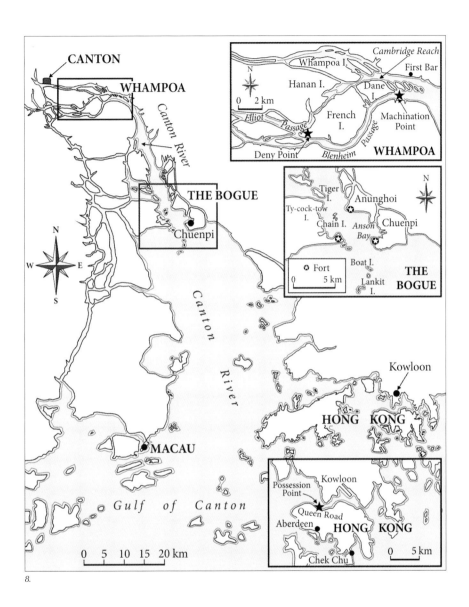

CANTON

WHAMPOA

Canton River

THE BOGUE

Chuenpi

Cambridge Reach
Whampoa I.
First Bar
Hanan I.
Dane I.
0   2 km
Elliot
Passage
French I.
Machination Point
Deny Point
Blenheim
Passage
WHAMPOA

Tiger I.
Anunghoi
Ty-cock-tow I.
Chain I.
Anson Bay
Chuenpi
⊙ Fort
Boat I.
0   5 km
Lankit I.
THE BOGUE

N
W   E
S

Canton

River

Kowloon

HONG KONG

MACAU

Gulf   of   Canton

Possession Point
Kowloon
Queen Road
Aberdeen
HONG KONG
Chek Chu
0   5 km

0   5   10   15   20 km

8.

8.   Map: Hong Kong and the Canton River (produced by Lee Li Kheng)

9.

10.

9. Nemesis *at the Bogue forts, 14 February 1841 (reprinted from Bernard, 1844)*

10. Nemesis *attacking batteries on the Canton River, 1841 (© National Maritime Museum, Greenwich, London)*

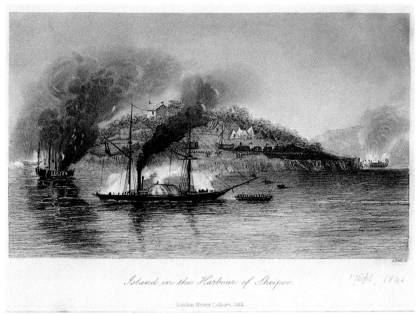

Island in the Harbour of Sheipoo.

17 Sept. 1841

London Henry Colburn, 1844.

11.

STORMING OF AMOY.

12.

11. Nemesis *in the harbour of Xiapu, 7 September 1841 (reprinted from Bernard, 1844)*

12. Nemesis *at Dinghai (reprinted from Ouchterlony, 1844)*

HONG KONG.

13.

14.

13. *Hong Kong (reprinted from Ouchterlony, 1844)*
14. *Afah (reprinted from Bernard, 1846)*

15a.

15b.

15. *Chinese caricatures of the invaders. Top: 'English Foraging Party', Bottom: 'Tartar and English Soldiers Fighting' (reprinted from Bernard, 1844)*

16.

17.

16. *The capture of Dinghai, Zhoushan, 1 October 1841:* Phlegethon *to the right (reprinted from Allom & Wright, 1859)*

17. *The bay at Dinghai, Zhoushan, 1841 (reprinted from Ouchterlony, 1844)*

18.

19.

18. Close of the attack on Xiapu, 17 May 1842 (reprinted from Allom & Wright, 1859)

19. Nemesis at Woosung, 16 June 1842 (reprinted from Bernard, 1846)

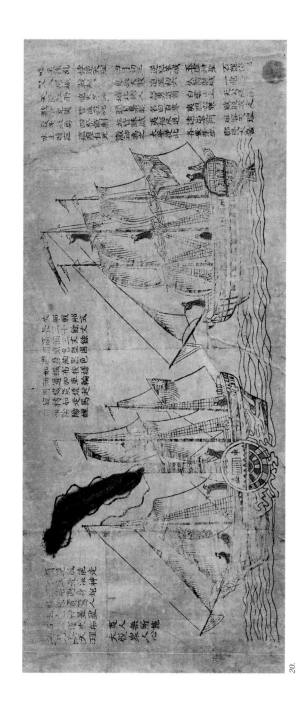

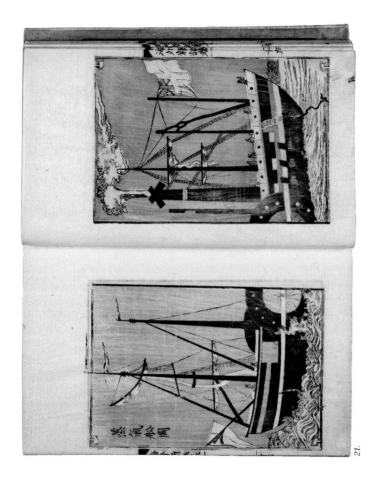

20. *Chinese scroll with illustration of the iron steamer Nemesis and a British man-of-war, with a 55-line Chinese poem and handwritten English translation, ca 1841.*

21. *The Opium War in Japanese Eyes: An Illustration from Kaigai Shinwa, 1894 (from Beinecke Rare Book and Manuscript Library, Yale University)*

B15

22.

22. 'Dent's verandah: Mr Durand, W.C.Hunter and Captain Hall', George Chinnery, Macau, 1842 (private collection).

{ 13 }

A BARREN ISLAND

"And all you have obtained is the cession of Hong Kong,
a barren island with hardly a house upon it."

—Lord Palmerston in his letter of dismissal to
Captain Charles Elliott, 21 April 1841[1]

When the British flag was first raised over Hong Kong in January 1841 the island was largely uninhabited – "a mountainous desolate looking place with only a few fishermen's huts to be seen" according to Surgeon Cree of the *Rattlesnake*.[2] The principle village was Chek-chu on the southern coast with perhaps 2,000 inhabitants, possibly a further 3,000 being scattered elsewhere. When Hall had visited the island in 1816 as a 19-year-old midshipman on HMS *Lyra*, she had anchored close to Chek-chu, but in fact the north shore opposite the Kowloon peninsula offered a much more sheltered harbour and it was here that the British set up shop. By April some thousands of Chinese were employed on the island, "all the ruffians of Canton" according to Cree. On 7 April "in the evening two boats with about 30 girls came alongside the ship, but Commodore Brodie very properly would not allow them to remain," Cree as a doctor of course well understanding the risks. Lob Lob creek, about 10 miles below Canton, and Whampoa's own Bamboo Town, had for many years been famous for the comforts they provided. In the 1770s William Hickey, travelling from Canton to Whampoa, had enjoyed what was on offer but was somewhat disconcerted when later told that he would probably have cause long to remember Lob Lob Creek, "there being no more than six women to satisfy the lusts of a fleet of five-and-twenty ships."[3]

The British, placing considerable emphasis on the value of hard work and brisk exercise to overcome 'impure' thoughts, generally seem to have been rather poorly organised compared with other European imperialists when it came to their troops' sexual requirements. None the less, in India regimental brothels, 'lal bazaars', were provided, there being 'first-class' ones, regulated and inspected, to serve British soldiers and unregulated ones for Indian troops. Certainly the work for the women must have been particularly gruelling; the lal bazaar in Amballa had only 6 women for 400 men and that in Agra less than 40 for 1,500. Unsurprisingly, health inspections not uncommonly found units with over 40 per cent of the men afflicted with venereal diseases.[4]

But in Hong Kong more respectable entertainments were soon available for Surgeon Cree. Twenty days later he "...went over to Kowloon to see a cricket match between the officers of the Navy and Army," adding optimistically "The Chinese looking on appeared to be greatly interested."

It has been said that in a new colony the first thing that the French built was a fort to defend what was already part of the mother-country, the Spanish a church to convert the heathen, and the English a factory to trade with all comers. And in Hong Kong the English were true to form. Temporary 'godowns', warehouses, soon made their appearance along the shore-line, with houses, barracks and a hospital behind. Captain Elliot spent much time organising the new township, Victoria; he was determined not to allow haphazard development, and in particular did not want to alienate land from the Crown. In June he organised the first land sale, actually an auction of annual plot rentals for the first 34 building sites, and in July appointed Lieutenant William Pedder, First Officer of the *Nemesis*, as Harbour Master and Marine Magistrate to control the comings and goings.[5]

That month the harbour was truly crowded, foreign merchant ships and Chinese junks vying for good anchorages with warships, store ships and transports of the British forces. When towards the middle of the month the weather turned sultry, with large storm clouds and much lightning, the British watched with some amusement as the Chinese began to decorate their homes with paper lanterns apparently against the coming storm. But when their junks began moving across to Kowloon and then further towards the Canton River, the crews beating gongs and letting off firecrackers, the foreigners began to realise that something pretty severe would soon be upon them.[6] Early on the morning of Wednesday 21 July, after a quiet night off Hong Kong, Hall took the *Nemesis* across to the mainland seeking shelter by Kowloon, there lowering the topmasts, putting out both fore-anchors but not dousing the boilers. By 8 am a strong northerly gale was blowing straight into the harbour and soon ships began to suffer. Close by the *Nemesis* a Chinese junk sank and the crew watched helplessly as all on board were drowned. By 10.30 am the typhoon was at its worst, the wind howling and the air so filled with rain and spray that visibility was reduced to a few yards. Every now and then the crew caught further glimpses of the destruction being wrought about them, pieces of ship both foreign and Chinese drifting passed and then a whole desperate family, men, women and children, clinging to the remains of their boat. By 2 pm the storm appeared to be abating and by 4 pm the weather had cleared sufficiently to see the full extent of the devastation. Ashore the havoc was terrible: all the temporary buildings had gone – the hospital, the barracks, the godowns – and the harbour was littered with wreckage. Six ships, including the transport *Prince George*, were totally lost, four were driven ashore, and at least 22 had suffered considerable damage, masts lost, rigging fouled. But the *Nemesis* was untouched. Steaming about the harbour on the 22nd, she managed to rescue many.

In the calm before the storm, on the evening of the 20th, Charles Elliot and Sir Gordon Bremer embarked in Macau on the cutter *Louisa*, commanded by Lieutenant Thomas Carmichael, to go to the *Wellesley* at Hong Kong. This vessel, bought in China and of only 75 tons, was allocated specifically to the Chief Superintendent which perhaps explains why they took so small a boat with the weather so threatening. That night as the winds increased Carmichael anchored in the lee of a small island, but soon after dawn they were struck by a huge wave, the captain was washed overboard and lost, the *Louisa* then drifting off at the mercy of the storm. Captained now by Elliot, that afternoon they managed to come ashore on another small island, the boat entirely wrecked but all 23 on board saved. There, with very few clothes but, happily, with eight bottles of gin for comfort they spent the night, fearfully cold and wet. As dawn broke a party of fishermen appeared, plundering the bodies of Chinese thrown up on the beach. As luck would have it, one of them was a man known to them in Macau, Ming-fong, and he led them to a village. Although there the castaways were robbed of their few possessions, the fishermen eventually accepted an offer from Elliot of $3,000 to carry four of them back to Macau.[a] Two small boats were provided, Elliot and Bremer lying in the well of one boat covered by mats. Later passing an armed junk their boat was hailed, asking for news of any wrecks, but the fishermen kept their silence. Considering that the price on the head of both Elliot and Bremer was $50,000 alive and $30,000 dead (ten times that placed on a naval captain and 500 times that on an ordinary soldier or sailor),[7] it is amazing that they were in fact carried safely to Macau, reaching there on the 23rd. Elliot immediately sent off a boat for the rest of the party, the remaining 19 reaching Macau on the 25th. The *Louisa* proved to be the only Royal Navy vessel lost during the entire campaign.

On 29 July 1841 a long low ship steamed into Hong Kong from the west and those watching her arrival no doubt at first mistook her for the *Nemesis*. The *Phlegethon*, sister ship to the *Nemesis*, had left England the previous September under the command of R. F. Cleaveland.[8] Somewhat smaller than her sister, 530 tons rather than 660, with engines of just 90 hp compared with 120, her keel had been laid in Laird's yard in April 1839 but she was not launched for 12 months. Why she languished on the stocks for a year while, between August 1839 and March 1840, the *Nemesis* was built, equipped and dispatched to China is not known. But when she did finally leave England she had two distinct improvements over her sister ship: proper bulkheads running down each side of the engine-room compartments, these providing not only greater bunkering but more importantly much greater longitudinal strength; and a more effective 'disconnecting apparatus' allowing a single engine to power a single paddle wheel. Unfortunately the mechanism is not described, its existence mentioned only in a letter from Peacock in May 1845 which said of 'the *Phlegethon* disconnection' that 'for small engines, I do not think that a simpler disconnection has yet been made.'[9]

The *Phlegethon* sailed from England in company with the *Proserpine*, at 400 tons and 90 hp the smallest of the four sliding-keel vessels to sail to the east, but they managed to keep together only as far as the Cape Verde islands. Soon after, the *Proserpine* ran into difficulties and, although hoping to put into Ascension or St Helena, was swept west, arriving at Salvador (then Bahia) in Brazil on 20 November. There Captain Hough report back to London "I am sorry I cannot report favourably on the

---

[a]   Equivalent to £750.

state of the *Proserpine's* bottom: but the truth must be told. Her bottom is thickly covered with large barnacles, seaweed and green slime. We knew this long before reaching here, for her great falling off in both steaming and sailing was proof positive. ... I must also state that she has not half sail enough."[10]

The *Phlegethon* reached Cape Town on 15 December, a month ahead of the *Proserpine*, leaving on the 29th, the second of the Secret Committee's sliding-keel vessels to round the Cape. Like the *Nemesis* before her she took the Mozambique Passage and again met very stormy weather, but she suffered no damage at all thanks to her improved longitudinal strength.[11] Stopping at the Comoros, they found poor Sultan Alloué still beset by the problems he had explained to Hall the previous September and, fearing for his life, Cleaveland gave him passage via Ceylon to Calcutta which the *Phlegethon* reached on 22 May. Immediately docked for urgent repairs, within four weeks she was again ready for sea, now with 79 men on board under the command of her First Officer Lieutenant McCleverty. Leaving the Hooghly on 27 June with dispatches for Hong Kong, she stopped in Singapore from 15 to 18 July before passing on to China.

Whilst Charles Elliot was delighting in his safe return to his family in Macau, the news the *Phlegethon* brought was hardly welcomed. From the dispatches he learnt not only that his hard-won Convention of Chuenpi had been rejected in London but that he himself was to be replaced.

Elliot and Lin were both cashiered by those above them for failing to do what was expected of them.[12] Lin failed through no fault of his own because what he was ordered to do was, given the military might of the British, impossible; furthermore, it was felt in Peking that his dismissal might mollify the British. But Elliot deliberately ignored his instructions and demanded less of the Chinese than his government ordered. Queen Victoria, who from her accession in 1837 aged just 18 always showed the greatest interest in her empire, was tutored on the Chinese campaign by her mentor and friend the Prime Minister, Lord Melbourne. To a relative she wrote: "*All* we wanted might have been got, if it had not been for the unaccountably strange conduct of Charles Elliot ... who completely disobeyed his instructions and *tried* to get the *lowest* terms he could."[13]

But since 1833 when the British Government had substituted a commercial free-for-all in place of the autocratic rule of the Company it had had, in its ignorance of China, quite unrealistic expectations of its Superintendents. Despite repeated requests from them over five years for proper guidance, all they ever received were instructions about what not to do. Palmerston, adamant that Elliot must communicate directly with Lin and not through the Co-hong merchants, gave him no instructions about how he was, under the actual circumstances of Lin's refusal, to behave.[14]

On 30 April Palmerston told the Cabinet that his patience with Elliot had finally run out and that he must go. In his place Sir Henry Pottinger (1789–1856) was appointed 'Plenipotentiary, Minister Extraordinary and Chief Superintendent of British Trade in China'. Pottinger, a colonel in the Company's Bombay army with 30 years experience in western India, recently the political agent in the province of Sind, had retired to England aged 50 just the year before. Politically skilful, he was well regarded and tough minded. Appointed with him, to command the naval forces in China, was Rear-Admiral Sir William Parker (1781–1866),[b] one of the Lords of the Admiralty, another tactful negotiator and skilful campaigner, famous as a disciplinarian.[15] Both men, ordered to hurry east by the Overland Route, left England on 4 June with the June mail for Bombay. There they spent ten days, leaving on 17 July for China in the Company's steamer *Sesostris* without visiting the Governor-General Lord Auckland in Calcutta, perhaps as it was already known that he was soon to be replaced. The *Sesostris*, passing Singapore on 31 July to 2 August, arrived in the Macau roads on the afternoon of Monday 9 August, only 67 days after her illustrious passengers had left England, "an astonishingly short passage", and the very next day the *Nemesis* carried these two to Macau to consult with Elliot, Bremer and Gough.[16] Although the nature of his dismissal must have hurt, perhaps it was with some relief that two weeks later on the 24th Charles Elliot with his wife and son, accompanied by Sir Gordon and Lady Bremer, embarked on the steamer *Atalanta* for India, leaving the seemingly intractable problems of British/Chinese relations for the comforts of an English home. And there, confident and well-connected, he was certainly not harshly treated, holding further diplomatic posts and ending his career as Rear-Admiral Sir Charles Elliot. In his own defence he wrote "It has been popularly objected to me that I have cared too much for the Chinese. But I submit that it has been caring

---

[b]   Vice-Admiral from 23 November 1841.

more for lasting British honour and substantial British interests to protect a helpless and friendly people", a people whom he elsewhere described as in many ways "the most moderate and reasonable people on the face of the earth."[17]

{ 14 }

THE VIKINGS SAIL NORTH

The British had come to realise the previous year that until the seat of power in Peking was more directly threatened success was unlikely, but clearly the expedition of June to November 1840 had not had the resources to do this effectively. Now Pottinger was determined to go north again and Gough and Parker commanded forces strong enough for success. Two alternative strategies were available. Firstly they could go via the Bei He river towards Peking and so threaten the emperor directly. But the problem here was that the river was too shallow for adequate naval support, and it was felt that to actually attack the capital would cause unnecessary bitterness. Secondly they could cut the Grand Canal where it crossed the Yangtse and so threaten the emperor indirectly. Palmerston had originally favoured the first plan, but in early June Lord Melbourne's Liberal government lost a vote of censure and the subsequent general election was won by Sir Robert Peel's Conservatives,[a] and Pottinger knew that the new Foreign Secretary, the Earl of Aberdeen, favoured the second plan.

---

[a]   'General election' is a somewhat euphemistic term, as at the time only about 7 per cent of adults were eligible to vote. Those standing for Members of Parliament were required to own property, MPs receiving no salary until the 1880s (Cook 1999, Pool 1993).

The heartland of historic China lies around the Yellow River, the Huang He.[1] Here, at the time of the Warring States (463–222 BCE), a number of minor fiefdoms formed the 'Central States', a term commonly mistranslated as 'The Middle Kingdom'. In 589 CE the founder of the Sui dynasty fixed his capital at Chang'an, modern Xi'an, on the Huang He. This had been a major city for 1,600 years but, with a system of government ensuring a bloated bureaucracy, from an early date it proved difficult to provide the ruling class with the requisite food and luxuries. As the land round the Yangtse to the south developed, so it became the rice bowl of the country but adequate supplies could not be brought to Xi'an as the Huang He was too shallow for effective navigation. So a large canal was planned to carry goods to the capital. Luoyang on the Huang He was linked to Yangzhou (Yangchow) on the north bank of the Yangtse in 605 CE. Then in 610 a southern extension was constructed from Zhenjiang (Chinkiang) on the south bank of the Yangtse via Wuxi and Suzhou to Hangzhou, this immense work undertaken by the forced labour of 5.5 million people. Finally the northern section to Tianjin and Peking, which first became the capital of the whole of China in 1267, was constructed during the reign of the Mongol conqueror Kubilai Khan in the 1280s. The Grand Canal, running for over 1,100 miles (1,800 km) from Hangzhou to Peking was in continuous use until the great flood of 1855 changed the course of the Huang He and virtually emptied large sections of the canal. What the British planned was to cut the canal at the Yangtse crossing, placing "a grip on the very lungs of the Chinese government".[2]

Immediately upon their arrival in Hong Kong, the new leaders set about preparing for the journey north. Within ten days a fleet of over 40 ships had been assembled and, leaving about half a dozen vessels and 1,300 men to protect Hong Kong, 36 set sail for the north on Saturday 21 August 1841: nine Royal Navy warships including the Third Rates *Wellesley*, Admiral Parker's flagship, and *Blenheim*; four Company steamers, the *Queen* carrying Sir Henry Pottinger, *Sesostris*, *Nemesis* and *Phlegethon*; the *Rattlesnake* troopship and *Plover* survey vessel, and 21 transports[b] and storeships, the *Marion* transport acting as General Gough's headquarters. On board were about 2,700 fighting men, with field artillery and a rocket-brigade, 400 new percussion muskets,

---

[b]   Transports carrying troops carried coal as ballast, fuel for the steamers.

thousands of 32-pound shot, tons of powder and enough food for over 3,000 people for two months.[3]

And so the British set out for the north, sacking one coastal town after another, a progress likened by the great Chinese scholar Arthur Waley to that of Early Victorian Vikings.[4] Sailing in fine weather the fleet reached Xiamen on the 25th, an important commercial town, lively and well fortified (then Amoy, and still so called by the Fujianese). After a reconnaissance in the *Phlegethon* the following morning by the three leaders, orders were given to attack the forts at 1.30 pm, on the grounds that the Chinese had ignored a request from Gough to 'retire'.[5] By 3 o'clock many of the batteries had been silenced and the *Nemesis* carried the general and some troops to the main battery; by 5 o'clock the whole of the outer defences were in British hands. Seeing this, the citizens started fleeing in droves, and when next morning the invading forces entered the town itself there was virtually no resistance. Later the loss of the town was nicely explained to the emperor: having captured six British warships and set them alight, "The south wind blew the smoke in our soldiers' eyes and Amoy was lost."[6] Then followed what became all too typical throughout the war. Although Gough had reminded his troops that "the individual appropriation of the goods of others, which in England would be called robbery, deserves no better name in China,"[7] looting started almost immediately, both by the invaders and by the local riff-raff who poured in as the citizens poured out.

Throughout the conflict with China the British leaders were strongly of the opinion that Chinese people unconnected with the government or military forces should not be harassed. Karl Gutzlaff, an interpreter travelling north with the fleet expressed this opinion forcefully: "...we should do our utmost to conciliate by unequivocal acts of kindness, and we should prove ourselves Christians by honest dealings, and philanthropists by our religion."[8]

Karl Friedrich Augustus Gutzlaff, nicknamed unsurprisingly by the sailors 'Happy Bowels',[9] was a singular character: a short squat figure usually shabbily dressed, described by Waley as "a cross between parson and pirate, charlatan and genius, philanthropist and crook."[10] Those who knew him well seldom trusted him and were irked by his conceit, but they admired his command of the Chinese language and found him often kind-hearted. Born in Prussia in 1803, the son of a tailor, he gained entry to a school for missionaries in Berlin. Continuing his studies in Rotterdam, in 1824 he was sent by the Netherlands Missionary Society to

Siam where he started learning the Chinese language. At Malacca in 1829 he married the first of three English wives, the first Mrs Gutzlaff dying soon afterwards, leaving him a considerable sum of money. With this, he embarked for China to spread the gospel and distribute medicines. In 1832 his command of Chinese gained him the post of interpreter on the Company's ship *Lord Amherst* during an illegal trading voyage up the Chinese coast, and later that year on Jardine Matheson's *Sylph*, trading in opium. There followed employment on other opium ships, and in 1834 marriage to the second Mrs Gutzlaff, a teacher and missionary. Settling in Macau, he became well known in commercial circles in Canton, and when the British expeditionary force sailed north in June 1840 he went with it as interpreter, recruiting a number of Chinese spies along the way. After the fall of Zhoushan he was appointed civil magistrate there, returning to Macau in February 1841. Now again sailing north with British forces, ahead of him were further stints as magistrate, first at Ningbo and then Zhenjiang and then a valued role as one of three British interpreters at the treaty concluding the conflict. After the war he busied himself as administrator and missionary, and after the death of his second wife in 1849, launched forth on a European lecture tour about evangelising China. When in England in September 1850 he married the third Mrs Gutzlaff, returning with her to China early in 1851 where in August he died, aged only 48.

Gutzlaff was perhaps a somewhat unusual missionary, but many Christians stormed the outer reaches of Empire with the bible in one hand, a gun in the other, leading a posse of merchant-adventurers. All too often their work was hampered by their strongly held views that the locals were in fact semi-barbarous idolaters in need of rescue. Such views were particularly damaging in China for the people of the Middle Kingdom whom they sought to convert and to civilise in fact viewed the white man as uncivilised, the British mere rebels revolting against the emperor. Here was a great civilisation that had never developed an indigenous religion, wonderfully had never known religious wars, and one that appeared to have little desire to change its ways, ways that could be infuriatingly practical to an earnest missionary. A boy on the island of Gulangyu (Kulangsu) near Xiamen after many months of elevating Christian instruction was asked what God he worshipped: "Oh, I am not at all particular, anyone whose birthday happens to come along."[11] It is hard today to understand how a man like Gutzlaff in such a role believed he could bring such a religion to such a people. But doubtless he believed in miracles. He certainly believed in the opium trade, no doubt like other missionaries expressing sadness at its effects but none the less seeing the war as God's way of opening China to his Word. "Only Christ can save China from opium. And only war can open China to Christ. And the war ... has arisen from the traffic in opium."[12] And when the fighting was over the Reverend Dr Leifchild could tell a meeting of the London Missionary Society concerning China "How wondrous are the ways of Providence, how mysterious to our apprehension, that this little nation – this handful of people – should be the means of saving, by her civil, moral, intellectual and spiritual condition, the teeming and swarming population of the globe!"[13]

On 5 September the fleet sailed on, leaving three ships with 550 troops to garrison the island of Gulangyu. But the *Nemesis* had to take her own route north; ten days earlier immediately after the attack on the forts Hall had found himself trapped in a coral lagoon, and to escape he had run his ship full tilt at the most likely passageway. Escape he had, but below the engine room the bottom had been gashed right through. Although the damage had been adequately repaired from the inside she was still leaking and it was decided that she should keep close in shore rather then travel with the rest of the fleet. This was not the first time, nor would it be the last, that Hall appeared rather careless of his ship, but he strongly believed in the future of iron for ship construction, and as Fay remarks he "was determined that nothing could stop his iron ship, and nothing did."[14]

In mid-September the north-east monsoon suddenly set in and Hall sought shelter near Xiapu (Sheipoo). As the harbour entrance seemed particularly narrow a local fisherman was persuaded to act as pilot, promised $10 if successful and to be swung from the yardarm if he failed. As the poor man had never seen a steamship before, let alone piloted one, it must have been a rather nerve-wracking experience but all went well and when he was eventually freed he was apparently astonished to receive his $10 reward.[15] After a small fort and three war-junks were destroyed and a wooding-party had successfully brought back 70 tons of fuel-wood taken from some wood-carrying junks, the *Nemesis* continued north. She arrived at the appointed rendezvous off Zhoushan on 18 September to find only the *Sesostris* there, but the rest of the fleet, somewhat scattered by the stormy weather, drifted in over the next week, the admiral on the *Wellesley* on the 21st, then the plenipotentiary on the *Queen* and finally the general on the *Marion* on the 25th.

The initial plan had been to attack Zhenhai (Chinhai) on the mainland first, but with the north-east monsoon now blowing it was decided to first secure Dinghai (Tinghai), the capital of the island of Zhoushan. Reconnaissance of the place's defences greatly impressed the British by the extent of the repairs carried out since their departure in February. Typically, Lieutenant Ouchterlony expressed "a high opinion of the indefatigable perseverance which these people can devote to labours having for their object the acquisition of gain, the preservation of their property, and the support of the arrogance and authority of their bigoted rulers."[16] One can imagine that some of the Chinese, viewing the fleet that came from half a world away preparing for attack, may well have shared these very sentiments.

The attack on Dinghai took place on Friday 1 October, the two iron steamers ferrying troops ashore from dawn, the forts pounded into silence by the *Wellesley* and *Blenheim*. Gough, as usual bravely leading from the front, was wounded in the shoulder though not seriously. By afternoon all the important sites had been taken and Pottinger and Parker landed from the *Nemesis* accompanied by Hall. Sometime later that day Hall came across a young Chinese boy wandering amongst the ruins. Although apparently only about ten years old he seemed very self-possessed, stating that his name was Afah, that his father, a soldier, had been killed, and asking if he could return with the captain to the fireship. This Hall allowed, sending him back to the island the following day to look for the rest of his family but as they had apparently all fled to the hills Afah returned to Hall. The *Nemesis* had recently taken on as stokers, by far the most unpopular job on a steamship, eight Chinese crewmen who had come north from Hong Kong on the *Wellesley*. And amongst these Afah happily settled down. And so began an unlikely friendship between the English captain and the Chinese boy, a boy eventually destined to meet Queen Victoria herself.[17]

Early in October news reached the expedition of the loss of the steamer *Madagascar*, an event which illustrates all too well one of the major dangers facing early steamships.[18] This wooden paddle steamer of 350 tons and 120 hp had been built in Portugal in 1838 for commercial use, sailing the next year for Calcutta where, with war in China looming, she was bought by the Bengal Marine (Table 8). On 16 August 1841 she left Calcutta under the command of Captain John Dicey with dispatches for the expedition from the Governor-General. Reaching Hong Kong in mid-September she left for the north on Friday 17th carrying a crew of 93 and six soldiers as passengers. Two days later at 9 pm, steaming in rough seas about 150 miles to the east, off the coast near Huilai, the after-cabin began to fill with smoke. Previously she had suffered from repeated fires in the coal-boxes, but this time it was the bulkhead abaft the boilers that was alight. Despite strenuous efforts, within two hours much of the bulkhead had been consumed and the coal in the after-hold was on fire; by 3 am her sides were well alight, and by 4 am Dicey decided to abandon ship.

The *Madagascar* carried four ships' boats, three cutters and a gig. The first to leave was the small gig with seven men, but, in the stormy seas, this was almost immediately crushed by the bows of the steamer and all were drowned. Next the smallest of the cutters, an old boat, was launched with 20 men but again was crushed by the ship and only one man saved. Now one of the remaining cutters was launched, but was cut adrift with only 30 men on board. This left the captain and 41 men to board the remaining cutter, a boat only 24 ft long and 7 ft wide. By 5 am on Monday 20 September all had left the doomed ship which was now ablaze from stem to stern.

The two cutters rowed northwards in the stormy darkness, and had covered about 12 miles when, just before 10 am, they heard a great explosion as the steamer blew up. With the seas still running high and the cutter's freeboard tiny, Dicey had all the men sit packed together around the gunwale, a human barrier to keep the water out, but even so the boat was almost swamped a number of times. Around noon the other cutter disappeared, presumably sunk. As night fell there was still no sight of land, but then at 10 pm in the pitch darkness they heard the sound of breakers. Spending the rest of the night fending the boat off the rocks, at last as dawn broke they found a safe place to run ashore, the men drenched and cold, worn out and very hungry.

Within an hour or so they were discovered by local men, taken to a nearby village and there locked up. Luckily they had with them the ship's two Chinese carpenters and so could communicate with their captors. On the 23rd they were marched 20 miles to Huilai where, pretending to be Americans, they managed to get word to James Matheson in Macau. After protracted negotiations and the payment of $6,000, they finally arrive back in Macau on 6 January 1842, all having been relatively well treated throughout their captivity, including the Chinese carpenters. But of the 99 who had sailed four months before only 42 returned.

Although in battle British forces seemed all too often to engage in unnecessary slaughter, when captives were taken both sides seem to have treated them well. The British generally released all prisoners soon after their capture, Gough ordering that each should be given $3, perhaps rather mean when the Chinese returned 'white' prisoners with $30 and 'blacks' with $15. Amongst those thus returned were two crew members of the *Nemesis* captured on Zhoushan, one English and one black, "a negro lad, who had been a slave at Macau, but had escaped and came on board the *Nemesis*, where he turned out a very smart useful lad," his appearance a cause of some amusement to the Chinese.[19]

If as the war progressed appalling numbers of Chinese soldiers were killed, it is also undoubtedly true that the British leaders wished only that military forces and the Chinese government should suffer, and that civilians should be inconvenienced as little as possible. When a Chinese junk filled with timber had its cargo confiscated near Zhoushan, Parker ordered that its captain must be paid. And when some captives had their queues cut off before release, an action that put the men at risk of execution in Qing China, Gough ordered that in future they should be merely disarmed and then released without such degradation. Certainly, telling combatant from non-combatant was often not easy. According to Ouchterlony, Chinese soldiers were distinguished only by a blue cotton jacket "and can thus by discarding it promptly change their profession."[20]

On 8 October the *Nemesis* and *Phlegethon* carried Pottinger, Parker and Gough 50 miles west to the mainland to reconnoitre Zhenhai. There it was decided that naval forces would attack the town, which lay on the left or northern bank of the Yung River, and the army would attack the Chinese forces on the right bank. The assault took place on Sunday 10 October and followed the usual pattern, the steamers landing troops and towing sailing ships into position. On the right bank of the river the Chinese, mostly men of the Green Standards, were caught in a pincer movement and many slaughtered, "hemmed in on all sides, and crushed and overwhelmed by the fire of a complete semicircle of musketry … Every effort was made by the General and his officers to stop the butchery, but the bugles had to sound the 'cease firing' long and often before the fury of our men could be restrained." By 2 pm the town and all defences on both sides of the river were in British hands with the loss of only 3 killed and 16 wounded. Cree estimated that perhaps 1,500 Chinese had been either killed or wounded, with hundreds of prisoners taken, these released the following day.[21]

With Zhenhai in their hands the British forces moved on towards Ningbo about 12 miles up-river to the south-west. With perhaps one third of a million people, this was one of the greatest merchant cities in China, monopolising the trade with Japan and Korea – a city later to become 'a city of the dead' in the disasters of the Taiping Rebellion of 1850 to 1864.[22] Most importantly, Ningbo lay only 100 miles east of Hangzhou which was the provincial capital and the southern terminus of the Grand Canal, and the British commanders felt that to threaten Hangzhou might indeed put pressure on Peking. On the 12th the *Nemesis* took Parker to view Ningbo, "dressed, as was his custom [when off-duty], in a white jacket and pith helmet, and a pair of flannel inexpressibles."[23] Seeing that many of the inhabitants had already fled, and fearing that the place would be looted before the British got there, Parker ordered four steamers towing four sailing vessels up to the city, carrying only 750 fighting men as well as some artillery and sappers. With Kulangsu, Dinghai and Zhenhai all garrisoned, each with about 500 men, the force was dangerously weakened but they could not delay. In fact Ningbo was taken without a shot being fired, on the evening of the 13 October the band of the 18th Royal Irish Regiment playing 'God Save the Queen' by the city's eastern gate. And here, with the weather deteriorating and the forces depleted, it was decided to over-winter.

Now the *Nemesis* and the other steamers were busily employed ferrying people and goods to and fro between Ningbo, Zhenhai and Zhoushan, making excursions up various rivers and attacking any fortifications found. In January 1842 a new line-of-battle ship, the 74-gun *Cornwallis*, arrived to replace the flagship, and the *Wellesley* set sail for England, soon followed by the *Blenheim* carrying Pottinger to Hong Kong. Arriving there on 1 February 1842 Sir Henry was pleased to see how rapidly the new colony was growing. In fact his obvious support for the settlement upon his first arrival five months before, despite the London government's coolness, had greatly spurred development. As the troops over-wintering there were still living on ships, Pottinger instructed that permanent barracks, storehouses and magazines and a hospital be built, meanwhile commandeering some of the new warehouses and ordering the troops ashore. And business was thriving too. Throughout the winter good quantities of opium had been arriving,[24] Lieutenant Pedder, late of the *Nemesis* and now Hong Kong's Harbour Master and Marine Magistrate, estimating that every fourth ship carried the drug. Jardine Matheson's receiving ship, the *General Wood*, moored off Victoria was certainly a hive of activity. And it wasn't just opium the Chinese were buying. Both British and Portuguese merchants were happily rearming them. Between the previous October and January it was estimated that 500–600 cannon, both brass and iron, as well as hundreds of cases of pistols, muskets and bayonets had been sent up the Canton River.[25] Free trade was indeed flourishing.

{ 15 }

AT THE TIGER HOUR

"What was the hour and what the season when he drew up his troops in this formation? It was a tiger year, a tiger month, a tiger day, a tiger hour."

— "The Story of Han Ch'in-hu", the legendary sixth-century boy-hero[1]

Meanwhile in the north as the winter wore on the situation at Ningbo deteriorated, more and more atrocities being committed by both sides. A soldier kidnapped and killed, a house plundered, respectable Chinese insulted – and thus the citizens increasingly fled and the city fell ever further into the hands of the Chinese rabble and the bored and greedy invaders, soldiers shooting down fleeing Chinese as if they were game.

In January Hall took the *Nemesis* over to Zhoushan for an overhaul. The ship was pulled up on a suitable sandy beach, and over the next few weeks the bottom plates damaged near Xiamen were replaced and other repairs carried out, local Chinese craftsmen proving eager to help. There the first death on board since leaving England occurred, the krooman Tom Liverpool dying on 10 February. When the *Nemesis* returned to Ningbo at the end of that month carrying the 26th Regiment, rumours were rife there of a build-up of Chinese forces in the region, but despite this Hall was ordered to carry both Gough and Parker to Zhoushan again on 3 March. Just before their departure, on 2 March, the popular Chief Engineer John McDougall was accidentally shot dead. How is not revealed, but a precise account is given of the monies owed his family: one week's extra pay for his efforts at Delagoa Bay in August

1840 – £5.00; bonus from the Government of Bengal – £50.00; sale of his effects – £14.79; total – £69.79.[2]

At Zhoushan on the 5th the *Nemesis* met HMS *Clio* (16 guns) "fourteen days only from Hong Kong, bringing the mails, and the joyful news of promotions in the service, consequent upon … the exploits in the Canton River." "[Hall's] performance was so outstanding that the Admiralty obtained an Order in Council to enable him to become a Lieutenant…"; this promotion backdated to 8 January 1841.[3]

When in late 1841 the Emperor heard of the fall of Zhenhai and Ningbo, he ordered his cousin I-ching (1793–1853) to prepare a counteroffensive to recapture these places. I-ching was a scholar and fine painter, a frugal man of comparatively modest tastes, trusted by the Emperor but with very little military experience. Travelling south to Suzhou where the army was to gather, he there set about recruiting local scholars for his staff. Amongst those who signed up was a young man of about 30, Pei Ching-chiao, who, when the fighting was over, wrote a detailed account of what proved to be a disastrous campaign. This gives us a rare Chinese perspective on the conflict and, in Arthur Waley's excellent translation, one blessedly unlike the literal translations beloved of Victorians.[4]

The initial plan was to gather at Suzhou an army of 12,000 Manchu Bannermen and 33,000 Green Standards, and to launch a counter-offensive on 9 February, the eve of the Lunar New Year. On the 31 January I-ching instructed the many literary men on his staff to compose announcements of victory and he spent happy hours placing the 30 received in order of merit. "At that time," says Pei, "it seemed only a question of counting the days and waiting till the news of victory arrived." However, when praying for victory at the temple of the God of War at Hangzhou, the omens given to I ching mentioned tigers. And as tigers tied in with traditional Chinese war magic, he decided that the attack should be delayed to the tiger hour of the tiger day of the tiger month in the year of the tiger – which translated to between 3 and 5 am on the morning of 10 March 1842.[a]

Pei's first assignment was to go to Ningbo to report on the strength of the invaders and how best the city could be approached. He found in the city less than 300 foreign troops and only two warships in the harbour,

---

[a]   More recently a similar belief proved equally ineffective. In Burma, students seeking to overthrow the military dictatorship called for a general strike to start at eight minutes past eight on the morning of 8 August 1988 (Myint-U, 2007).

but "at no place have the pillage and rapine of the foreigners been worse than at Ningpo." His next assignment was to build 500 rocket-mortars but Pei was ashamed to say that, owing to the complete lack of experience of all concerned, functional weapons proved impossible.

Meanwhile up at the advanced base 80 miles north-west of Ningbo all was not well. The man that I-ching had placed in command for the great attack, Chang Ying-yün, proved totally unsuitable. Not only was he found to be of lower rank than certain of the regional commanders who thus would not take orders from him, but he was also an opium addict and, when the crunch came, quite incapable of command. Furthermore, secret agents were passing intelligence to the invaders and relaying fictitious stories to the Chinese headquarters. When these were compounded with the often equally fictitious stories passed back by officers who were not spies, it is little wonder that I-ching felt that the recapture of the two towns was going to be "as easy as turning over one's hand".

And then there were the problems associated with gathering an army consisting of many regional forces. Whole brigades, unfamiliar with the territory, got lost. Others attacked fellow Chinese forces thinking that they were in the pay of the invaders. Of course every commander and his staff needed bodyguards, and Pei says that six out of every ten soldiers were held in reserve for this purpose. And when the advance finally came on 5 March the troops were sent forward unburdened with rations as it was believed that they could cater for themselves in this well-populated country. But the peasants, fearing pillage, fled with all their food and the sufferings of the famished troops, Pei said, "were unendurable".

Of course the advancing army needed guns and baggage, these to be transported along the Yao River. As the river was shallow, only small boats could be used but these were in short supply so porters were hired to take the stuff by land. "We hired 2,400 men, half of whom were beggars of very poor physique and incapable of covering much more than 10 miles a day. The winter ice was beginning to melt, moreover for several days it had been raining in torrents, so that the roads and paths were deep in mud. Half and more than half of our porters decamped before their task was over."

The attack was to start by sending fireships amongst the invading fleet, but as at Canton this proved a total failure. And a new method of fire-raising proved no more effective. Someone suggested that firecrackers should be tied to the backs of monkeys who would then be flung on board the British ships, where they would spread fire rapidly in all directions which with luck would reach the powder-magazine and thus the whole ship would blow up. Nineteen monkeys were bought and taken to the advanced base, but as Pei wrote "The fact is that no-one ever dared go near enough to the foreign ships to fling them on board, so that the plan was never put into effect."

On 9 March Karl Gutzlaff, now magistrate at Ningbo, heard further reports that an attack was imminent, these confirmed that day by some local boys who were helping in the barracks. But the British took no special precautions and so when the South and West Gates were simultaneously assaulted at 3 am the following morning the garrison was taken by surprise. This was the first time they had faced a considerable body of Manchu Bannermen, and now and later they were much impressed by the physical stature and discipline of these men and by their bravery, but their tactics and weapons were woeful; indeed, many had mistakenly left their guns behind and were armed only with swords and spears. The South Gate fell briefly and the Chinese reached the marketplace before being driven back. At the West Gate the attackers, with their swords and spears and a few matchlocks, were driven into the narrow streets by a force of about 130 armed with percussion rifles and two howitzers. And there an appalling slaughter took place. As the Chinese advanced the howitzers opened up, firing three rounds of grape-shot from a distance of no more than 30 yards before being replaced by disciplined platoon firing. Those at the back of the Chinese column, not knowing what was going on at the front, pushed forward and so a mound of the dead and dying formed, which filled the street from side to side, "the writhing and shrieking hetacomb" horrifying Lieutenant Ouchterlony. "The corpses of the slain lay heaped across the narrow street for a distance of many yards, and after the fight had terminated, a pony, which had been ridden by a mandarin, was extricated unhurt from the ghastly mass in which it had been entombed so completely as to have at first escaped observation."[5] In this skirmish a single British soldier was killed and a few wounded; the estimates of the Chinese losses were from 400 to 600, with only 39 prisoners taken.

It seems that the assault on both Ningbo and Zhenhai involved no more than 5,000 Chinese troops, little more than 10 per cent of the total army in the region, and at Zhenhai they fared no better, much of the attacking forces getting lost in the darkness and arriving at the scene

12 hours after the assault had been repulsed. The defeated armies regrouped on the hills by the town of Tzu-chi, 18 miles to the north of Ningbo and there, on 15 March, they were again routed.

The *Sesostris*, the only steamer at Ningbo on the night of the 9th, easily evaded the fire-raft attack and at dawn left to bring news to the leaders at Zhoushan. Gough returned immediately to Ningbo on the *Sesostris* followed on the 14th by Parker with the *Nemesis*, *Phlegethon* and *Queen*. The British forces at Ningbo now amounted to about 1,250 fighting men, the 900 men of the garrison under Gough and 350 seamen and marines accompanying Parker from Zhoushan. On the 15th about 1,000 were embarked on the *Nemesis*, *Phlegethon* and *Queen*, with Gough and Parker on the *Nemesis*, and moved a few miles up-river to attack the main body of Bannermen, perhaps 7,000 men, near Tzu-Chi. Again superior tactics and arms readily won the day with the loss of only three killed and 22 wounded whereas Chinese losses were again estimated at many hundreds. W. D. Bernard, a friend of Captain Hall, reckoned this to be the most classic battle of the war and it was, typically, watched with interest and little fear by many local peasants gathered on the surrounding hills. By the 17th the British were again back at Ningbo.

Now I-Ching attempted to retake Dinghai on Zhoushan but this was an even more dismal failure. A flotilla of 276 small boats under the command of Cheng T'ing-ch'en were gathered from all parts of the coast, but most were at a complete loss amongst the uncharted shoals and sandbanks, so when the seasick sea-braves heard of the defeats on land "they lost all heart for the fray, and putting out again to sea cruised around aimlessly for more than a month without the courage to commence an assault."[6] Needless to say this is not the story that I-ching heard. Cheng, hearing that he was about to be court-martialled for his inaction, suddenly reported that his boats had launched a brilliantly successful fire-raft attack, destroying one English warship and 21 other boats at the cost of hundreds of English lives but with only 3 Chinese dead. Doubt was expressed as to the truth of this but in the end the report was passed to Peking with the result that Cheng was promoted to the Fourth Rank and awarded the Peacock Feather.

The two months following the Chinese attack saw comparatively little military activity, the *Nemesis* being largely employed ferrying people and materials about and in occasional operations against war-junks and fire-boats. In other ways too she showed her metal, as it were, to any doubters in the navy. On one occasion she ran at full speed on to a conical rock off southern Zhoushan, and as the tide fell was held by the rock in front, her stern deep in the water and part of her keel exposed, supported by neither rock nor water, a position a wooden ship would have been unlikely to have survived. As the tide rose again it was hoped that she would float free but a large indentation made by the rock held her fast. So Hall sent out boats to seek local junks for assistance and this was readily given. As the tide was rising for the second time six were brought along side, three to port and three to starboard, strong hawsers passed underneath between pairs of junks and as the water rose she was lifted off, suffering only the large dent but no other material injury.

On board, young Afah's English was coming on apace and he was proving to be a most useful interpreter, much more reliable than the two Cantonese usually used, who tended to cheat the local suppliers. So on 15 January Hall registered him as a member of the crew, 'Afar Nemesis', a 'boy' at £1.50 per month.[7] At dinner one day Sir Charles Burdett of the 41st Madras Native Infantry challenged Afah to pronounce his name, promising to give him a pistol if he succeeded. After a little instruction from Hall the boy proudly returned to Sir Charles, spoke well and received his reward. A few days later he found a use for his prize; accompanying Hall to Ningbo as interpreter, he entered a house allotted to the troops as a residence to find a Chinese soldier there who would not leave. Afah suddenly produced his pistol, which was unloaded, aimed it at the man and shouted, "'Suppose he no get up, he makey shoot.' The fellow, in great alarm, roared out,, 'No fire! I go! I go!' and ran out of the house to the great amusement of all present."[8]

The British had always intended to occupy Ningbo only as winter quarters and so on 7 May they moved out and sailed north, anchoring on the 13th off Chapu, on the northern arm of the Bay of Hangzhou. On the 17th the fleet moved closer inshore, the *Cornwallis* (74 guns), *Blonde* (46), *Algerine* (10), *Columbine* (18), *Modeste* (18), *Plover* (10) and *Starling* (6) carrying the considerable total of 182 guns (Table 9b). The attack on Chapu began at dawn on Wednesday 18th, the fleet opening fire as the *Nemesis* and *Phlegethon* again usefully ferried troops directly to the shore. The Chinese garrison, numbering perhaps 7,000 but hopelessly out-gunned, were soon in retreat but again the coolness and bravery of the Bannermen greatly impressed their opponents. Later upon entering Manchu houses the British were horrified to see whole families who together had committed suicide rather than be captured. Again the Chinese losses were formidable, Hall estimating that perhaps 1,200 had been killed or wounded against the loss of 13 killed, including two crew members of the *Nemesis*, and 52 wounded. But if in China the British were suffering comparatively little, elsewhere in the Empire things were not going so smoothly.

{ 16 }

A TROUBLE IN OUR HEART

"The Yangtze River is a region like a throat, at which the whole situation of the country is determined. Now they have already cut off our salt and grain transportation and stopped the communication of merchants and travellers. This is not a disease like ringworm, but a trouble in our heart and stomach."

—Chang Hsi, assistant to plenipotentiary Yilibu, August 1842[1]

On 12 January 1842 many thousands of miles to the west of Ningbo, a solitary man rode into the western Indian town of Jelalabad. He was a Scotsman, a doctor named William Brydon, and he brought news of the virtual annihilation of the British garrison of Kabul (*see* chapter 20).[2] This disaster appalled the British government and people and it was the progress of the Army of Retribution sent to Afghanistan in revenge, and not the conflict in China, which held the attention of the rulers of both Britain and British India throughout 1842. But Governor-General Lord Ellenborough, who had replaced Lord Auckland early in the year, also saw that the China venture, which was costing a great deal of money, had to be pressed to a swift conclusion – and a profitable one, for the Afghan war was certainly going to be horribly expensive. He thus determined that the forces in China should be substantially reinforced and, despite the demands of the Afghan campaign, the land forces received an additional regiment from Britain and six from India, as well as more artillery, sappers and miners. So that whereas at the start of the year Gough had commanded about 3,000 troops, by June he commanded 10,000.

And the naval forces were likewise greatly expanded.[3] Fortunately neither the Royal Navy nor the Company's navies were currently involved in major ventures elsewhere, and the fleet around Zhoushan was reinforced over April and May by warships, troopships and store ships. Between 2 April and 26 May, a total of 55 ships left Singapore for China. The steam fleet almost tripled in size, from 4 to 11 ships (Table 9a). The *Nemesis, Phlegethon, Queen* and *Sesostris* were joined by six more Company steamers. From the Bengal Marine came the wooden *Tenasserim* (769 tons), a copy of the *Queen* built the previous year in Moulmein in Burma, and two more of the Secret Committee's iron steamers *Pluto* and *Proserpine*. And a similar trio arrived from the Indian Navy, the wooden *Auckland* (964 tons), built at Bombay in 1840, and Laird's *Ariadne* and *Medusa*. A twelfth Company steamer, the *Hooghly* (158 tons), had been employed around Hong Kong since the previous August. Joining this Company fleet towards the end of June was the first Royal Navy steamer to be employed in the East, HMS *Vixen* (180 ft, 1,065 tons, 280 hp). This wooden paddle steamer had been launched in February of the previous year, commissioned that December and sent straight to China.

Two other steamers from England arrived in China after hostilities ceased. The Company's *Akbar* sailed from Falmouth on 22 May 1842 and arrived at Singapore on 25 August, a journey of 95 days of which 80 had been at sea but more than half solely under sail. That same day the *Vixen's* sister ship, HMS *Driver*, reached the Yangtse; the ship later to become the first steamer to circumnavigate the world although she did so largely under sail, travelling 75,696 miles via Borneo, New Zealand and Rio to reach England again on 14 May 1846. It says much about the life of a sailor at the time that of her crew of 149 men, 32 died on this voyage and 47 were invalided.[4]

By mid June all six of the Secret Committee's 'sliding-keel vessels' were gathered off Zhoushan. The *Proserpine*, leaving England with the *Phlegethon* in September 1840, had arrived in Calcutta in June 1841, working between there and Moulmein in Burma until 11 May 1842 when, still under the command of John Hough, she left for China. The *Pluto*, leaving England in October 1841 under John Tudor sailed straight to China as the *Nemesis* had done before her, passing Singapore in late April and arriving off Hong Kong on 15 May.[5]

The journeys of both the *Ariadne* and *Medusa* to the war were filled with drama, these little flat-bottomed iron ships being patently unsuited for long sea voyages.[6] Since their launch in Bombay in 1840, the two vessels had been acting as packet boats between there and the Indus River delta to the west. Perhaps it was when Sir Henry Pottinger and Admiral Parker stopped in Bombay on their way to China in July 1841, well aware of the sterling work that the *Nemesis* was accomplishing, that they were ordered east. On Wednesday 29 September, the pair left their home port together, the larger *Medusa* commanded by Lieutenant Harry Hewitt, the *Ariadne* by his junior, Lieutenant John Roberts. Passing through Singapore on 19–22 October, the two little ships were by the end of the month steaming north in the South China Sea towards the Philippines, making very slow progress against contrary winds. But on Tuesday 2 November, just 120 miles short of Manila, the *Ariadne* finally ran out of coal and Hewitt ordered Roberts to return to Singapore.

The *Ariadne*, crewed by only two officers and 15 men, first moved south, obtaining some fuel wood from islands near Palawan, but then a fierce storm swept her 90 miles to the east "owing to the vessel having so slight a hold of the water." On 12 November she managed to beat back to the extreme northern tip of Borneo. Landing again for fuel, the wooding party was attacked but safely regained their ship after killing three of the attackers. By the end of November the *Ariadne* was back at Palawan, with little food, no grog and no fuel. But having wooded successfully, Roberts decided to try for the north again, and then by chance on 8 December they met the *Cornwallis* on her way to join the fleet off Zhoushan. Having obtained some coal and supplies from the Third Rate, the *Ariadne* sailed for Manila, waiting there for further fuel, finally reaching Macau on 22 January 1842. There she worked for a few months, probably sailing north for Zhoushan with her sister ship in May.

The *Medusa* upon parting with the *Ariadne* on 2 November headed on to Manila, which she reached the following day, desperately short of fuel. But all that was available there was a little coal of the poorest quality and some wood. Having loaded 30 tons, even the cabins now wood-filled, she set off north again on the 9th. And then on the 13th, within a day's sailing of Hong Kong, she ran into a nasty storm. With her compass inaccurate and fuel virtually finished, she was swept westwards towards Hainan, the dreadful weather preventing any navigational observations, the ship in imminent danger as she approached the island. Hewitt now gave up hope of reaching Hong Kong and turned his ship back towards Singapore, ordering the crew to find fuel wherever they could, breaking up the cabin fittings, even the wooden bulwarks. Swept south they finally reached safety at Camranh Bay in Cochin-China on the Thursday 18th. There they rested for six days, resetting the compass and taking on wood and water. But the wood proved too green to burn well so they moved on south largely under sail, reaching Singapore again on Monday 6 December, 45 anxious days after their departure.

There, Hewitt learned that just a week after they had left the steamer *Forbes* (302 tons) had arrived from Calcutta with orders for the two not to proceed to China but to go instead to Moulmein in British Burma where trouble was expected. So, after necessary repairs, the *Medusa* left Singapore on the 19th for the Tenasserim coast but in fact found at Moulmein that she was no longer needed. As the *Friend of India* reported on 2 December, "While this great storm has been gathering upon the mountains of Afghanistan, the squall which appeared to threaten us on our eastern frontier has blown off."[7] So the *Medusa* steamed on to Calcutta where in April she helped embark troops for China on the assembled transport ships. She herself left again for the east on the 24th, arriving in Singapore on 5 May and leaving two days later for China accompanied by *Vixen* and HMS *Dido*, a much safer way to travel over the South China Sea.

The *Medusa* finally arrived in Hong Kong on 19 May 1842, leaving nine days later for the north probably accompanied by the *Ariadne*. But the two were not destined to work together for long. On 23 June the *Ariadne* ran on to an uncharted rock off Zhoushan and was badly holed, the engine room flooded and three Chinese crewmen drowned. A sail was immediately passed under her to stem the leak and she was taken in tow by the *Sesostris*, but entering Zhoushan harbour she sank in 30 ft of water and was lost.

On 9 May the two plenipotentiaries sent south by the Emperor to assess the foreigners' assault reached Hangzhou. On the 20th, knowing of the loss of Chapu, Yilibu and Qiying sent word via a junior military officer that they wished to negotiate but Pottinger would not receive him, determined to negotiate face to face only with the plenipotentiaries themselves. By now the majority of the reinforcements had arrived, and it was decided to proceed up the Yangtse towards Nanjing (Nanking), the ancient capital and the greatest city on the river. On the 29th the fleet anchored about 40 miles off Chapu, and on 8 June in foggy weather eventually rendezvoused at the mouth of the river. The *Nemesis*, with Gutslaff on board as interpreter and accompanied by the *Phlegethon* and *Modeste*, was sent ahead to reconnoitre the defences of the fort at Woosung. This lay about 25 miles up-river on the right or southern bank where the Hwangpu River flowed in from the south, the town of Shanghai lying a dozen miles up this tributary.

The fleet, warships and transports, finally anchored off Woosung on Monday 13 June and at first light on the 16th five warships were towed into place opposite the fort by five steamers: the flagship *Cornwallis* paired with the *Sesostris* and the Fifth Rate *Blonde* with the *Tenasserim*, the unrated *Modeste, Columbine* and *Clio* being towed respectively by the iron steamers *Nemesis, Phegethon* and *Pluto*, the *Medusa* being kept in reserve. Joined later by the *Algerine* (10 guns) and *North Star* (26), the fleet pounded the fort for two hours before seamen and marines landed and captured it. That day the veteran General Chen Hua-cheng was killed during the bombardment, a man still regarded by the Chinese as one of the heroes of the war. Somewhat to their chagrin, the British army was never engaged, though no doubt their disappointment was somewhat offset by finding amongst the 250 guns captured 42 of brass, so useful for the prize fund.

Meanwhile the *Nemesis*, having released the *Modeste*, continued up the river to attack a fleet of junks. Amongst these, to the crew's surprise and amusement, were five newly-built 'wheel-boats'. These strange craft, each powered by two pairs of 5-foot diameter paddle wheels turned manually from below the deck by a capstan via wooden cogs, were thought by the British to be the Chinese answer to their paddle steamers. But in fact such vessels had been made in China at least since the fifth century CE. In 1161 the Song navy had defeated a fleet sent by the Jin off the southern coast of Shandong using wheel-boats powered by treadmills and equipped with quite formidable weaponry – iron rams, rockets, catapults for hurling incendiary missiles, explosive bombs using gunpowder, and fire-rafts.[8] Evidently, in former times the Chinese navy might have made a formidable foe but now Hall gave them no chance to show their prowess, sowing havoc with grape and canister from the bow gun. In the middle of the engagement Afah appeared on the bridge "to see the fun", but with shots flying around Hall quickly ordered him below.

On 14 June HMS *Dido* (18 guns) 'a beautiful corvette, one of Symond's best' arrived off Zhoushan.[9] Her captain was Henry Keppel (1809–1904) of whom we have already heard a little – as the son of an earl, his rapid promotion compared with Hall – and of whom we will hear more. Less than 5 ft in height, with bright red hair and sparkling eyes, Keppel was not only a man of great presence and charm but a fine sailor, energetic and brave. Respected by all, from the lowliest of his midshipmen to his Queen, he rose to become Admiral of the Fleet Sir Henry Keppel, Victoria's 'little Admiral', dying full of years and honour in 1904.[10]

The *Dido* had left Falmouth on the 23 January and, sailing via Rio, Cape Town and Singapore, which she left accompanying the *Vixen* and *Medusa*, reached Hong Kong on the 30 May, a voyage of 127 days to compare with the *Nemesis'* 245 days, 18 months earlier. But her record was easily beaten three months later by HMS *Vindictive* (50 guns) which took only 90 days from England, twice covering 296 miles on a single day.[11] In Hong Kong Keppel immediately reported to Pottinger, and was ordered to pick up a convoy of transports carrying 2,500 men from India and shepherd them north to Zhoushan, sailing on from there to Woosung on 16 June just as the engagement finished.

The following day, well-connected as he was, Captain Keppel dined on board the flagship with the Admiral and on the 18th landed with the General. "Waterloo Day. General Sir Hugh Gough landed in my gig, when I witnessed the horrors of war. Mutilated carcases of men and horses by the hundreds. Houses burning, villages deserted, etc. Struck by the prevalent feeling so strong for destruction. Sir Hugh Gough … directed an orderly to ascertain whether a Chinaman separated from the others was dead or alive. The corporal turned the body over with his bayonet in it, answering 'Dead, your Honour', which he certainly was then."[12] And this despite Gough's pious instruction that "the unarmed, or the suppliant for mercy, of whatever country or whatever colour, a true British soldier will always spare."[13]

With the army now greatly swollen, it was necessary to give it a bit of fighting to do to keep up morale. And so on Sunday 19 June the force was divided into two divisions to advance on Shanghai. One advanced overland up the left bank of the Hwangpu River, a proper army with horse-drawn artillery, the horses shipped in from India, and duly assisted by the locals who apparently volunteered to free stuck guns and to carry scaling ladders. The countryside was "a perfect flat as far as the eye could reach, and in as high a state of cultivation as the market gardens around London."[14] The second division steamed up, courtesy of the navy, again men-of-war towed by steamers. The *Sesostris* had run aground and damaged her rudder and was left behind. The *Tenasserim* towed the *North Star* and the three iron steamers the same ships they had helped at Woosung, all led by the *Medusa* carrying the General, the

Admiral and the sociable Keppel. No opposition was met with and the city taken without bloodshed, the invaders amazed at the great wealth of the place, the large warehouses and well-stocked timber yards. They were also amazed, with the temperature soaring to 97°F (36°C), to find abundant ice in well-constructed ice-houses, used by the Chinese for the preservation of fish but by the grateful invaders to cool their drinks.[15] Gough again sent out an order forbidding looting, but when the troops, numbering over 3,000, were quartered in the city for four nights, many in shops and private houses, it is unsurprising that the place was comprehensively plundered, with much of the loot then being sold back to the Chinese.

An account of that day has been left by a Shanghai scholar called Tsao Sheng who helped organise a sort of Home Guard.[16] Rumour was rife that the Manchu Bannermen were going to massacre everyone in the town as mobs had damaged the government offices – a nice comment on Manchu/Han relationships. In the afternoon "news came that the General Chi Lun was advancing upon the western gate. Terrified voices came from every door down the street, screaming 'He's come to massacre us all!' The panic had not subsided when the sound of a long and continuous cannonade began. Again the cry went up, 'He's massacring the city!' As a matter of fact Chi Lun had gone away again; the guns that were being fired were those of the foreigners! I knew now that the worst was at hand … Suddenly fire arose from the Prefecture, and at the same time the foreign soldiers arrived in force, both by land and from their ships. When they first came there were six ships, two of them what are called fire-wheel ships. These anchored at the southern quay of the main bay."

The next day Tsao "went home by the small path and when I got to my gate I found several foreigners there, beating it down with their muskets. I thought of my wife still hidden within and determined that if death was to be her fate, I would share it. I rushed up and attempted to thrust myself between them and the gate, but was seized and held. They then went into the house and ransacked all the chests and boxes, taking money, headdresses, trinkets – everything they could lay their hands on." And what Tsao did not lose to the British he lost to local robbers. On the 21st "at about the Second Drum-beat (9 pm) the rain at last stopped and the moon shone fitfully. A band of local brigands now arrived, having got in by pushing down part of the wall. They said that they had only come to shelter from the rain; but there were twenty or thirty of them, and they soon began a search even more thorough than that of the enemy. In fact everything that the foreigners had not taken they made a bundle of and took away. As I was single handed there was nothing for it but to stand by and let them do as they pleased. A check-up after they had gone showed that they had not left a single farthing or a single grain of rice. Coverlets, trousers, coats, shoes – everything that could be eaten or used – had practically all disappeared. This really was, as they say, the calamity of calamities!"

The invaders certainly looted what they could, but they were not particularly bloodthirsty. "Actually the foreigners have contented themselves with loot and rape, but as the city fell without resistance, there has been no general slaughter ... But they are pressing the people into their service to do all their heavy work, such as shifting gun emplacements and gunpowder, and utensils of all sorts. They take anyone they come across – Buddhist monks, Taoist monks, notables and well-to-do people, and keep them all day and all night."

On the 21st the *Nemesis*, carrying the Admiral, other officers and a party of 50 marines, and accompanied by the *Phlegethon* and *Medusa*, continued up the river to see if a passage was available to Suzhou, thought to be the most important manufacturing town in China. "No opposition for 60 miles. Country thickly populated, and the natives astonished rather," as Keppel observed. But the river became too shallow and the ships turned back, only later to learn that they had been so close to Suzhou that the steamers' smoke had been seen from the city walls.[17] With all this steaming around in a highly populated and treeless landscape, there was apparently no problem in fuelling the steamers for coal, commonly mined in China, was readily available.

In mid-June Sir Henry Pottinger arrived back at Zhoushan from Hong Kong with further reinforcements, on the 22nd reaching Woosung on the *Queen* where he was met by both Gough and Parker, the *Proserpine* also travelling from Zhoushan to the Yangtse at about this time. Now all was ready for the end-game, the cutting of the Grand Canal and the threatening of the second city of the Empire, Nanjing. Ever since the capture of Ningbo the previous October, the Chinese had been putting all their efforts into strengthening the defences of Peking, apparently unaware of the British designs on Nanjing whose defences remained derisory.

The end of June was marred by squally weather, quite unsuitable for sending a fleet up an uncharted river known to have strong currents and shifting sandbanks. The Yangtse is the world's third largest river, rising on the high plateaux of Qinghai and running almost 4,000 miles to the sea, and so of course carries immense quantities of silt and, during the summer monsoons which had now set in, huge volumes of water. And the British intended to sail up this river with a fleet of many dozens of ships, including two 74s which drew at least 23 ft of water, Parker's flagship *Cornwallis* and the *Belleisle*, now a troopship. On the 29th the *Phlegethon* with two survey vessels was sent ahead to mark the most suitable channel, returning a few days later having buoyed it as far as the Grand Canal. Now the fleet prepared for its journey inland, an armada of 73 ships: 11 sailing warships, 4 armed troopships, 10 armed steamers and 48 transports carrying about 9,000 troops and 3,000 marines and seamen of which 2,000 could be employed ashore. Add to this two warships left to blockade the river at Woosung, and an unknown number of vessels supporting garrisons of about 500 men each at Zhoushan, Zhenghai and Xiamen. And then compare this to the forces gathered 11 months earlier at Hong Kong to sail north – 36 vessels, of which 5 were steamers, carrying 2,700 fighting men – and the determination of the British that the war should be concluded quickly and on their terms becomes fully apparent.

Without doubt this expedition was a truly remarkable feat of planning and of seamanship. The logistics were certainly formidable: over 70 ships, well over 13,000 men of many different ranks and races, the clothing and the food, the matériel for war, all gathered thousands of miles from home. And yet they were well supplied with all necessities, none of the first-hand accounts marked by significant complaint. To illustrate the former and perhaps explain the latter, each military officer on board a transport "was allowed, per diem, three bottles of beer, one of wine, and a pint of brandy."[18] The successful outcome of the campaign would suggest that not all of this was consumed.

For the journey up the Yangtse the fleet was divided into six sections: an Advanced Squadron and five Divisions, all five iron steamers in the Advanced Squadron which also included Admiral Parker on the *Cornwallis*, and each Division with one wooden steamer, the First with the transport *Marion* carrying General Gough, and the Third with the *Queen* carrying Sir Henry Pottinger.[19]

Wednesday 6 July dawned misty but soon cleared, a day that was to witness perhaps the most stunning spectacle of the whole campaign. There, strung out along the Yangtse, lay the armada, each division well separated from the next. On board the *Dido*, towards the back of the line, Captain Keppel waxed lyrical. "The whole, anchored in a single line – with room to swing, required space. It was a beautiful sight. On a signal from Flag for fleet to weigh, in a few minutes you would see a white cloud, three miles in extent, moving up the river. While the seamen went aloft to loose sails, troops manned sheets and halyards. Wind heading, the reverse took place, and a forest of masts succeeded the white cloud."[20] And from his troopship Lieutenant Ouchterlony was also bowled over: "nothing interfered to mar the brilliant effect of this striking spectacle."[21]

The *Nemesis* led the advanced squadron, giving soundings by signal flags to those following in her wake. It was a slow process, most ships grounding more than once but without damage as the bottom was muddy, but some requiring the combined efforts of two or three steamers to get them free and on their way again. On 8 July they moved above the influence of the tides and, against a current of 5 to 7 knots and often contrary winds, the procession moved, if at all, at a snail's pace. On board the old *Belleisle* (74 guns) Captain Cunynghame observed "…we got into one of those whirlpools which render even steamers of considerable burden unmanageable … such was the power of the eddy in which we lay, that although a strong breeze was blowing at the time, and every stretch of canvas that could be set was well aback, she did not move from the spot in which she lay spellbound, as though it were the work of enchantment."[22]

So it was two weeks before the whole fleet was assembled off Zhenjiang, a fine walled city about 150 miles above Woosung, lying on the right bank of the Yangtse by the entrance to the southern branch of the Grand Canal. Here the river was about 1 1/2 miles wide, and the *Calliope* was sent across to blockade the entrance to the northern branch of the Canal near Yangchow. During their journey up-river to Zhenjiang the British fleet had intercepted no fewer than 700 junks which gives some indication of the great importance of river trade in this part of China.

On the 18th Pottinger on the *Queen* accompanied by the *Nemesis* moved a dozen miles above Zhenjiang, anchoring by the small town of Esching. There, the local mandarin was invited on board the *Nemesis*, coming with small gifts, and with apparent interest was shown over the ship, young Afah acting as interpreter. After nine months on board Afah, now 'almost adopted' by Hall, could speak English fluently. On the 19th the *Nemesis* was joined by the *Dido* and *Childers*, and that evening Hall took Keppel and others ashore to call upon the mandarin, where they were politely received in a most impressive place of many courtyards and buildings. Keppel apparently charmed the mandarin into volunteering to provide fresh supplies for which the British would pay, and a little market was set up. But not every food-gathering was so gentlemanly. A few days later Keppel reported: "Started with Hall in *Nemesis* on a foraging expedition ... The best plan was to catch a fat Chinaman, generally the chief of a village. The people always pleaded poverty as an excuse. Having dropped on to such as I have described, I gave him until 4 pm to supply twenty-five bullocks or have his tail cut off, which had the desired effect."[23] But Keppel was a little unfair. With the Chinese army gathered for the defence of Zhenjiang living off the land, food was indeed at a premium.

One of the more cheering aspects of this conflict was the remarkable consideration with which the Chinese often treated their invaders. Surgeon Cree, out with a duck-shooting party on Zhoushan, bought food at a butcher's shop, the butcher's wife cooking it for them and a friendly crowd watching the foreigners eat; and later, picking his way through the ruins of Zhenjiang after its capture, Cree was eagerly sold fresh fruit and vegetables.[24] One afternoon Bernard "walked for the distance of five or six miles into the interior, attended by crowds of the peasantry, who appeared to be a strong, hardy, well-disposed race, and offered no kind of violence or insult".[25] Lieutenant Forbes, visiting villages in search of coins for his collection, found himself "in the midst of as amiable, kind, and hospitable a population as any on the face of the globe, as far ahead of us in some things as behind us in others."[26]

On Thursday 21 July Hall, Keppel and their colleagues, still enjoying the hospitality of the mandarin at Esching, could hear the sound of gunfire from down the river. The attack on Zhenjiang had started early that morning, the landing rather chaotic, some men being put ashore when it was still dark and in the wrong place, others not landed until it was all over. Fighting went on throughout an exceptionally hot and sultry day, again the Manchu Bannermen, their numbers estimated at between two and four thousand, fighting bravely against overwhelming odds – "such steady coolness and indomitable courage".[27] By evening it was all over, uncounted numbers of Chinese dead and wounded, the invaders suffering 40 dead, of which 17 were killed by sunstroke, and 128 wounded. With temperatures approaching 100° F (38°C) men in the 98th Regiment particularly suffered. "We lost but five men, killed by the enemy's fire, but before night, about twenty of H. M.'s 98th had perished from the effects of *coup de soleil*. This, indeed, was a sad thing; but we were soon obliged to grow callous to such scenes, for ere the week was past, forty more men of that regiment alone had perished of cholera ..."[28] Surgeon Cree was less sanguine about sunstroke than Captain Cunynghame. "Besides, men in one regiment were kept standing in the sun buttoned up to their throats with stiff leather stocks and heavy shakos, three days' provisions and sixty rounds of ammunition, till a dozen of them dropped in the ranks from sunstroke."[29] Cholera was certainly a disease much feared; with no known cure, death through dehydration from diarrhoea was often very rapid – sometimes within five hours of the first symptoms – and always very nasty. Cree, helpless, watched "two fine young sailors *in articulo mortis*, blue features and sunken eyes and gasping for breath; three others tormented with cramp, groaning and tossing in their beds."

The poet Zhu Shi-yün has left a graphic if biased account of the actions of Lieutenant-General Hai-lin, in command of the Manchu garrison.[30] On 9 July the General in order to calm the population announced, "A brilliant plan has been made which assures us of complete victory; so there is no reason to panic or stampede." But then, "Inside the city his whole activity consisted in arresting passers-by day and night, on suspicion of their being traitors. Whenever women or children saw Manchu soldiers, they fled in terror; upon which the soldiers ran after them and slew them, announcing to Hai-lin that they had disposed of traitors; for which he gave them rewards." Two days later "... at Chinkiang militia have been concentrated to guard the harbour and river-mouth. But Hai-lin still sits tight in the city, amusing himself with wine and women, and never even asks what is going on outside ... Tonight at the Second Watch (9 pm on the 14th) the street was blocked with fugitives. I opened my gate and questioned some of them ... What happened was that when the foreign ships reached the Sui-shan they fired a large gun and knocked out the Sui-shan battery. Our troops were scattered in every direction by the explosion and fled back to the city ... There were some thirty or forty gunners at the battery, but they had no gunpowder. When the attack began they sent a runner to the city to ask for some, but Hai-lin sent none. That was why they fled." And so the sorry saga continued, with the usual stories of plunder by bandits, citizens fleeing in helpless confusion, and ill-led and ill-fed soldiery. By the 20th many of the troops had not had a solid meal for five days. "Tonight, Commander Liu's troops, owing to the gate being shut and there being nowhere where they could buy food, have collected under the walls, threatening to storm the city, capture General Hai-lin and eat him raw!" In fact the General died during the attack, either in battle or perhaps from suicide.

As the fighting subsided so the looting began, both members of the invading forces and the locals taking advantage of the chaos, so that by the following day this elegant city of perhaps 200,000 inhabitants was a shambles. "We rowed up a canal as far as the west gate, the scene of the grand explosion, a terrible scene of ruin, all the houses round smashed and the city gate and the guardhouse above, which the Tartars so hotly defended, a smoking ruin."[31] Again there were horrible scenes of suicide and murder in the Manchu houses, Ouchterlony in one house counting 16 women and children dead either by poison or with their throats cut from ear to ear. Keppel landed that day from the *Dido*. "On going through the town, there were piles of dead Chinese soldiers at the corners of the streets. While contemplating one of these heaps, a body sprang up and performed a somersault: it was a Chinese soldier whose fuse had reached his magazine."[32]

Despite the disaster at Zhenjiang the Chinese were still unwilling to send negotiators of sufficient rank, and the British leaders decided that they would continue to Nanjing. However, they were happy to negotiate with the leaders of Yangchow on the north bank, agreeing not to attack if paid a ransom of half a million dollars. News of the happenings of the 21st reached Peking on the 26th and duly alarmed the Court. As Chang Hsi, plenipotentiary Yilibu's assistant, had written: "The Yangtze River is a region like a throat, at which the whole situation of the country is determined. Now they have already cut off our salt and grain transportation and stopped the communication of merchants and travellers. This is not a disease like ringworm, but a trouble in our heart and stomach." Only then does it seem that reality was faced and serious negotiations sanctioned.

With the wind in the west, it was not until the beginning of August that the fleet set out for Nanjing, just 40 miles further up the river, 200 miles from the sea, leaving a small force to secure but not garrison Zhenjiang. Now the countryside seemed deserted, not the hive of activity seen earlier in the invasion. Admiral Parker arrived off the city in the *Cornwallis* on the 3rd, followed two days later by Pottinger and Gough in the *Marion* towed by the *Queen*, the General impressed by the place. "This vast city, which contains a population of one million souls, is surrounded by a wall twenty miles in circumference, and in some parts seventy ft high; and the garrison numbered fifteen thousand men, of whom six hundred were Tartars, exclusive of militia."[33] By Tuesday 9th the fleet was in position for an assault – if one proved necessary. Over the next couple of days troops were landed, including for the first time a troop of horse artillery from Madras with their Arab mounts still apparently in fine condition although they had been on board for four months. By now the two Chinese plenipotentiaries, Yilibu and Qiying, had presumably received instructions from Peking for on the 11th they sent word from Wuxi offering an immediate ransom for Nanjing of $3 million and stating that they themselves were now willing to negotiate. This is exactly what Pottinger had been waiting to hear.

From this moment the war drew rapidly to a conclusion. Pottinger immediately invited the plenipotentiaries to attend discussions on the *Queen*, mentioning that without a satisfactory outcome the city would be attacked on Sunday 14 August. At about 1 am that morning he received a positive response from the Chinese, meeting the two plenipotentiaries again on the 15th and on the 17th informing Gough that hostilities were suspended, that they 'must now be considered as in temporary occupation of a friendly country'.[34] Meanwhile the Chinese sent word to Peking by horse relay, messages being able to cover the 766 miles between the two cities in three or four days. On the 19th the *Medusa* was sent up a canal to receive the Chinese delegation, bringing them down to the river where Parker's barge ferried them out to the *Cornwallis*. There they were received by Pottinger, Gough and Parker with due ceremony, everybody dressed in their finest, suitable salutes fired, many speeches given and much cherry-brandy drunk. Shown over the ship, the Chinese appeared to find little surprising – except that boys so young could be midshipmen learning war instead of students studying at an academy. Three days later the Chinese returned the hospitality, over 100 British officers all in full uniform and accompanied by the requisite guards-of-honour being royally entertained at a fine temple, or 'joss-house', in the city.

Meanwhile those not engaged in negotiations could enjoy the sights of Nanjing, sights which deeply impressed them. Particularly popular was to visit 'the far-famed Porcelain Pagoda', a marvellous building probably never before seen by Europeans and destroyed a few years later in the Taiping Rebellion. Standing 261 ft tall, octagonal with 9 stories, from the top a remarkable view was obtained over the great walled city, home of more than a million people. Of equal surprise to many British was their reception "Dense crowds wedged us in on all sides ... I did not, however, observe a single rude or uncourteous action ... From every class of people near Nanking we invariably received the greatest civility."[35]

On the 27th the Chinese received permission from Peking to conclude negotiations, and the Treaty of Nanking was signed in the after-cabin of the *Cornwallis* on Monday 29 August in front of a large crowd of senior officers, Captain Hall being invited to attend although he was not of the prescribed rank. Two days later the *Sesostris* accompanied by the *Tenasserim* was sent post haste to Calcutta with the good news, leaving Hong Kong on the 10 September and Singapore on the 21st. The Emperor's ratification of the treaty was received on Thursday 15 September, and the following day the steamer *Auckland* left for Bombay and Suez, dispatching the treaty to London by the Overland Route. Almost exactly three years had passed since the conflict began with 'the Battle of Kowloon'.

{ 17 }

INDIA AT LAST

The Treaty of Nanking, by which Britain was confirmed in her possession of Hong Kong, obtained the right to trade and settle not only at Canton but also at Xiamen (Amoy), Fuzhou (Foochow), Ningbo and Shanghai, and received an indemnity of $21 million, has frequently been discussed and need not detain us here.[1] But it is worth recalling that this success was achieved by a most unusual force, and one with no unified command. There were two navies, Royal and Company, and similarly two armies; and there was no formal connection between these armies and navies, between Gough and Parker. And added to this was political leadership in the person of Pottinger. So it says much for these three men as individuals – they sensibly had the habit of frequently dining together – that the force was successfully gathered, was transported as far as Nanjing, and came away with a treaty that satisfied their often belligerent but ignorant superiors back home.

For the British forces the war was a job well done, the Chinese taught a necessary lesson. As Bernard put it "the Chinese ... were inclined, in the first instance, to believe that we were nothing more than lawless plunderers, seeking our own profit, instead of being servants of a great nation, seeking redress for innumerable wrongs."[2] But for the Chinese their defeat was truly traumatic. The social disorder in southern China resulting from it culminated eventually in the Taiping Rebellion of 1850 to 1864, perhaps the most calamitous event in their long history. Indeed, for many Chinese historians 1842 is a watershed in that history, heralding a new era, one of humiliation and painful adaptation in which it became all too apparent that Chinese civilisation could no longer regard itself as central to the world.[3]

Considering that the Chinese had been comprehensively defeated the terms of the treaty were far from severe. And nowhere was opium mentioned, a surprising omission if, as is generally claimed, the war was indeed 'an opium war'. Certainly the treaty was not followed by any attempt to restrict its sale. In fact within seven days of its signing the poet Zhu Shi-yün could write "The English ... are also telling people to go to Sui-shan, where 'opium is on sale very cheap – an opportunity not to be missed.'"[4] So how did this huge effort affect the trade? Fay gives some telling figures for the number and average price of chests of opium sold in Calcutta and bound for China for the first six months of the two years spanning the war. In 1839, 18,563 chests were sold at an average price of Rs 537, and in 1842, 18,362 chests at Rs 768.[5] So as the soldiers and sailors sweated and bled, and the Chinese died in their thousands, the volume of trade was virtually unaffected and the price rose nicely. In 1843, Jardine Matheson with a fleet of 30 to 40 ships made a profit of £200,000.[6] The following year, with a million people employed in British India in opium production, 48,000 chests were shipped to China and sales continued to increase for almost 30 years, peaking at 93,000 chests in 1872. The trade finally ceased in 1911 but this was due to neither controls nor lack of demand; rather, by this time the Chinese themselves produced all that they required. Mao Zedong and his comrades on their 'Long March' through rural China in the 1930s passed through fields of poppies "which stretched as far as the eye could see."[7]

Back in the mother country throughout 1842 the public eye was on the Afghan campaign rather than on China. None the less the treaty, like the war, drew vehement criticism. In an editorial on 3 December 1842 The Times stated, "We owe some moral compensation to China for pillaging her towns and slaughtering her citizens, in a quarrel which could never have arisen if we had not been guilty of this national crime." In parliament Lord Ashley, later Earl of Shaftesbury, was moved to say, "I cannot rejoice in our success; we have triumphed in one of the most lawless, unnecessary and unfair struggles in the records of history," later declaring that the opium trade "was utterly inconsistent with the honour and duty of a Christian Kingdom ... I am fully convinced that for this country to engage in this nefarious traffic is bad, perhaps worse than encouraging the slave trade." Yet the Foreign Secretary of this Christian Kingdom had instructed Pottinger to "strongly impress upon the Chinese plenipotentiaries how much it would be to the interest of the Government to legalise the trade," whereas the pagan Emperor had told Yilibu that "gain-seeking and corrupt men will for profit and sensuality defeat my wishes, but nothing will induce me to derive revenue from the vice and misery of my people."[8]

Of course the problem was that revenue: Great Britain and its merchants derived too much money from the trade to wish to see it reduced. So all that James Matheson felt impelled to do was to ask the commander of his opium fleet to show discretion: "The opium trade is now so very unpopular in England that we cannot be too cautious in keeping it as quiet and as much out of the public eye as possible."[9]

Around the time of the treaty, William Gladstone had confided to his diary "I am in dread of the judgement of God upon England for the national iniquity towards China."[10] And if he had known of the condition of the British forces soon after their triumph he might well have felt that God's judgement was already being wrought. At the capture of Woosung in June the health of the troops had been remarkably good, but on 20 July Captain Keppel had noted "Ships now swarming with rats, and crews getting unhealthy", and Surgeon Cree remarked that mosquitoes were both "abundant and venomous".[11] By the time the fleet arrived off Nanjing in August, dysentery and malaria, 'intermittent fever', had taken a terrible toll and only about 3,400 soldiers, a third of the force, were fit for combat. By mid-September Keppel, himself down with malaria, reported that 97 of the *Dido's* crew of 145 were on the sick list.

At about this time the first ship to leave Nanjing made her way slowly back down the river. The troopship *Belleisle* had left England the previous December for China packed with almost 1,300 people. Amongst these were 650 men of the 98th Regiment with their equipment and provisions. And 87 of their wives and children who were taken as far as Hong Kong; in Britain wives could, with permission, live with their husbands in the barracks, but the number allowed to follow their men to war was strictly limited, usually one per 8 cavalrymen or 12 infantrymen, drawn by lot.[12] Leaving Nanjing, Captain Cunynghame, aide-de-camp to Major-General Lord Saltoun who had travelled out on her, could report that of her crew of about 250, 50 had died, 120 were ill and only 80 fit for service; and of the regiment there were 150 dead, 380 ill and only

120 fit for service. By the end of the year a further 100 men of the 98th had died, a loss of one third. Although admitting that most deaths were due to dysentery and intermittent fever, Cunynghame bizarrely blamed the Chinese for "a scheme so barbarous as was put into practice by way of destroying our troops – that of sending abandoned females amongst them, solely for the purpose of engendering diseases."[13]

But if Europeans suffered, the Indian troops were even more seriously affected. Of the 900 Bengal Volunteers who arrived in China in June, only 400 returned to Calcutta, a loss of more than half. Hindu sepoys faced particular problems; mainly high-caste, they were unable to dress suitably for cold weather, did not like food cooked on board a ship, could not share it with others or even drink from the same water-casks, and so they were often cold and undernourished. Muslim troops remained much healthier.[14]

As the fleet slowly followed the *Belleisle* down-river, a difficult passage averaging only about 20 miles a day, a little ship set sail from Taiwan (Formosa) to meet the British garrison at Xiamen carrying a motley band of 10 European and Indian men with a strange and disturbing tale to tell.[15]

On the 8 March 1842 the brig *Ann* belonging to Jardine Matheson set sail from Zhoushan to return to Hong Kong carrying $50,000 in silver, the result of a successful voyage to the north selling opium. On board were 57 men, Captain Denham and a crew of 54 – 16 Europeans, 4 Chinese and 34 lascars – and two passengers, Mr Gully, a friend of Captain Hall's, and his Chinese servant Francis. Just after midnight on the 10 March in thick and squally weather the ship ran aground and quickly started to break up. She carried only three boats and soon the jolly-boat was washed away and a second crushed by the fall of a mast. At dawn all 57 men managed to leave in the longboat and sail safely to the shore about five miles distant, landing with the loss of only two men. There, by Tanshui on the north-east coast of Taiwan, they were soon captured. After a forced march southwards during which a further two died they reached the capital, Tainan (Taiwan-fu). Then thrown into prison, they were amazed to find amongst their fellow prisoners about 150 Indian lascars.

In late August of the previous year the *Nerbudda* transport had arrived in Hong Kong from Calcutta carrying 29 Europeans, two Filipinos and 243 Indian recruits, largely camp-followers – bearers, cleaners and hospital orderlies rather than soldiers – for the British army in the north.

After loading water and provisions she set off again, but in the storms of September 1841, which had driven the *Nemesis* to take shelter in Xiapu, she was damaged and anchored off Taiwan. The next morning she was seen to be slowly sinking and all the Europeans – including Captain Smoult, two mates and the officer commanding the lascars – together with the Filipinos and three Indians, commandeered all the boats, those still on board being resisted with fixed bayonets, and sailed away. The 240 men left to their fate on the sinking ship immediately set about constructing rafts as best they could, about 150 eventually making it to the shore where they were soon rounded up and imprisoned.

Meanwhile those in the boats after eight days adrift were picked up by the schooner *Black Swan* and taken to Hong Kong; there, the *Canton Press* reported her loss on 16 October 1841, attaching no blame to Captain Smoult. Captain Nias, the senior officer in Hong Kong immediately sent HMS *Nimrod* with Smoult to look for the *Nerbudda* but unsurprisingly nothing could be found. Immediately rumours started swirling around Hong Kong questioning the truth of Captain Smoult's report, and he was apparently arrested, but his fate is unknown.

In Tainan the conditions under which the captives, now totalling over 200, were kept were initially grim, but in June 1842 they were moved to a new prison with better facilities, Denham and Gully now starting to draw and sell pictures in order to buy food. Then on 12 and 13 August, by orders of the local governor Yao Ying, all except Denham and seven others from the *Ann* – four Europeans, two lascars and one Chinese – and two lascars from the *Nerbudda*, were taken away and publicly executed, a total of 197 men. Why so many were killed, and why ten were spared remains a mystery, although rumour had it that the ten were to be sent to Peking for trial. On 31 August it was reported in the Hong Kong press. "The *Nemesis* steamer proceeds to Formosa to reclaim the crews of the *Ann* and *Nerbudda*" but for some reason she never went. Instead, in October the few survivors were returned from Taiwan to the British garrison at Xiamen.

This sad story is instructive as it shows both British and Chinese officers in an uncharacteristically ruthless light. For naval officers, either military or civilian, to desert their ship leaving crew or passengers behind was seen as deeply reprehensible and the story of the loss of the *Nerbudda* greatly shocked the British. And for the Chinese to massacre prisoners was very much at variance with their usual behaviour, most being well-treated and quickly repatriated, and so the massacre on

Formosa excited much anger amongst the British. But fortunately news of the atrocity reached them after peace had been declared and so led to no further bloodshed.

By the end of October the harbour at Zhoushan was crowded with at least 150 vessels either the property, or in the pay, of the British government, as well as a scattering of opium ships. Bernard found the sight inspiring: "I never remember to have witnessed so picturesque and striking a scene as was there presented to view. Both the outer and inner harbours were crowded with men-of-war, transports, and steamers ... The troops on board the transports, the boats constantly passing and repassing, the bands playing, and the perfect good feeling and friendliness which prevailed throughout our forces ... added greatly to the real satisfaction derived from the glorious termination of the war."[16] The *Nemesis* was again hauled on shore and examined but was found to be in excellent condition. Keppel, relaxing, records a typically social time, excursions to Ningbo and to the many-templed Putuo Shan (Potoo) island sacred particularly to the Goddess of Mercy, Guanyin, interspersed with fine dinners on one ship or another. On 25 October he entertained Hall and other officers on the *Dido* – the two men seemed to like each other as, back in England, they met on and off for dinner until Hall's death in 1878 – and on 4 November dined with Admiral Parker "who talked of sending me Senior Officer to the Straits. Like the idea much" – a post that would again bring him and the *Nemesis* together. Interestingly Keppel had, like Hall, adopted a Chinese boy for, at Penang on his way to Calcutta in February 1844, he noted: "Left my China boy Chopsticks at school in Penang, and sailed." Chopsticks![17]

In mid-November Sir Henry Pottinger left on the *Queen* for Hong Kong, followed by the *Marion* with Sir Hugh Gough, and four naval ships carrying the first instalment of the Chinese indemnity, $6 million, bound eventually for Calcutta and London. That month the five remaining 'sliding-keel vessels' parted, and would not meet again for almost ten years when another colonial war brought them together in Burma (*see* Table 11). By the end of November the *Nemesis* and *Pluto*, with much of the rest of the fleet, were anchored off Hong Kong. There on 5 December they were joined by the *Proserpine* which was to remain in China, around Hong Kong, until March 1845 when repairs necessitated her return to Calcutta, the port from which she sailed for the rest of her career. The *Phlegethon* and *Medusa* did not leave the north immediately, being retained there to survey those uncharted waters. Sometime early in 1843 the *Phlegethon,* working off the port of Fuzhou, anchored for the night in five fathoms of water. Soon after, in a heavy swell she swung on the ebb of the tide and struck heavily astern. The Captain's steward, rushing down, found the after cabin filling rapidly and immediately sealed the watertight bulkhead. Without this she would undoubtedly have been lost with all hands, for when she was finally hauled ashore the hole in her bottom was found to measure no less than 12 by 8 ft. Through this huge rent had tumbled two or three dozen cases of Captain McCleverty's claret but fortunately not the chest containing the crews' pay for the next few months.[18] After temporary repairs she sailed for Calcutta in May 1843 and was there thoroughly refitted. The *Medusa* spent three more years in the north surveying the seas around Zhoushan, finally sailing from Hong Kong in November 1845 for her home port, Bombay, which she reached in December, and from there she worked for the next six years.[19]

At Hong Kong the *Nemesis* discharged the eight Chinese firemen who had been on board for about 15 months, Hall remarking how they had been happy to work for him as volunteers at $12 a month, and had shown no ill feelings when the northern Chinese were attacked, in fact enjoying the opportunity to go ashore for plunder.[a] But young Afah stayed with the ship.[20] It was probably at this time that Hall met "old Chinnery", the painter George Chinnery (1774–1852) who lived in Macau, this resulting in a delightful oil painting, the only known one of Hall, *'Dent's verandah: Mr Durand, W. C. Hunter and Captain Hall.'*[21]

When the *Nemesis* had sailed for the north 15 months before, the fledgling British settlement, less than six months old, had just been devastated by the typhoon of 21 July. Now those returning saw an amazing transformation. Victoria was a thriving community set along a good main road which ran for four miles along the north coast of the island. Large stone warehouses lined well-built wharfs and jetties. And which were the most splendid? Captain Cunynghame gives the answer: "The buildings, which [are] far more magnificent, as well as better situated than any others, are the storehouses or 'go-downs' of Messrs Matheson and Jardine, the merchant princes of the far East;

---

[a]   In the second 'Opium War', the 'Arrow War' (1856–60), the nicely named Canton Coolie Corps served the British faithfully, apparently happy to see their northern cousins defeated (Gelber 2004).

they lie eastward of the town and are of immense extent."[22] There was a busy Chinese bazaar and European market, both a Catholic church and an American Baptist chapel, and a 50-bed Seamen's Hospital and a school, Morrison's Institute, were under construction. English-speaking residents were served by two European hotels and a billiard-room, and three newspapers, *The Hong Kong Gazette*, *The Eastern Globe* and *The Hong Kong Register*. The *Canton Register* was still published in Macau. ("Macao, poor Macao! From the day on which the Union Jack was hoisted on the neighbouring island, your fate was sealed, to decay and die like Goa."[23]) And all this had been achieved in little more than a year and while still at war.

The following April Pottinger was appointed the first Governor and Commander-in-Chief of the new Crown Colony although it is questionable whether his tenure was entirely successful. When he left Hong Kong in June 1844, the *Canton Register* welcomed his departure with a nice turn of invective: Pottinger "with all his brilliant talents appears either to have been utterly devoid of a sense of the moral obligations imposed upon him ... or deliberately living in seclusion among a few adoring parasites whose limited intellects were devoted to pandering to the great man's vanity."[24]

In the week before Christmas 1842 much of the fleet, including the *Pluto*, passed on towards Singapore and India, leaving only a few ships and about 1,250 men to garrison the newly-won territory. At 3 am on the morning of 23 December the *Nemesis* left Macau alone, not exactly slipping quietly away in the night but marking her departure with celebratory rockets and gunfire. On board was Hall's friend W. D. Bernard whom he had first met that year in China, and it was during this voyage that Hall suggest that Bernard should compile from his diaries an account of the *Nemesis'* journey to the east[b] and its role in the China war, part of the profits of the venture going to the families of those who had been killed or had died on board.[25] In fact there had been only five deaths since leaving England, and all of these in 1842.

Keeping close to the Chinese coast the *Nemesis* steamed westwards and then turned south along the east coast of Hainan Island. On Christmas day they entered a sheltered bay, Liengsoy, where Hall,

---

[b]   This book has ensured the lasting fame of the *Nemesis* but, cited so often to epitomize the power of the invaders, it has perhaps led to an overemphasis on her role compared with that of other Company steamers.

Bernard and others went ashore, finding the locals friendly and eager to sell them fresh provisions. The next day in the beautiful harbour of Yin-lin-kan they took two small boats and ran a couple of miles up-river and walked into the interior. "The population was by no means dense, but the people were everywhere civil and good humoured. The mountains were covered with woods, often to the very highest point, and deer and pheasant seemed abundant". They took tea at a welcoming tea shop where Bernard was surprised at the people's literacy, and the people greatly surprised by the looks of the West African krooman who accompanied them. On turning back, they were overtaken by a local dignitary on horseback who promptly dismounted to offer a ride to a young midshipman.

From Hainan the *Nemesis* continued south to the coast of Vietnam, to the fine harbour of Phu Yen on 29 December and so to Singapore on 5 January 1843, entering the roads colourfully decorated with Chinese flags. The previous day in Calcutta the first opium sale of the new year had netted the government a handsome profit of £500,000.[26] A week later she continued on, steaming north to Malacca where Hall spent a couple of nights with his friends the Salmonds. Stopping at Penang on the 17th, she continued her leisurely progress up the coast of the British territory of Tenasserim to Moulmein, an attractive town lying across the river from the ancient capital of Martaban, a range of low hills running through the town crowded with temples and pagodas in various stages of construction and decay. There the *Endymion* carrying General Gough back to India lay at anchor, and on the 30th Hall joined a party of naval officers led by the Governor to some fine limestone caves, the Farm or Ka-yôn Caves, crowded with sacred carvings, travelling both by boat and, to his amusement, by elephant. [27]

On Monday 6 February 1843 the *Nemesis* finally entered her home port, Calcutta, for the first time. Again gaily decorated with Chinese flags and banners, she sailed up the Hooghly, saluted by Fort William and watched by a crowd of thousands as news of her exploits was already widespread. Later, she took Gough up-river to review the garrison at Barrackpore. Sir Hugh, as Commander-in-Chief India, was to go on to command in the Sikh War and, although "with his mane of white hair ... he is always found where the fire is hottest," he eventually retired safely to England as 'Baron Gough of Chinkiangfoo in China and of Maharajpore and the Sutlej in the East Indies' with a pension of £4,000 per year.[28]

After three years of strenuous work the *Nemesis* was now thoroughly inspected and found to be still in fine condition. "She displays in no small degree the advantages of iron. Her bottom bears the marks of having been repeatedly ashore; the plates are deeply indented in several places, in one or two to the extent of several inches ... Her bottom is not nearly so much corroded as I expected to have found it, and she is as tight as a bottle."[29] Back in England that November Hall reported in person to the Admiralty on his ship. Later, in 1847, Admiral Sir George Cockburn would tell the Select Committee on Estimates that Hall's report, together with those from Bombay and Portsmouth Dockyards, were the main factors in the Board's decision to order the construction of a large number of iron ships for the Royal Navy during the mid 1840s. A year later Hall himself gave further evidence before that Committee, stating that the *Nemesis* had once been struck 14 times by shot, and ""one shot went in at one side and came out at the other, it went right through the vessel""; but there were no splinters, ""it went through just as if you put your finger through a bit of paper ... Several wooden steamers were employed upon the same service, and they were invariably obliged to lie up for repairs, whilst I could repair the *Nemesis* in 24 hours and have her always ready for service; indeed, many steamers were obliged to leave the coast of China and go to Bombay for repairs. Repairs which would have taken a wooden steamer several days would take us as many hours only."[30]

The night before his departure for England Captain Hall was guest-of-honour at a splendid farewell dinner in the Town Hall, much touched by being presented with a fine sword. "The crew of the *Nemesis* have presented to their Commander a beautiful dress sword, a pair of handsome epaulettes, and a cocked hat, as a token of the respect they bear towards him, and to mark their admiration of his conduct throughout the war with China. The sword bears the following inscription: 'Presented as a tribute of respect to Captain Hall, Commander of H. C. Steamer *Nemesis* by the crew of that vessel, March 4th 1843.'"[31] The following day Hall finally "left the dear old *Nemesis* for England", sailing with his friend Bernard and the 'China boy' Afah south in the steamer *Tenasserim* first to Madras and then on to Bombay and to England by the Overland Route, visiting the Pyramids in Egypt and so through France to London.

On the 19 July that year in western England Prince Albert arrived in the port of Bristol by train from London, there to officiate at the launching of the world's largest steamship. Isambard Kingdom Brunel, encouraged by the success of his wooden paddle steamer *Great Western* on her maiden voyage across the Atlantic in 1838, had determined to build an even larger and more luxurious vessel for the Great Western Steamship Company, again of wood and powered by paddles. But later that year, 1838, Laird's iron *Rainbow* fitted with Airy's compass correctors visited Bristol, and the Company's Directors were persuaded by Brunel that his new ship could now safely be of iron. And so, on 19 July 1839, the keel of the *Great Britain* was laid, now to be an iron paddle steamer. But then another change: in May 1840 the *Archimedes*, of wood but screw-powered, steamed into Bristol and so impressed Brunel that he determined that a screw should also power his new vessel. And so the ship that Albert launched that July day in 1843 was indeed a true pioneer in ship design. Of iron and powered by a huge screw, with five watertight bulkheads, 322 ft long and of 3,675 tons, her engines developing 2,000 hp, the *Great Britain* was by far the largest ship of her time and a vessel vastly different from that other iron pioneer, the *Nemesis*, which had, over the past three years, so ably demonstrated the utility of small iron ships in coastal warfare.[32]

{ 18 }

NEMESIS HALL

On Monday 29 August 1842, the very day that the Treaty of Nanking was signed aboard the *Cornwallis* on the Yangtse, the Queen and Prince Albert, travelling by steam train from Windsor to London,[a] boarded the Royal Yacht *Royal George* on the Thames at the start of their first visit to Scotland. The *Royal George,* a sailing ship of 330 tons, had been used for King George IV's visit to Scotland 20 years before, towed down the Thames by the Royal Navy's very first steam vessel, HMS *Comet.* Now the accompanying squadron consisted of nine naval vessels of which seven were paddle steamers, including the Navy's second oldest steamer *Lightning.* And again the yacht was towed all too slowly up the east coast of Britain, reaching Leith, the port for Edinburgh, after three long days.[1] There followed a triumphant visit to her northern kingdom which clearly delighted the royal party, but the Queen felt that her method of sea travel was both outdated and beneath her dignity, and for the return journey the paddle steamer *Trident* (1,000 tons) was chartered. On 21 September she wrote to the Prime Minister, Sir Robert Peel, a strongly worded letter on this topic and Sir Robert replied the next day promising a new steam yacht. The new vessel, by the great

---

[a]   Just two months before, on 13 June 1842, the Queen had made her first journey by train, travelling on the one-year-old Great Western Railway from Slough to London, pulled by the locomotive *Phlegethon* (Crump 2007).

ship designer Rear-Admiral Sir William Symonds, Surveyor of the Navy, was ordered on 31 October, the keel laid at Pembroke on 9 November and the *Victoria & Albert*, for the first year of her life known simply as *Royal Yacht*, was launched on 25 April 1843, a wooden paddle steamer of 1,034 tons. The speed of construction, similar to that of the *Nemesis* but remarkable for a wooden ship, attests to what could be achieved if the order came from someone with the very strongest interest.[2]

William Hall and Afah arrived in London in April 1843, Hall immediately arranging for the boy to stay with Dr Jonas Pope of Number 3 Manchester Square. Dr Pope, a widower living with his 27-year-old daughter Agnes, was either a friend or relative (his middle name was 'Hall'), and had agreed to have the boy taught written English and be instructed in religion. On the recommendation of the Rector of St Marylebone Afah was placed in the junior school attached to the Rectory and proved to be both clever and well behaved. Baptised by the Rector in March 1844 'Leang William Afah', Hall transferred him to a good boarding school at Hanwell, West London, where again he did well, popular with both teachers and his fellow pupils.[3]

It was with the greatest of satisfaction that on 10 June Lieutenant Hall heard of his promotion to the rank of Commander, again through an Order in Council, this allowing the Admiralty to count his service on the *Nemesis* 'as though on a queen's ship'. Three weeks later, on 1 July, Hall was appointed Commander of the *Victoria & Albert* under Captain the Rt. Hon. Lord Adolphus Fitz-Clarence whom we have met before as someone with an unusually strong interest; as a natural son of King William IV he had been appointed Captain of the royal yacht in 1830, aged 28, on the accession of his father. Considering that in 1843 about two thirds of Royal Navy Lieutenants were on half pay ashore or acting at lower ranks and nearly half the Post-Captains had never served at sea at that rank, to obtain such a position so rapidly says much for Hall's reputation.[4]

At 9 o'clock on the morning of Monday 9 September 1844 the *Victoria & Albert* set out from Woolwich Dockyard on the Thames for Dundee on the east coast of Scotland, a two-day journey in sometimes stormy weather.[5] On board were the Queen and Prince, both of whom had fallen in love with the Highlands on their first visit two years earlier. The Queen had just been delivered of her fourth child, Prince Alfred, and her husband, feeling that she needed a holiday, had asked Lord Glenlyon if they could take Blair Castle in Perthshire for about three weeks – as Albert wrote "they would wish to go perfectly quietly and without *any state*, in fact just as *any nobleman* would go down for a little shooting etc."

The royal couple were accompanied by their eldest child Princess Victoria, 'Vicky' aged almost four, and, 'without *any state*', by Sir Robert Peel, the Prime Minister; Lord Aberdeen, the Foreign Secretary; Lord Liverpool; Lord Charles Wellesley, Equerry to the Queen; Sir Edward Bowater, Equerry to the Prince; Lady Charlotte Canning, Lady-in-Waiting; Lady Caroline Cocks, Maid-of-Honour; George Anson, Treasurer to Prince Albert; Sir James Clark, the Royal Physician; and over 60 servants from the Royal Household. Ten carriages and 40 horses were required to transport the Royal party from Dundee to Blair Castle where Lord Glenlyon provided housekeepers, housemaids, laundrymaids, dairymaids and one kitchen maid as well as all the gamekeepers required for the shooting.

Also on board the Royal Yacht was Afah from Zhoushan, now about 13 years old. During the journey north the royal couple had noticed him and asked after his family. Young Vicky wanted to shake his hand, "and sweetly expressed her sorrow when told by Prince Albert that his father had been killed." Perhaps the boy had been delighted by that particular attention, but at times he seems to have found his role as 'the China boy' a burden. Earlier that month as the ship was being prepared on the Thames, Hall had been called away to the Admiralty and the boy had gone missing, to the consternation of the crew. Upon his return Hall called out for him. "'I am here sir!' he instantly answered from his cabin. The Captain asked why he had locked himself in. "Soon you go away, plenty of people come on board the yacht; all want to see China Boy; China Boy no want to see them: they no your friends, everybody friends. I tired and go into your cabin, and lock myself up until you came back: all the sailors look for me and call China Boy: I no answer till I hear your voice." At Dundee he came on deck one day without shoes and stockings and asked Hall for permission to go ashore. "Go on shore without shoes and stockings! Certainly not!". "The women in Scotland no wear shoes and stockings; why should I not go without them all the same?"[6]

Returning to England with the royal party, Hall was on 22 October 1844 finally promoted Post-Captain, a truly red-letter day for him for from now on further promotion would be automatic as those senior to him died. Now truly Captain Hall – and often known as 'Nemesis Hall' to distinguish him from other naval Halls – on the 30 April 1845 he married the Hon Hilare Caroline Byng, the third daughter of his very first captain 34 years before, George Byng, later Rear-Admiral the Viscount Torrington.[7]

The Halls set up home at Shipbourne Lodge in Kent not far from the Byngs' home at Yotes Court. Inventing iron bilge tanks and 'Hall's patent anchor', Hall was elected to a Fellowship of the Royal Society in 1847. For four months that year he took command of HMS *Terrible*, the largest paddle warship ever built for the Royal Navy (Table 3). On 1 March 1846 Captain Keppel had visited her just after her launch. "By steamboat to ... Woolwich ... I went over the *Terrible*, an enormous vessel, 1847 tons bm, 3189 tons displacement, 800 horsepower."[8] Later Hall took command of the paddle frigate HMS *Dragon* (1,297 tons), for two years conveying food to the famine-stricken Irish, and in 1850 taking her to the Mediterranean.

With the outbreak of the Russian War (the 'Crimean War') in March 1854 Hall was unable to obtain a vessel corresponding to his seniority and so accepted HMS *Hecla* (815 tons), a small paddle sloop. Leaving Portsmouth on 28 March, the *Hecla* joined the British fleet in the Baltic and for the following few months engaged in various actions there, not returning to Portsmouth until the 31 October "bearing many marks of the severe fire to which she was exposed." As in China Hall seemed happy to be in the thick of things, on one raid having a rifle ball pass through the collar of his coat and being bruised on the right leg by a spent bullet. During the attack on Bomarsund in the Åland Islands on the 21 June the *Hecla*, again playing a central role, was almost lost when a lighted shell fell on her deck, but this was thrown overboard by the young mate, Charles Lucas (1834–1914).[9] For his gallantry Lucas was immediately promoted Lieutenant, and then on 26 June 1857 invested by the Queen with the very first Victoria Cross ever awarded. That same day Victoria first received word from Lord Palmerston about disturbances in India, the first stirrings there of the great Mutiny or Rebellion. In 1879 Captain Lucas VC, later Rear-Admiral, married the Halls' only child, Dolly, born on 23 April 1851.

After his return to Portsmouth Hall was at last appointed, on 18 November 1854, Captain of a ship worthy of his rank, HMS *Blenheim*, well known to him 13 years before in China. Although old, built in 1808, she was at least large – a Third Rate converted a, few years before to a screw blockship and now carrying 60 guns and 600 men. On 4 April 1855 the *Blenheim* sailed from Portsmouth for the Baltic, serving with the British fleet there until November when she returned to Portsmouth. While in the Baltic Hall was made a CB. (The British Honours system is certainly intricate; suffice it to say that the Order of the Bath was the only order generally available to naval officers, and came in three grades: Companion, CB; Knight Commander, KCB; and Knight Grand Cross, GCB.) After a cruise to Lisbon in early 1856 and participation in the Grand Naval Review of 23 April at Spithead, the *Blenheim* was finally paid off on the 3 June 1856, this proving to be the end of Hall's active service. Hall was promoted to Rear-Admiral on the active list in April 1863 and retired the following year. Awarded a KCB in March 1867, Sir William was made a Vice-Admiral on the retired list in July 1869 and a full Admiral in December 1875. Admiral Sir William Hutcheon Hall, FRS, KCB, 'Nemesis Hall', died in his eightieth year at 48 Phillimore Gardens, Kensington, his home in London, on 25 June 1878.

If we know a certain amount about Hall's career, what can we ascertain about him as a man? The best source is his personal diary, a small one-page-a-day volume for 1853 but with the briefest of daily entries up to 1869, obviously written only for himself, and presumably presented after his death, along with a few cuttings and letters, by his family to the National Maritime Museum in London. Hall was clearly a loving family man. 'What a delightful change being happily once more moored at home sweet home.' His mother, always 'Dear Mama', lived with them at Shipbourne in her old age, and her death in 1868 clearly greatly distressed him. His wife was always "My dear wife" or "Dear Hila". "Poor Dolly taken ill of measles – sat up with her all night", not something that every Victorian father would have done for his daughter. A practising Christian, he attended Church of England services regularly and if the weather was poor held Sunday prayers at home.

Hall's book on the *Nemesis* was written in good part so that profits could be used to support the families of those crew members who had been killed or injured in China, and this concern for the welfare of sailors was deeply felt. He had been appalled by the conditions he had found in Liverpool when recruiting a crew for the *Nemesis* in 1839, the first time he had undertaken such a task in such a port: the dreadful lodging houses, the drunkenness, the 'crimps' who preyed upon newly arrived sailors to relieve them of their hard-earned cash. In Calcutta in 1843 he had, as promised, arranged for his two remaining kroomen, Thomas Benaly and Jack Wilson, to return to Africa via London, providing them with £20 each for their onward passage. But when Hall arrived in London these men called upon him virtually penniless, their money taken by 'crimps', Hall himself finally arranging their passage home to Principe.[10]

Typically, Hall acted upon his concern. A 'Sailors' Home' had first been established in London in 1835 but now he worked to spread them to other ports so that by 1853 eight were open. "Here the sailor finds the advantages of a lodging house, club, school, church, bank and shipping office, all in one." In September 1852 'The Institution for the Establishment of Sailors' Homes and Destitute Sailors' Asylums at the Principal Seaports of the United Kingdom, India and Colonies' was initiated, with Hall as Chairman and Managing Director (and also donating the considerable sum of £200), and the following year he founded *The Sailors' Home Journal and Chronicle of the Royal Navy & Mercantile Marine*. So it is of no surprise that at a Trafalgar Day dinner in London on 21 October 1852 a special toast was drunk to Captain Hall "the ardent and successful advocate of Sailors' Homes." And then of course there were the various committees – the Inland India Board, the Red Sea Board, the P & O Board, the Lifeboat Board. But as touching as any of these facts are the titles of a number of little cuttings from journals folded into his diary: "Early rising", "Health", "Sorrow", "A word to young men", "Success", "A brave man", "Woman's love", "Self-made men". So if, as a naval officer, Hall was clearly both brave and decisive, then personally he was clearly kind and compassionate, seeking to lead a good and purposeful life.

Of the subsequent life of the 'China boy' there are only fragmentary clues. Hall's diary notes on 22 March 1848 "Afah and I dine with the Admiral." On 22 August 1866 a list of items buried below the foundation stone of the new conservatory at Shipbourne is signed by 'Affa, Admiral Hall's Interpreter in China', then a man of 35. So at least we can say that Afah settled in England and remained close to the Halls.

{ 19 }

THE INDUS FLOTILLA

On Thursday 6 April 1843, a month after Captain Hall's departure for England, the *Nemesis* accompanied by the *Pluto* left Calcutta for Bombay with Lieutenant William Fell Acting Commander and Thomas Wallage (1815–51) First Officer, a man later to play a significant role in her story. The *Pluto* had reached Calcutta from China on 19 February and there Lieutenant Tudor had relinquished command to his First Officer, Lieutenant George Airey who was destined to captain the ship for the next eight years – although when appointed in England in October 1841 he had been given leave of absence from the Royal Navy for only two years. Both vessels arrived at Bombay on 10 May where they were soon docked for a thorough overhaul.[1] When again in good order, both were put to work as packets, carrying troops and documents between Bombay and the Indus River delta to the west.

The Punjab, the Land of the Five Rivers, lies across the route to India from the west.[2] Bounded by the Himalayas to the north and watered by the great Indus and Sutlej rivers, it proved a place of endless warfare and there developed a distinctive people, the Punjabi, with a distinct religion, Sikhism. Founded in the fifteenth century the Sikh faith gave rise through centuries of conflict with their Muslim neighbours to a military order, the Khalsa. In 1801 the 20-year-old Ranjit Singh proclaimed himself Maharajah of the Punjab, turning his country into a nation, its capital Lahore. Mindful of his powerful neighbour to the south and east Ranjit, 'the Lion of the Punjab', built the Khalsa into a formidable force, powerfully armed and beautifully drilled, using it to expand his country to the north and west, into Kashmir and the Afghan province of Peshawar.

By 1836 when a new Governor-General, Lord Auckland, arrived in Calcutta the three Company Presidencies covered more than half of India, amongst the Indian states only the Punjab posing any real threat to British domination of the entire subcontinent. But Auckland well recognised that there were external threats, these centring around Afghanistan. There, Dost Mohamed, the Amir of Kabul, remained threatened by Ranjit from the east, but the British were unwilling to assist as Ranjit was both powerful and nominally their ally. Thus spurned but needing friends, Dost Mohamed turned westwards, to Russia and its ally, Persia. And so the 'Great Game' began, the struggle between Britain and Russia for control of the central Asian gateway to India.[3]

Auckland – supported by Lord Melbourne's Cabinet in London, particularly by Lord Palmerston, the Foreign Secretary, and Sir John Hobhouse, President of the Company's Board of Control – believed that the status quo was untenable. As the Sikhs could not be discomforted, they concluded that the only way forward was to replace Dost Mohamed withwith a ruler friendly to Britain. For this Shah Shuja was chosen, a former Afghan ruler now in exile in the Punjab, and an army raised to carry him back to Kabul. 'The Army of the Indus', 10,000 soldiers and about 40,000 camp-followers, began the invasion of Afghanistan on Sunday 10 March 1839, the very day on which, far to the east, Commissioner Lin arrived in Canton intent upon suppressing the opium trade. After much drama and difficulties the army finally arrived before the walls of Kabul on 6 August, Dost Mohamed fleeing north and Shah Shuja being installed in his place. Unsurprisingly the new ruler, a despot friendly with the Sikhs and forced upon them by an outside power, proved far from popular with his subjects. So clearly British troops would have to remain to support him, this garrison soon settling down to the life of a typical British outpost, the officers confident enough to send for their wives and families – and confident enough to neglect the town's defences. Over the following year the Company, now heavily indebted, both reduced the size of the garrison and the annual 'subsidy' paid to allied tribesmen to retain their allegiance. So when on 2 November 1841 an insurrection exploded the garrison was totally unprepared. Cooped up in an indefensible cantonment were 4,500 troops, 700 of which were Europeans, and their 12,000 camp followers including 30 European women and children. After two months of privation and death, on New Year's Day 1842 an agreement was reached with the Afghans that, in return for a payment of £145,000, the garrison would be given safe passage to Jelalabad, 80 miles to the east through high snow-covered passes.

The retreat from Kabul began on 6 January, almost 15,000 persons leaving the shelter of the town in vicious winter weather without adequate food or clothing and immediately, despite the agreement, meeting fierce sniper fire. By the 9th thousands were dead, shot down or frozen, and by the 11th the fighting force was reduced to no more than 300 men. On 12 January Dr William Brydon, the 30-year-old assistant surgeon of a native regiment, finally reached the fort at Jelalabad, the sole European to avoid either death or capture during the retreat.

In London the previous August Lord Melbourne's Whig administration had been defeated and replaced by Sir Robert Peel's Tories, the Earl of Aberdeen replacing Palmerston as Foreign Secretary. And new governments meant new Governors-General in India. In March Lord Auckland, reeling from the disaster, was replaced by Lord Ellenborough. Ellenborough, more hawkish than his predecessor, immediately raised an 'Army of Retribution' which entered Afghanistan to rescue the remaining British garrisons, capturing Kabul in September and laying waste whatever could be destroyed. Considering the western approaches to India, Ellenborough became convinced that Sind, a still independent state straddling the lower Indus River, must be brought under full Company control. Despite the fact that the two amirs who ruled Sind had just signed a treaty highly favourable to the British, Sir Charles Napier, the general charged by Ellenborough with securing the province, invaded it in February and finally defeated the two amirs the following month. With an army of 2,500 men, only 500 of whom were British, against a Baluchi army of 35,000 Napier "saw no safety but in butchery: it was we or they who must die." "We have no right to seize Scinde," he said, "yet we shall do so, and a very advantageous, useful, humane piece of rascality it will be."[4] For this rascality the general was awarded £70,000 as prize money and the governorship of Sind. Napier was certainly eccentric enough to have announced his victory with a one-word dispatch to the Governor-General, 'Peccavi' (I have sinned) but sadly the story is apocryphal. Ellenborough was delighted with the new acquisition, but not so his masters in London who were aghast at the thought of the cost of administering yet another rebellious province. So Ellenborough was recalled the following year, replaced by his brother-in-law, Lieutenant General Sir Henry Hardinge, who though no lord was a friend both of the Duke of Wellington and of Sir Robert Peel.

It was into these conflicts and acquisitions that, in about September 1843, the *Nemesis* sailed from Bombay, now captained by William Oliver, her task largely to help sustain the new province of Sind. Working with the *Pluto* for the next year, the two vessels shuttled back and forth mainly to the mouth of the Indus, about 550 miles to the north-west, each round trip taking two to three weeks (the destination is given as 'Kurrachee' but the coordinates indicate somewhere near Keti Bandar in the Indus Delta). Sometimes they were sent on shorter journeys, to Surat 150 miles north of Bombay or Vengurla 180 miles south. The nature of these journeys can best be illustrated by an extract from Captain Oliver's log (somewhat modified).[5] The Nemesis had arrived in Bombay from the Indus on 16 February 1844 and was apparently there for four weeks before sailing again for the north-west.

> **Friday 15th March**. Bombay. Take on 35 tons coal and 1,000 gallons of water.

> **Saturday 16th March.** Bombay. 4 am, embarked a detachment of H. M. 78th Highlanders for Kurrachee, 74 officers, 2 ladies, 110 rank and file, 21 public and private followers, 15 women and 18 children. 5 am, lit fires. 6.20 steam up. 8 am, weighed and proceeded full power out of harbour and made all plain sail.

> **Sunday 17th March**. 10 am, mustered by division and performed Divine Service. Boilers blown off every hour.

> **Monday 18th March**. Midnight, light variable airs and fine. 1.30 am departed this life, David White, child. Noon, light airs and fine, thermometer 112°. Set jibs and forward trysail.

> **Tuesday 19th March**. Fresh gales with heavy sea. Found crosshead and side rod of the air-pump bent. Port bilge pump choked with coal dust. Found a quantity of provisions damaged owing to the heavy rolling and straining of the vessel and shipping much water forward. Drop rudder separated during the day. Set

trysails double reefed and hove too. Sent down masts and spars.

Wednesday 20th March. Fresh gales with heavy sea. Ship labouring much. Bilge pumps working very badly being blocked occasionally by small coals from the bunkers. 10.55 am stopped the engines, took floats off and put fires out.

Thursday 21st March. Sea calmer, made good progress. Travelling about 120 miles per day. At dusk anchored off Kiddawarie *(at 24.06 N so in the Indus delta)*.

Friday 22nd March. *Comet* came along side to discharge men and baggage for Indus.

Saturday 23rd March. 12.30 am ship grounded. Daylight commenced scraping a great quantity of barnacles off ship's bottom. 12.35 pm ship floated. 4.40 received mails. 5.45 weighed and drifted towards fairway buoy. Received from *Comet* 5 European officers, 1 native officer, 3 medical subordinates, 148 rank and file, sick, from various regiments for Bombay."

During her service from Bombay the crew of the *Nemesis* numbered about 75 men: six officers and six engineers, all European, 14 engine-room crew and 49 others, all Asian (Table 7).[6] Add to these the 240 people embarked on 16 March, the necessary segregation between men and women and between the 88 European adults and the Asians, a temperature reaching 112° F (45° C) and a decent storm, and the seven-day journey for these 315 souls is hard to imagine: the long, narrow ship rolling horribly, the uneven thudding of the engines, the wind howling in the rigging; and, the hatches battened down, in the airless darkness below the children crying, the slopping chamber pots, the vomit. But the log, sadly but unsurprisingly, gives no details of such things although the brief mention of David White is telling.

During 1844 it became clear that the two iron steamers still in China must return to India for repairs, and it was decided to replace the *Proserpine* with the *Nemesis* and the Indian Navy's *Medusa* with the Bengal Marine's *Pluto*. So late in 1844 the *Nemesis* was recalled to Calcutta, leaving Bombay for the last time on 17 November, heading south. Later, the Indian Navy at Bombay would report to London: "The iron vessels are acknowledged in the transport of troops to have saved many times their cost, independent of the many advantages attendant upon their certainty and celerity."[7] The voyage around India proved so stormy that upon arrival at Calcutta she had to be docked for repairs, and it was not until April 1845 that she was again ready for sea, her lascar crew replaced by a largely European one. On 1 May she formally 'entered Her Majesty's service' under the command of Captain J. Russell, her First Officer still Thomas Wallage, leaving that day for the east, towed down the Hooghly, "80 miles of dreary river", to the sea by the *Enterprize* in order to save fuel. Two weeks later the *Pluto* too left Bombay, bound not for Calcutta but for Singapore, seeing service there and in Borneo before reaching China in mid-September.[8]

At this time the Bengal Marine ran 17 steamers, 7 for river work and 10 for sea-going: the four sliding-keel iron vessels and the *Enterprize, Tenasserim, Ganges, Irrawaddy, Diana* and *Hooghly*. Although they worked really for the Royal Navy rather than the Company, the running costs of the iron steamers in 'the China seas', the *Proserpine* and *Medusa* in China and the *Phlegethon* around Singapore, had up till now been met by the Company. And these costs were considerable (Table 6). For the year to 30 April 1845 the *Nemesis*, sailing out of Bombay with a largely lascar crew, had cost £3,683 (36,831 rupees) to run, and in the following year, with a larger and mainly European crew, £5,135. And then there were the repairs. After her return from Bombay in late 1844 repairs to the *Nemesis'* hull cost £1,015 and to her engines £724; and a major refit in 1847/48 cost £6,718.[9] So in 1844 the Company happily came to an agreement with the home government that in future when Company vessels 'entered Her Majesty's service' they would be paid for by Her Majesty's government. This would cover not only all running costs but also an annual fee of 10 per cent of the vessel's 'initial cost', to cover all ordinary repairs. Thus from subsequent accounts we know the precise initial cost of the *Nemesis*: £28,943 (*see* chapter 4).

{ 20 }

OF SULTANATES AND SETTLEMENTS

When the *Nemesis* first steamed down the Straits of Malacca in October 1840 British influence in the region stemmed very largely from three settlements there, Penang, Malacca and Singapore, although a fourth, in Borneo and of a quite different nature, was at that very moment being born. The three, ruled since 1826 from India as the Straits Settlements, were essential staging posts between the Company's dominions in India and their growing interests in China. Malacca was by far the oldest centre of European influence but by the nineteenth century certainly the least significant, whereas the newest, Singapore, settled just 21 years before, was already the most powerful.[1]

The history and the status of the fourth territory were entirely different, Sarawak in western Borneo being in many ways more reminiscent of an Englishman's private estate than of a British colony. James Brook (1803–68) was born in Benares, India, the son of a High Court Judge and a Scottish mother.[2] Sent to England at the age of 12 for education, he refused to stay at school and, after a period of private tutoring, was commissioned in 1819 as an Ensign in the Company's 6th Native Light Infantry and returned to India. Fighting in Assam in the First Burmese War (*see* chapter 27) he was seriously wounded at Rangpur in February 1825 and was sent home to England to recuperate.

In England he found too little to occupy him and was eager to return to India but his first attempt in 1829 came to a premature end when the

Carn Brae was wrecked just off the English coast. The following year the *Castle Huntley* successfully carried him to India but he arrived just after his five-year leave of absence had expired. Resigning his commission he sailed on via the Straits of Malacca to Canton, not returning to England until June 1831. Hankering after the East, he again spent what he later felt were wasted years in England, dabbling in this and that, at one time purchasing a brig to trade with China; but his total lack of commercial sense meant almost instant failure.

In late 1835 Brooke's father died, leaving James, his only surviving son, the tidy sum of £30,000. With part of this he bought the *Royalist*, an elegant yacht of 142 tons, carrying four boats and armed with six 6-pounders and a number of swivel guns. Importantly, as she had belonged to the Royal Yacht Club she had the same privileges as a man-of-war and could fly the White Ensign. In 1836–37 he sailed in her to the Mediterranean, enjoying enormously the experience of captaining his own ship but still dreaming of the east. And then in 1837 he came across G. W. Earl's newly published *The Eastern Seas*.[3] Here Earl spoke strongly against the Dutch in Batavia, a place not only horribly unhealthy but ruined by slavery and penal taxation, arguing that Britain had a mission to pacify and to civilise whether or not profit accrued, the creed of the 'white man's burden', the British working with local people and Chinese immigrants to bring wealth and happiness. This Brooke saw was exactly what he himself believed and he determined to try his fortune on those seas. On 16 December 1838 he set out in the *Royalist* from Devonport with a handpicked crew of 19 for Singapore, the port which his great hero, Sir Stamford Raffles, had founded just 20 years before.

Brooke was a man of great charm, brave and energetic. His good friend Captain Henry Keppel considered that when he was young he lacked discipline and was much too lively and happy-go-lucky to make a good soldier. Clearly loving the role of leader, and never a good follower, "too fond of having his own way and too impatient of interference in his plans", he tended to surround himself with relatives and friends, "too many useless hangers-on" according to Keppel.[4] If lacking the rigours of a formal education, Brooke was none the less extremely well read, devouring books on a great variety of subjects, fascinated by history and law, theology and biology. But he was certainly no businessman – 'As a man of commerce, I am a fool'[5] – with little interest in the intricacies of commerce or in money, subjects that might have stood him in much better stead in the role he was about to undertake. Again according to

Keppel "My friend Brooke has as much idea of business as a cow has of a clean shirt."[6]

The *Royalist* sailing via Rio and Capetown arrived in Singapore on 1 June 1839, the captain ill and the ship in urgent need of repairs. With his good connections and charm Brooke was soon welcomed by the small British community, and Governor Samuel Bonham, hearing that he planned to sail further eastwards, asked if he would take a message of thanks to the ruler at Sarawak in western Borneo where the crew of a ship recently wrecked had been kindly treated. Leaving Singapore in late July, the *Royalist* finally anchored in the Sarawak River off the little town of Kuching (sometimes itself called 'Sarawak') on 15 August where he was welcomed by that ruler, Rajah Muda Hassim, an uncle of the Sultan of Brunei.

Brunei, sometimes called 'Borneo' or 'Borneo Proper', was established as a Malay sultanate in the fifteenth century, an offspring of the rise of the Malacca sultanate. The strategic position of the major settlement in a time of rapidly increasing trade allowed it to grow quickly, becoming the largest market of the region, perhaps at its height with over 100,000 inhabitants. But then decline set in, so that by the early nineteenth century, although still the nominal ruler of the whole of the north coast of Borneo, from Tanjung Datu in the west to Marudu Bay in the east, the Sultan of Brunei controlled little more than his capital, and that often tenuously.

The founding of Singapore in 1819 and its rapid rise influenced the lands of the Brunei sultanate. In 1828 a new sultan, Omar Ali Saifuddin II (ca 1800–52), came to the throne and throughout the 24 years of his reign his own power waned just as that of Britain waxed. While apparently a weak and indecisive ruler, Omar Ali was also considered by the British with whom he dealt deranged, though this may have arisen in part from their desire to justify the taking of his lands, in part because of his physical deformities, for he had both cancer of the mouth and a twisted hand. The *Straits Times*, with typical invective, called him 'His Dinginess the Sultan of Borneo'.[7] But he seems to have been generally respected by his courtiers and survived as sultan for 24 years, dying peacefully. In the western part of the Sultan's lands, along the Sarawak River, antimony had been found, a substance prized by the merchants of Singapore. And lying as it did next to the well populated Sambas region of Dutch Borneo, Sarawak was conveniently placed for the smuggling of goods, notably opium, into Dutch territory. Unfortunately the governor,

Pangiran Makhota, had through his own corruption driven the local Malay chiefs to revolt, and the Sultan sent his uncle Hassim to restore order, a task that had proved too great for him.

Brooke rather took to Hassim, a little man about 45 years old, intelligent and mild, unsuited for the role he had unwillingly undertaken. Surrounded by a tribe of brothers Brooke listened patiently to his tales of woe, learning that Hassim's difficulties arose as much from intrigue within his court as from attacks from without. But he felt that he could do little, offering only advice and no practical help. After a fascinating six weeks, in which Brooke explored the surrounding country and, to his evident delight, first met the indigenous people, the Dayaks, he returned to Singapore.

Leaving Singapore again in late November 1839 the *Royalist* spent the following six months cruising in the archipelago.[8] Returning to Singapore in late May to find the harbour crowded with the ships of the China expedition Brooke, again ill, intended to rest and restock and then sail on to the Philippines and China before going home. But on his way east he decided to make one last visit to his friend Hassim in Sarawak, anchoring again at Kuching on 29 August 1840. Here he learnt that Hassim's situation was, if anything, worse than the year before, his position still threatened by Makhota, and piracy and headhunting rife on the rivers. It seems to have been then that the message that Earl had expounded so forcefully struck home. Yes, he could do something here, he could bring peace to these rivers. But to do that he needed both time and authority. Clearly Hassim would be happy to wash his hands off Sarawak and its problems and return to Brunei yet he remained uncertain about allowing this enthusiastic white man to help.

On 4 November, the day that the *Nemesis* steamed out of Singapore towards the coast of Borneo and so to China, Brooke told Hassim that he was finally going to leave and Hassim, aghast at the thought, promised him the government of Sarawak. Within a few weeks Brooke and his followers had put down the rebellion, and as peace was restored so trade picked up. If some of the locals saw their chances for plunder and slaves diminished, so others welcomed the new sense of security that the foreigner brought. But as Brooke hankered after ever greater authority so Hassim continued to procrastinate. At last on 24 September 1841 James Brooke was invested as Rajah of Sarawak in Kuching, his title being confirmed by the Sultan the following July during a triumphant visit to Brunei.

The territory that James Brooke now ruled extended from Tanjung Datu in the west to the Sadong River in the east, encompassing the watershed of the Sarawak River. It was peopled by four main groups. The indigenous Dayaks were basically forest people, the Land Dayaks (Bidayuh) living largely to the west, inland and for security away from the rivers, the Sea Dayaks (Iban), fiercer than their cousins, in their great longhouses along the rivers to the east, the most warlike beyond the jurisdiction of Sarawak. The Malays, followers of Islam, were mostly fishermen and farmers, but they also provided the rulers of many river mouths, thus controlling trade, particularly salt, a vital item for the inland people. And finally the Chinese, dominating the commerce of Kuching, but found mainly around the antimony mines up the Sarawak River at Bau.

Over the following decades the influence of the Brooke Raj gradually spread north-east to encompass much of the Brunei sultanate. To say that this was accomplished by force of arms is in some sense true. But these arms, destroying piracy, slavery and headhunting, brought security and the rule of law and it was this peace that the majority of all groups clearly desired. Without doubt Brooke viewed his kingdom as an instrument by which he could bring civilisation to the local people and not as an estate from which he could extract profit. His views on European influence in the Archipelago were radical: "The first voyages from the West found the natives rich and powerful, with strong established governments, and a thriving trade with all parts of the world. The rapacious European has reduced them to their present condition. Their governments have been broken up; the old states decomposed by treachery, by bribery, and intrigue; their possessions wrested from them under flimsy pretences; their trade restricted, their vices encouraged, their virtues repressed, and their energies paralysed or rendered desperate."[9]

The Sarawak of James Brooke and his nephew Charles, the second Rajah, grew like the earliest of Southeast Asian societies, groups of people coalescing around a powerful individual, a 'mandala state'. It certainly was an unusual state: an Englishman whose primary loyalty must be to the British Crown acting as feudatory ruler for a foreign sultan. So what was the legal status of Sarawak and its Rajah? Was the state independent or a vassal of Brunei, and, if independent as the Rajah professed, could its ruler as a British subject owe allegiance to Queen Victoria and call upon her government and navy for assistance? These questions, in which the *Nemesis* became intimately involved, would haunt James for many years.

{ 21 }

PIRATES AND PROFITS

> "If I have travelled on the sea, I will then understand that war, trade and piracy are fundamentally like the Trinity, inseparable and indivisible."
>
> —*Faust Part 2*, Act 5, J. W. von Goethe

From the founding of modern Singapore in 1819 her traders were exercised by the problem of piracy.[1] Certainly the problem was very real; boats trading along the coast were often plundered, those coming down on the north-east monsoon from China, Cochin-China and Siam frequently waylaid, and European ships sailing to and from China sometimes attacked. And the culprits were many. Most fearsome were the Illanun from Illana Bay in Mindanao, and the Balanini from the Sulu Archipelago which stretches south-west from Mindanao to Borneo. Their fleets would set forth generally around the month of May on voyages lasting many months, seeking both plunder and slaves, sweeping through the archipelago on easterly winds, the 'pirate wind', during the south-west monsoon. Their boats, 'prahus', could be of considerable size, up to 90 ft long and 10 ft wide with perhaps 60 rowers, slaves, and as many fighting men, armed with a couple of guns mounted fore and aft and numerous small brass cannon, 'lelah'. Such fleets or 'balla', perhaps 30 travelling together each with an average of 35 men, would terrorise coastal communities, robbing, killing and enslaving, and could attack and capture quite considerable cargo vessels.

Then there were the Malays and the *orang laut*, the former from coastal villages, sometimes acting as fishermen, sometimes as robbers, the latter sea nomads living in their boats. For Europeans those Malay chiefs who were in alliance with them were considered legitimate rulers, whereas those with conflicting interests were mere pirates.[2] When Temenggong Abdul Rahman of Singapore died in 1825 with his successor only 15 years old, control of the *orang laut* in the neighbouring seas broke down. As Earl reported "The Malay pirates absolutely swarm in the neighbourhood of Singapore, the numerous islands in the vicinity, the intersecting channels of which are known only to themselves, affording them a snug retreat, whence they can pounce upon the defenceless native traders..."[3] Their prahus were generally smaller than those of the Sulu fleets but were at least as well armed, carrying perhaps a 12-pounder in the bows, broadsides each of six lelah, and numerous muskets. Around the Malay Peninsula they were particularly prevalent along the sheltered east coast during the south-west monsoon in April and May, moving south to Johore from June to September (the largest market for their slaves was at Endau in eastern Johore), and then up the Straits of Malacca during the north-east monsoon from October to January.

Thirdly there were pirates from China. In the 1830s these seemed to confine themselves largely to their own shores and those of Cochin-China, but in the 1840s, with the ending of the Chinese War, fleets began to go further afield and by the 1850s they were a significant scourge throughout the South China Sea.

And finally there were the Iban or Sea Dayaks of Borneo. Their practice of headhunting fascinated and shocked the Victorians, the taking of heads, drying them and then displaying them in the head-house – or the 'skullery' as Keppel nicely called it.[4] Sea Dayak boats, 'bangkong', although sometimes as long as prahus were both faster and lighter, made of planks bound together with rattan and thus easily disassembled, and more lightly armed, perhaps with only one or two lelah and a few muskets. The feats of their crews, 60 to 80 men, could be prodigious: paddling, they could sustain a speed of 6 mph for 18 hours, covering 100 miles in a day, and could reach 12 mph if closing on a prize.

When steamships arrived in eastern waters in the 1820s the people of Singapore soon saw how beneficial it would be to have one stationed at their port. Not only would this enhance communication between them and the settlements at Malacca and Penang and with the government in India, but such a ship would also add greatly to British prestige when conducting negotiations with native rulers, and could play a decisive role against the twin evils of piracy and slavery.[a] From the early 1830s Calcutta was bombarded with petitions to this effect and finally agreed that, as part of the Bengal Marine, a small steamer should be based at Singapore. At the end of October 1836 the wooden paddle steamer *Diana*, the second of that name, was launched at Currie's yard near Calcutta, 168 tons and using the two 16 hp Maudslay engines from the first *Diana*. Leaving Calcutta on 5 February 1837 she reached Singapore on the 2 March and was immediately handed over to Captain Samuel Congalton.

Samuel Congalton (1796–1850) was already well known in Singapore for his efforts against piracy, his boldness and good humour endearing him to many. John Thomson, a young surveyor in Singapore and a great fan, enjoying hot coffee and biscuits on board the *Diana* in the company of Congalton's pet orang utan and tame otter, describes him well: "He was a man of small stature, but compact and active. Though trained as an apprentice in a tough school – that of the Sunderland coal trade – he was a man of the utmost delicacy of feeling, and of high principle. His manners were of the old school – bluntness and honesty happily blended with acute perception of propriety. His ready and pungent wit rendered his conversation animated and engaging."[5] Born in North Berwick, Congalton ran away to sea as a young boy, working first in the coastal trade but eventually finding himself gunner on a ship bound for Calcutta. Serving then on 'country' ships, in 1821 in Penang he joined the Company's armed schooner *Jessy*, on which he saw service in the First Burmese War, and for the rest of his life served the Company. In March 1826 he received his first command, the schooner *Zephyr*, and was soon actively pursuing pirates up and down the coasts of the Peninsula. Indeed, it was in large part the successes of the *Zephyr* that inspired the merchants of Singapore to campaign for an anti-piracy vessel of their very own, a steamer. So when the *Diana* steamed into Singapore in 1837 she was handed to a man well versed in the ways of pirates. And it is gratifying to know that his salary was raised from $100 per month on the schooner to $350 on the steamer.

It was over a year before Congalton had the opportunity to test his new ship, crewed by himself, two European officers and 30 Malays,

---

[a]   It is worth noting that at this time their colonial neighbours, the Dutch in the Netherlands East Indies, were buying slaves in Bali and Lombok for their plantations at only £20 a head (Earl 1837).

against a pirate fleet. On 18 May 1838 HMS *Wolf* (18 guns), which for the past two years had been helping Congalton in his hunt for pirates, was lying off Trengganu on the east coast of the Peninsula when she sighted a fleet of Illanun prahus bearing down upon a large Chinese junk. The *Singapore Free Press* reported: "HMS *Wolf* was a sailing vessel, so of course the little steamer went ahead; and the pirates in six large prahus, seeing the smoke, thought it was a sailing ship on fire; so they left the Chinese junk which they were attacking, and bore down on the steamer, firing on her as they approached. To their horror, the vessel came up close against the wind, and then suddenly stopped opposite each prahu and poured in a destructive fire, turning and backing quite against the wind, stretching the pirates in numbers on their decks. A vessel that was independent of both wind and oars was, of course, a miracle to them." From prisoners it was later ascertained that there had been about 360 men aboard the prahus, pirates and slaves, of whom 90 were killed and 150 wounded. Eighteen pirates were brought to trial in Singapore on 7 June and sentenced to be transported to Bombay. Later the *Singapore Free Press* in an angry report said that when the *Wolf* left Singapore later that year her captain, Edward Stanley, was presented with a 100 guinea sword by the merchants of the city and was guest of honour at a public dinner – and Congalton received no recognition at all. This lack of public recognition of the services of officers of the Indian navies certainly rankled. On 23 May 1843 Admiral Parker, from the China campaign, felt it necessary to write to Governor-General Lord Ellenborough about it, pleading that the officers of Company steamers be rewarded for their excellent services "exactly as the officers of the Royal Navy and the Queen's and Company's Land Forces ..."[6]

With his position as Rajah of Sarawak confirmed by the Sultan of Brunei in July 1842, James Brooke set about his rule with considerable confidence. Holding absolute power he wielded it humanely for his times. To those who knew their place whether his social superiors, equals or inferiors, he was a man of great charm, but his weakness was his inability to take criticism, an impatience with diplomacy, and a certain ruthlessness to anyone he considered a rival.

Brooke was at this time, as his friend Spencer St John later wrote, "...very much alone, with only four followers: a coloured interpreter from Malacca, an illiterate servant, Peter; a shipwrecked Irishman, Crymble; and a doctor, Mackenzie, a fine companion but with no interest in the country (subsequently killed by Chinese pirates)."[7]

But he quickly grew to love Sarawak and its people, delighting in the company of the Malay gentry and becoming especially fond of the Land Dayaks. "It is the Land Dyaks for which I particularly feel, for a more wretched oppressed race is not to be found, or one more deserving of the commiserations of the humane. Though their country is rich, the produce is all yielded to the oppressors. Though industrious they never reap what they sow. Though caring of their families, they can rarely preserve half of their children, and often, too often, are robbed of all of them and of their wives."[8] The Sea Dayaks he admired, their high spirits and their openness, their love of freedom and adventure, the Malays their sophistication and good manners, and the Chinese their hard work and business sense.

As his influence spread over the territory of Sarawak Brooke became persuaded of the necessity of taking action further afield. Particularly exercising him were the Sea Dayaks of the Saribas and Skrang rivers beyond Sarawak to the east, these with Malay help continually raiding Sarawak's Land Dayaks for heads and slaves. But to teach the Sea Dayaks the lesson which he felt was necessary would require much stronger forces than he could currently muster. "What a train of reflection does not this necessity lead to! Am I then really *fond* of war? This is a question that I ask myself. And I answer – 'Certainly' – for what man is not? And, indeed, what else makes among my countrymen so many sailors and soldiers?"[9] A profoundly nineteenth-century reflection.

In March 1843 Brooke was again in Singapore, one night dining at the house of a local worthy, William Napier, the settlement's first law agent and the founder in 1835 of the first proper newspaper, *Singapore Free Press & Mercantile Advertiser*. Also at dinner was Henry Keppel of the *Dido*, and he and Brooke immediately took a great liking to each other, a lifelong friendship which had a profound effect upon Brooke's fortunes. In May the *Dido* carried Brooke back to Kuching, he delighting in his friend's ship – "She is, without exception, the handsomest vessel that ever I saw,"[10] and Keppel delighting at the reception the Rajah received there and later bemused at his first meeting with Rajah Muda Hassim, "We took our seats in a semicircle, on chairs provided for the occasion, and smoked cigars and drank tea. His majesty chewed his sirih-leaf and betel-nut, seated with one leg crossed under him, and playing with his toes. Very little is ever said during these audiences, so we sat staring at one another for half an hour with mutual astonishment; and after the usual compliments of wishing our friendship might last as long as the moon, and my having offered him the *Dido* and everything else that did not belong to me in exchange for his house, we took our leave."[11]

Here was Brooke's chance to enhance his authority: the presence in Sarawak of a man-of-war with a friendly captain and a crew of 145 battle-hardened men. And then, most conveniently, Keppel received from Hassim a letter begging him to act against the piratical Sea Dayaks. The captain needed no further encouragement. In early July Brooke and Keppel led a force from Kuching to the Saribas River, British sailors supported by numerous local warriors, and, leaving the *Dido* at sea, swept up the river in boats and over the next two weeks attacked and burnt three Dayak settlements. For this action the Court of Judicature in Singapore awarded the men of the *Dido* £795 in head money: 23 men killed at £20 each and £5 for each of the other 67 men engaged but not killed. Returning to Kuching to a people delighted to hear of the humiliation of the Saribas Dayaks, Keppel regretfully had immediately to leave for China, unable to help teach the Dayaks of the Skrang River a similar lesson.

Head money? The concept of paying a reward for each pirate killed or attacked looks, in retrospect, suspiciously similar to the much despised 'headhunting' of the Dayaks, the Bornean carrying back in triumph a head, the Briton a handsome £20. Under an Act of 1825 aimed at the suppression of piracy in the West Indies, crews of HM ships engaged in anti-piracy work were entitled to such rewards.[12] But might not the existence of such awards encourage unnecessary savagery, and even, Heaven forbid, cloud the judgement of a naval officer as to both the number and the nature of his opponents? Were they indeed really 'pirates' – and not just local warriors resisting a foreign invasion? A nice example can be taken from Captain Sir Edward Belcher's (1799–1877) account of his voyage in HMS *Samarang* (26 guns) which, being in his own words, is not influenced by the fact that, able but bad-tempered, he was widely disliked in the Royal Navy (as his obituarist observed "Perhaps no officer of equal ability has ever succeeded in inspiring so much personal dislike…").[13] In 1844 the *Samarang* was engaged in survey work off the island of Jilolo (Halmahera) to the west of New Guinea when, at 2 am on the night of 3 June, her boats, a gig with six men and a barge with 20, were attacked. Belcher's account of this outrage is accompanied by a wonderful etching of five huge pirate vessels, for all the world like Viking warships, bearing down upon a little gig from which proudly flutters the Union Jack. Having successfully driven off this night-time attack, the following morning Belcher sent out four boats manned by 47 men to punish the remainder of the pirate fleet, five even larger vessels and 10 others. Although local Dutch officials denied there were pirates in the vicinity, Belcher claimed that these were the much feared Illanun, and upon his return to England he applied for the award of the bounty, stating that 1,580 pirates had been engaged of which 350 had been killed and 27 vessels destroyed or disabled. Not bad for a few little boats manned by a handful of brave British against these most fearsome of warriors – and at night! For this, the officers and men of the *Samarang* were awarded £10,000, Captain Belcher for a wound suffered also receiving a pension of £250 a year.

But to return, if somewhat indirectly, to Sarawak. On Tuesday 22 May 1844, exactly a year since she had last left Singapore, the *Phlegethon* anchored in the roads there, now thoroughly refitted and under the command of Joseph Scott (1797–1845). That March, Henry Keppel, knowing that he was to return to the Straits as Senior Naval Officer, had inspected her in Calcutta and decided that she should be stationed in Singapore to act against pirates, assisting Congalton and the *Diana*. Meanwhile the *Dido* had sailed from India to China, and now returned from Macau to join the steamer in Singapore on 19 July.

Six days later the *Dido* and *Phlegethon* left for Borneo, arriving in the Sarawak River on 1 August where Keppel immediately started planning with Brooke the completion of the unfinished business of the year before – an attack on the Skrang Dayaks. On the 5th the expedition left Kuching, a flotilla of boats towed by the steamer: boats from the *Dido*, the *Phlegethon's* four cutters, and the *Jolly Bachelor*, Brooke's locally built boat. On board were 13 officers, 108 seamen and 16 marines. Amongst the *Dido's* officers was a young midshipman on his first visit to Borneo, Charles Johnson (1829–1917), the nephew of James Brooke and destined to become, as Charles Brooke, the second Rajah of Sarawak.[14] Accompanying the steamer were a swarm of boats carrying about 300 local men loyal to Brooke under the command of Budrudeen, brother of Hassim and a particular favourite of the Rajah. That evening the boats anchored at the mouth of the Batang Lupar, there about four miles wide. The following day the *Phlegethon* steamed eastwards up the river, anchoring within musket range of the Dayak forts at Patusan, and by that evening the whole settlement had been looted and burnt, with the capture of 56 guns. Some of these were of brass and when later auctioned in Singapore fetched £900, a useful prize. It was rumoured that in fact a number were bought back by those from whom they had just been taken.

On the 11 August the flotilla advanced further up the river towards its confluence with the Skrang from the north and the Undop from the south. Leaving the *Phlegethon* on the Batang Lupar, a fort up the Undop was attacked on the 12th before the boats pulled up the Skrang to their main objective, the rivers in places almost impassable as numerous great trees had been felled across them. The engagement on Monday 19th, vividly described by Keppel, was typical of these expeditions.[15]

> As the stream was running down strong, we held on to the bank, waiting for the arrival of the second cutter. Our pinnace and the second gig having passed up, we remained about a quarter of an hour, when the report of a few musket-shots told us that the pirates had been fallen in with. We immediately pushed on, and as we advanced the increased firing from our boats, and the war-yells of some thousand Dyaks, let us know that we had met.
>
> It is difficult to describe the scene as I found it. About twenty boats were jammed together, forming one confused mass – some bottom up; the bows and sterns of others only visible, mixed up pell-mell with huge rafts – and amongst which were nearly all our advanced division. Headless trunks, as well as heads without bodies, were lying about; parties hand to hand spearing and krissing each other,[b] others striving to swim for their lives; and entangled in the common mêlée were our advanced boats, while on both banks thousands of Dyaks were rushing down to join in the slaughter, hurling spears and stones on the boats below.
>
> For a moment I was at a loss what steps to take for rescuing our people from the position in which they were, as the whole mass, through which there was no passage, were floating down the stream, and the addition of fresh boats only increased the confusion. Fortunately, at this critical moment, one of the rafts, catching the stump of a tree, broke this floating bridge, making a passage through which my gig (propelled by paddles instead of oars) – the bugler, John Eager, in the bow – was enabled to pass.
>
> It occurred to Brooke and myself simultaneously, that by advancing in the gig we should draw the attention of the pirates

---

b   The kris is a dagger with a wavy blade widely worn in the Malay Archipelago.

towards us, so as to give time for the other boats to clear themselves. This had the desired effect. The whole force on the shore turned, as if to secure what they rashly perceived to be their prize. We now advanced mid-channel, spears and stones assailing us from both banks. Brooke's gun would not go off, so, giving him the yoke-lines, I, with the coxswain to load, had time to select the leaders from amongst the savage mass, on which I kept up a rapid fire.

Allen (R. C. Allen, master of the Dido) in the second gig, quickly coming up, opened upon them from a Congreve rocket-tube such a destructive fire as caused them to retire behind the temporary barriers where they had concealed themselves previous to the attack on Patingi Ali, and from whence they continued, for some twenty minutes, to hurl their spears and other missiles, among which were short lengths of bamboo loaded with stone at one end. The sumpitan (blow-pipe) was likewise freely employed, and although several of our men were struck, no fatal results ensued. Mr Beith, our assistant surgeon, dexterously excised the wounds, and what poison remained was sucked out by comrades of the wounded men.

From this position, however, the Sekarrans retreated as our force increased, and could not again muster courage to rally. Their loss must have been considerable. Ours might have been light had poor old Patingi Ali attended to orders, but he was over confident. Instead of falling back, as particularly directed by me, on the first appearance of any of the enemy he made a dash, followed by his little division of boats, through the narrow pass. The enemy at once launched large rafts of bamboo and cut off his retreat. Six war-prahus bore down, three on either side, on Patingi's devoted followers. One only of a crew of 17 escaped to tell the tale.

When last seen by our advanced boats, Mr Steward and Patingi Ali were in the act (their own boats sinking) of boarding the enemy. They were doubtless overpowered and killed, with 29 others. Our wounded in all amounted to 56.

A few miles further up was the capital of Karangan, which we carried without further opposition. Having achieved the object of our expedition, we dropped leisurely down the river; slept in our boats, with a strong guard on shore. On the 20th we reached the steamer, where we remained all the next day attending to the wounded."

Not until 4 September did the expedition finally leave the Batang Lupar, the *Phlegethon* towing the naval boats back to Kuching. Although Brooke had long wanted the assistance of a shallow-draught iron steamer, he was later scathing about the *Phlegethon*: "We are put into an inefficient steamer, manned with a weak crew of wretched blacks, and obliged to crawl from place to place, with intervals of ten or twelve days, for wood cutting at each place ... of her crew there are not five men who have ever seen a large gun fired."[16]

About a year earlier Brooke had come to realise that it was essential that Rajah Muda Hassim and his family – 13 brothers, their wives and sundry followers – should leave Kuching and return to Brunei. Although he personally enjoyed their company and was grateful for their assistance against marauding Sea Dayaks, he had come to see that their continued presence in Kuching undermined his authority. Indeed, they themselves were eager to return home. Thus on the night of 14 October 1844, Hassim and his family were embarked on the *Phlegethon* at Kuching, canvas awnings being spread and the crew confined forward to protect the modesty of the 24 women passengers. Throughout the voyage the poor women were all confined to the Captain's cabin, a space cramped for half that number, one actually dying there. Brooke, eager to support Hassim on his return to the intrigues of the Brunei court, accompanied the party with Captain Belcher on HMS *Samarang*, the two well-armed vessels being thought to enhance the prospects of successful discussions with the Sultan.

But Brooke's journey also had another aim – the ceding of the island of Labuan off the coast of Brunei, not to Sarawak but to the British crown. He felt sure that such a possession would not only prove an impetus to trade and a curb on piracy but would also stir the British government and navy to take a more active interest in the affairs of Borneo. His tactics were successful, the *Phlegethon* with her guns trained on the palace helping to persuading the Sultan to agree to the cession, although two years were to pass before the British flag was raised over the new colony.

With Labuan in mind, the Foreign Secretary in London, Lord Aberdeen, agreed early in 1845 to the appointment of Brooke as 'Her Majesty's Confidential Agent in Borneo', and in March in this role he sailed to Singapore for discussions with the new naval Commander-in-Chief, Rear-Admiral Thomas Cochrane[c]. He was particularly concerned about the safely of Hassim and his family in Brunei where his friendship with Brooke had won him many enemies, most notably his cousin Pangeran Usop (Yusuf), the 'Prime Minister'. Conspiring with Usop and others was one Serips Usman of Marudu Bay at the northern tip of Borneo, described as a half-bred Arab and leader of a cruel band of pirates 2,000 strong, largely Illanuns. In fact Usman was in many ways typical of local leaders, a bold man in uncertain times attracting a healthy band of followers. Brooke very much wished to extirpate what he viewed as a nest of brigands and Cochrane agreed to help, although Brooke had to wait, impatient as always, until August for this to materialise.

---

[c] In contemporary reports Admiral Cochrane (1789–1872) is sometimes plain 'Thomas', sometimes 'Sir Thomas'. Born on 5 February 1789, he entered the Royal Navy on 15 June 1796, aged 7, supposedly as a First-class Volunteer on HMS *Thetis* (42 guns), commanded by his father Captain Alexander Cochrane. On 29 May 1812 Thomas, aged 23, was knighted as a proxy for his father Alexander who had been awarded a KCB. Thomas was not awarded a KCB in his own right until 29 October 1847. So in 1845 he was correctly both 'Thomas' and 'Sir Thomas', another marvel of the British Honours system.

{ 22 }

GUNBOAT DIPLOMACY

The year 1845 saw Singapore welcome all five of the Secret Committee's sliding-keel vessels to the harbour. Throughout that year the *Phlegethon* was stationed there, cruising from Penang to Cochin-China and Borneo. Returning from their service in China, the *Proserpine* arrived on 19 March on her way to Calcutta for a well-earned overhaul, and the *Medusa* on 29 November bound for Bombay. Their replacements travelling east, respectively the *Nemesis* from Calcutta arriving on 14 July and the *Pluto* from Bombay on 3 June, were both destined first for service in Borneo.

When the *Nemesis* steamed into Singapore on 14 July her sister ship *Phlegethon* lay at anchor there, the first time that the two had met since November 1842 off Zhoushan. In Penang in early July First Officer Thomas Wallage, who had now been with the ship for over three years, had his will witnessed by Captain John Russell and the ship's surgeon, Mr Robinson, perhaps realising that the days ahead promised to be more exciting than those recently passed in India. Travelling with Wallage were his wife Elizabeth and their one-year-old son, but when the *Nemesis* sailed on from Singapore on the 17th, Elizabeth and the boy, although destined for China, stayed behind.[1] There on Monday 4 August they may have witnessed an historic event, the arrival of the paddle steamer *Lady Mary Wood* (533 tons, 230 hp), from Galle in Ceylon which she had left eight days before. Her arrival had been widely anticipated and was warmly welcomed, for she heralded the start of the first regular monthly mail service from Britain to India and on to Singapore and Hong Kong by the Peninsular & Oriental Steam Navigation Company, the P & O. As she steamed into the harbour European residents gathered at the Post Office near the mouth of the Singapore River, soon delighted to learn that their letters from London had taken as little as 41 days.

Since the end of the Napoleonic Wars the Admiralty had been responsible for the dispatch of mail to the Mediterranean. Employing the first steamers in 1830, they extended their route from Malta to Alexandria in 1835, sending mails overland to Suez where they were picked up by the Company's steamer *Hugh Lindsay* for passage to Bombay. This route certainly seemed more satisfactory than the long journey around the Cape, but the *Hugh Lindsay* was not capable of maintaining a regular service by herself.

On 1 September 1837 the contract for the carriage of mails from Britain to Gibraltar was awarded to the newly formed Peninsular Steam Navigation Company, the company adding 'Oriental' to their name when they extended their route to Alexandria exactly three years later.[2] But to make the 'Oriental' a reality more efficient steamers were needed on the Suez to India run. On 24 September 1842 the P & O steamer *Hindostan*, 2,018 tons, left England with the mail for India, travelling via the Cape to Bombay. There, early in 1843, she took over from the Calcutta Steam Navigation Company the task of bringing the mail from Suez, steaming to Galle in Ceylon to leave the Bombay mails and then on via Madras to Calcutta. Later that year the *Victoria* (230 tons) a wooden paddle steamer built in Bombay in 1839, started the first steamer service between India and the Straits, but the dignitaries of Singapore felt that a P & O service would better serve their needs. A contract was signed with the company specifying the number of hours to be taken between ports, about six days from Galle to Penang, two days to Singapore, a two-day stopover there, and seven days on to Hong Kong. Thus letters could now be expected in Hong Kong about 50 days after leaving London instead of the four to five months only recently required.

When the *Lady Mary Wood* steamed on eastwards on 5 August 1845 the *Singapore Free Press* could report "The P. & O. Company have now in service and in progress of construction 30 steamers, 26 are sea-going and 4 for river service: 14 of them are from 1,200–2,000 tons and of 450–520 horse power ... All of them are capable of carrying armaments, the first 14 as heavy as any steam frigate." But Elizabeth Wallage and her son were not on board the *Lady Mary Wood*, no doubt because of the cost of such a passage. The year before Captain Cunnynghame, returning to England from the China war, had paid £163 to the P & O for the passage from Calcutta to Southampton, an enormous sum.[3] Instead the Wallages embarked for Hong Kong on the 17th on a country ship, the *Cowerjee Family*, certainly less luxurious but also very much cheaper.

Both the *Nemesis* and *Pluto* on leaving Singapore were bound first not for China but for Borneo, part of Admiral Cochrane's response to Rajah Brooke's request for help. On Friday 8 August 1845 a British squadron arrived off the mouth of the Brunei River, impressive enough to alarm the most sanguine of sultans. Cochrane's flagship HMS *Agincourt* (72 guns) was accompanied by the *Vestal* (26), *Daedalus* (20), *Cruiser* (18), *Wolverene* (16) and the steamers HMS *Vixen, Nemesis* and *Pluto*.[4] Pangiran Budrudeen, to Brooke's great pleasure, came off to greet them – a most colourful spectacle as Surgeon Cree, now on the *Vixen*, reported. "Bedrudin ... passed in his boat, a long, low proa with 18 paddles, a 4-pounder gun on the bow, red silk umbrella with green fringe, a large yellow ensign ... some of the nobs had on sky-blue jackets and yellow pyjamas. The *Agincourt* saluted him with seven guns and the Admiral sent him back on the *Nemesis*."[5] The following morning the three steamers moved up the river, carrying Cochrane, Brooke and about 500 sailors and marines, the river winding through forests with a little grassland where the forest had been burnt. The town, a place of perhaps 10,000 people, straggled along the banks for a couple of miles, the wooden houses raised on piles above the water. There in the centre stood the palace and the steamers anchored opposite it at about 6 am, the Admiral and the Rajah landing in their finery. "The Admiral ... is at times disagreeable about dress, and very pompous. He is himself a regular old buck, and looks as if he kept himself in a bandbox."[6] At an audience at the palace Cochrane assured the Sultan that his force posed no threat to Brunei but that he must discipline Usop for various misdeeds. The Sultan replied that he was not powerful enough to accomplish this but gave the Admiral permission to do what was necessary, exactly what Cochrane wanted. The next morning the steamers moved up-river until opposite Usop's stockade where, seeing no signs of Usop's submission, their guns flattened it within 15 minutes, Usop fleeing, only to be killed a few weeks later by those with whom he sought refuge. From his house the British recovered 20 cannon, again later auctioned in Singapore for prize money. Although none of the British force were hurt by enemy action "... one unfortunate man of the *Nemesis* was blown from his gun, through carelessness in loading."[7]

Leaving the Brunei River the fleet first stopped at Labuan to wood the steamers, then sailed for the north, entering Marudu Bay on Sunday 17 August. The next day the three steamers towed 24 ships' boats, nine being well-armed gunboats, carrying a total of almost 550 seamen and marines to the mouth of the Marudu River where they anchored for the night. At daybreak on the 19th the boats alone set off upstream towards Serip Usman's stronghold, the river being too shallow even for the iron steamers. Soon after 9 am, the leading boats rounded a bend to find themselves confronted by formidable defences. Across the river lay a boom formed of large tree trunks bound together by wire rope and attached by this to trees on the banks. Trained on the boom were the guns of two forts – four 18-pounders, two 12s and three 9s – one fort directly ahead on a point of land where the river branched, the other and larger one on the left bank. For almost an hour the attackers worked to force an opening in the boom under sustained fire from the forts, this answered much more accurately by the gunboats and to even greater effect by a rocket battery set up on the left bank. In the forts the chiefs, marked by their brightly coloured coats, could be seen bravely directing the fire, but then the boom was breached, boats swarming through and soon the smaller fort was taken which, being on higher ground, commanded the larger fort. Before long the defenders were in full flight and the victors, entering the forts and village, saw the carnage they had wrought: the bodies of Illanun in their bright warcoats, of Serips in their white turbans and robes, the remains of a Chinese slave, a women with her arm shattered by grape-shot still nursing her child. Although Usman's body was never found it was confidently reported that both he and his son had indeed been killed. The British casualties amounted to 8 killed and 13 wounded; as Cochrane reported to the Admiralty "When the great strength of the position is referred to ... it is rather astonishing than otherwise, and a source of thankfulness, that the casualties were not more numerous."[8]

Once the fortifications had been comprehensively destroyed, the guns either spiked or taken as prizes, the flotilla returned to the steamers in the bay. The bodies of five of those killed were recovered and from the *Nemesis* they were respectfully buried at sea, each man sewn into his hammock with two iron shot at his feet. The squadron now assembled off the island of Balambangan; from there the *Cruiser* carried Brooke back to Kuching, before continuing on to Singapore, whilst the rest sailed north for China. The *Nemesis* reached Hong Kong on 11 September, the first to arrive, before soon moving north to the island of Zhoushan.[9]

In Canton trouble was brewing.[10] Ever since the Treaty of Nanking in 1842 the politics of the Canton province and Hong Kong had been dominated by the refusal of the Cantonese, the most individualistic and troublesome of Chinese according to the British, to open their city to foreigners, an important provision of that treaty. The treaty had also stipulated that Zhoushan would be returned to the Chinese when the last instalment of the $21 million indemnity had been received. Now at last that hour was at hand, the final payment due on 22 January 1846. So the British, wishing to force the Canton issue, threatened to withhold the handover of the island until the city was opened. The mandarins, sensing a diplomatic victory at Zhoushan, finally bowed to British demands and on 13 January proclaimed that foreigners would be allowed to enter.

Over the years a belief had grown amongst the Cantonese that the invaders could be defeated if only the Chinese stood firm, and here were their rulers disgracefully kowtowing to the foreigners. On 15 January the city prefect, Liu Hsin, believed to be returning from a meeting with the British, was chased back to his house by an angry mob, the house burnt to the ground, Liu escaping from his garden into the governor's residence. At this the governor-general, Qi-ying, and his officials lost their nerve and gave in to the 'righteous' people. The British plenipotentiary, Sir John Davis,[a] more sensitive than many of his countrymen, saw that Qi-ying had lost much face and, wishing to retain his moderating influence, decided to neither press his demands over Canton nor to withhold Zhoushan. And so on 5 July the *Nemesis* left Ningbo for Zhoushan carrying four mandarins who were to take possession of the island in the name of the Emperor.

Three days later in Canton an irate British merchant attacked a Cantonese stallholder, beating him and then arresting him.[11] A crowd rapidly gathered demanding their compatriot's release, armed foreign merchants left the factories to disburse the mob, and three Chinese were shot dead. For years the British had demanded that the Chinese authorities punish any person who misbehaved towards them and generally the Chinese had complied. Now the tables were turned – and Qi-ying demanded the punishment of the guilty parties. With

---

[a] Davis, an experienced China hand, had replaced Pottinger in 1844.

Qi-ying egged on by the Cantonese and Davis fending off merchants baying for retribution, the situation did not look promising but both were determined to compromise. On 17 July the *Nemesis* was recalled from Zhoushan and stationed off Canton to prevent further incidents, the merchant who had precipitated the incident was fined $200, and the families of the three dead men were 'adequately compensated'. By the end of August the incident was over, but for the Chinese it left an indelible mark – again, the Cantonese had been sold out by their Manchu rulers, rulers so weak that they could not prevent uncivilised foreigners murdering the sons of the Han.

Back in Singapore the *Phlegethon* was engaged in more peaceful pursuits, but now under a different commander. Captain Scott had succumbed to malaria whilst she was in Singapore that January, his place initially taken by First Officer Coverly until the arrival from Calcutta in early June of Captain B. S. Ross. On 20 September 1845 Ross took his ship north from Singapore, the *Singapore Free Press* reporting in early October: "The Honourable Company's steam vessel *Phlegethon* left this last week for Turon in Cochin-China (Tourane, now Da Nang). The object of the *Phlegethon's* voyage is to convey to the King of Cochin China an Autograph Letter from the Governor General of British India expressing the high estimation in which the conduct of His Majesty is held in extending his protection to, and sending to Singapore, the shipwrecked crews of the *Mellish* and *Allowie*. The *Phlegethon* also conveys sundry presents from the Governor General to his Cochin China Majesty." This mission took the best part of two months, the *Phlegethon* not returning to Singapore from Nha Trang (Nientrang) until 14 November.

In early January 1846 the aging *Diana* was replaced in Singapore by a new steamer, the *Hooghly*, Captain Congalton immediately transferring to her. This change was met grumpily by the *Singapore Free Press*. "We really see no reason why the Bengal Government should palm upon the Straits Settlements such steamers only, as are not worth much at Calcutta for the same reason they are worth little in the Straits." Clearly the writer assumed she was the first of that name, a ship launched in 1828, but in fact she was the *Hooghly (ii)*, built just the year before in Calcutta, and at 193 tons and 50 hp a modest advance on the 10-year-old *Diana (ii)*, 168 tons with her 32 hp engines dating back to the very first steamship in eastern waters (*see* Table 8).

But soon such griping was driven from the pages of the local newspapers. On 12 December 1845 a Sikh army had crossed the Sutlej river into British India, meeting the British forces under Sir Hugh Gough first on the 18th. Over the next 54 days four major and bloody battles were fought, ending on 10 February at Sobraon, 'the Waterloo of India', the British there finally crushing Sikh resistance, although a further war was needed before the Punjab was formerly annexed in 1849.[12]

In early 1846 the government in Singapore received complaints from Chinese merchants about raids on their ships coming down from China, the culprit apparently the ruler of the east coast state of Kelantan. Rather than send the new *Hooghly* Governor Butterworth decided that the *Phlegethon* would create a stronger impression.[13] Leaving Singapore on Tuesday 31 March the *Phlegethon* steamed north up the east coast, stopping first at Trengganu to pay a courtesy visit to the well-behaved rajah of that state, "one of the most respectable amongst the rulers of the native states." The little town on the river bank just a quarter of a mile from the sea proved typical of coastal settlements: a terrace of Chinese shops along a single street by the waterfront backed by the Malay quarter, a scattering of wooden houses raised on stilts, a simple mosque, the ruler's house by far the largest building. There on 3 April with due pomp a party of officers called upon the rajah, the following day the rajah returning the visit, honoured with a salute of ten guns and a plentiful feast. Then on northwards, anchoring on the 6th at the mouth of the Kelantan River. The nature of their mission had clearly preceded them for they were met by an emissary of the rajah, but one, according to Ross, too nervous to deliver his message. The following day Ross and two officers embarked on the gig and with two well-armed cutters set forth up the river, travelling 9 miles to the capital. There they landed and marched to the rajah's house where Ross demanded an audience, ordering the return of the stolen goods and a promise to desist from piracy. Unsurprisingly they received full satisfaction, and so sailed on 9 April, reaching Singapore again on the 14th.

Six days earlier Rajah Brooke had welcomed Captain Egerton of HMS *Hazard* (18 guns) to Kuching, only to hear that his friends Rajah Muda Hassim and his brother Budrudeen, together with 11 other members of their families, had been murdered in Brunei around the turn of the year. Brooke was outraged, angry with himself for encouraging them to return to the dangers of the Brunei court, furious with the Sultan for what he saw as treachery. He immediately sent a dispatch to Admiral Cochrane in Madras pleading for a rapid and severe response. Early in the morning of Friday 19 June 1846 a squadron of seven ships under

Cochrane's command set sail from Singapore for Brunei.[14] This time accompanying the flagship *Agincourt* were the *Iris* (26 guns), *Hazard* (18), *Ringdove* (16), *Royalist* (8), and the paddle steamers HMS *Spiteful* (1,055 tons) and *Phlegethon*, providing a force of 230 marines and 500 seamen. Collecting Brooke at Kuching on the 25th, they sailed first to the Rejang River and then on to Brunei which they reached on 6 July. There followed an action similar to the one the year before: the steamers threatening the Sultan's palace, the Sultan lamenting the murders and professing good intentions, the British finding an excuse to attack, the Sultan's forces utterly routed. "So ended the 8th of July" wrote Captain Rodney Mundy of the *Iris*; "thirty-nine pieces of cannon, mostly of large calibre, fell into our hands, nineteen of which were brass. The sultan, his boasted army, and all the inhabitants had fled."[15] On the *Phlegethon* two men lay dead and seven wounded.

After further alarums and excursions up the coast of Borneo, the fleet sailed on to China, leaving Mundy with the *Iris*, *Hazard* and *Phlegethon* to attend to Borneo. On 27 August Brooke could write to Mundy from Brunei; "I have quite a menagerie of old women and young children aboard the *Phlegethon*, with a few young men, the unhappy survivors and dependants of Muda Hassim's family."[16]

Returning to Singapore Mundy there received on 25 November via HMS *Wolf* (18 guns) instructions from Admiral Cochrane to press the treaty of November 1844 with the Sultan, particularly to take possession of Labuan Island. On 1 December the *Iris* and *Wolf* left Singapore for Borneo, stopping briefly at Kuching to meet Brooke who could not come on to Brunei as he was about to leave for Singapore on the *Hazard* for discussions with Cochrane. On the 18th the Sultan signed a treaty ceding Labuan to the British, and on Thursday 24 December 1846 the Union Jack was for the first time raised over the island.[17] In a foretaste of the disasters soon to strike the little colony, Commander James Gordon, the 28-year-old captain of the *Wolf*, succumbed to malaria less than two weeks after the ceremony and was buried close by the first encampment.[b]

During the attack on Brunei on 8 July the *Phlegethon* had been damaged, a roundshot hitting the paddle-box and killing the cook in the galley behind, and, more seriously, she had been holed by nine grape-shot below the waterline abreast of the foremast, that compartment flooding. Temporary repairs had proved quite satisfactory but on her return to

---

[b]   Son of Rear Admiral Sir James Gordon, hence his youthful command.

Singapore in early September it was obvious that only in Calcutta could she again be put in proper order, and she left for India on 11 October. There she remained under repair for many months, corroded hull plates being replaced, new boilers inserted and a new funnel fitted. Meanwhile Captain Ross was sent to Singapore as Harbour Master, and it was under the command of a new captain, G. J. Niblett, that she returned in August 1847 to the Straits. To fill the gap, the *Nemesis* was ordered back from China to Singapore which she reached on 21 December 1846, 13 days from Macau. Captain Russell, suffering from nerves, had been given a one year leave of absence in November, and it was Thomas Wallage who was now her acting commander.[18]

With Labuan now safely ceded, Lord Palmerston, again the Foreign Secretary, at last gave Brooke an official position, early in 1847 appointing him 'Her Britannic Majesty's Commissioner and Consul-General to the Independent Chiefs of Borneo' at a salary of £500 a year, and sending him a draft of a treaty to be concluded with the Sultan of Brunei. In his new role Brooke steamed up to Brunei on the *Nemesis* in May 1847, treaty in hand. On board with the Rajah and Captain Wallage was a crew now of 80 men, all but six of whom were British.[19] Rendezvousing at Labuan with HMS *Columbine* (18 guns) and *Royalist*, the *Nemesis* embarked Commander Charles Grey and 23 men from the *Columbine* and ferried them to Brunei town. After what Brooke thought were successful talks, the steamer started back for Labuan at about 9 am on the 30th, almost immediately running into a fleet of 11 suspicious-looking prahus, soon seen to be Balanini.[20] As the steamer turned towards them they cut free the small boats they were towing and headed west. The chase lasted for over three hours, which says much for the rowers' stamina, before they turned to the shore and there lined up stern-first to the beach, about 30 ft apart with a hawser run between them. The *Nemesis* approached slowly until within 200 yards, anchoring broadside to the shore in 6 ft of water, rolling heavily in the swell. The action opened at 1.30 pm when a shot from the pirates killed a seaman on the *Nemesis*, the steamer then pouring in grape and canister from her two 32-pounders and her long-sixes while three ships' boats under Commander Grey rowed in to attack the west flank. Although that day the *Nemesis* fired a total of 160 round shot and nearly 500 charges of grape and canister (and canister at 300 yards would spread to 30 yards), accuracy was clearly wanting for after a couple of hours bombardment the pirates cast off the hawser and nine boats, obviously not much damaged, pulled away to the east, only two being too crippled to follow. Wallage immediately turned eastwards and gave chase; seeing this, six again turned to the beach, the steamer continuing after the other three. But then, looking back, Wallage saw that the six had not been beached but were now bearing down on Grey's boats. Again the *Nemesis* turned, now steaming westwards to rescue Grey. By the time darkness fell Grey and his men were safely back on board, five of the pirate boats had been destroyed or captured and six had escaped, although apparently only three made it back to Sulu.

From their captives the British learnt that they were indeed Balanini, returning home from a year-long journey around Borneo, laden with booty and with captives. The largest boats were manned by over 50 men, the total force a band of about 350, not counting the 100 or so men and women, both Malays and Chinese, whom they had taken as slaves. Of the total Wallage estimated that perhaps 80 to 100 had been killed, both pirates and their captives, with a similar number wounded. British losses were three killed and five severely wounded. The following day the Rajah wrote to Captain Wallage:[21]

> Sir, I have great satisfaction in expressing to you my sense of the judicious and gallant manner you fought the Honourable Company's steamer Nemesis under your command in the late action with the Balanini Pirate Fleet. You must allow me at the same time to express my sense of the gallantry and good conduct of the officers and crew of the Steamer under your command.
>
> I have the honour to be Sir
> Your obedient servant,
> J. Brooke.
> Commissioner to Her Majesty

{ 23 }

OF CONVICTS AND COLONIES

By first light a considerable crowd had already gathered outside the jail. There, over night, carpenters had erected a low scaffold, broad enough for three men to die side by side. Usually in Singapore crowds for such events were largely Asian, the Chinese being specially interested in these spectacles, particularly if it was one of their number who was to hang. But today there were a surprising number of Europeans grouped together to one side, standing silently. As the first glimpse of the sun was seen over the river the gates of the jail opened and three men were led out and up to the platform. Their names were read out: Hew Ah Ngee, Low Sang Kee, Lo Ah Mung – their crime, mutiny and murder, and their punishment, death. All three appeared calm, and when given a chance to speak one spoke at some length but apparently in a dialect unfamiliar to most of Chinese watching for they showed signs of impatience. Then the three were led forward, ropes placed about their necks and the order given. As the bodies fell some cheering – or was it jeering – broke out, and later some Europeans were to complain that not only had an unseemly number of their kind attended the event but that some had actually had the vulgarity to applaud. The day was Friday 26 May 1848. The story had started over six months earlier.[1]

The *General Wood*, a brig of 740 tons, was certainly past her prime. She had been employed as a receiving ship off Hong Kong when that island had first been taken in 1841, but now, with the opium trade again booming, she was back to her old task for the India–China trade, carrying opium for Jardine Matheson from Bombay to Canton and a variety of cargoes on her return to India. In early November 1847, having unloaded her opium at Whampoa, she received a somewhat unusual cargo in Hong Kong – 92 convicts bound for banishment in Bombay and, as men took much space but weighed little, a load of stone ballast. On Wednesday 10 November the ship left Hong Kong under the command of Captain William Stokoe with a crew of three European officers, a clutch of sepoys, and perhaps 90 sailors, mostly Indian lascars but with a handful of Chinese, and after an uneventful voyage reached Singapore on the 23rd .

There she remained for almost six weeks awaiting a nicely profitable cargo, sugar. The stone ballast was unloaded and the partitions on the prisoners' deck removed. As they could not be accommodated ashore the convicts were kept on board, now more crowded than ever and in sweltering heat. One prisoner died and two Chinese convicted in Singapore were added, bringing the total to 93. At last, on the first day of the new year with all the sugar safely stowed, four passengers embarked bound for Bombay: Mr Andrew Farquhar, Lieutenant William Seymour of the Bombay Cavalry, his wife and her amah. Sunday 2 January 1848 dawned fair and at first light the *General Wood* sailed, bound for Penang and Bombay. But as the day advanced both tide and wind turned against her so Captain Stokoe decided to spend the night at anchor off the Carimon Islands, beating up the Straits of Malacca the next day. After a fine dinner hosted by the Captain the Europeans, officers and passengers, turned in at about 9 pm. Forward of their cabins most of the prisoners lay crowded together, a chain passed through their leg-irons; but 14 were unchained, either sick or acting as cooks, and none were handcuffed. Indeed there were only 53 pairs of handcuffs on board but the prisoners had been so well-behaved that Stokoe had needed to use only seven pairs. A single sepoy stood guard, holding the key to the leg-chain.

At about 1 am on the 3rd the passengers were awakened by a great commotion. No sooner had Seymour and his wife scrambled out of bed than the Captain rushed in from his cabin adjoining followed by Farquhar. The Captain seemed quite out of his mind and Seymour despite repeated questioning could get no sense from him. Instead he rushed up and down the cabin, sometimes firing his pistols randomly at the door, exclaiming in anguish, "Oh blessed Jesus save us! Oh merciful father, what have I done that this should happen!"

What indeed the Captain had done was to post a totally inadequate guard on what were, unsurprisingly, desperate men, men being taken from their homeland to they knew not where nor for how long a time. Sometime after midnight one of the unchained prisoners had killed the guard, removed his keys and unfastened the leg-chain. Those free had immediately moved to a box of arms kept unguarded on deck while others broke off their shackles. The men were not leaderless: over the weeks on board a group of about 16 had taken command, and now set about ordering the capture of the ship. Seizing pieces of timber as weapons the men were told first to find and kill the European officers. This they quickly accomplished, the last of the four to die being the captain who leapt overboard in the darkness and was seen no more. With his wife and amah beside him, Seymour decided to stay in his cabin in the hope, which proved correct, that the convicts would not harm the passengers. Crouching there, they listened as at least five people were beaten to death over their heads and their bodies thrown overboard. Perhaps 40 of the crew were thus killed.

As dawn broke on the 3rd the prisoners' leaders tried to restore some order. Then the ship's head was turned eastwards and slowly she made her way back whence she'd come, giving Singapore a wide berth before turning north. The four passengers were not ill-treated, but on the third day the Seymour's amah, maddened by worry, suddenly rushed to the rail, leapt overboard and could not be saved. And so they continued northwards, stopping frequently at various islands to gather provisions and fresh water. But on the morning of Saturday 21st the *General Wood* grounded on a reef about 9 miles from Pulau Laut, a small island to the north of Great Natuna and, severely holed, rapidly began to settle. The boats were launched but being only three in number were unable to take everyone on board and so, leaving 15 convicts and 16 crew members for a second passage, the boats pulled for the island. But when no more than half way to shore they saw the *General Wood* slowly slip off the reef and go down by the bows.

As the three boats pulled in to Pulau Laut one was badly damaged but all managed to get ashore, perhaps over 70 convicts and 40 crew and passengers. The Chinese wished to immediately move on northwards, towards home, but with only two serviceable boats not all could be accommodated so when they sailed 16 of their number were left behind. Now of course the remaining convicts were greatly outnumbered by the crew and soon, with the help of the four families of fishermen on the island, all 16 were caught and bound, together with three of the Chinese crew who had helped their fellow countrymen. The fishermen proved remarkably hospitable to this sudden invasion but, overwhelmed by the numbers, all the newcomers were ferried on the 24th to a larger island nearby. And there they remained for three weeks while arrangements were made to take them back to Singapore. It was at this time that news of the fate of the *General Wood* first filtered to Singapore, so when on the morning of the 20th February the boat carrying the survivors, including Lieutenant and Mrs Seymour, Andrew Farquhar and 19 Chinese prisoners, reached Singapore it was met with enormous interest.

On 5 April the barque *Celerity* from Siam anchored in Singapore with rumours that boatloads of Chinese had landed on an island off Cambodia a month or two before. Believing that these might be convicts from the *General Wood*, Governor Butterworth ordered Captain Niblett to immediately take the *Phlegethon* to investigate. After rapid coaling and provisioning the ship sailed on the morning of the 8th, reaching the island, Pulau Ubi (possibly the island now called Con Son), on the 11th. At 2.30 am that night two well-armed boat parties landed and found in a hut there items taken from the *General Wood*. Within two weeks, 29 convicts had been captured and one killed. Although about an equal number of convicts remained unaccounted for, on 5 May, with fuel and provisions running low and four officers and 24 crew suffering from fever, the *Phlegethon* turned for home, finally reaching Singapore again on Monday 8 May under tow from the paddle steamer HMS *Fury*, 1,124 tons, whom she had met en route. On that journey two convicts were lost. One tried to hang himself, dying later in Singapore, and another leapt overboard only to be pulped by a paddle wheel. A third more sensibly leapt overboard aft of the wheels, but then was saved, although this was of little benefit for Loh Ah Mung was one of those hanged three weeks later outside Singapore jail.

Two trials were held. The 19 brought from the Natunas were tried on 26 to 28 April, the jury finding all guilty of mutiny but, to the judge's amazement, not guilty of violence. So although he condemned five to death he had to commute this to transportation for life, the others being transported for upwards of eight years. The reason why the jury acted somewhat leniently appears to be because there was a strong feeling in Singapore that the mutiny was in part the fault of the authorities; if convicts from China or anywhere else were to be transported, and this itself seemed undesirable, then they should not be transported on private ships, particularly those carrying passengers, and they should be provided with an adequate armed guard at government expense. At the second trial, on 18 and 19 May, these concerns had apparently been adequately demonstrated for here the jury convicted all 27 convicts of both mutiny and violence, and four were condemned to death, one being reprieved before the dawn of Friday 26th.

Although the newspapers received a number of complaints about the leniency of the sentences, only three to die for so many deaths, the European community clearly felt that they had responded honourably to the outrage. And when the day following the trial HMS *Maeander* (46 guns) sailed into harbour they put their cares behind them in a considerable celebration, for the ship was captained by that favourite son of Singapore, Captain Henry Keppel, and carried from England the now famous Rajah of Sarawak.

Almost a year before, on 20 June 1847, James Brooke and his assistant Hugh Low had bid a lengthy and colourful farewell to Sarawak, embarking on the *Nemesis* for Singapore on the first leg of their journey to England.[2] Reaching Singapore on the 23rd, 12 days later they boarded the P & O steamer *Pekin* bound from Hong Kong to Galle in Ceylon, where, after a month's wait, they changed to the *Hindostan* for Suez and thence overland to Alexandria and so on to England by 1 October. Back in Singapore the *Nemesis* was still present when, on 7 July, a brand new P & O liner anchored in the roads, now joining the *Pekin* on the Galle – Hong Kong run. The *Sir Henry Pottinger* had been launched in March 1846 at Fairbairns' yard on the Thames, the same yard that had launched the *Pluto* and *Proserpine* for the Secret Committee less than seven years before.[3] Now the largest iron steamer known apart from the *Great Britain*, she measured 206 ft from stem to stern (240 ft overall) and 1,405 tons, with eight watertight iron bulkheads and oscillating engines of 450 hp powering her paddle wheels. With four decks, two running the entire length, she could carry up to 130 passengers in considerable comfort, a remarkable contrast to the *Lady Mary Wood* of just two years before.

James Brooke's first visit home since he left there, unknown, on the *Royalist* almost nine years before was a triumph. His friend Henry Keppel's book published the year before, called *The Expedition to Borneo of HMS Dido* but in reality very largely about Brooke's deeds in Sarawak, had made him a household name amongst the ruling classes, a true Victorian hero. And Keppel, well connected, was determined that his friend should be properly fêted by Society, knowing he would relish every minute of it. Within a month he had been invited to spend a night at Windsor Castle with the Royal Family, had met Prime Minister Lord John Russell at Downing Street, dined with Lord Palmerston the Foreign Secretary, been honoured at a large dinner at the United Services Club, been granted the Freedom of the City of London and dined with the Lord Mayor, and been given an honorary degree by Oxford University and honorary memberships of various clubs. There followed visits for hunting and shooting to some of the great houses of England – to Bowood, to Woburn and to Holkham, and sittings for Frank Grant, the foremost portrait-painter of his day, later Sir Francis Grant PRA.[4] That magnificent portrait, now in the National Portrait Gallery, London, epitomises the early Victorians' vision of Empire: the heroic, handsome Englishman carrying to dark and distant lands the torch of civilisation.

For some years Brooke had been seeking to rationalise to the British Government his position in Sarawak, a British citizen owing feudatory duties to a foreign ruler, the Sultan of Brunei. So he was delighted to learn in October that Palmerston had added to his official title that of 'Governor of Labuan', instructing him in that role "to afford to British commerce the support and protection needed … in consequence of the prevalency of pirates."[5] Not the least of his pleasures must have been to learn that his salary was to be quadrupled to the handsome sum of £2,000 per year. Now that Brooke held official appointments, Lord Auckland, First Lord of the Admiralty, was persuaded to send him back east on a naval ship, and instructed Keppel to prepare HMS *Maeander* for the voyage.

The *Maeander* left Portsmouth on 1 February 1848 commanded by Keppel and carrying Brooke and Low.[6] Also on board in specially constructed cabins was the new Lieutenant-Governor of Labuan, William Napier, usually resident in Singapore, with his wife and teenage daughter Kitty (he had handed over editorship of the *Singapore Free Press* to his friend Abraham Logan in 1846 before leaving for England). After a slow and stormy start the ship called at Rio and then passed south of the Cape and on to the Sunda Straits, reaching Singapore on Saturday 20 May. Over the next few weeks preparations were made for the new settlement on Labuan: staff appointed, buildings prefabricated, supplies bought. Amongst these arrangements was the construction of a little steam tender, nominally for the *Maeander* but really for Sarawak, the first steamer built in Singapore. The *Ranee*, designed by the *Maeander's* carpenter Mr Bulbeck, was built of teak at Messrs Wilkinson, Tivendale & Company, one of two shipyards on the left bank by the mouth of the Singapore River. Long and narrow, 61 ft by 8.5 ft, she was powered by a single engine of only 4 hp which proved much too small.[7]

In August of the previous year the *Phlegethon* had joined the *Nemesis* in Singapore for three months before the latter was recalled to Calcutta. So it was the *Phlegethon* that on 9 June 1848 embarked the pioneer settlers for Labuan, Lieutenant James Hoskens RN as Harbour Master and Mr John Scott, an engineer, as Surveyor General, later the second Governor (1850–56). The arrival of the *Phlegethon* at the island relieved the Indian Navy's steamer *Auckland* (964 tons), which returned to Singapore to pick up further people and supplies for the new settlement.[8] Later the *Phlegethon* passed on to China, reaching Hong Kong from Manila on 25 November, there to replace the *Pluto* which, after three years strenuous work, including an accident in 1846 in which she was very nearly lost, was in urgent need of a thorough overhaul.

In January that year the *Straits Times* in Singapore had announced that Brooke was to receive a knighthood, so the community were somewhat surprised when he returned in May still a mere Mister rather than 'Sir James'. But on 7 August news arrived confirming the award of the KCB, and a grand investiture was held on Tuesday 22nd in which Lieutenant-Governor Napier of Labuan officiated – Governor Butterworth of the Straits Settlements being a servant of the Company and not of the Crown was ineligible for this honour. This proved to be the most elaborate ceremony yet staged by Europeans in Singapore, the 240 guests dancing until dawn, but unfortunately, due to some oversight, the editor of the *Straits Times*, Mr Robert Woods, was not invited, an unintended insult which had rather unpleasant consequences.

A week later Sir James embarked again on the *Maeander* with various of his followers, including Hugh Low as Colonial Secretary now married to the youthful Kitty Napier, and sailed for Kuching. There the Rajah was welcomed home in great style, the river crowded with boats, the shore with people, to Keppel yet further confirmation of the genuine love and respect felt by the people of Sarawak for his dear friend.[9] But the Rajah was disturbed to hear that this respect still did not pertain to the Dayaks of the Saribas and Skrang rivers, whose fleets continued to raid coastal communities for plunder, slaves and heads, the most recent being up the Sadong River, just a few miles east of Kuching. But dealing with these would have to wait: it was Labuan now which demanded attention. On

13 September the *Auckland* returned from Singapore with Napier and the Rajah's nephew and heir-apparent, Captain Brooke Brooke,[a] and ten days later the *Maeander* set out for Labuan with the Rajah and his party, landing them there at 'Victoria' on the 29th, together with a party of marines, Keppel returning to Singapore to collect a company of the 21st Native Infantry as a garrison.

The colony of Labuan had a slow and unhappy start, not through ill preparation but through ill health.[10] Victoria was on low swampy ground which exuded 'mephitic exhalations' and malaria was rife. When the *Maeander* returned in early December virtually every European civilian was ill. As Spenser St John, the new secretary for Labuan, wrote: "The Governor, the Lieutenant Governor, the Doctor, Mr and Mrs Low, Captain Hoskins (sic), Mr Grant, Captain Brooke and the marines were all down with fever at the same time. The only civilians to escape were Mr Scott and myself."[11] Keppel immediately embarked Sir James, who was too weak to walk, and some of the other Europeans and on Monday 4 December set out on a cruise to restore their health. Sailing north-eastwards they rounded the north of Borneo and, with Sir James recovering, decided to visit Sulu, seeking an audience with Sultan Muhammed Fadl, the nominal chief of both the Balinini and the Illanun pirates. This they achieved on 30 December, the British party being cordially welcomed although no formal agreements were made. Sailing on via the Spanish fort and penal settlement at Zamboanga on the western tip of Mindanao, Keppel landed Sir James and his colleagues, much improved in health, back on Labuan on the 28 January 1849. There the *Maeander* found both the *Nemesis* and *Pluto* at anchor. The *Pluto*, returning from China to Calcutta still under the command of Lieutenant George Airey, continued on with the *Maeander* to Singapore. Reaching her home port in late February, she was docked in the same dock recently vacated by the *Nemesis*, and there over the next two years was virtually rebuilt.[12]

---

[a]   James Brooke's favourite sister Emma married the Reverend Charles Johnson. Their two eldest sons, Brooke Johnson (1821–68) and Charles Johnson (1829–1917), both came to Sarawak in the 1840s to work for James, who never married, eventually taking the family name Brooke. Hence Brooke Brooke. Charles Brooke became the second Rajah on the death of his uncle in 1868.

1. John Turnbull Thomson. J. T. Thomson, "Singapore town from the Government Hill looking southeast", 1846, watercolour on paper. (Hocken Collections, Uare Toaka O Hakena, University of Otago)

C1

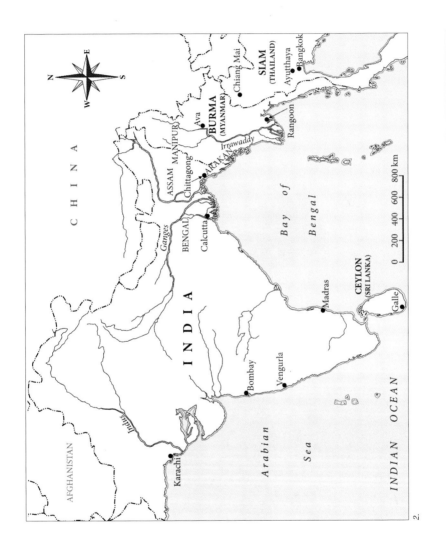

2. *Map: India and the Bay of Bengal (produced by Lee Li Kheng)*

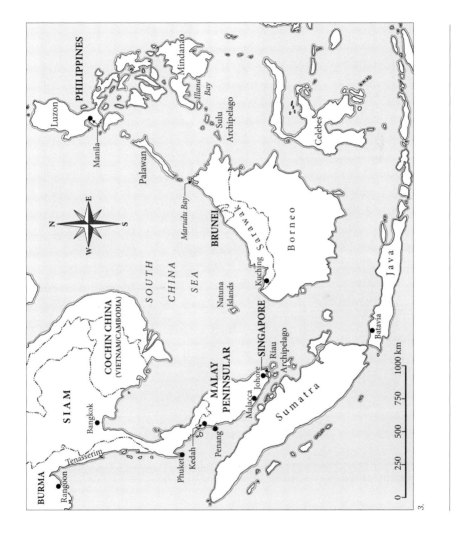

3. *Map: The South China Sea: Sumatra to the Philippines (produced by Lee Li Kheng).*

4.

4. *Captain William Hutcheon Hall, CB, FRS, about 1860, shown holding the sword presented to him by the crew of the Nemesis in February 1843 (© National Maritime Museum, Greenwich, London)*

5. *'James Brooke, Rajah of Sarawak, 1847' (reprinted from* Illustrated London News, *9 October 1847)*

6. *Admiral of the Fleet Sir Henry Keppel in old age (reprinted from West, 1905)*

5.

A.Debenham Eowes & Ryde Photo   Emery Walker Ph.sc

6.

7.

8.

7. *Hong Kong's Queen's Road 1846 (reprinted from Tam 1980)*

8. *Hong Kong from Kowloon, ca 1850 (reprinted from Allom & Wright, 1859)*

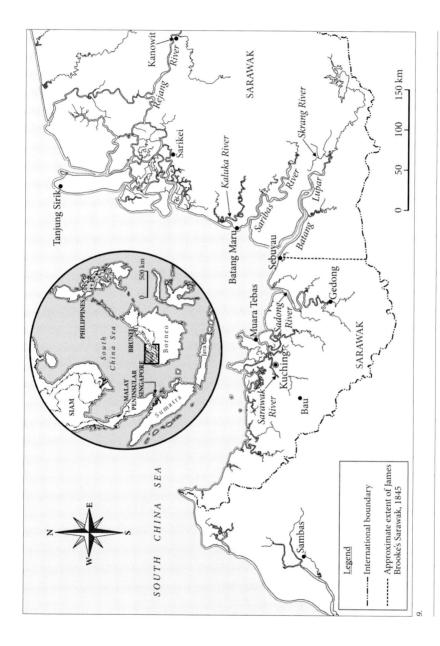

9. *Sarawak, Borneo (produced by Lee Li Kheng)*

The Town, Brunai – 'Vixen' 'Pluto' Nemesis   The Albert Watson 2

10

10. *Vixen, Pluto and Nemesis at anchor in Brunei harbour, 10 August 1845 (© National Maritime Museum, Greenwich, London)*

11.

12.

11. HMS Dido *at Sarawak, 1843 (reprinted from Keppel, 1846)*

12. *The attack on Brunei town, with* Phlegethon *towing HMS* Spiteful *and assorted boats, 8 July 1846 (reprinted from* Illustrated London News, *3 October 1846)*

13.

14.

15.

---

13. *Captain Thomas Wallage, Singapore, April 1850 (from Roff, 1954, reproduced with permission from Sarawak Museum Journal)*

14. Maeander *passing astern of* Hastings *towed by* Fury, *off Labuan 24 November 1848 (reprinted from Keppel, 1899)*

15. *'Sir James Brooke' by Sir Francis Grant (© National Portrait Gallery, London). He was also known as the 'Rajah of Sarawak'.*

16.

16. Phlegethon *at Labuan, August 1848 (reprinted from* Illustrated London News, *9 December 1848)*

17.

17. *The Battle of Batang Maru, 31 July–1 August 1849 (reprinted from* Illustrated London News, *11 November 1849)*

18.

19.

18. *The Chinese pirate Shap-ng-tsai (reprinted from* Illustrated London News, *14 June 1851)*

19. Phlegethon *with* Columbine *and* Fury *attacking pirates in Gulf of Tonkin, 21 October 1849 (© National Maritime Museum, Greenwich, London)*

20.

21.

20. Phlegethon *on the Kanowit river, June 1846 (reprinted from Mundy, 1848)*

21. *Georgetown and Fort Cornwallis from the roads, Penang, 1846 (watercolour by Charles Dyce)*

22.

22. *SS* Himalaya, *iron screw passenger ship, launched 1853 for the P & O. At that time the largest vessel in the world, 3,452 tons, length 340 ft, beam 46 ft. 200 first class passengers and 213 crew. Sold 1854 to the Royal Navy as HMS* Himalaya, *troopship (reprinted from* Illustrated London News, *4 February 1860).*

23. *Map: Burma (produced by Lee Li Kheng)*

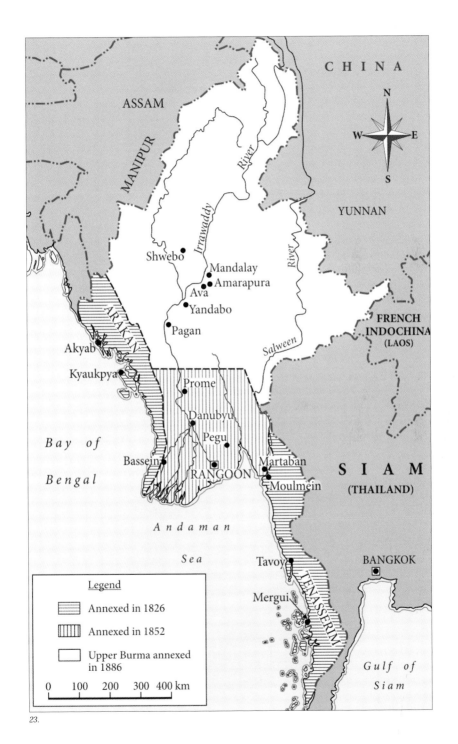

CHINA

ASSAM

MANIPUR

Irrawaddy River

River

N
W E
S

YUNNAN

Shwebo
Mandalay
Ava Amarapura
Yandabo
Pagan

Salween River

FRENCH
INDOCHINA
(LAOS)

ARAKAN

Akyab

Kyaukpya

Prome

Bay of
Bengal

Danubyu
Pegu
Basseins
RANGOON
Martaban
Moulmein

SIAM
(THAILAND)

Andaman

Sea

Tavoy

BANGKOK

TENASSERIM

Mergui

Gulf of
Siam

Legend

Annexed in 1826

Annexed in 1852

Upper Burma annexed
in 1886

0   100   200   300 400 km

23.

24.

C20

25a.

25b.

24. Phlegethon *at the attack on Rangoon, 11 April 1852 (reprinted from Laurie, 1853)*

25. *British ships at Rangoon, April 1852 (reprinted from* Illustrated London News, *26 June 1852)*

26.

26. *The* Great Britain *in her final resting place in Bristol, England (reproduced with permission from the SS Great Britain Trust, Dronex Images)*

{ 24 }

IN SPLENDID ORDER AGAIN

We hear that the little *Nemesis* is in splendid order again, and has been fitted out in a manner that reflects the highest credit upon the officers of the Honourable Company's Dockyard in Kidderpore.

—Bengal Hurkaru, 10 December 1848

After further duties between Singapore and Labuan the *Nemesis* was recalled to Calcutta in October 1847, reaching her home port on 3 November after an absence of two and a half years in China and the Straits. Now she required "a thorough repair of hull and machinery and new boilers", her first overall refit since her launch eight years before, a process destined to take a full 12 months.[1] Thomas Wallage was soon transferred to the steamer *Fire Queen* (371 tons), which he captained for some months in Burmese waters. John Russell had still not recovered from his nervous complaint so at the end of his one year leave of absence he was sent to replace B. S. Ross as Harbour Master at Singapore, Ross returning to take command of the *Nemesis* – but then he was promoted Naval Store Keeper at Calcutta. So as the refit drew to a close Wallage was finally appointed to full command, the Bengal Marine's equivalent of promotion to Post-Captain. As the *Bengal Hurkaru* remarked "A better officer and a braver man could not easily be selected".[2] His salary was now £50 a month as the *Nemesis* was rated First Class, Niblett on the Second Class *Phlegethon* drawing £40 and Congalton on the Third Class *Diana* £35.

The refit of the *Nemesis* was fundamental. Strong diagonal trussing was added throughout the whole length of her engine and boiler rooms to strengthen her amidships, her foremost sliding keel was removed as it made her steer badly, her engines thoroughly overhauled and new boilers provided, made locally at the Government Steam Factory. And many other modifications had also been made as the *Hurkaru* announced on 11 December.[3]

> We find that the H. C. steamer *Nemesis* leaves this morning with a European crew and a suitable armament, to take the place of the *Phlegethon* at Labuan, to assist in the operations for the suppression of Borneo piracy. The *Nemesis* will be towed down by the *Tenasserim*, being the first instance we have heard here of one steam vessel towing another.[a]
>
> The following interesting particulars of the manner in which the *Nemesis* has been fitted out for the expedition, we have taken from a demi-official paragraph which appeared in yesterday's *Hurkaru*: 'We hear that the little *Nemesis* is in splendid order again, and has been fitted out in a manner that reflects the highest credit upon the officers of the Honourable Company's Dockyard in Kidderpore. On deck the vessel exhibits all the means and appliances of a man-of-war efficient at every point. She has two large guns, one forward and one aft, and four small broadside guns. She has been fitted with Captain Smith's paddle-box boats, each capable of containing forty men, besides two large boats, and one hoisted up at the stern; and she has a European crew of fine young fellows, selected out of about two hundred who offered for the service. The accommodations of the commander and of the officers are so handsomely fitted up that they give the steamer quite the appearance of a yacht. The pillars in the commander's sleeping and dining cabins are elegantly carved, and these cabins throughout are most tastefully painted, the cornices are gilded, and there are silk curtains which draw out and screen off the couches of the sides; the deck of the cabins is covered with oil-cloth, &c. Captain Wallage, who naturally takes a pride in the vessel in which he has distinguished himself, has gone to considerable

---

[a] In fact she had been towed down by the *Enterprize* in May 1845.

expense in supplying some of the elegancies which embellish his accommodations.'

And the expenses were indeed considerable – a total of £6,718; but then the Company was being paid a hire charge of £2,994 a year to cover such eventualities.

If it seems surprising that 200 European sailors should be available in Calcutta for service, it is worth recalling the dire conditions then prevailing in much of the British Isles. 'The Hungry Forties' both started and finished with periods of disastrous harvests (1839–42 and 1849–53), culminating in 1845 with the failure of the Irish potato crop and appalling famine in Ireland (then of course part of the United Kingdom). In 1847 the *Singapore Free Press* mentioned in passing: "Ireland still continues in a bad state, 'dead bodies lie unburied by the wayside or cast into shallow pits, and the sound of desolation spreads over the land.'" Furthermore, the Company was thought of as a good employer, better than the merchant service, and it was easy to find merchant seamen wishing "to take the bounty of 50 rupees" to join for the usual period of three years. As a Bombay paper said "Jack willingly submits to a month's imprisonment for leaving his (merchant) ship, if he has only a chance of being 'passed' at the Marine Office."[4]

On the same day as Sir James Brooke's audience with the Sultan of Sulu, 30 December 1848, the *Nemesis* left the Hooghly River below Calcutta for Singapore, Captain Wallage accompanied by his wife Elizabeth and their three young sons, the youngest only six months old, the First Officer now Robert Goodwin, destined later to take command. Arriving at Singapore on the 13 January 1849 she sailed on to Labuan a week later, the *Maeander* finding both the *Nemesis* and *Pluto* anchored in Victoria Bay when she returned there from Sulu with Sir James. On 14 February she left Labuan to take the Rajah back to Kuching, continuing to Singapore.

On 1 March raiding into Sarawak territory began again.[5] That night a fleet of bangkong manned by both Dayaks and Malays rowed far up the Sadong River, almost to Gedong, seeking plunder, slaves and heads, about a hundred people along the river banks being killed or captured. The Rajah realised that some immediate response was necessary, and when the *Nemesis* returned on 20 March he gathered together a force of 'friendlies' at Kuching and on the 24th sailed for the Batang Lupar.

By the time they reached the estuary many other 'friendlies' had joined them, excited by such excursions, so that the fleet now numbered almost 100 boats and 3,000 men. Leaving the steamer with Wallage to guard the entrance to the Saribas River, over the next few days Brooke led the boats, including four from the *Nemesis*, up all the navigable rivers between Kuching and the Saribas, destroying any fortifications encountered but meeting no significant resistance. Now it became clear to him that if he wanted to put an end to pirate fleets he would need to attack the fleets themselves; to attack their villages merely allowed them to disassembled their boats and hide them, ready to be rebuilt for the next raid. In February the *Maeander* had left Singapore for China with Keppel already aware that his friend expected further trouble, and so when he arrived at Hong Kong he informed Admiral Sir Francis Collier, the new Commander-in-Chief, about the problem and Collier agreed to send HMS *Albatross* (16 guns) under Captain Arthur Farquhar to Borneo.

On 21 April the *Nemesis* left Kuching for Singapore carrying the Reverend Francis McDougall (1817–86) on his first visit there since arriving in Kuching the previous year, his task to arrange the necessary supplies for his new mission in Sarawak. Returning to his family on the 24th, Wallage found his third son, 10-month old Frederick, gravely ill. The boy died on the 28th and was buried that same day by McDougall.[6]

In 1846 Keppel and other friends of Brooke had formed the Borneo Church Mission Institute in London to appoint and then support a priest to serve the Church of England in Borneo.[7] On 22 November 1847 Frank McDougall was introduced to a packed meeting of the Institute in the presence of the Rajah, over a thousand people attending, mostly women. A month later he and his wife Harriette (1818–86) embarked on the *Mary Louisa* (333 tons) for Borneo via the Cape, leaving their eldest son at school but taking their second son, one-year-old Harry, with them. Arriving in Singapore on Tuesday 23 May 1848, just three days after the *Maeander* which had made a much quicker passage, the McDougalls spent a month there before sailing on to Kuching. A busy year lay ahead: founding a church, St Thomas', building a house, starting a school – and celebrating the birth and then mourning the death of their third son that November. Some years later Harriette would write "1853 was the first year since we came to Sarawak that we had not lost a little one... The flowers all died along the way."[8] It was that year in June that their seventh child and first daughter, Mab, was born, the first to reach adulthood, a sad reminder of the perils faced by colonial families in the east.

The McDougalls were a remarkable and devoted couple. Frank, both a qualified surgeon and priest and later first Bishop of Sarawak, has been described as "a rollicking mixture of Bishop, Surgeon and Sea-captain – a man of a good deal of shrewdness and observation." Very energetic, an excellent seaman and horseman, his hearty manner and loud voice did not always go down well in the tiny European community of Sarawak. Impulsive and patriotic, an enthusiastic 'High Church' Anglican, he proved better at command than leadership, tending to insult his young missionaries to their faces – "muffs and fools and donkeys" – admitting that he found it "difficult to keep my tongue behind my teeth". Harriette, 'Harrie', was in contrast both calm and patient but, typical of a new generation of English women arriving at that time in far-flung parts of the empire, she was both earnest and censorious, suffering no fool gladly. Conservative by nature, she enthusiastically embraced her role as the only European lady in Kuching, educating children, teaching cooking and sewing, caring for the sick, and entertaining often – "The Rajah's and our's are the only public houses and it entails no small cost in this most expensive of places." But she would never accept Asians of any class as social equals, and was appalled at liaisons between the Rajah's British staff and local women which unsurprisingly were not uncommon.

The *Nemesis* carried McDougall back to Kuching on the 12 May 1849 where Wallage entertained his family on board, young Harry McDougall playing happily with the large bulldog, Pompey, belonging to Dr Miller, the ship's surgeon, while the company was regaled by the ship's Scottish piper.[9] The Rajah, waiting impatiently throughout April for a suitable naval vessel, was delighted in mid-May to welcome Captain Farquhar and the *Albatross* to Kuching, but as all seemed quiet on his eastern front he decided to now use the steamer to again visit Sulu, hoping this time to get the Sultan not just to mouth pleasantries but to actually sign a document to which he could be held. Steaming first to Labuan they left that island for Sulu on 23 May, celebrating Queen Victoria's 30th birthday the next day at sea. Back in Kuching these celebrations were marred by a nasty accident: a seaman on the *Albatross* was seriously injured when a cartridge exploded while loading a gun for the birthday salute. McDougall, assisted by Dr Treacher, the Colonial Surgeon for Labuan who was on his way to Singapore, successfully amputated both arms using the new anaesthetic chloroform.[10] Prior to the advent of ether in 1846 and chloroform the following year, all that a wounded man under the knife could hope for was laudanum and copious alcohol – and great fortitude.

On 28 May Brooke paid his second visit to the Sultan of Sulu, this time accompanied by three members of his staff, Charles Grant his private secretary, Spenser St John and Mr Ruppel of the Labuan secretariat, and Captain Wallage and officers of the *Nemesis*, all dressed in their finest and escorted by a marine guard-of-honour, and led, it would be nice to think, by the Scottish piper.[11] The Sultan's palace was an impressive place, well fortified, the walls 15 ft high with numerous embrasures for cannon, the guns themselves however apparently old and rusty. The British party crossed a compound crowded with men, all colourfully dressed, each one of course wearing his kris, and entered the meeting hall up a broad flight of steps. Here, behind a long table covered in a green cloth ranged a brilliant semicircle of courtiers, the Sultan in the centre on a raised seat. Evidently pleased to see the Rajah again he came forward, shook hands with each visitor and conducted them to a row of chairs. There followed a pause of a few minutes for mutual admiration. The Sultan himself appeared quite young, beautifully dressed in red and green silk and well bejewelled, and, continually chewing betel, closely accompanied by a handsome cup-bearer carrying a finger-glass into which His Highness frequently spat. To his side stood guards in ancient chain-armour from throat to knee, each armed with sword, spear and kris except for two who carried old Tower muskets. In all, a sight well set to impress his visitors.

The Rajah then addressed the Sultan and his court in his excellent Malay, a language other than their own but which they could understand. Telling them of his pleasure at his last visit and his purpose in returning, he delivered two copies of the proposed treaty and asked them to examine it to see if it met with their approval. The British party then returned to the *Nemesis* and awaited developments. Hearing the next day that the Sultan was happy to sign, the Rajah returned to the palace without ceremony at 7 that evening, and after a friendly conversation over coffee, chocolate and sweetmeats, the treaty was duly signed, one copy for the Sultan, one for the Rajah, the party not breaking up until after 2 the next morning.

On the 30th the *Nemesis* steamed on to Basilan, the largest of the Sulu islands and then to Zamboanga to pay a courtesy visit to the

Spanish Governor, Don Cayetano de Figueroa. Although well received and hospitably entertained, it was clear that the Governor was less than happy with one of the treaty's clauses, that requiring the Sultan not to alienate any territory without the consent of Her Britannic Majesty. But Brooke was unpersuaded, believing that previous treaties between Spain and Sulu, in 1737 and 1836, in no way compromised the independence of the Sultan.

Amongst Sir James' many strengths was not that of the patience necessary for diplomacy. This weakness undid him a year later when he visited a much more sophisticated court, that of the King of Siam. But in Sulu, with a local sultan before him, he was in his element, his personal charm, his excellent Malay and the support of a modern warship placing him in a position not requiring patience. Thus the *Singapore Free Press* could later report: "We learn that Sir James Brooke was completely successful in accomplishing the object of his visit. He found the Chiefs of Sulu eager to renew and strengthen those friendly relations which subsisted between Sulu and the English in former times." But the British government had no desire to return to 'former times'; just as it suited them to let the Dutch hold sway in the Netherlands Indies so they were happy to let Spain control the Philippines. So Brooke's treaty was never ratified.

The *Nemesis* reached Labuan on 10 June, Sir James spending 12 days there as governor before returning to Kuching. On the 17th the following appeared in the *Singapore Free Press*: "Sarawak. The Sakarrans are again reported to be on the alert for fresh victims, but Captain Kepple who is soon expected in Borneo, will we trust, in conjunction with the *Albatross*, speedily commence reducing these pests to the peace of Borneo to order. We are not of those who imagine that this much to be wished for consummation will be affected in a day, or even months. A stringent and vigorous policy must be pursued. The numerical strength of these powerful hordes has gone on increasing – the absence of those who had previously inflicted such deserved punishment has emboldened them, combined with their late successes, to assume a position even more formidable than that of former times." Arriving back at Kuching on the 24th, Brooke found the *Albatross* already anchored there. With further rumours of a fleet being prepared for sea up the Saribas and Skrang rivers, he realized that the time had at last come to pursue just such 'a stringent and vigorous policy'.

{ 25 }

THE BATTLE OF BATANG MARU

As the sun rose the scene on the river at Kuching was the liveliest imaginable. The water was crowded with boats of every description, the *Albatross* towering over large bangkong and tiny dugouts, naval cutters and Malay prahus. On the right bank the bazaar was packed, Malays and Dayaks streaming between the Chinese shops and the shore carrying all manner of goods. Opposite, the lawns of the Rajah's house were also alive with men, some still hardly awake for the partying had gone on long into the night. Now they were dressing in their finest, the Dayaks wrapping their chalwats about them, the Malays their sarongs, adjusting head-dresses to jaunty angles, examining swords and krisses.[1]

Downstream lay HMS *Royalist* (8 guns) and the *Nemesis*, both at anchor. By mid-morning a string of eight boats had been attached to the steamer: three from the *Albatross*, one from the *Royalist*, three from the *Nemesis* herself (the two paddle-box boats and the cutter) and the little steam-tender *Ranee*, left at Kuching by the *Maeander*. By mid morning the *Royalist* had also been tied alongside the *Nemesis*. By now the local boats were in better order, Sir James Brooke on his new prahu, the *Singh Rajah*, with 70 men surrounded by a melee of 17 other boats carrying over 500 warriors, flags and pennants flying, drums and gongs sounding, all accompanied by much shouting and merriment. And so the fleet descended the river, leaving only the *Albatross* behind, Captain Farquhar as senior officer travelling on the steamer.

Throughout the afternoon more boats joined them from Lundu, Sadong and elsewhere, so that when they anchored that evening at the Muara Tebas entrance they numbered over 1,000 men. The date was Tuesday 24 July 1849.

That night was spent in a happy confusion at the river mouth, further boats joining the fleet – 300 men from Lundu, 800 from Lingga – so that by morning there were perhaps 70 local boats with over 2,400 men assembled. The next two days were busy ones for Wallage and his crew, the *Nemesis* first towing the naval boats eastwards to the mouth of the Batang Lupar, then returning for the *Royalist* and by nightfall taking her up that estuary to lie off the Lingga River, then the next morning towing the boats beyond the *Royalist* to the mouth of the Saribas River. That evening the Europeans were fascinated to watch a huge flock of fruit bats, 'flying foxes', flying overhead to their feeding grounds, darkening the sky for nearly half an hour, a propitious omen according to the assembled Dayaks. The following day was quietly spent, but on the 29th news was received that a fleet had indeed set out from the Saribas and Skrang rivers a few days before, heading north. Later it was learned that they had gone first to Sarikei on the Rejang River but had found the town too well defended and so had continued to Matu, capturing two prahus carrying sago and one with cotton goods.

Scout boats were immediately sent north to glean what news they could, while the motley fleet was divided into two divisions to intercept the pirates on their return. Sir James with his nephew Captain Brooke in the *Singh Rajah* with two cutters and a number of prahus sailed north to blockade the mouth of the Kaluka, anchoring concealed from the north by a bend of the river. Between the mouth of the Kaluka and the Saribas lay a sandy flat, its southern-most point called Batang Maru, and off this the *Nemesis* with Farquhar anchored, all the remaining boats stretching from her south-east across the Saribas.

The following two days were spent in great suspense, but at last on the 31st they received the news that they had been waiting for. "At about 7 ½ P.M.," wrote Mr Urban Vigors, "we were engaged in a rubber of whist on board the *Nemesis*, and had almost abandoned all hope of surprising the enemy, when a spy boat returned at best speed, with the long and anxiously-looked-for intelligence that the piratical fleet had rounded Tanjong Siri, and was rapidly approaching our position."[2] The fleet, perhaps 150 boats strong, swept south on a strong flood tide. Seeing the

Kaluka was guarded they continued south towards the Saribas. Brooke, now ill with malaria, sent up a rocket to warn the *Nemesis* lying five miles distant.

The first knowledge of the approaching fleet for those aboard the steamer was the sound of their paddles in the darkness. Then, as the pirates spied the steamer and the other boats lying nearby the sound of gongs was heard, accompanied by defiant yells. But it was not long before those approaching realised the strength of the forces ranged against them. Now the 'friendlies' started firing on the pirates who, in great confusion, were rapidly hemmed in. With Brook's forces well organised, all the men-of-war boats carrying blue lights to distinguish them, the darkness greatly favoured them. The *Nemesis* was "everywhere, and everywhere cutting up the pirates; rockets, shells, shots, musketry flying in all directions," the scene eerily lit by moonlight, the flashes of the guns and the glare of rockets.

> "The moon was now a little more observed, and partial darkness hung over the sea, allowing us to remark in all its beauty the dazzling brilliance of the rockets as they curvetted and bounded over the waves. Heavy cannon were flashing in the distance, and the rapid volleys of muskets appeared to light up the whole scene, which was as novel and exciting as can be imagined. For several hours the conflict was maintained in all its fury... The *Nemesis*, meanwhile, had got up her steam and, advancing straight upon the enemy's fleet, rolled in her broadsides of grape, canister, and round shot from her heavy 32-pounders."[3] "We then pursued five other prahus, and destroyed them in detail, passing round each and pouring in a constant fire of grape and canister, musketry and rifles, until they drifted past us helpless as logs, without a living being on board. That discharge of grape was a fearful sight, as at point-blank range it crashed over the sea, and through the devoted prahus, marking its track with the floating bodies of the dying, shattering prahus, planks, shields, and fragments of all sorts."[4]

Realising they could not escape many of the bangkong, perhaps 80, were run ashore and abandoned. Others set out westwards to sea, whilst 17 were run down by the steamer, the boats capsized and many of their crew pulped by the paddle wheels.

The next morning revealed a scene of devastation, great numbers of prahus lying empty on the shore, others abandoned bobbing in the sea amongst a tangle of wreckage and countless bodies. The casualties amongst the British forces were only two killed and six wounded, all local men, but how many 'piratical' Dayaks died in that slaughter cannot be known. Brooke forbade his forces from pursuing those who had escaped ashore, feeling that the punishment already inflicted was enough; later he estimated that perhaps 300 had been killed in the action and 500 died later of their wounds. Captain Farquhar in his report claimed that the fleet contained 3,430 pirates of which 500 had been killed in the course of the action, with 98 boats taken or destroyed. Finally, Sir Christopher Rawlinson, Recorder of the Court of Judicature in Singapore, in his wisdom ruled that 88 boats had been captured or destroyed, 500 men had been killed (at £20 per head) and a further 2,140 had been involved and neither killed nor captured (at £5 per head). Thus he awarded a total of £20,700 to the crews of the *Albatross, Royalist* and *Nemesis*, Farquhar himself earning £2,757, a huge sum (over £150,000 today) for one night's work.[5] Although head money ostensibly went solely to HM ships, in this case the crew of the Company's steamer benefited too. Captain Wallage received £735 3s 9d (over £40,000 today) while the five lowest-rated men each received £18 7s 7d, Wallage acting scrupulously in the division of the spoils.[6] To give an indication of the value of this award for a night's work, Wallage would receive a total of £650 for a year's work and the most junior member of the crew £13.

After conferring with Farquhar, the Rajah decided to push on up the Saribas, aiming to destroy any strongholds found there rather than further pursue fugitive Dayaks. On the 2nd, the *Nemesis* and the heaviest prahus remaining behind, a dense mass of smaller boats together with the *Ranee* started inland, swept up the river on the tide, the men excited, keen on plunder. In the midst of this advance an overhanging tree branch carried away the *Ranee's* funnel and, grounding forward, she was swept sideways across the stream. Now, almost blocking it, she suddenly let off steam, the white cloud and the piercing noise causing consternation to those crowded near, and the confusion was immense.

Finding Paku rebuilt after its destruction in 1843 it was again destroyed, the boats then returning downstream to join the *Nemesis* on the 7th. Then they sailed north for the Rejang, first wooding by the mouth, on the 11th anchored off Sarikei and by the 14th off the Kanowit

River, still accompanied by about 2,000 'friendlies' in a vast array of boats. Brooke then led a flotilla of smaller boats up the Kanowit, for four days destroying houses as they went "to make them feel that they were no longer secure from punishment, even in their remotest retreats."[7] Back on the steamer, they anchored off two huge longhouses, each raised on piles about 40 ft high and containing perhaps 300 families. There Brooke invited the chiefs on board, men whom Brooke knew were involved in piracy, telling them he would fine them for their misbehaviour. It says something for his nerve, and indeed for his reputation amongst the Dayaks, that although he was way beyond his jurisdiction they accepted his judgement. The brass cannon and valuable Chinese jars taken were loaded on board the *Nemesis*, later to be sold by auction in Kuching and the proceeds divided amongst the 'friendlies'. Before leaving, Jawi, a young chief, "asked to look over the dreaded fireship that had done such fearful execution on the night of the fight – they had never seen one before. They looked about, and after partaking of brandy and water appeared quite at their ease."[8] The fleet finally reached Kuching again on the 24 August.

Six weeks later on Monday 8 October, far to the north across the South China Sea, the steamer HMS *Fury* (1,124 tons), towing the *Phlegethon* and HMS *Columbine*, left Hong Kong to try to find and defeat a pirate fleet led by the famous Shap-ng-tsai. Sailing west along the coast, they paid courtesy calls on various fishing villages where they were well received, learning on the 12th that the pirates had recently sailed for the Gulf of Tonkin. Entering the channel between the Leizhou Peninsula and Hainan Island on the 13th, they landed at Haikou where the local leader, Wang Hai-quang, fat and 40 and cheerful, offered to accompany them with eight war-junks. Continuing round the northern coast of the Gulf of Tonkin Shap-ng-tsai's fleet was finally engaged on Saturday 20th. By the next day 58 junks had been destroyed, about 1,700 men killed, perhaps a further 1,000 escaping ashore, many to be later killed by the locals. Only six junks escaped with perhaps 400 men, and only 49 prisoners were taken, of which 8 were women and 6 children. For this a total of £42,425 was awarded as head money, over twice that for the Borneo engagement.[9]

The following year, 1850, the government in London asked Parliament for over £100,000 for head money, the majority, over £63,000, for Batang Maru and the action off Cochin-China. The sum caused outrage amongst MPs but was upheld in court. Although a bill for the repeal of the Act of 1825 had been prepared a couple of years before it had never been submitted but this demand spurred MPs to action, and the awarding of head money was finally abolished in 1852.

The battle of Batang Maru was, in terms of Victorian warfare, a minor skirmish, but none the less had a profound effect both upon James Brooke personally and upon the history of Sarawak. Although it was by no means a decisive engagement in the long-running campaign by the British against piracy in the Archipelago, it none the less led to the successful, and peaceful, absorption of many of the Saribas and Skrang people into Brooke's Sarawak. In August 1852 Captain Brooke, the Rajah's nephew, could write to Keppel telling him that he was about to set out to visit the Saribas and Skrang "though the object this time is peace not war ... The whole coast, from having been one incessant scene of bloodshed, is now as safe as the British Channel."[10]

But unfortunately the engagement became caught up in parliamentary politics in London, becoming briefly a *cause célèbre*, arguments raging and enquiries sitting until the end of 1854. The matter is complex and not immediately relevant to this story – and it has been exhaustively covered elsewhere.[11] Suffice it to say that within a couple of months of the fighting the *Straits Times* in Singapore, anti-Brooke almost since its founding in 1845 by Robert Woods, the man unaccountably omitted from the guest list for Sir James' installation as KCB, was saying that the battle was a massacre of the innocent. This was taken up by the London *Daily News* and then by John Hume, MP for Montrose, and Richard Cobden, MP for Manchester, the latter shocked by the fact that at Batang Marau "the loss of life was greater than in the case of the English at Trafalgar, Copenhagen, or Algiers ..." In a debate in Parliament in July 1850 entitled 'The Charges Against Sir James Brooke', Brooke's detractors were defeated 169 to 21, and in a similar motion a year later by 230 to 19. What were these charges? Basically, that the natives were not pirates; that if they were, they were too harshly treated; and that the Royal Navy should not be allowed to support a mere adventurer.

Although Brooke wished to encourage trade between Sarawak and Singapore, his determination not to allow his people to be exploited by Europeans, and indeed not to allow any Europeans in any way to dispute his authority on the north coast of Borneo, won him some enemies in Singapore. And then he had fallen out with the Eastern Archipelago Company, a company aiming to exploit the riches of Borneo which he himself had helped form and which, based on London, had powerful friends there. Certainly the press attacks on him were surprisingly personal and vindictive, perhaps because the adventurer Mr Brooke was now Sir James, 'Governor of Labuan' and 'Consul-General and Commissioner to the Native and Independent Chiefs of the Indian Archipelago', clearly loved in Kuching and lionised in London.

And it was at Brooke that nearly all the venom was directed. That the action had been authorised by the naval Commander-in-Chief, Admiral Collier, and had involved Captains Farquhar and Wallage, and indirectly Henry Keppel, was hardly mentioned. That Brooke received in November 1849 an address in his support signed by 22 people in Singapore, representatives of all but three of the merchant firms established there, was ignored. That Sir Christopher Rawlinson, Recorder of the Court of Judicature of the Straits Settlements, heard credible evidence in September from Dayaks captured that July night that they were indeed engaged in activities he deemed piratical, was apparently irrelevant. Nor was mention made of the action in the Gulf of Tonkin, clearly a much more ruthless engagement than Batang Maru but of course nothing whatsoever to do with the Rajah of Sarawak. Certainly those who actually knew James Brooke were, almost to a man, incensed by the charges against him; however, even if false, the attacks both weakened him personally, for he took them much to heart, and diminished his position in Sarawak amongst certain groups opposed to his rule.

Henry Keppel was particularly vehement in his support of his friend the Rajah, spending about a fifth of his 580-page book on the voyage of the *Maeander* in a comprehensive refutation of Hume's charges. Of course, he felt the charges personally too and could echo Brooke's anger at attacks "made on my reputation as a public man, and my character as a private one." After all, it was his *Dido* that had first helped Brooke against the Saribas and Skrang, and in his first book, on the *Dido*'s voyage, he had related these actions in detail, an account which had met with the approval of the British and Indian Governments, of the Royal Navy, and of the British press.[12]

Although in 1852 Lord Palmerston, the Foreign Secretary, announced that "Sir James Brooke retires from this investigation with an untarnished character, and with unblemished honour", the controversy refused to die. With a change of government, the new Prime Minister, the Earl of Aberdeen, seeking to pacify Hume and his allies asked the Governor-General in India, Lord Dalhousie, to institute a Commission of Enquiry in Singapore. This was held between September and November 1854 and entirely exonerated the Rajah.

The last word can reasonably be left to a comment that December in the *Straits Times'* rival newspaper, the *Singapore Free Press*, whose editor, Mr Aitken, had in fact acted as the Rajah's legal advisor at the enquiry:

> Sir James Brooke, after clearing the seas around Sarawak of pirates was suddenly assailed by accusations of having butchered unoffending natives. The Aborigines Society took up the cause of the Dyaks. The unscrupulous malignity of a dismissed agent was aided by the mistaken philanthropy of hundreds, and the incessant invective of a newspaper. The Rajah was supported by the House of Commons, and the House twice acquitted him. But the tide turned with a new government, the coalition ministry eagerly supporting the Rajah's opponents. But the Commission found on their arrival in Singapore that their task was an absurdity. Not only were there no grounds for the charges, but there were no charges at all. Thus the Rajah found a strong defence in a Dutch Resident, who alike by instinct and policy was hostile to him, whereas a knot of individuals at Singapore have chosen to run down one of the most successful of British pioneers. They have accepted every calumny, rejected every reply, taken advantage of misguided people, and at last when the enquiry was ordered, have shrunk from substantiating even a single charge. We leave them to the contempt they have so assiduously earned.

{ 26 }

A MISSION TO SIAM

Siam, now Thailand, is notable amongst Southeast Asian nations for never having experienced colonial rule, in good part because in the nineteenth century its kings and their officials were wise enough both to understand the threats they faced and to learn from those who threatened them; but also because the rival colonial powers, the British in Burma and Malaya and the French in Indo-China, viewed Siam as a buffer state.[1]

Eighteenth-century Siam was in many ways a typical 'mandala' state, a powerful dynasty centred on a fertile valley surrounded by lands where their control might be slight but where they expected their interests to prevail. Thus on their southern border they were not pleased when the Sultan of Kedah ceded Penang to the British in 1786 and Province Wellesley in 1800; suspicious of all European interest in the region they had placed every possible restriction on trade. The Government of India, under pressure from merchants, sent letters and presents to Bangkok in 1818 and 1819 but to no avail and so in 1821 dispatched an official envoy, John Crawfurd, to Siam but again with little benefit.[2]

In July 1824, soon after the start of the First Anglo-Burmese war, the Siamese king Rama II died. Prince Maha Mongkut, his eldest son by a royal mother, was expected to succeed him, a man who later proved to be one of the most remarkable of Siamese monarchs. But Mongkut was a monk at the time of his father's death, and a strong party at court placed his brother on the throne as Rama III (r. 1824–51). The defeat of the Burmese by the British in 1826 with the consequent annexation of Arakan and particularly Tenasserim bordering Siam, put fresh impetus into the desire of British merchants to obtain favourable conditions for trade with the Siamese. But the British India government strongly desired good relations with Siam and thus in 1826 Captain Henry Burney was sent to Bangkok on a friendly mission with orders to obtain a treaty that would regulate relations between Siam and the Company. The Siamese, learning from the fate of the Burmese, were by then eager for some regulation of trade, not least because the Court received its taxes in kind and these goods needed to be sold on. After some difficulty in persuading the Siamese that what was done on behalf of the Governor-General of India was done on behalf of the British King and his government, Burney successfully concluded a treaty that, firstly, defined spheres of influence – the British recognising Siamese rights in the Malay sultanates of Kedah, Kelantan and Trengganu and the Siamese British rights in Penang – and, secondly, put trade on a much firmer basis. But as time passed the main problem with this trade became all too apparent; although the British were eager for Siamese exports – teak, sugar, rice – the small population of Siam, probably about 5 to 6 million and mostly poor, meant that it could absorb few British imports: "white and grey shirtings, maddapolems, etc., figured shirtings, cambrics, jaconets, lappets, fancy muslins, gold and printed long-cloths, chintzes, Turkey red twist, light woollen cloths, metals generally, hardware, muskets, earthenware, &c. and numerous other articles of small importance."[3]

With the defeat of China in 1842 and the subsequent growth of Hong Kong and development of Singapore, British merchants were eager to further expand their markets. Considering Siam they readily found fault with Siamese adherence to the Burney treaty, complaining about the sugar monopoly and other perceived injustices, and sought its renegotiation. As the *Daily News* reported: "The commercial regulations of the Siamese government are illiberal as becomes barbarians," the *Straits Times* commenting, "The Siamese ... are, at one and the same time, timid, jealous, unwarlike, and arrogant." But both Governor Butterworth of the Straits Settlements and the Court of Directors considered it best to leave well alone.

In October 1848 the Singapore Chamber of Commerce approached the Foreign Secretary, Lord Palmerston, concerning trade with Siam. Palmerston, eager to thwart any French ambitions in the region, was willing to consider some approach. Although the India Board remained unenthusiastic, they accepted Palmerston's suggestion of an informal Naval mission rather than a formal embassy, and Palmerston instructed the Admiralty and the government in India accordingly.

In February 1850 Lord Dalhousie (1812–60), the Governor-General, made the briefest of visits to Singapore, landing from the Company's largest steamer *Ferooz* (1,447 tons) on the morning of Monday 18th and leaving two days later. On the 19th when replying to an address from the Chamber of Commerce he announced, to their pleasure, the appointment of Sir James Brooke as the British Plenipotentiary to go to Siam to seek a new commercial treaty.[4] Brooke himself was not present and word of his appointment was sent to him in Sarawak, together with a letter from Palmerston which clearly expressed his limited expectations: "It is very important that if your efforts should not succeed, they should at least leave things as they are …" And Brooke himself, writing to his friend John Templer that June, clearly saw that the mission was one of conciliation. Knowing that the Siamese King was old and ill he wished to "remove apprehensions and obstacles, and pave the way for the future", a future with a new king, Mongkut "an educated man, reads and writes English, and knows something of our literature and science", whom he elsewhere calls "a highly accomplished gentleman, for a semi-barbarian."[5] If the 'barbarian' epithet seems insensitive to modern ears, particularly when applied to such a gifted man, it is worth noting that later Mongkut himself talked of his "half barbarous and half civilised nation".[6]

Towards the end of 1849 Brooke's health had not been good, and he determined to take some time off to recuperate, planning to visit Penang where he had been offered the use of Governor Butterworth's bungalow on Penang Hill. On 3 December the *Nemesis* left Singapore for Labuan and Sarawak where she was stationed for the next couple of months, ferrying Brooke, Hugh Low and others on various excursions to the court at Brunei. On hearing of his mission to Siam, Brooke in late February left Kuching on the *Nemesis* for Singapore which he reached on 2 March. Both his health and the lack of a suitable warship to accompany him, something vital to impress the Siamese with the status of his mission, precluded an immediate start, so he arranged with Butterworth for Captain Wallage to go without him to Bangkok to make arrangements for a formal visit later. Wallage left Singapore for the north on Wednesday 13 March.

After a slow trip up the east coast of the Malay Peninsula the *Nemesis* arrived on 21 March off the mouth of the Chao Phraya River, the Menam Chao Phraya often just called the 'Menam'. Unable to obtain a pilot, Wallage took her, with some difficulty, over the bar at the river mouth and anchored off Paknam, a scruffy settlement by a large island fort some three miles from the sea. The arrival of such a steamship unannounced caused some anxiety amongst the Siamese, and Wallage sent two officers by boat to Bangkok, 35 miles up-river, with letters to European and American residents there explaining the purpose of his visit, and requesting that the Siamese send down a suitable official to receive a letter formally announcing the impending embassy. After a slow journey of about 15 hours, both sailing and rowing, the officers arrived at the town on Sunday 24th, returning the same day with a Siamese delegation to Paknam where the letter was handed over with due ceremony, the *Nemesis* firing a salute which was returned by the fort. So on the 26th she sailed again for Singapore, passing in the river the US ship *Plymouth* carrying the US Consul in Singapore, Mr Balestier, arriving presumably with the hope of pre-empting any British treaties. Whereas the journey north had taken just 8 days, the return took 18, fueling stops in Kelantan and Trengganu being made more hazardous by the fact that smallpox was raging there.

Brooke did not wait in Singapore for the return of the *Nemesis* from Siam, instead travelling north towards the end of March to Penang with some of his colleagues from Sarawak – his secretary in Labuan Spenser St John, his young private secretary Charles Grant (nephew of the portrait painter Francis Grant), and Frank and Harriet McDougall. There in the cool weather 2,200 ft above sea level they rested for six quiet weeks, a time that they all were to remember as a particularly happy one.[7]

Meanwhile the *Nemesis*, after nine days in Singapore, left again for Labuan and Sarawak, arriving back in Singapore on 13 May soon after Brooke's party returned there from Penang. But there was still no suitable warship to lead the mission, the party waiting impatiently throughout June and much of July, a couple of cruises in the *Nemesis* up the coast of the Peninsula alleviating the boredom. Meanwhile the attacks by the *Straits Times* on all those involved in the battle of Batang Maru the previous July continued. Now an officer of the *Nemesis*, Dr Miller the surgeon, was accused of giving false information to that paper. On the 7 July Rear Admiral Charles Austen held a Board of Enquiry on his flagship HMS *Hastings* which quickly exonerated the doctor, every witness calling the statements false, statements described by the rival *Singapore Free Press* as "a fresh assortment of calumnies, couched in a style so virulent and vulgar as to reveal the animus of the writer, – a style devoid of all pretension to manliness or honesty of tone ..." But doubtlessly these attacks upon Sir James filtered through to Siam, making his later negotiations there all the more difficult.

At last, on Wednesday 24 July a ship deemed suitably impressive for the mission steamed into Singapore. HMS *Sphinx* (originally *Sphynx*) had sailed from Plymouth on the 2 March under the command of Captain Charles Shadwell, dispatched to Singapore to replace the *Fury* and for the mission to Siam. Launched on the Thames in 1846, she was a paddle sloop of 1056 tons, 180 ft long with a beam of 36 ft, and a draught of 14.5 ft, hardly ideal for river travel. Powered by a two-cylinder oscillating engine of 500 hp she could carry 360 tons of coal, using up to 40 tons per day under full power, and 50 tons of water, enough for 100 days. She was armed with two 10" pivot-guns, two 68-pounders and two 42-pound carronades as well as smaller guns for the paddle-box boats and field pieces, and carried a compliment of 160 men, of which 16 were officers.[8] Certainly a considerable advance on the *Nemesis*.

On Saturday 3 August 1850 the *Sphinx* carrying Brooke and his party and towing the *Nemesis* left Singapore for Siam. Brooke took suitable presents for his hosts but, tactlessly, the Foreign Office had seen fit to provide him with letters only from Lord Palmerston, and these a year out of date, rather than with one from Queen Victoria to the King of Siam. The voyage north was uneventful and, without fueling stops, the Chao Phraya was reached within six days. There they were met by what the Singapore press reported as 'rumours of an unfriendly nature'; an army of 20,000 assembling to man the river-mouth batteries, booms to block the river ready to be launched, fireships prepared to be sent against them, but "most formidable of the preparations were those of a certain Armenian Jew, who was reducing the motley army of Siam into an efficient state of discipline."[9] His efficiency must indeed have been impressive to have so quickly assembled 20,000 men.

On the morning of Saturday 10th, the *Nemesis* crossed the bar and steamed up to Paknam carrying Sir James Brooke, Mr St John and Captain Brooke, the Rajah's nephew. At the fort the party was received with courtesy, the letter from Brooke to Chao Mun Way Voranath, later to become Prime Minister, being accepted, pilots being assigned to the visitors, and a salute from the guns of the *Nemesis* being met by an answering salute from the fort. After a night at Paknam the steamer returned to the mouth of the river and, with the pilots' help, the *Sphinx* successful crossed the bar into the river that evening. But there misfortune struck: taking in more water for her boilers, the *Sphinx's* engines became blocked with mud and, drifting in the gathering darkness, she left the channel and settled on a mud bank amongst fishing traps. There for two days she remained until, sufficiently lightened, she finally refloated on a rising tide. Later it was considered that this accident had harmed the mission. Rumour had it that the Siamese had been expecting HMS *Hastings* to accompany Brooke, a 74-gun Third Rate, the likes of which the Siamese had never seen and 'were looking forward to with mingled feelings of curiosity and dread', so the *Sphinx* was something of a disappointment anyway, and this mishap added nothing to her reputation.

On the 14th Brooke and his party returned to Paknam on the *Nemesis*, there to meet the Minister for Foreign Affairs, Chao Phya Phra Klang, who had hastened down from Bangkok. The audience was held on the 16th in a specially built hall outside the walls of the fort where, after the exchange of the necessary courtesies, the Siamese appeared to welcome the mission although they initially had some difficulty in understanding from whom it came, a company of merchants or the British Queen. Anyway, a Siamese state barge was sent off to the *Nemesis* to collect Palmerston's letter to Phra Klang which was taken ashore under salute, the Siamese firing "two or three field pieces near the audience hall, and did it remarkably well, good time and very rapid". Although a letter from Victoria herself would have been far preferable, this one was apparently felt adequate for the following day Phra Klang's eldest son paid a courtesy visit to Sir James on board the *Nemesis*.

Clearly, progress could only be made by discussions in the capital, and on the 18th St John and Captain Brooke went up to Bangkok to make arrangements for Sir James' visit. The Siamese had determined that no steamer should go up the river, for fear they said of frightening the inhabitants, and so the journey was made not on the *Nemesis* but by state barge. In Bangkok they were offered the house which Mr Balestier had used earlier in the year, but, although six bedrooms had been added, they considered it too small and also unhealthy for it was built over swampy ground. Luckily a British merchant, Mr Brown, came to the rescue, offering the party accommodation at the British factory which was considered worthy. Thus on the 22nd an impressive flotilla of seven barges left Paknam for the capital carrying Sir James and his party and a detachment of Royal Marine guards, soon to be joined by four more barges carrying Siamese dignitaries.

The journey was initially through flat country, the Chao Phraya broad and lined with mangroves, but after a stop for refreshments generously provided at the fort at Praklat, the scenery became more picturesque. As they drew near the town boat yards became ever more frequent, for timber was cheap and many merchants in the region ordered Siamese trading vessels; then came the floating houses, and behind them houses on stilts scattered with wonderfully coloured temples. By evening the British party was safely ashore at the British factory, waiting there for four days before serious negotiations began. On Monday 26th Brooke was invited to the palace, a huge walled compound of splendid temples, fine houses and barracks. The audience hall was an open building set on a broad field. First the British delegation were politely seated and then the Siamese dignitaries entered, each in a sedan chair preceded by a man carrying a silken cushion on which was placed a sword, teapot and sirih box, and followed by about 20 colourfully dressed attendants. The dignity of this impressive display clearly pleased Brooke and his party, but nothing substantive was achieved other than that negotiations should now be continued in writing.

Up to this point the British had had little cause for complaint, and Brooke felt that all was proceeding as planned. But within a few days rumours reached the visitors that the King was opposed to any form of agreement. None the less, on 4 September Brooke delivered his proposals in the form of three letters to Phra Klang, written in both Siamese and English, proposals that he considered eminently reasonable. Firstly, he asked that permission be given for a British consul to reside in Bangkok, that ground be set aside for British merchants' houses and godowns, and that there be no arbitrary right of deportation. Secondly, for commerce he sought the abolition of certain monopolies, freedom to export rice, and a reduction in export taxes, the King's revenues being compensated by the retention of eight monopolies and taxes from the great increase in trade that would result. But the Siamese viewed these matters rather differently: the earlier appointment of two Portuguese consuls to Bangkok had not resulted in an increase in trade; recently a British merchant resident in the city had been caught importing opium, entirely against Siamese law; and the export of rice was forbidden unless there was a three-year supply stored in the country.

The delivery of the proposals was followed by two weeks of total silence from the Siamese, weeks in which many negative rumours circulated. During this time the King, now seriously ill, discussed the British proposals with his ministers and also with Mongkut who, though still in the priesthood, was to succeed to the Siamese throne. After a further exchange of correspondence the British heard on the 26th that all their proposals had been rejected, and in a tone they considered 'insolent and decidedly inimical'.

Sir James, no diplomat, was furious at this summary refusal of his proposals and decided to leave Bangkok immediately. This he did on Saturday 28th, though not without further protestations from the Siamese of goodwill and friendship, and the conveyance to Sir James of a letter from the Foreign Minister to Lord Palmerston, and the exchange of presents. Amongst those Sir James received was a splendid Siamese royal barge, green with a fine awning, and amongst those he gave was a smart set of court clothes, much admired the following year by Ludvig Helms, later to work in Sarawak, when he saw them worn at the Siamese court.[10] The barge was with some difficulty hoisted onto the *Nemesis* for passage to Sarawak, and there for many years it added to the lustre of the Rajah.

On the morning of the 29th final communications were sent to the Siamese court, and the *Nemesis* joined the *Sphinx* at anchor outside the bar. This time they sailed independently, the *Sphinx* with Sir James reaching Singapore on 4 October and the *Nemesis* two days later. There, the press greeted the mission with typically different reports, the *Singapore Free Press* as always supporting Sir James' actions, and the *Straits Times* as always viciously attacking him, "The envoy asked for free trade in everything, reduction of duties, relinquishment of royal right of pre-emption, and a resident consul. After a month's dangling, a plump refusal was given to every one demand, as might surely have been expected. The envoy withdrew in dudgeon..."[11] After a couple of weeks in Singapore, Sir James and his party on the 22nd boarded the *Nemesis* for Sarawak after an absence from his state of over seven months.

The failure of the Brooke mission to Siam was taken seriously by the British Government. Rejecting Brooke's call for the Burney treaty to be enforced by military means if necessary, they determined to pursue, but only by peaceful means, improved relations with the Siamese. When preparing for the mission Brooke was well aware that Rama III was both old and ill, and that his probable successor, Mongkut, was much more internationally minded. Due to his ill-health, Brooke left Sarawak for England in January 1851 and there that August he received a letter from Phra Klang's eldest son telling him that Rama III had died in April and had indeed been succeeded by Mongkut (r. 1851–68). At his suggestion, the Foreign Office agreed that Brooke should return to Siam that October, but then word came that the Siamese wished to postpone further negotiations until after the late king's cremation planned for April 1852. But when April came Brooke felt that, because of his health, he was not yet ready to leave England.

That same month word came that reforms were already underway in Siam. It was perhaps the defeat of China by Britain in 1842 that was the decisive event in the thinking of Mongkut and his more liberal advisers. If China, to whom Siam had paid tribute for centuries, could not resist then Siam had to accommodate if she wished to retain her independence. In early January 1852 the Siamese Court issued a proclamation which granted nearly all the wishes of foreign powers concerning trade: duties reduced, opium importation allowed as a government monopoly, the export of rice permitted. Hearing this the India Board doubted that a new mission was necessary, and when that December a new government came to power in London the new Foreign Secretary, Lord John Russell, sided with the Board. But in fact, the British Government's lack of enthusiasm for a new agreement with Siam was short-lived. With the appointment of a new Superintendent of Trade in Hong Kong in 1854, the Foreign Office instructed Sir John Bowring, 'the Governor of Hong Kong and British Plenipotentiary in China', to negotiate with Siam and the treaty which he signed with them on 18 April 1855 was deemed eminently successful. The following year similar treaties were concluded by the Siamese with the USA and France, in good part to provide some protection against Britain whom they saw as rapacious. For Siam these treaties proved a turning point, not only in her relations with western nations but in her internal economy.

On 10 February 1851 the *Nemesis* left Singapore for Calcutta, Thomas Wallage accompanied by his wife and their expanding family; in November 1949 Elizabeth had borne their fourth child and first daughter, and a fifth child following in late 1850. In March Wallage obtained a Pilot's Licence for the River Hooghly and, handing over command of the *Nemesis* to his First Officer, Robert Goodwin, took over the Company's steamer *Enterprize* then working out of Calcutta. But in September while attending a brother officer's funeral Wallage caught a chill, dying on 6 September aged only 36 years, one of the 80 per cent of Britons who, leaving Britain for India, never saw their native country again.[a] In Bengal the sudden temperature drop in September after the very hot and mosquito-ridden summer was known to cause chills which precipitated malarial attacks. Wallage was buried at Chowringhee, Calcutta in "one pukka grave"; this to modern eyes may appear to indicate the great respect in which he was held but in fact 'puckah' is a type of mortar, hard as stone. His widow and the four surviving children sailed for England towards the end of the year in the *City of Poonah*, and their sixth and last child was born en route in Mauritius on 25 January 1852. Family rumour has it that Mrs Wallage carried the great fortune of £27,000 back to England, the prize money won by her husband on the *Nemesis*, but given the amount awarded after Batang Maru this would appear apocryphal.[12]

---

[a]   By 1900 two million Britons lay buried in India (Gill 1995).

{ 27 }

FROM RANGOON TO MANDALAY

> Come you back to Mandalay,
> Where the old Flotilla lay:
> Can't you hear their paddles chunkin' from Rangoon to Mandalay?
> On the road to Mandalay,
> Where the flyin'-fishes play
> An' the dawn comes up like thunder outer China 'crost the Bay!
>
> —"Mandalay", Rudyard Kipling

The country called Burma or Myanmar is one of great ethnic diversity.[1] In attempting to untangle its history it is helpful to realise that the heartland of the Burman people lay at Ava, near Mandalay. Here the great Irrawaddy River runs through a land with a highly seasonal climate, a land enclosed by mountains to the west and north and east and by the great wet delta to the south. And from this apparent fastness the Kings of Ava, sometimes strong and aggressive, sometimes weak and vacillating, waged endless wars upon their neighbours, wars fought for slaves and for loot rather than for land, moving west and north-west into Manipur and Assam, north-east into Yunnan, east through the Shan states towards Laos, and south-east into Siam. But their greatest interest lay in the coastal regions to the south and west, to what were at times independent kingdoms, to the land of the Mon around Pegu and the Irrawaddy Delta and to Arakan along the Bay of Bengal.

Burmese kings, like rulers of 'mandala' states elsewhere, sought absolute control over the heartland but were quite content to accept that in outer areas their control might be slight but their interests must prevail. So borders were flexible, a concept inexplicable to the British.

Conflicts within Burma meant that people were continually moving across the border between Burma and British India, and this did not amuse the British. In 1819 a new king ascended the Burmese throne, Bagyidaw (r. 1819–37) who, though weak himself was strongly influenced by the ambitious and competent general Thado Maha Bandula. Lord Amherst (the same who had made an abortive embassy to the Chinese court in 1817), arrived in Calcutta as Governor-General in August 1823, apparently with no desire for war with Burma. But within a year continual incursions all along the frontier had convinced him that the Burmese were bent upon the conquest of Bengal.

On 5 March 1824 the British declared war on Burma. The plan of campaign was to draw Bandula's forces from the frontier by mounting a full-scale invasion of Lower Burma, capturing the seaport of Rangoon, a ramshackled place of perhaps 20,000 inhabitants, and thus commanding the entrance to the highway to the capital at Ava, the Irrawaddy river; and at the same time seeking the conquest of Assam, Manipur, Arakan and Tenasserim, thus hemming the Burmese in to their heartland. But not for the first time the British underestimated their foes. Viewing the Burmese people as essentially indolent, friendly and happy-go-lucky, and their monarchs as monsters, they had neither a concept of the people's belief in kingly divinity nor of their capacity to fight for their homeland. Indeed, it was one of the things that endlessly surprised Victorian imperialists – that people would rather live under their own corrupt and rapacious rulers than under the just and noble British.

The First Anglo-Burmese War, one of the more inept of Britain's imperial adventures, at least started propitiously: having gathered a force of 63 ships and over 11,000 British and Indian troops and camp followers in the Andaman Islands under Lieutenant-Colonel Sir Archibald Campbell, Rangoon was captured on 10 May without a shot being fired. But the place was deserted (despite this, much of it was set ablaze by drunken troops) and the army logistically ill-prepared for advance up-river or indeed for remaining in Rangoon with the four-month rainy season (May to August) just beginning.[a] As Major Snodgrass, Campbell's military secretary wrote: "Deserted, as we found ourselves, by the people of the country, from whom alone we could

---

[a]   In April the temperature is at its hottest and the Irrawaddy at its lowest. By August the river above the tidal reach could have risen by 40 ft, falling rapidly in September. December to February sees the coolest and driest weather.

expect supplies – unprovided by the means of moving either by land or water, and the rainy season just setting in – no prospect remained to us but that of long residence in the miserable and dirty hovels of Rangoon, trusting to the transports [from Calcutta] for provisions, with such partial supplies as our foraging parties might procure from time to time by distant and fatiguing marches into the interior of the country."[2]

This conflict marks the first occasion in which steamships were used for warfare, and if their role in the actual conflict was marginal their use illuminated their potential as fighting vessels in calm and shallow waters, as troop carriers and as packets carrying urgent dispatches (see chapter 8). The *Diana*, when launched at Calcutta in July 1823 the first steamer east of the Mediterranean, arrived on the Irrawaddy in May 1824 at the time of the capture of Rangoon and was joined there by the tiny *Pluto* in early 1825. Both were used as true fighting vessels, the *Diana* armed with Congreve rockets, the *Pluto* a floating battery carrying six guns, four 24-pound carronades and two long 6-pounders. The larger *Enterprize*, recently arrived from England, joined them in January 1826 just before the war ended, but was used only as a packet carrying dispatches.

The capture of Rangoon in May 1824 did, as planned, draw Bandula away from the frontier region. Initially he hoped to hold the British in Rangoon until fevers and frustration caused them to tire of their campaign, but although dysentery, malaria and scurvy were indeed playing havoc with the invaders, as the year advanced there was no sign of them withdrawing. In fact, they used this enforced delay to move east to occupy Tenasserim, the province bordering Siam; first Mergui in the south fell, then Tavoy, and finally Moulmein in the north to a force led by Lieutenant-Colonel Henry Godwin (1784–1853), later to lead the army in the Second Anglo-Burmese War. Towards the end of the year Bandula was encamped outside Rangoon with a huge force of over 20,000 men, although the British feared there were up to 60,000, their estimates of the numbers of their opponents being notoriously fickle. But Bandula's attack on 1 December had by the 15th been comprehensively repulsed with the loss of great numbers of Burmese; British losses were only 30 killed and 220 wounded.

Since the end of the rainy season Campbell had been receiving reinforcements, including the little *Pluto*, and by the start of the new year his troops numbered over 12,000. Thus strengthened he decided to go up-river to Prome. Bandula gathered his army at the stronghold of Danubyu whose fort commanded the river route to the north, telling

Campbell, "If you wish to see Danubyu come as friends and I will show it to you. If you come as enemies, land!" But on 1 April 1825 the great general was killed by a mortar shell and his army fled in disorder, allowing the British to pass on to Prome where they spent their second wet season. Meanwhile in the west, British forces in March took Arakan, and drove the Burmese from both Assam and Manipur. It was during the campaign in Assam in February 1825 that the 21-year-old James Brooke, later Rajah of Sarawak, was severely wounded.

The capture of Prome greatly disquieted the Court of Ava, and at the end of the wet season they attempted to retake it by surprise, gathering an army at Pagan and sending down a fleet of great teak war-boats, each over 100 ft long carrying 6- and 12-pounder guns and up to 60 oarsmen and 30 musketeers.[3] But with the help of the *Diana* and *Pluto* the attack was repulsed, the Burmese commander carrying this news to the court being immediately executed. The way to the capital was now open to a British force strengthened with fresh troops and adequate river transport (56 small vessels led by the *Diana*) and they now presented their demands to the Burmese: the cession of Arakan, Tenasserim, Assam and Manipur, and the payment of an indemnity of £1 million in rupees. These so staggered the Burmese that they tried every form of persuasion to get them reduced, but without success. Not until the British were within three days march of the capital, 70 miles, were they willing to agree, the Treaty of Yandabo bringing hostilities to an end on 24 February 1826.

Official records show that in the early years of the nineteenth century the Indian Government had no particular designs on Burmese territory. Rather, they went to war due to what they considered as Burmese threats to their interests in India. The war gave the British all the territory they deemed necessary for India's security, and with it even greater domination of the Bay of Bengal, but at a heavy cost.[4] At least 15,000 out of 40,000 men serving in the expeditionary forces died, the great majority from malaria, cholera and dysentery. Of the 12,845 men at Rangoon in January 1825, only 225 were subsequently killed in action but 4,853 died of disease; and, if the overall death rate was about 40 per cent, that amongst the European troops was even higher. In Arakan, of two regiments of 1,004 men not one was lost in action but 595 died of disease within eight months of arrival and a further 200 soon after leaving Burma – a loss of 80 per cent.[5] But these figures were hushed up, and of course the deaths of much greater numbers of Burmese went uncounted. Uncounted too was the cost of inadequate clothing and shelter, insufficient food, and a shameful lack of medical supplies. So to the British at home the outcome of the war, another conquest, was greeted with considerable enthusiasm. And the Governor-General was rewarded with the title of Earl Amherst of Arracan.

For the Burmese, exhausted by three-quarters of a century of expansionist efforts, the defeat broke their military power beyond recovery. Although they kept their three main ports, at Bassein, Rangoon and Martaban, they had lost two large coastal provinces, not to mention their vassal territories of Assam and Manipur, a generation of leaders and soldiers had been wiped out, and to add insult to injury they had had to partly pay for their defeat. None the less, the Court of Ava learned little from this disaster; their pride was hurt, but their ignorance of the outside world remained so that they were still unwilling to treat with a power that was much greater than theirs. The Treaty of Yandabo had stipulated that the two nations should exchange envoys, a British Resident at Amarapura and a Burmese Ambassador at Calcutta. But although the former was appointed, the Burmese could in no way be persuaded to send an ambassador to the court of a mere Governor-General. And yet weighty matters needed discussion and decision – the exact boundaries of Arakan and Manipur, and whether Tenasserim should be retained, returned or sold.

The British initially administered their two new provinces directly from India. Although neither was of any economic significance, the retention of Arakan was seen to be vital for the safety of India, and in 1828 it was transferred to the Bengal administration under the Commissioner for Chittagong. Because Tenasserim was of little strategic value and merely a drain on resources, consideration was initially given to handing it back to the Burmese or even selling it to Siam. But in 1835 it too was transferred to Bengal.

By the mid 1830s King Bagyidaw was showing increasing signs of insanity, that curse of Burmese kings. And when in 1837 a rebellion broke out led by the King's brother, Tharrawaddy (r. 1837–45), the British Resident, Major Henry Burney, unwillingly found himself deeply involved as mediator. In this he was notably unsuccessful: having got the brothers to agree that the King would abdicate in favour of Tharrawaddy if there was no bloodshed, the latter promptly massacred all the King's family and their followers. In June 1837 Burney was recalled by Governor-General Lord Auckland, but two subsequent

Residents were both treated with contempt by the new King who appeared to believe that he could recover the lost provinces by force of arms. And it was probably fear of this possibility that persuaded the Secret Committee to strengthen the Bengal Marine with four sliding-keel vessels all designed for river service (see chapter 2). Although conflict was avoided, early in 1840 the Government of India withdrew the Resident and severed diplomatic relations with the Court of Ava, these not being restored until 1851.

Alarums and excursions continued throughout the early 1840s, the Indian Government unwilling to act decisively to curb Tharrawaddy's ambitions. But then the King like his brother before him became insane. The ensuing power struggle amongst his sons was won through his scheming mother, Taung Nanmadaw, by Pagan Min [r. 1846–53], his reign, the ninth of the Alaungpya dynasty, starting with the usual bloodbath, rivals, their families and followers all being slaughtered. But the new king was in fact a man of mild manners if of feeble mind, quite unsuited to his role, and as his control of the kingdom weakened so his officials, receiving no salary but living on a percentage of the taxes they could extract, became ever more avaricious.

The British in Burma at this time were largely confined to Rangoon. Here, in a settlement on the very fringes of empire many of the dregs of the European commercial world washed up, living in a culture for which they had no respect and under the authority of officials for whom bribes were essential. "Rangoon has long been notorious as an asylum for fraudulent debtors and violent and unprincipled characters from every part of India ..."[6] And here in 1851 the Governor of Pegu, Maung Ok, charged two British sea-captains and members of their crews with embezzlement and murder. An early bribe would have settled the matter, but in the end their freedom cost the stubborn captains £1,920, an amount they immediately asked the Government of India to reimburse. As luck would have it, the Governor-General, Lord Dalhousie, had recently presided over the defeat of the Sikhs on one frontier and was in no mood to allow British subjects on another to be treated with apparent contempt. "The Government of India", he wrote in a minute, "could never, consistently with its own safety, permit itself to stand for a single day in an attitude of inferiority towards a native power, and least of all towards the Court of Ava."[7]

On 18 October 1851 Dalhousie despatched to Rangoon Commodore George Lambert (1795–1869), an officer of the Royal Navy but now the deputy Commander-in-Chief of the Company's naval forces. Lambert sailed in HMS *Fox* (46 guns), supported by the Company's steamers *Proserpine* and *Tenasserim*, with a demand for the removal of Governor Maung Ok and for compensation. Despite Lambert's arrogant behaviour and the nature of his demands, the King did his best to please, immediately appointing a new governor. U Hmone arrived in Rangoon on 4 January 1852, and that very day Lambert sent a junior officer to meet him, a studied insult, and then when that meeting failed complained that he himself had been insulted. And of course insults must be met by action – military action.

{ 28 }

UP THE IRRAWADDY AGAIN

After returning Sir James Brooke to Sarawak in October 1850, the *Nemesis* spent a few more months in Singapore waters, shuttling between there, Kuching and Labuan. Packet work was now all that was required of her for the activities of British, Dutch and Spanish naval vessels had by this time largely broken the great fleets of Illanun and Balanini raiders.[1] On 17 January 1851 she left Sarawak for Singapore, carrying the Rajah on the first leg of a journey to England, his second visit since his arrival in Borneo 12 years before.[a] In urgent need of repairs, the steamer left Singapore for Calcutta on 10 February, arriving at her home port on 1 March where she was immediately placed in the dock recently vacated by the *Pluto*. The *Pluto*, now virtually rebuilt, left Calcutta on 28 March to replace the *Nemesis* still commanded by Lieutenant Airey who had been with her since her departure from England almost ten years before. But in Singapore George Airey suffered the fate soon to befall Thomas Wallage; on 20 April dying probably from malaria.[2]

Although thoroughly overhauled in 1848, the *Nemesis* again needed extensive repairs: at water level her hull plates had worn so thin that two strakes (rows) had to be replaced all round, and her engines

---

[a] Brooke arrived in England in May 1851, the month that 'The Great Exhibition of the Industry of All Nations' opened in London, visiting the Crystal Palace with Henry Keppel that August (Keppel 1899).

thoroughly serviced. By August she was again ready for sea and that month Robert Goodwin, lately her First Officer but now her Captain, set about recruiting a new crew, most men signing for three years service on 20 August 1851. On the 21st the ship sailed for China to relieve the *Phlegethon*. Calling at Singapore from 12–17 September she reached Hong Kong on 19 October, there joining the squadron of Rear-Admiral Charles Austen, youngest brother of the novelist Jane Austen.[3]

The *Phlegethon* after three years in Chinese waters under Captain Niblett sailed from Hong Kong for India on 1 November 1851, reaching Moulmein on the 23rd where she was "ordered to hold herself to follow the *Proserpine* to Rangoon".[4] On 6 January 1852 Commodore Lambert seized the King's ship *Yenanyin* anchored off Rangoon, and then ordered all British residents and merchants to leave the city. "The *Proserpine* steamer ran close into the main wharf, and eight or ten of the boats from the frigate (HMS *Fox*) and steamers came to the shore to protect and receive the fugitives."[5] The following day she carried almost 400 people to Moulmein, passing en route the *Phlegethon* bound for Rangoon. On the 9th, in a further provocation, Lambert ordered the *Fox*, the paddle steamer HMS *Hermes* (828 tons) and the *Phlegethon* to sail close to a fort where they were fired on. During the consequent two-hour bombardment about 300 Burmese were killed and a similar number injured.[6]

If there is little doubt that Lambert hankered after war with the Burmese, did the Governor-General also? Although in official dispatches Lord Dalhousie repeatedly said he wished for peace, it is notable that he did not recall the 'combustible commodore', as he later called Lambert, even after Lambert clearly disobeyed written orders, and in numerous dispatches wrote admiringly of his actions and continued to call him his friend. And that Lambert served his masters well is indicated by the fact that when he died in 1869 it was as Admiral Sir George Lambert.

On Thursday 12 February 1852 the British India government decided to send a military expedition to Burma. On the 15th the *Phlegethon* returned to Calcutta with conciliatory letters to Dalhousie from both King Pagan Min and Governor U Hmone, but the Governor-General ignored these, sending back on the *Phlegethon* an ultimatum demanding a further £100,000 from the Burmese court to cover the cost of war preparations, an outrageous demand that the King obviously could not accept. In true imperial fashion the Burmese were informed "that the English were sincerely desirous of peace, but that, if a reply were not received from Ava by the 1st of April, fully agreeing to the terms proposed by the Governor-General, our forces would inevitably invade the country; and that the guilt of having provoked the war would rest with them."[7]

On 21 February the Indian Navy in Bombay received orders from the Governor-General to send six steamships to Burma, the *Berenice, Ferooz, Medusa, Moozuffer, Sesostris* and *Zenobia* (Table 10). That same month the P & O steamer *Precursor* (1,555 tons, 251 ft overall and 600 hp), usually on the Suez to Calcutta run, was hired to carry troops to Arakan. As the *Straits Times* reported, "When the huge *Precursor* made her appearance at Kyook Phyoo (Kyaukphyu) all the native boats fled, frightened by her size."

Rear-Admiral Austen, recalled from China to take command of the expedition, reached Penang in his flagship HMS *Hastings* (74 guns) in March. Leaving the *Hastings* there as her draught made her unsuitable for the Burma campaign, he transferred to HMS *Rattler* (867 tons), the world's first purpose-built screw warship, made famous for her tug-of-war with her sister ship the paddle steamer *Alecto* in April 1845 for in winning she helped convince the Lords of the Admiralty of the superiority of screw propulsion. The *Rattler* accompanied by the paddle steamer HMS *Salamander* (818 tons) arrived in Burmese waters on 1 April, the day that the British ultimatum expired. The following day, Lieutenant-General Sir Henry Godwin,[b] the land forces commander, the same who had fought in the First Burmese War, arrived off the Irrawaddy on the *Hermes* together with the steamers *Enterprize* and *Tenasserim* and four transports from the Bengal Marine.

During March the six steamers from Bombay ordered to Burma assembled in Madras, sailing on from there on the 31st towing four transport ships and carrying almost 4,400 soldiers and camp-followers, 960 sailors, and a detachment of European artillerymen and marines. Arriving off the Irrawaddy on Wednesday 7 April, the British commanders now had at their disposal a formidable force of over 8,000 fighting men[c] supported by 160 heavy guns on 18 warships and 14 transports (Table 10).[8] Of the fighting ships only two were sailing ships,

---

[b]   His knighthood was actually conferred just before his death in 1853 aged 69.
[c]   Certainly a diverse mix: 2,727 European soldiers, 3,040 Indian soldiers, 808 sailors of the Royal Navy, 952 of the Indian Navy and 510 of the Bengal Marine (Low 1877).

the *Fox* and HMS *Serpent* (12 guns). Of the 16 steamers, 3 were Royal Navy and 13 from the Company's navies, one of the 16 being screw-propelled and 5 built of iron. Such a fleet stands in remarkable contrast to that which had greeted the *Nemesis* in China just 12 years before, but it was to be another few months before she herself could join the squadron in her second and final colonial war.

Clearly, Dalhousie was determined that this war should be conducted quite differently to that of 30 years before. He ensured that the naval forces were both powerful and suited for rapid communication between Calcutta and the Irrawaddy, that construction materials for barracks were prepared ahead of need, and that good food and adequate medicine was always available for the troops. Indeed, health provision was so effective that mortality from sickness amongst the troops in Burma was actually lower than in peacetime India. And most importantly he tackled with enthusiasm the problems of employing a fighting force divided both between Army and Navy and between Crown and Company. This was no easy task as his land commander, Godwin, an irascible man in his late 60s, was notorious for his jealousy of the Navy whose role was of course absolutely central. And unfortunately naval command seemed usually to be in the hands of the combustible commodore rather than those of Admiral Austen, a man renowned for his relaxed charm and sunny character. Charles was the youngest of eight Austen children in this cheerful and devoted family. A favourite of his sisters Cassandra and Jane, "our particular little brother", Jane could write of his homecoming in 1813 "dear Charles, all affectionate, placid, quiet, cheerful, good humour."[9]

On 3 April 1852 the Admiral on the *Rattler* and the General on the *Hermes*, together with the *Proserpine* and *Salamander*, sailed east to Moulmein, capturing the Mon port of Martaban opposite on the 5th and returning to the Irrawaddy by the 8th. From there the steamers *Ferooz* and *Medusa* were sent to secure Martaban and the *Phlegethon* up-river to examine the defences of Rangoon. On Easter Sunday 11 April the city and Dalla opposite were attacked. On the *Sesostris* Commander Campbell ordered that 68-pound shot be heated red-hot before firing from the 8" guns whose range was over a mile. "The effect was tremendous. The whole place was set on fire, and two-thirds of it burnt down … the Indian Navy seems to stand high in the good opinion of all."[10] Though probably not of the citizens of Rangoon. On the 12th troops were landed: "Guns and carriages dismounted, wheels lying here and there, boxes of medicines, boxes of shot, rations of beef, powder arrack, and ladders, all in one confused mass, while the troops moved in the midst of them to form into position." "On the night of the 13th," wrote a citizen, not Burmese but Armenian, "orders came to send us up to the great Pagoda ... Rockets and shells poured down on every side. Our escape must solely be ascribed to the mercy of Providence. To have escaped from the shells, some of which burst near us – from the Governor's hand, and the hands of the Burmese soldiery, that had already commenced pillaging the new town – must be set down as a miracle ... We at first returned to our abodes, but found them uninhabitable. A portion of the houses in the new town were in a blaze from the rockets ... This night was a night of flight." The last resistance at the Shwedagon pagoda crumbled on the 14th, the shrines of the great pagoda, the finest in Burma, then looted by the invaders. As Lieutenant Laurie on board the *Berenice* wrote, tongue certainly not in cheek, "The Navy had acted as a pioneer of true civilisation."[11]

With this quick and easy victory disagreements between the combustible commodore and the irascible general flared. Lambert wanted to use the wet season, May to August with the rivers high, to go up the Irrawaddy as far as Prome. Of course then glory would go to the sailors. But Godwin was determined to wait for the dry season; indeed, he appeared to have learnt nothing from the near disasters in Burma 30 years before. But then a delay would mean that the rivers would be too low for the steamers and the glory would go to the soldiers.

But the commodore would not wait. On Monday 17 May, a week after the start of the rainy season, Lambert together with 800 naval men on the *Sesostris, Moozuffer, Tenasserim* and *Pluto*[d] left Rangoon for Bassein which, although only about 90 miles due west, meant a journey by river and sea of about 220 miles, "following the little *Pluto* as our guide, having no pilots and but a poor map, dated 1754!"[12] Reaching the town on the afternoon of the 19th, it was captured within two hours. Leaving the *Sesostris* there, the expedition returned to Rangoon on the 23rd. A couple of weeks later another expedition was launched from Rangoon, the *Phlegethon* crowded with men and towing more in six boats steaming up-river on 3 June towards Pegu, 60 miles to the north-west. About 16 miles below the town the river became too shallow for

---

[d] This is of course the sliding-keel *Pluto*, not the vessel from the First Burmese War. She had left Singapore for Burma on 2 April 1852.

the steamer and so on the 4th the troops were landed, marched to Pegu and captured it that evening. Now the three main Burmese cities of the coastal plain between the British provinces of Arakan and Tenasserim were in British hands.

Pegu, once a royal capital, had been modelled in the sixteenth century after the splendours of Pagan, a perfect square with the moated royal palace at its centre, scattered with many beautiful buildings. Although by the nineteenth century much had been lost to wars and neglect, the temples were still exquisite, white and gold with occasional splashes of red and blue, every surface covered with carvings, each crowned with a graceful *htee* or umbrella, the whole dominated by the great Shwemawdaw Pagoda rising to over 320 ft. The British, after destroying the granaries and seizing what loot they could, handed the town back to the Peguese and the expedition steamed back to Rangoon – whereupon the Burmese quickly retook the town. The next expedition to leave Rangoon departed at the beginning of July, five paddle steamers under the command of Captain Walter Tarleton of the *Fox* – four of the sliding-keel vessels, *Phlegethon, Pluto, Proserpine, Medusa,* and the *Mahanuddy* – but again Godwin adamantly refused to allow any soldiers to go along. Aiming closer to the Burmese heartland they steamed up the swollen Irrawaddy to Prome, about 250 miles north of Rangoon by creek and river, yet lying only 30 miles above the furthest reaches of the vast delta. Arriving on the 9th they immediately landed and, with little opposition, took the town, the next day descending the river again. And again, without an adequate garrison the place was soon retaken by the Burmese.

With the ending of the rainy season in August the rivers would rapidly shrink, broad stretches falling by as much as 20 ft in September alone, and such expeditions become increasingly fraught, no doubt to Godwin's pleasure. Perhaps it was this expectation that caused the recall of the *Nemesis* from China to Burmese waters. On the 21 June she took her final departure from Hong Kong, the barren island whose colonisation she had witnessed 12 years before and now a town of at least 30,000 Chinese. At Manila she was delayed by atrocious weather which forced her back to port twice and she did not finally leave there for Singapore until 13 July. Captain Goodwin had been asked to look out for a Royal Naval survey ship, HMS *Royalist* (8 guns), in the vicinity of Ulugan Bay, Palawan, but he could not find her, and so sailed via Labuan, where he found the colony short of provisions, to Singapore, arriving on

27 July. On Friday 30 July 1852 the *Nemesis* steamed out of Singapore for the last time bound for Penang and Rangoon, reaching Burmese waters with her companion from Siam, HMS *Sphinx*, Captain Charles Shadwell now taking over from Tarleton command of the Irrawaddy flotilla.

On 21 July 1852 the Governor-General, perhaps with the wet season about to end wishing to encourage at least a little cooperation between his field commanders, left Calcutta for Burma on the *Ferooz*, holding discussions in Rangoon from Tuesday 27th to Sunday 1 August. Although Dalhousie ostensibly did not want to annex more territory but rather to force Pagan Min to negotiate, sometime in June he had apparently decided to annex the old kingdom of Pegu and so informed London. This would link Arakan and Tenasserim, giving Britain control of the complete coast and thus greatly impoverishing the Court of Ava.

On 27 September a squadron of eight steamers, the *Sesostris* and *Medusa* of the Indian Navy and the *Fire Queen*, carrying both General Godwin and Commodore Lambert, *Enterprize*, *Mahanuddy*, *Nemesis*, *Phlegethon* and *Proserpine* of the Bengal Marine, left Rangoon for Prome, "and after a fortnight's tedious navigation, with numerous groundings and detentions due to the lack of water, arrived off Prome on the 9th October."[13] That same day Admiral Austen aged 74 died from cholera on board the *Pluto* at Rangoon, "winning all hearts by his gentleness and kindness, when struggling with disease," his body taken by the *Rattler* to Trincomalee, Ceylon, where his wife Fanny was staying.[e] Prome was captured again on the 15th and the town of Pegu on the 21 November. By that time London's agreement to the plan for annexation of the province had reached Calcutta, and Dalhousie ordered it carried out without delay. Thus on 20 December the annexation of Pegu province was proclaimed with due ceremony in Rangoon, Major Arthur Phayre – a 'political', a military officer in an essentially civilian posting, being appointed its first Commissioner.

Of course this entirely unilateral action did not mean the end of hostilities, and skirmishes continued well into the following year. On 21 January 1853 "that far famed vessel the *Nemesis*" as the *Rangoon Chronicle* called her,[14] left Bassein carrying Captain Albert Fytche, the

---

[e]   At the time of Charles Austen's death his sister Jane's novels, hugely popular then as now, could be bought in London for 3/6 each (17.5 p, about £9.60 in today's money) in the cheapest edition yet published. This was about the daily wage of a skilled labourer or twice the daily wage of an unskilled one.

Deputy Commissioner for Bassein, and Captain Rennie of the Indian Navy's steamer *Zenobia* in command of 80 seamen and marines and a force of over 300 Karens – a crowded voyage. Travelling north and then east towards Kyaungonn (Khyoung Gou), after two days the men were landed and marched 15 miles inland to destroy an enemy camp, and then back to the ship and up-river until the water became too shallow, and then another march lugging one 12-pounder and three 3-pounder guns to what turned out to be a deserted camp, "the men having marched between thirty and thirty-four miles since one a.m., no mean exploit, and that they had to drag the guns over rough roads and sometimes over paddy fields..."[15] There the Karen were used to lure the Burmese who had fled back to the river where they were met with a shower of grape and canister from 200 yards, killing 50 outright and wounding hundreds, with 50 prisoners taken as well as 300 muskets and much other loot.

In early November 1852 the *Phlegethon* had suffered a large rent in her starboard boiler and had to be towed by the *Berenice* to Calcutta for repairs. There she remained for the rest of the year, leaving on New Year's Day for Rangoon towing the troop-boat *Soane*. In early February 1853 she was dispatched to Danubyu with a detachment of 145 sailors and marines and 360 sepoys under the command of Captain Granville Loch of HMS *Winchester* (52 guns), their task to put paid to Myat Htun, a Burmese in rebellion against the annexation of Pegu. Loch was another of those remarkable early Victorian characters.[16] Born in 1813, he volunteered for the Navy at the age of 11 and remained at sea until he was 21 when he was appointed Lieutenant. Realising the importance of steam Loch went privately to Glasgow to study the science and practice of steam engines at Napier's factory, a path later taken by Nemesis Hall. Then appointed Captain on the South America station he took ship to Rio de Janeiro, but arriving there found that his command was on the Pacific coast. So he rode across the continent to join her. In January 1842, with nothing better to do, he sailed with Keppel on the *Dido* bound for China and the Opium War: "My other friend, Granville Loch, lately promoted to the rank of Captain – full of zeal, but being too junior for a command – was glad to accompany me to China."[17] In 1846 Loch was appointed to the West Indian station, and, after further shore time, to command the *Winchester*, leaving from Plymouth for Burma on 23 May 1852.

On 3 February Loch and his troops left Danubyu and marched inland. As was typical of the times, British officers led from the front arrayed in all their finery, undoubtedly brave but also foolhardy. Burmese officers more practically placed their ethnic conscripts ahead. The following day by a deep ravine the British were suddenly ambushed. Loch, crying "Winchester to the charge! Forward men! Follow me!" dashed forward but almost immediately a ball hit his pocket-watch and carried it into his body and he fell. A retreat was soon ordered which turned into a rout with 3 officers and 96 men killed or wounded, and many guns lost. Loch was carried in great agony back to Danubyu, and with the other wounded placed on board the *Phlegethon* which sailed immediately for Rangoon, but he died on board on the 6th before the town was reached. Ten days later a writer reported, "many were the hair-breadth escapes that day. A corporal had eight balls in his body but is now hearty ... And Glover of the *Sphinx* had a most wonderful escape, a ball entering his right temple and coming out under or rather before his right ear ..." And Glover lived long, eventually dying as Sir John Glover.[18]

Granville Loch epitomised a characteristic typical of many Victorian fighting men which seems very foreign to us today – a genuine and open love of war. Certainly they saw the horrors of war, but none the less hankered after it. No one showed this more clearly than a young ensign who was instrumental in the taking of Myat Htun's stockade a month later. Garnet Wolseley (1833–1913, later Field-Marshal Lord Wolseley), aged only 19 and fiercely ambitious, had arrived in Burma at the beginning of the year, fearful that he was too late for action. Now volunteering to lead the assault, he wrote towards the end of his life, "What a supremely delightful moment it was! No one in cold blood can imagine how intense is the pleasure of such a position who had not experienced it himself ... In a long and varied military life ... I have never experienced the same unalloyed and elevating satisfaction, or known again the joy I felt as I ran for the enemy's stockades at the head of a small mob of soldiers, most of them boys like myself."[19]

To Dalhousie's surprise the annexation of Pegu drew no response from the Court of Ava and, visiting Rangoon on the *Tenasserim* in March, he reluctantly concluded that it would be necessary to advance on the capital. But what he did not know was that another revolution was in progress in the capital which, in February 1853, resulted in Pagan Min being replaced as king by his half-brother Mindon Min (r. 1853–78). Mindon was certainly different from most of his forebears – a sincere Buddhist, he did not slaughter Pagan and his household but allowed him to retire honourably, and then seriously sought peace with the British. Initially he could not believe that the British intended to keep Pegu, but negotiations with Phayre, Godwin and Lambert between March and May finally convinced him that the territory was indeed lost to Ava, and he wrote to Phayre telling him that he had ordered the end of hostilities along the new border. On 4 July 1853 Dalhousie accepted peace. "All that is known of his character and past history", he wrote of Mindon, "mark him among Burmese rulers as a prince of rare sagacity, humanity and forbearance, and stamp his present declarations with the seal of sincerity."[20]

That month, far to the east, another eastern power confronted for the first time the naval might of a western nation. On 8 July a United States squadron under Commodore Matthew Perry steamed into Uraga Harbour near Edo (modern Tokyo), Perry with his 'black ships' determined to open the Japan of the Tokugawa Shogunate to western trade.

Although it took a further three years to bring Pegu under complete control, relations between the two combatants rapidly improved. In 1854 Mindon actually sent a mission to Calcutta, and the following year at his invitation Phayre led a British mission to the Court of Ava. Although the British greatly desired a treaty which was resolutely refused by Mindon, these missions resulted in much good will. The credit for this lay largely with Phayre, a scholar of Burmese language and culture with a fine reputation for courtesy, and with Mindon who, like King Mongkut of Siam, had the wisdom to perceive that the interests of his kingdom could only be forwarded by having good relations with more powerful neighbours.

The British initially administered Pegu much as they did Tenasserim, working through a native administration. For the ordinary villager life was perhaps little altered, but now they lived in a society where official extortion was illegal, banditry was effectively curbed, and those in power believed that the general welfare of the governed was at least of some concern. Arakan had at one time been a large exporter of rice, but under Burmese rule half the population had fled and exporting rice had been deemed illegal. With a more settled and just administration, and the close proximity of the Indian market, Akyab, its capital, soon became a flourishing commercial centre. Tenasserim had always been sparsely populated but its annexation opened up its valuable teak forests and for a while Moulmein became a thriving port. But the rapid development of Rangoon after 1853 quickly eclipsed Moulmein. Soon it was seen that the maintenance of three separate provinces was costly and inefficient, and in 1862 they were amalgamated to form the province of British Burma, with Rangoon the capital and Phayre its first Chief Commissioner.

But a Burma thus divided could not last. It was Mindon's son Thibaw (r. 1878–85), the eleventh and last king of the Alaungpya dynasty, another ruler both weak and capricious, who finally lost the Burmese heartland in the brief Third Anglo-Burmese War of 1885. And so it was the British who in the end defined today's Burma, drawing neat boundaries on their maps, these enclosing areas, notably the highlands around the Irrawaddy valley that had never been truly Burmese, boundaries that today are still cause for conflict.[21]

{ 29 }

SO OLD A SHIP

It was so old a ship – who knows, who knows?
And yet so beautiful, I watched in vain
To see the mast burst open with a rose,
And the whole deck put on its leaves again.

—"The Old Ships", James Elroy Flecker

The transformation in the nature of British naval power between the invasions of China in 1840 and of Burma in 1852 was truly startling. In 1824, just 16 years before the *Nemesis* joined the fleet in southern China, the very first steamer to be used as a fighting vessel saw action in the first Burmese war. Three years later the last battle ever to be fought between sail-only fleets took place at Navarino. The Royal Navy ordered their first iron ship, the packet *Dover*, in 1839 (launched 1840); their first screw ship, *Rattler*, in 1842 (launched 1843); and their last paddle warship, *Valorous*, in 1847 (launched 1851). By 1850 the Royal Navy was committed to a screw-driven battle fleet, large sailing-only vessels never again being ordered.[1]

In June 1854 soon after the start of the Russian (Crimean) War (1854–6) the British and French Baltic fleet consisted of 47 men-of-war of which 25 were steamers.[2] Of the 19 British ships of the line 11 were screw-powered, including the old *Blenheim* from the China War, now a screw blockship soon to be captained by our friend Nemesis Hall. Also present was Henry Keppel, late of the *Dido* and *Maeander*, now captain of a new type of warship, the *Saint Jean d'Acre*, 3,400 tons, wooden hulled with engines of 600 hp turning a single screw, with 101 guns on

244

two decks and a crew of 900 officers and men. Amongst the ships in the other theatre of naval operations, the Black Sea, were the *Valorous*, the Royal Navy's last paddle warship, and the *Terrible*, their largest (*see* Table 3), commanded briefly in 1847 by Nemesis Hall and now captained by another veteran of the China campaign, Captain McCleverty, late of the *Phlegethon*.[3]

The merchant fleets of the world had also greatly altered over the past dozen years though not so radically as the fighting fleets. In Britain, Lloyds Register in 1853 listed 9,934 merchant ships of which only 187 were steam powered, but of these 68 per cent were built of iron rather than wood, and 43 per cent powered by screws rather than paddles.[4] In contrast, in the United States, of a total steam marine of 624 vessels largely on inland waters with only 15 per cent ocean-going, only 11 per cent were powered by screws. In June 1852, alongside news of the capture of Rangoon, the *Straits Times* reported that currently on the River Clyde in Scotland there were 37 steamships under construction, 28 paddle steamers and nine screw-powered, ranging in weight from 300 to 2,500 tons, all but seven built of iron, and all but eight of the paddle ships being sea-going. To the south on the Mersey Laird's had now built over 90 ships, amongst these the Royal Navy's only iron paddle frigate, HMS *Birkenhead* of 1,405 tons and 536 hp. Launched in 1845 she was converted to a troopship in 1851, large holes being cut in the previously watertight bulkheads to improve ventilation, a modification with terrible consequences. Leaving Cape Town on 25 February 1852 with 638 people on board, at 2 am the following morning she struck a rock off Danger Bay, sinking within 25 minutes with the loss of 445 lives, a disaster still famous for the exemplary courage and discipline displayed.[5]

That same month, February 1852, witnessed the arrival in Singapore of the first screw vessels to call there. The P & O *Shanghai* (546 tons) arriving on the 27th on her first regular India – China run, had left England late the previous year, reaching Calcutta in 90 days, 78 days at sea of which 51 had been under steam. The *Paou Shan*, a cargo vessel of 400 tons and 80 hp owned by Messrs Dent & Company of Hong Kong, arrived the same day, 89 days direct from Plymouth. Eight months later a second P & O screw vessel arrived in the roads but this time from the south. The *Chusan* (700 tons) had left Sydney on 31 August and travelling via Adelaide, Swan River (Perth) and Batavia reached Singapore on 13 October. Her arrival, promising a start to a much desired service to Australia, was celebrated on 26 October by a splendid party given by Captain Marshall, the P & O agent, in the company's spacious new office.[6]

Three weeks after the *Nemesis* left Singapore for the last time on 30 July 1852, a very different vessel left a very different port for a very different destination. On Saturday 21 August Brunel's iron screw ship, the *Great Britain*, left Liverpool bound for Australia with 630 passengers, a crew of 138 and a full cargo. Despite having to put back to St Helena she reached Capetown on the 10 October and Melbourne on the 11 November, a voyage of just 82 days. Never again did she carry so many passengers on this route – gold had first been discovered in Australia in February of the previous year– nor so fast.[7] But this feat, for a vessel already considered past her prime (but none the less at sea until 1886), built around the same time as the *Nemesis*, only emphasises just how revolutionary she was.

The advent of peace between Britain and the Court of Ava caused the Honourable Company to consider carefully the future of their marine establishments. At this time the Indian Navy of Bombay consisted of about 30 steamers including the *Medusa*, a dozen sea-going and the remainder for river and harbour duties.[8] The smaller Bengal Marine contained nine steamers: the four iron steamers of the Secret Committee, *Nemesis, Phlegethon, Pluto* and *Proserpine* in Burmese waters, the *Enterprize, Fire Queen, Tenasserim* and *Sesostris* (recently transferred from Bombay) around Calcutta and Burma, and the *Hooghly* stationed in Singapore.[9] Not only were many of these vessels old and worn but they were of decreasing utility: the Royal Navy was finding it ever easier to reach Britain's eastern possessions, and the P & O was growing apace and providing greatly improved communications between China, India and the home country. Whereas when the *Nemesis* first set sail from England the P & O owned seven ships; by 1855 they had 42. In 1851 they launched their first screw vessel, the *Shanghai*; in 1852 the *Chusan* reached Australia; and 1853 saw the launching on the Thames of the *Himalaya*, larger than the *Great Britain*, a screw vessel of 3,540 tons and 700 hp, her length at 372 ft considerably longer than the largest British fighting ship, HMS *Duke of Wellington* at 240 ft overall.[10] That same year, 1853, also saw the start of a revolution in travel within the subcontinent itself, with the opening on 16 April of the first Indian passenger railway, running for 21 miles from Bombay to Thane (Tannah).[a] In September of

---

[a]   The first railway from Howrah, across the river from Calcutta, was opened

the following year the P & O was able to deliver the mail to the delighted inhabitants of Singapore just 34 days after it had left London.[11]

Peace in Burma in July 1853 found all five of the iron vessels ordered by the Secret Committee 14 years before in Burmese waters: the *Nemesis* at Bassein, towing ships up and down the river to the sea, transporting stores and carrying troops to various skirmishes, the *Phlegethon* then at Rangoon but later that month sent to Kyaukphyu in Arakan for general duties, the *Pluto* likewise serving Tenasserim from Moulmein, the *Proserpine* and *Medusa* still on the Irrawaddy. All five were clearly showing their age, known to be nearing the end of their useful lives.[12]

At the Bengal Marine's dockyard at Calcutta a new vessel was taking shape, launched on 7 September 1853 as 'the new *Proserpine*' to receive the engines of the old vessel of that name, this a common practice at the time – to transfer the name with the engines. So the *Proserpine* was the first of the five to go, followed three months later by the Indian Navy's *Medusa*. Stationed on the Irrawaddy at Prome on the new northern boundary of British Burma, the *Medusa* on 9 December there suffered the same fate as befell her sister ship *Ariadne* 11 years before off Zhoushan. Steaming a few miles north of the town she stuck an uncharted rock which holed her in her second compartment "and the vessel being in a state of extreme weakness, owing to old age and decay, the sudden rush of water destroyed compartment after compartment," and she sank in 26 ft of water, without loss of life and little lamented.[13]

On 2 November the *Nemesis* arrived in Calcutta from Bassein to be surveyed to see whether she should be repaired or rebuilt, and it was decided that, at this stage, repairs could be undertaken "which will allow her to run for some months longer." On 30 January 1854 she left the dock with her hull and boilers in much better order and her engines thoroughly overhauled, and for the next seven months worked again in Burmese waters. In July the brig *Rob Roy*, carrying opium from Calcutta to Canton, was wrecked on the Andaman Islands, and the *Nemesis* from the Irrawaddy and *Zenobia* from Calcutta were ordered to salvage what they could.[b] The *Nemesis*, first to arrive, took on board 350 chests of the

---

in February 1855, running 55 miles to Burdwan. Lord Dalhousie, the Governor-General between 1848 and 1856, had played an enthusiastic part in railway development in Britain as chairman of the Advisory Board on Railways in 1844/45 (SFP).

[b]   In 1854 in the seas around the British Isles, 987 vessels were wrecked with the loss of 1,549 lives, amongst which was the screw steamer *Nile*, sinking on the

drug and carried them to Rangoon, a nice reminder of her role when first she arrived in eastern seas 14 years before.[14]

In Calcutta on 24 August 1854 many of the crew of the *Nemesis* were discharged, their three years of service completed since they had joined her in August 1851 on the eve of her last voyage to China. But Captain Goodwin stayed on and, recruiting a new crew, returned to Rangoon for service on the Irrawaddy, there joining the *Enterprize*, now commanded by Captain Niblett. Niblett had in mid-1853 been transferred from the *Phlegethon* to the *Enterprize*, "his proper vessel", larger and so allowing him to be paid £50 a month rather than £40, although his new ship now aged 15 years and with engines dating from 1824 was fit only for river service. The *Phlegethon*, now in Arakan under Acting Commander T. H. Hodge, had last been thoroughly overhauled in 1846, with further extensive repairs in late 1852. In February 1855 she became unserviceable and, as in November 1852, had to be ignominiously towed to Calcutta, this time by the *Fire Queen*. There she was condemned and over the next few months dismantled, apparently even her engines being of little value for history does not record a 'new *Phlegethon*'.

And February 1855 also saw the end of her larger and more famous sister ship *Nemesis*, just 15 years old.[c] On Wednesday 28th Captain Goodwin and many of the crew left the *Nemesis* for the new *Proserpine*, which on the 6 March steamed from Calcutta for Arakan to replace the *Phlegethon*. That same day saw the appointment of Captain H. Barrow to the '*Nemesis* troop boat' currently under construction at the Company's dockyard at Kidderpore, a smaller vessel officered only by '1st and 2nd mates' which apparently inherited her namesake's engines. On 1 April the Third Officer of the *Nemesis* under Goodwin, Mr J. Slade, was appointed Officer-in-Charge of her dismantling. But her hull was saved: later that year the annual report mentions the expenditure of 5,140 rupees on "Hulk *Nemesis* partly for accommodation of Harbour Master's assistants." And so she ended her days, a hulk on the banks of the Hooghly River, her engines beating in another hull.

Stones of St Ives which had so nearly been the graveyard of the *Nemesis* 14 years before (Editorial, *The Life-Boat*, vol 2, no. 17, July 1855).

[c]   In contrast, the Navy's very first steamship *Comet*, launched in 1822, was not broken up until 1869 after 47 years of service; but then she was of wood – and never saw action in distant waters. And Brunel's *Great Britain*, of iron and built at the same time as the *Nemesis*, sits even now in the dock where she was built, in Bristol.

And what of the *Pluto* which had started her career in 1839 so inauspiciously? In 1854 the sea steamers of the Bengal Marine came under the control of the Indian Government, and with the demise of the Honourable Company in 1858 after the Indian Mutiny, the Bengal Marine ceased to exist as an independent force. Their last report says that on 31 July 1860 the *Pluto*, the second of that name to serve the Bengal Marine, was still stationed in Tenasserim. And apparently she ran for a year or two longer for not until 1863 is *Pluto (iii)* mentioned, replacing that year the old *Hooghly* in Singapore.[15] So the first of the Secret Committee's six iron vessels to be launched was the last to die.

Epilogue

The Annual Report of the Bengal Marine Department for 1858/59 listed on 31 July 1858 Captain R. Goodwin as commander of the 'sea steamer *Nemesis*', not a troop-boat for her complement of officers and engineers was as large as for our ship. The command of Goodwin's previous ship, the new *Proserpine*, had now passed to W. H. Eales. On the following 30 April this ship was based in Arakan, a year later Goodwin retiring from command, replaced by Eales of the *Proserpine*. The last existing Annual Report states that on 31 July 1860 the *Nemesis* under Eales was stationed at Calcutta.

What was this ship? Surely not our ship, the hulk repaired, the engines returned. But then, what indeed was our ship, our *Nemesis*? Certainly more than Laird's hull and Forester's engines, repaired and renewed over the years. She was also her captains and her crews, her voyages and her exploits. If in her time she captured people's imaginations, as she undoubtedly did, so now a century and a half later we can more fully understand her pioneering role as a ship and her role in history, and, seeing this, can pay sincere tribute to those who gave her life. When indeed does such a vessel ever die?

APPENDIX 1   Tables

Table 1. Royal Navy ships in commission, 1 May 1840

Data from Anon (1840), Anon (2003), Kemp (1976), Lyon & Winfield (2004).

Rating	Number of ships	Number of guns	Approx crew	Present station
Line of battle				British waters 65, Mediterranean 44, West Indies 28, South America 24, Coast of Africa 21, East Indies 14, North America 4, Australia 2.
First Rate	6	Over 110, 3 gundecks	840	
Second Rate	8	90–110, 3 gundecks	740	
Third Rate	14	80–90, 2 gundecks	500–720	
Below the line				
Fourth Rate	2	60–80, 1–2 gundecks	350	
Fifth Rate – frigates	8	32–60, 1 gundeck	220–300	All steamers were in British waters, the Mediterranean or the West Indies.
Sixth Rate – frigates	21	Up to 32, 1 gundeck	140–200	
Unrated				The 73 ships in the West Indies, South America and the coast of Africa were largely employed in anti-slavery patrols.
Sloops	40	16–18	120–140	
Brigs	37	3–10	80–120	
Surveying vessels	12	4–12		
War sloops fitted as packets	23	4–10		
Yachts	3			
Steam vessels	28			
TOTAL	202			

Table 2. *Nemesis*: dimensions and form

Data from Anon (1840), Data largely from Creuze (1840). Dimensions in feet and inches.

Length overall	184′
Length from stem to taffrail	173′
Length between the perpendiculars	165′
Breadth, beam	29′, including paddle-boxes about 47′
Depth	11′
Semi-circumference	23′ 6″
Burthen in tons (old measurement)	660 bm
Draught	Fully laden 6′, unladen 5′
Speed	Max under steam or sail about 9 knots
Engines	Two, each one cylinder 44″ diameter (dia), 4′ stroke, supported with wrought iron framings. Two rectangular boilers each with three fires
Horsepower, nominal	120 hp
Paddle-shaft	78′ abaft fore-end of waterline
Paddle-beams	Oak 12″ square, passing through sides of vessel in sockets and connected on all four sides by angle-iron
Paddle wheels	17′ 6″ dia to inner edge of rim. Width about 8′. Weight about 2 tons each. Basic disconnecting apparatus
Floats	16 per wheel, each 6′ 9″ by 14′ 6″, of elm or pine. Fixed, not feathering, but could be unshipped for sailing
Paddle-boxes	Wood. No paddle-box boats initially
Bridge	Running between paddle-boxes
Funnel	Perfectly smooth at top, no ornamentation

Stays and rigging	Funnel stays and main rigging of chain at top and rope thereafter
Foremast	32′ abaft fore-end of waterline, rakes 2′ in 20′, from deck to hounds 42′, from head 8′, dia 15″
Mainmast	111′ 6″ abaft fore-end of waterline, rakes 1′ in 20′, from deck to hounds 42′ 6″, from head 8′, dia 15″
Fore top-mast	24′, dia 10″
Fore head	4′
Sliding gunter-mast	28′, dia 6″
Sliding pole	8′
Main top-mast	33′, dia 10″
Main pole	13′
Fore gaff	23′, dia 7.5″
Main gaff	23′, dia 7.5″
Fore-yard, cleated	52′, dia 10.5″
Fore-yard, arms	3′, dia 10.5″
Fore-topsail-yard, cleated	36′, dia 8.5″
Fore-topsail-yard, arms	2′, dia 8.5″
Fore-topgallant-yard, cleated	25′, dia 6″
Fore-topgallant-yard, arms	1.5′, dia 6″
Bowsprit, out-board	21′, dia 15″
Bowsprit steeves (rises)	5′ 6″ in 20′
Jib-boom, out-board	13′, dia 8″
Jib-boom, in-board	13′ 6″

Cross-section	Oblong, with base curved down 6" in 15', corners rounded off to an arc of a circle about 3' dia, sides curve slightly outwards
Stern post	Plumb
Stem	Rakes forward of the perpendicular by an angle of 16°
Keel plate	1' wide, slightly curved, convex side down
Frames	3" wide angle-iron, 18" apart amidships, increasing to 3' apart fore and aft. Run up to and end on the metal angle-iron gunwale
Planking	Iron sheets 8' by 2' 6". Lower 6 strakes from keel to turn of bilge clinker-built, strake at turn of bilge and 6 strakes up sides carvel-built. Keel plates 7/16" thick, clinker 3/8", carvel 5/16 to 1/4'
Riveting	3/4 iron rivets put in from inside. Sheets riveted to frame every 3". Outer part of hole to take rivet counter-sunk so outer surface perfectly smooth. Rivets applied at almost welding heat, contracting when cooled so fitting very tight. Clinker seams riveted without strengthening bands, carvel plates to a strip of iron-plate on the inside. Caulked by blows of cold chisel
Wood/iron connections	All with felt sandwiched between
Floor	To the vertical flange of the frames along the bottom of the ship riveted every 6" another angle-iron with about 9" vertical flange, 4" horizontal flange. The floor, of red pine 12" square, bolted to this with 1" bolts (sleepers and keelsons). Bolt-heads sunk about 1/2" and hidden by plugs of white lead so hardly visible
Deck	Deck-beams of two bars of angle-iron back to back with a bar of iron 9" deep and 1/4" thick sandwiched between. To these the deck of 3" fir bolted as with floor
Gunwale (planksheer)	Oak 4" thick, 10" broad, screwed to 3" angle-iron gunwale

Bulkheads	6 bulkheads dividing the vessel into 7 watertight compartments, 4 of 5/16" iron, 2 at ends of 3/16" iron. Wooden sleepers pass through but joint watertight. In stoke-hold, between engines and boilers, a partial bulkhead to strengthen vessel. Small hand pump in each compartment
Coal holes	Against bulkheads fore and aft of engine room, and perhaps elsewhere, holding about 145 tons
Sliding keels	Two, one just before engine-room, one just abaft, each in watertight trunk 1' thick from base to deck made of iron 7/16" secured by angle-iron to a bulkhead which it helps support. Each keel 7'x7', can protrude 5', made of 4 1/2" wood. Raised by small windlass and endless chain
Rudder	True rudder, wood, goes to base of stern post. Iron drop-rudder attached by pivot to lower part of true rudder with chain from its outer edge to taffrail, and can be lowered to the same depth as sliding keels, 5'
Wheel	Aft
Hawseholes	Simple holes for anchor cable both fore and aft, the stern anchors allowing the vessel to be drawn off shore
Painting	Outside of vessel several coats of red lead, then varnished

Table 3. *Nemesis*: other armed paddle steamships compared.

Dimension	H.C.S.V. *Nemesis* 1839–55	HMS Alectoa 1839–65	HMS Cyclopsb 1839–64	HMS Terriblec 1845–79
Type	Iron paddle steamer	Wooden paddle steamer	Wooden paddle steamer	Wooden paddle steamer
Launch/Completion date	L. 23 Nov 1839 'ready for sea' Jan 1840	L. 7 Sep 1839 C. 12 Dec 1839	L. 10 Jul 1839 C. 4 Feb 1840	L. 6 Feb 1845 C. 25 Mar 1846
Length (main deck)	173'	164'	190'	226'
Beam	29'	33'	37'	42'
Draught	4'–6'	–	17'	20'
Tons (bm)	660	800 (878 tons displacement)	1,191 (1,862 tons displacement)	1,847 (3,189 tons displacement)
Machinery	Side-lever, 2-cylinder (44" dia, 48" stroke)	Direct-acting, 2-cylinder	Direct-acting, 2-cylinder (64" dia, 66" stroke)	Direct-acting, 4-cylinder 'Siamese' type (72" dia, 8 ft stroke)
Nominal horsepower	120	200	320	800
Maximum coal, tons	175	–	420	–

Paddle wheels, diameter	17.5'	—	26'	34'
Crew	60–90	—	175	200
Main armament	2 x 32pdr swivels 5 x 6pdr broadsides	2 x 32pdr pivots 2 x 32pdr broadsides	2 x 98pdr/10" pivots 4 x 68pdr/8" broadsides	8 x 68pdr 8 x 56pdr 3 x 12pdr
First cost	£29,943	£27,268 (incl. machinery £10,700)	£53,931 (incl machinery £22,103)	£101,842 (incl machinery £41,820)
Data mainly from	Creuze (1840), Bernard (1844), IOR/L/PS	Lyon & Winfield (2004)	Lyon & Winfield (2004), Brown (1993)	Lyon & Winfield (2004), Brown (1993)

a   Similar in size to Nemesis. Later famous for her tug-of-war with the screw-powered Rattler.

b   When launched the largest steam warship in the world.

c   The most powerful paddle warship ever built, and when built the most powerful steam warship of her day. In 1847 she was captained briefly by W. H. Hall, late of the Nemesis, and at Sebastopol in 1854 by J. J. McCleverty, late of the Phlegethon.

Table 4. *Nemesis*: construction costs compared

Data from IOR/L/MAR

Vessel	Hull	Tons bm	Launch date; builder	Item	Item cost	Total cost (£)a
Nemesis	Iron	660	23 Nov 1839; Lairds, Birkenhead			28,943b
Phlegethon	Iron	530	30 Apr 1840; Lairds, Birkenhead			24,288
*Pluto*c	Iron	450	ca Jul 1839; Fairbairn, Thames			40,315
Queen	Wood	760	6 Jun 1839; Young & Co, Thames	Vessel	15,367	30,890
				After-cabin accom	600	
				Engines	14,500	
				Other partsd	423	
Sesostris	Wood	876	1839; W. & H. Pitcher, Thames	Vessel	16,959	36,114
				After-cabin accom	600	
				Engines	18,135	
				Other parts	420	

					Price		33,439
Zenobia (i)	Wood	684	1837, Ireland; bought 4 Jan 1839		25,000		
				Engine repairs	400		
				Outfitting	8,039		
Tenasserim	Wood	769	23 Apr 1841; Moulmein, Burma				39,885

a All costs given to the nearest £. Costs originally in rupees converted at 10rp = £1.

b 'Total cost' of the three iron vessels may not be strictly comparable to that of the wooden vessels; see text.

c Proserpine never rented to Royal Navy so cost unknown.

d 'Other parts' include anchors. pumps, etc.

Table 5. Expenditure in £ of HEIC Secret Committee on six iron steam vessels over three financial years (May–April): May 1838–April 1841

Data from IOR/L/MAR.

Item	1838/39	1839/40	1840/41	Total
Purchase of vessels and machinery	49,105	39,953	8,000	97,058
Freight & shipping	562	1,938	2,397	4,897
Law expenses	163	–	–	163
Stores	–	9,304	324	9,628
Coals	–	721	155	876
Dollars	–	250	500	750
Chronometers	–	225		225
Current expenses, including outfit and pay of officers and crew.	–	2,278	5,392	7,670
Pay of mechanics sent out with vessels in frame	–	1,791	924	2,715
Sundries	–	25	–	25
Total	£49,830	£56,485	£17,692	£124,007

Table 6. *Nemesis*: annual running costs in £ (May to April)

Data from IOR/L/MAR. Costs converted from rupees to nearest £ at 10 rp = £1.

	1844/45	1847/48	1848/49	1851/52	1852/53	1853/54
Location	Bombay to Nov, Calcutta to Apr	Singapore to Oct, Calcutta to Apr	Calcutta to Dec, Singapore to Apr	Calcutta to Aug, China to Apr	China to Jun, Burma to Apr	Burma
Total	£3,683	£4,066	£4,126	£3,616	£3,245	£4,930
Officers and engineers	797					2,094
Crew	342 (all native)					1,634
Fuel	231					409
Stores	399					659
Repairs to hull	1,015					9
Repairs to engines	724					–
Miscellaneous	175					125

Table 7. *Nemesis*: the crew.

Data from IOR/L/MAR, Anon (2003), Bernard (1844).

Note: In official crew lists four racial categories are given: 'European', 'East Indian' (Caucasians born in India, this probably encompassing 'Eurasians', those of mixed race), 'Native' (mostly Indians – 'lascars', but Filipinos – 'Manila men', and Malays also noted) and 'Chinamen'. The names only of officers and engineers are given except in the east when the names of all Europeans and East Indians are given and of a Native or Chinaman if an engineer. Most engineers were East Indian.

Table 7a. Crew numbers on four dates

Note. E = 'European' and 'East Indian'. N = 'Native' and 'Chinaman'.

Date	1 April 1840 (see Table 7b)	20 June 1844	1 Dec 1848 (see Table 7c)	May 1853
Location	Departing England for east	Departing Bombay for Karachi	Departing Calcutta for Singapore	In Burma
Officers	7E	6E	7E	7E
Engineers	3E	6E	7E	6E
Engine room crew	8E	14N	17N	21N
Warrant/ Petty officers	15E	49N	22: 14E + 8N	20 (E/N unknown)
Able/ Ordinary seamen, boys ('private men')	23E		40: 30E + 10N	30 (E/N unknown)
'European' or 'East Indian'	56	12	58	42
TOTAL	56	75	93	84

Table 7b. Crew on departure from Portsmouth, 28 March 1840

Position	Name	Joined	Discharged	Initial pay, £ per lunar month[a]
Officers (7)				
Commander	W. H. Hall RN	26 Dec 1839	28 Feb 1843, Calcutta	40
1st officer	W. Pedder RN	1 Mar 1840	31 Jul 1841, Hong Kong	15
2nd officer	E. L. Strangways RN	20 Jan 1840	15 Mar 1841, Macau	12
3rd officer	J. L. Galbraith	25 Dec 1839	28 Feb 1843, Calcutta	5
4th officer	F. W. Whitehurst	1 Mar 1840	28 Feb 1843, Calcutta	5
Surgeon	P. Young	1 Mar 1840	20 Jan 1841, Macau	15
Purser	J. Gaunt	21 Jan 1840	28 Feb 1843, Calcutta	8
Engineers (3)				
1st engineer	J. C. McDougall	01 Mar 1840	Accidentally shot 02 Mar 1842	20

a Prior to departure from England the officers of Company ships, but not other ranks, were given an allowance of £40–50 for outfitting and £80–100 for passage home from India. This is not specifically mentioned for the Nemesis.

| 2nd engineer | J. Kinross | 28 Mar 1840 | 21 Aug 1841 | 16 |
| 3rd engineer | H. L. Harley | 1 Mar 1840 | 28 Feb 1843 | 10 |

Others (46): position and initial pay, £ per lunar month

Warrant officers (3): Gunner 5, Carpenter 5, Boatswain 5,

Petty officers (12): Gunner's mate 3, Carpenter's mate 4, Boatswain's mate 4, 2nd master 4, Cook 4, Cook's mate 3, Steward 3.5, Captain's servant 3, Yeoman of signals 3, Armourer 4, Armourer's mate 2.6, Boiler-maker 2.5

'Private men' (31): 17 Able seamen at 3 each, 3 Ordinary seamen at 2.5 – 2.0 each, 7 Stokers at 2.5 – 1.6 each, 3 Boys at 1.5 – 1.0 each, Gunroom servant at 1

Table 7c. Crew on departure from Calcutta, 1 December 1848

Caucasian crew officially listed			Probable native crew
Officers	Engineers	Others	
Captain	1st Engineer	Carpenter	Stoker tindal x 2
1st Officer	2nd Engineer	Gunner	Stokers x 15
2nd Officer	3rd Engineer	Boatswain	Cook's mate
3rd Officer	1st class Apprentices x 3	Carpenter's mate	Stewards x 3
Clerk	3rd class Apprentice	Gunner's mate	Servants x 4
Surgeon		Armourer	Ordinary seamen x 5
Midshipman		Boatswain's mate	Boys x 5
		Gunner's yeoman	
		Quarter-master x 4	
		Purser's steward	
		Ship's cook	
		Able seamen x 30	
Total = 7	Total = 7	Total = 44	Total = 35

Table 7d. Commanding officers, with official dates appointed and discharged

Name	Appointed	Discharged
HALL, William Hutcheon, RN	26 Dec 1839	28 Feb 1843
FELL, W.	Mar 1843	ca Oct 1843
OLIVER, A. William	ca Oct 1843	ca Apr 1845
RUSSELL, J.	ca Apr 1845	30 Nov 1846
WALLAGE, Thomas (1st Officer from March 1843)	1 Dec 1846	30 Nov 1847
Unknown: ship under repair at Calcutta	1 Dec 1847	12 Apr 1848
ROSS, B. S. (temporary command)	13 Apr 1848	21 Dec 1848
WALLAGE, Thomas	22 Dec 1848	Mar 1851
Unknown: ship under repair at Calcutta	Mar 1851	04 Jul 1851
GOODWIN, Robert (1st Officer from December 1848)	5 Jul 1851	28 Feb 1855
SLADE, J. (officer in charge, overseeing dismantling)	1 Mar 1855	–

Table 8. The first steamships in eastern seas, 1823 to August 1842

Data from Bernard (1844), Gardner & Greenhill (1993), Gibson-Hill (1954), IOR/L/PS, Low (1877), Lyon & Winfield (2004), SFP. **Notes**. All vessels are paddle ships. Those marked * belonged to Bengal Marine (Calcutta); all other Company vessels belonged to Indian Navy (Bombay). Sometimes whether ownership was Company or private is difficult to ascertain (e.g., 'Peacock's Iron Chicks').

Name	Launch date & place	Hull, tons bm, nhp	Notes (BU = broken up)
A. HEIC vessels launched in the East			
*Diana (i)	12 Jul 1823, Calcutta	Wood, 132 tons, 32 hp	Built as passage boat/tug on Hooghly, bought 1824. BU 1836.
*Pluto (i)	1822, Calcutta	Wood, 8 hp	Built as dredger; the engine driving two bucket chains. Converted 1824 to troop boat and floating battery. Sunk 1829.
*Irrawaddy (i)	1 Jan 1827, Calcutta	Wood, 305 tons, 80 hp	Tug on Hooghly. BU 1839.
*Ganges (i)	15 Feb 1827, Calcutta	Wood, 305 tons, 80 hp	Tug on Hooghly, packet to Burma.
*Burhampootur	19 Jan 1828, Calcutta	Wood, 152 tons, 50 hp	Packet. Sunk Ganges 27 Jun 1832.
*Hooghly (i)	29 Mar 1828, Calcutta	Wood, 158 tons, 50 hp	Tug/packet on Ganges. Replaced 1845 by Hooghly (ii).

Name	Date, place built	Material, tons, hp	Notes
Hugh Lindsay	4 Oct 1829, Bombay	Wood, 411 tons, 160 hp	Built for Bombay-Suez run. 1843 transferred to Madras. BU 1858.
*Experiment	1830, Calcutta	Wood, 150 tons, 32 hp	Barge-like accommodation vessel on Hooghly.
*Lord William Bentinck, Thames, Megna, Jumna	Built 1832–33, Thames, launched Apr 1834–Jan 1836 Calcutta	All four iron, 275 tons, 60 hp	'Peacock's Iron Chicks', commissioned by Bengal Government, brought in parts to Calcutta for Calcutta Steam Tug Association. All still active 31 July 1853.
Euphrates	Dec 1834, Bir, Upper Euphrates	Iron, 186 tons, 40 hp	Built Lairds, in parts to Middle East for Euphrates Expedition 1835–37. Still in service 1867.
Tigris	Jan 1835, Bir, Upper Euphrates	Iron, 109 tons, 25 hp	Built Lairds, in parts to Middle East for Euphrates Expedition 1835–37. Sunk 21 May 1836.
Diana (ii)	Oct 1836, Calcutta	Wood, 168 tons, 32 hp	Engines from *Diana (i)*. Built for Straits Settlements, Singapore. Sold 1846.
Snake	1838, Bombay	Iron, 40 tons, 10 hp	In parts to Bombay, tender, still serving 1858.
Enterprize (ii)	July 1838, Calcutta	Wood, 572 tons, 120 hp	Engines from *Enterprize (i)*, still serving 1855.
Incus (ii)	1839, Bombay	Iron, 308 tons, 60 hp	Built Lairds, May 1837, in parts to Bombay, still serving 1853.
Assyria	1840, Basra	Iron, 197 tons, 40 hp	These three vessels built Lairds, in parts to Basra. Later with *Euphrates* added to Indus Flotilla.
Nimrod	1840, Basra	Iron, 198 tons, 40 hp	
Nitocris	1840, Basra	Iron, 154 tons, 40 hp	

Comet (ii)	1839, Bombay	Iron, 205 tons, 40 hp	These two vessels built Lairds, in parts to Bombay for Indus Flotilla.
Meteor	1839, Bombay	Iron, 149 tons, 25 hp	
Planet	1840, Bombay	Iron, 397 tons, 60 hp	These two vessels in parts to Bombay for Indus Flotilla. *Satellite* stationed Sind till 1873.
Satellite	1840, Bombay	Iron, 335 tons, 60 hp	
Ariadne	1840, Bombay	Iron, 432 tons, 70 hp	These two vessels built Lairds, in parts to Bombay. *Ariadne* sunk off Zhoushan 23 Jun 1842, *Medusa* sunk Irrawaddy 9 Dec 1853.
Medusa	1840, Bombay	Iron, 432 tons, 70 hp	
Victoria	Oct 1839, Bombay	Wood, 714 tons, 230 hp	Sold ca 1864.
Auckland	9 Jan 1840, Bombay	Wood, 964 tons, 220 hp	Sold ca 1874.
*Tenasserim	23 Apr 1841, Moulmein	Wood, 769 tons, 220 hp	Half-sister to Queen (below). Still serving 1853.
Semiramis (ii)	26 Feb 1842, Bombay	Wood, 1031 tons, 350 hp	Hulked 1863.
B. HEIC vessels launched in Britain, steaming East			
*Enterprize (i)	22 Feb 1825, Thames	Wood, 464 tons, 120 hp	Reached Calcutta 8 Dec 1825. Bought by Company Jan 1826. BU 1838.
Atalanta	1836, Thames	Wood, 616 tons, 210 hp	Reached Bombay 13 Apr 1837. For Bombay-Suez run. BU ca 1850.

Berenice	1836, Clyde	Wood, 630 tons, 230 hp	Reached Bombay 13 Jun 1837. For Bombay-Suez run. Burnt at sea 1866.
Semiramis (i)	1837, Thames	Wood, 800 tons, 300 hp	Reached Bombay 12 Apr 1838. Damaged Feb 1839, replaced by Zenobia. Later coal hulk at Aden.
Zenobia (i)	1837, Waterford	Wood, 684 tons, 280 hp	Reached Bombay 14 Jul 1839. Irish cargo vessel Kilkenny bought Jan 1839. Hulked ca 1850.
*Madagascar	1838, Portugal	Wood, 350 tons, 120 hp	Reached Calcutta 1839. Portuguese, bought 1840 for Opium War. Burnt at sea 20 Sep 1841.
Cleopatra	1839, Thames	Wood, 770 tons, 220 hp	Reached Bombay 29 Apr 1840. Lost without trace off Malabar coast 14 Apr 1847.
*Queen	16 Jun 1839, Thames	Wood, 766 tons, 220 hp	Reached Calcutta early 1840. Half-sister to Tenasserim (above). Listed to 1860.
Sesostris	1839, Thames	Wood, 876 tons, 220 hp	Reached Bombay 16 Jun 1840. Transferred from Bombay to Calcutta 1853.
*Pluto (ii)	Mid 1839, Thames	Iron, 450 tons, 100 hp	Reached Singapore 23 Apr 1842. Still serving 1860.
*Proserpine	Early 1840, Thames	Iron, 400 tons, 90 hp	Reached Calcutta Mar/Apr 1841. BU late 1853.
*Nemesis	23 Nov 1839, Birkenhead	Iron, 660 tons, 120 hp	Reached Singapore 30 Oct 1840. BU 1855.
*Phlegethon	30 Apr 1840, Birkenhead	Iron, 530 tons, 90 hp	Reached Calcutta 22 May 1841. BU 1855.

Memnon	1841, Thames	Wood, 1,140 tons, 400 hp	Reached Singapore 24 Jun 1842. Wrecked Cape Guardafui, Somalia, 1 Aug 1843.
Akbar	1841, Clyde	Wood, 1,143 tons, 350 hp	Reached Singapore 25 Aug 1842. Sold 1859.

C. Royal Navy vessels

Driver	24 Dec 1840, Portsmouth	Wood, 1,056 tons, 280 hp	Reached Zhoushan 28 Aug 1842. Wrecked West Indies 3 Aug 1861.
Vixen	4 Feb 1841, Pembroke	Wood, 1,056 tons, 280 hp	Reached Hong Kong 19 May 1842. BU 1862.

D. Other vessels – until 1835 cnly

[Steam yacht]	1819, Lucknow	Wood, 19 tons, 8 hp	Inland yacht for Nawab of Oude, very little known.
Vander Capellen	23 Nov 1825, Surabaya, Java	Wood, 236 tons, 50 hp	Built Java for merchant service around Java. Apr 1827 first steamer in Singapore. Sold 1840 to King of Cochin-China.
Emulous	28 Oct 1825, Thames	Wood, 226 tons, 100 hp	Reached Calcutta 21 Sep 1826. Passage boat/tug. BU 1838.
Telica	1824, Liverpool	Wood, 134 tons, 50 hp	Reached Calcutta Apr 1827 after working in South American. Used as tug. 1829 sold to Indian Navy as sailing vessel.

Comet (i)	1826, Calcutta	Wood, 76 tons, 20 hp	Passage boat/tug. BU 1836.
Firefly	1826, Calcutta	Wood, 76 tons, 20 hp	Passage boat/tug. BU 1836.
Forbes	21 Jan 1829, Calcutta	Wood, 302 tons, 120 hp	Tug on Hooghly. 1830 first steamer in China (Macau). Purchased 1835 by newly formed Calcutta Steam Tug Association.
Indus (i)	15 Aug 1833, Bombay	Wood, 13 hp	Tug. BU 1837.
Jardine	1835, Aberdeen	Wood, 115 tons, 48 hp	Reached China Sep 1835 as sailing vessel. Engines put in order but removed 1836.
Willem de Eerste	4 Aug 1823, Amsterdam	Wood, 595 tons, 120 hp	Sold to Netherlands Indies government 1835, reached Batavia 1836. Wrecked 1837.
Hekla	1835, Rotterdam	Iron, 80 hp	Sent in parts to Surabaya, Java, launched 24 Dec 1836.
Etna	1835, Rotterdam	Iron	Sent in parts to Surabaya, Java, launched early 1837.

Table 9. British naval ships engaged in the Opium War, 1839–42

Data from Bernard (1844), Clowes (1901), Low (1877), Lyon & Winfield (2004), Ouchterlony (1844), SFP.

Note: Throughout the war there were other British ships involved as transports, troopships and store ships, many privately owned.

Table 9a. Steamships

Name	Launch date & place	Hull, tons bm, nhp	Arrival in China seas
Royal Navy			
Driver	24 Dec 1840, Portsmouth	Wood, 1,056 tons, 280 hp	25 Aug 1842, Zhoushan, to end
Vixen	4 Feb 1841, Pembroke	Wood, 1,056 tons, 280 hp	19 May 1842, Hong Kong, to end
HEIC Indian Navy (Bombay)a			
Ariadne	1840, Bombay	Iron, 432 tons, 70 hp	22 Jan 1842, Hong Kong, sunk 23 June 1842
Atalanta	1836, Thames	Wood, 616 tons, 210 hp	20 Jun 1840, Hong Kong, to 24 Aug 1841
Auckland	9 Jan 1840, Bombay	Wood, 964 tons, 220 hp	13 May 1842, Hong Kong, to end
Medusa	1840, Bombay	Iron, 432 tons, 70 hp	19 May 1842, Hong Kong, to end
Memnon	1841, Thames	Wood, 1,140 tons, 400 hp	23 Jul 1842, Hong Kong, to end

---

[a] HEIC steamship *Ackbar* reached Singapore on her way to China on 25 August 1842.

Sesostris	1839, Thames	Wood, 876 tons, 220 hp	Aug 1841, Hong Kong, to end
HEIC Bengal Marine (Calcutta)			
Enterprize (ii)	July 1838, Calcutta	Wood, 572 tons, 120 hp	Jun 1840, Hong Kong, depart Singapore for Calcutta 3 Feb 1841
Hooghly (i)	29 Mar 1828, Calcutta	Wood, 158 tons, 50 hp	Aug 1841, Hong Kong, to end
Madagascar	1838, Portugal	Wood, 350 tons, 120 hp	16 Jun 1840, Hong Kong, burnt at sea 20 Sep 1841
Nemesis	23 Nov 1839, Birkenhead	Iron, 660 tons, 120 hp	25 Nov 1840, Hong Kong, to end
Phlegethon	30 Apr 1840, Birkenhead	Iron, 530 tons, 90 hp	29 Jul 1841, Hong Kong, to end
Pluto	Mid 1839, Thames	Iron, 450 tons, 100 hp	15 May 1842, Hong Kong, to end
Proserpine	1840, Thames	Iron, 400 tons, 90 hp	Jun 1842, Woosung, to end
Queen	16 Jun 1839, Thames	Wood, 766 tons, 220 hp	Jun 1840, Hong Kong, to end
Tenasserim	23 Apr 1841, Moulmein	Wood, 769 tons, 220 hp	6 May 1842, Hong Kong, to end

Table 9b. Royal Navy sailing ships

* in Chinese waters at end of the war, 29 August 1842

Rating	Name & gunsb	Total
3rd	*Blenheim 74, *Cornwallis 74, Melville 72, Wellesley 72	4
4th	*Endymion 50, *Vindictive 50	2
5th	*Blonde 46, *Cambrian 36, Druid 46, *Thalia 46	4
6th	*Alligator 28,c *Calliope 26, Conway 28, *Herald 28, *North Star 28, Samarang 28, Volage 28	7
Unrated	*Algerine 10, *Childers 18, *Clio 16, *Columbine 18, *Cruiser 18, *Dido 18, *Harlequin 16, *Hazard 18, Hyacinth 18, Larne 18, *Modeste 18, Nimrod 20, *Pelican 18, Pylades 18, *Serpent 16, *Wanderer 16, *Wolverene 16	17
Troop-ship	*Apollo (ex Fifth Rate), *Belleisle (ex Third Rate), *Jupiter (ex Fourth Rate), *Rattlesnake (ex Sixth Rate), *Sapphire (ex Sixth Rate),	5
Survey vessel	Louisa (cutter), *Plover (cutter), *Royalist (brig), *Starling (schooner), Sulphur (bomb vessel)	5
Hospital ship	*Minden (ex Third Rate)	1
		45

---

b   Guns from Lyon & Winfield 2004.
c   Alligator a troopship from July 1842.

Table 9c. British ships at two engagements

Type	July/August 1840 off Hong Kongd	6 July 1842 off Woosunge
HM sailing ships	15: *Algerine, Alligator, Blenheim, Blonde, Columbine, Conway, Cruiser, Druid, Hyacinth, Larne, Melville, Nimrod, Pylades, Volage, Wellesley*	9: *Algerine, Blonde, Calliope, Clio, Columbine, Cornwallis, Dido, Endymion, Modeste*
HM steamships – wood	-	1: *Vixen*
HM troop-ships	1: *Rattlesnake*	5: *Apollo, Belleisle, Jupiter, Rattlesnake, Sapphire*
HM survey ships	1: *Louisa*	2: *Plover, Starling*
HEIC steamers – wood	4: *Atalanta, Enterprize (ii), Madagascar, Queen*	4: *Auckland, Queen, Sesostris, Tenasserim*
HEIC steamers – iron	-	5: *Medusa, Nemesis, Phlegethon, Pluto, Proserpine*
Total naval ships	21	26
Transport & store ships	27	48
Total fleet	48	74

---

d   At this time the only British ships in Chinese waters were off Hong Kong/Macau.

e   At this time many British ships were elsewhere in Chinese waters (e.g., Zhoushan, Hong Kong). The only other steamship was the Bengal Marine's *Hooghly* at Hong Kong.

Table 10. British naval ships in Burmese waters, April 1852

Data largely after Low (1877); also from Laurie (1853), Lyon & Winfield (2004), SFP, ST.

Name	Launch date & place	Hull, tons bm, nhp	Heavy guns, men Fate	Arrival in Burma
Royal Navy				
Fox	17 Aug 1829 Portsmouth	Wood, 1,077 tons, (Fifth Rate, sail)	42 guns, 315 men BU 1882	Oct 1851
Hermes	25 Jun 1835 Portsmouth	Wood, 715 tons, 140 hp	3 guns, 135 men BU 1864	Jan 1852
Rattler (screw)	13 Apr 1843 Thames	Wood, 866 tons, 200 hp	9 guns, ca 135 men BU 1856	Apr 1852
Serpent	14 Jul 1832 Thames	Wood, 418 tons, (unrated, sail)	12 guns, 110 men BU 1861	By Jan 1852
Salamander	14 May 1832 Thames	Wood, 818 tons, 220 hp	6 guns, 135 men BU 1883	Apr 1852

HEIC Indian Navy (Bombay)

Berenice	1836, Clyde	Wood, 630 tons, 230 hp	Troop/store ship, 2 guns, 97 men Burnt at sea 1866	Apr 1852
Ferooz	18 May 1848, Bombay	Wood, 1,447 tons, 500 hp	8 guns, 230 men	Apr 1852
Medusa	1840, Bombay	Iron, 432 tons, 70 hp	2 guns, 60 men Sunk Irrawaddy 9 Dec 1853	Apr 1852
Mcozuffer	27 Jan 1846, Thames	Wood, 1,440 tons, 500 hp	7 guns, 230 men Sunk off Rangoon 15 Jul 1853	Apr 1852
Sesostris	1839, Thames	Wood, 876 tons, 220 hp	4 guns, 135 men	Apr 1852
Zenobia (ii)	1 May 1851, Bombay	Wood, 1,003 tons, 280 hp	6 guns, 200 men	Apr 1852

HEIC Bengal Marine (Calcutta)

Enterprize (ii)	July 1838, Calcutta	Wood, 572 tons, 120 hp		Mar 1852
Fire Queen	25 Sep 1843, Liverpool	Iron, 371 tons, 200 hp		Aug 1851
°*Mahanuddy*	After Aug 1842, Calcutta	Presumed wood		*early 1852
Phlegethon	30 Apr 1840, Birkenhead	Iron, 530 tons, 90 hp	2 guns BU 1855	*Jan 1852
Pluto	Mid 1839, Thames	Iron, 450 tons, 100 hp	1 gun Still serving 1860	Apr 1852
Proserpine	Early 1840, Thames	Iron, 400 tons, 90 hp	2 guns BU late 1853	*Oct 1851
Tenasserim	23 Apr 1841, Moulmein	Wood, 769 tons, 220 hp	Still serving 1853	Oct 1851

Steamers joining later

				12 Aug 1852
Nemesis	23 Nov 1839, Birkenhead	Iron, 660 tons, 120 hp	2 guns, ca 84 men BU 1855	
°*Damoodah*				*
°*Indus*	1839, Bombay	Iron, 308 tons, 60 hp		*
°*Lord William Bentinck*	1834, Calcutta	Iron, 275 tons, 60 hp		*
°*Nerbudda*				*

° = 'river steamers'; by July 1853 the Bengal Marine had 10, the above plus *Berhampooter, Hooringotta, Jumna, Megna, Thames.* Of their eight 'sea steamers', seven (as above) were employed in the Burmese campaign, the *Hooghly* in Singapore. These were soon joined by the *Sesostris,* transferred from the Indian Navy.

* = mentioned in ST 12 April 1853 as present 19 March 1853

Strength of forces 7 April 1852 (from Low 1877)			
	Men	Heavy guns	Warships
Royal Navy	818	80	5
Indian Navy	952	31	6
Bengal Marine	500	33	7
Troops	5,767	16	–
Total	8,037	160	18

Table 11. The dance of the sliding-keel ships

Location

'Bombay' : the home port and includes the seas to the west of India
'Calcutta' : the home port and includes Burma
'Straits'   : Singapore the home port and includes Penang, the South China Sea and Borneo
'China'   : Hong Kong the home port and includes the coast to the east.

Note: The sixth sliding-keel ship, *Ariadne*, sister-ship to *Medusa*, was launched in Bombay in 1840, departed Bombay with Medusa September 1841, arrived in China January 1842, and sank off Zhoushan, China, June 1842.

	Nemesis	Phlegethon	Pluto	Proserpine	Medusa
1839	Nov: launched England		ca Jun: launched England		Dec: completed England
1840	Jan–Mar: England Mar–Nov: voyage to east Nov–Dec: China	Apr: launched England. Sep–Dec: voyage to east	All year: England	ca Jan: launched England. Sep–Dec: voyage to east	In parts to Bombay and there launched
1841	All year: China	Jan–May: voyage to east May–Jun: Calcutta Jul–Dec: China	Jan–Oct: England Oct–Dec: voyage to east	Jan–Jun: voyage to east Jul–Dec: Calcutta	Jan–Sep: Bombay Oct–Dec: aborted voyage to China
1842	All year: China (depart Dec)	All year: China	Jan–May: voyage to east May–Dec: China	Jan–May: Calcutta Jun–Dec: China	Jan–Apr: Calcutta May–Dec: China
1843	Feb–Apr: Calcutta May–Dec: Bombay	Jan–May: China Jun–Dec: Calcutta	Feb–Apr: Calcutta May–Dec: Bombay	All year: China	All year: China
1844	Jan–Nov: Bombay Dec: Calcutta	Jan–May: Calcutta May–Dec: Straits	All year: Bombay	All year: China	All year: China

1845	Jan–May: Calcutta Jun–Aug: Straits Sep–Dec: China	All year: Straits	Jan–May: Bombay Jun–Aug: Straits Sep–Dec: China	Jan–Mar: China Apr–Dec: Calcutta	Jan–Nov: China Dec: Bombay
1846	Jan–Dec: China Dec: Straits	Jan–Oct: Straits Nov–Dec: Calcutta	All year: China	All year: Calcutta	All year: Bombay
1847	Jan–Oct: Straits Nov–Dec: Calcutta	Jan–Jul: Calcutta Aug–Dec: Straits	All year: China	All year: Calcutta	All year: Bombay
1848	All year: Calcutta (depart Dec)	Jan–Nov: Straits Nov–Dec: China	All year: China	All year: Calcutta	All year: Bombay
1849	All year: Straits (arrive Jan)	All year: China	Jan: China Feb–Dec: Calcutta	All year: Calcutta	All year: Bombay
1850	All year: Straits	All year: China	All year: Calcutta	All year: Calcutta	All year: Bombay
1851	Jan–Feb: Straits Mar–Aug: Calcutta Oct–Dec: China	Jan–Nov: China Nov–Dec: Calcutta	Jan–Mar: Calcutta Apr–Dec: Straits	All year: Calcutta	All year: Bombay
1852	Jan–Jun: China Aug–Dec: Calcutta	All year: Calcutta	Jan–Mar: Straits Apr–Dec: Calcutta	All year: Calcutta	Jan–Feb: Bombay Mar–Dec: Calcutta
1853	All year: Calcutta	All year: Calcutta	All year: Calcutta	ca Sep: dismantled Calcutta	Jan–Dec: Calcutta Dec: sunk Irrawaddy
1854	All year: Calcutta	All year: Calcutta	All year: Calcutta		
1855	From Mar: dismantled Calcutta	From Mar: dismantled Calcutta	All year: Calcutta		
			[Jul 1860: still serving from Calcutta]		

APPENDIX 2

The Engines of the Nemesis[1]

The *side-lever engine*, which powered most steamers in the 1830s, was a direct development of Watt's beam engine, the single overhead beam being replaced by two beams, the *side-levers*, low down on either side. How did they work? The *piston* in the single vertical *cylinder* was attached by the *piston-rod* to the centre of the *cross-head* which moved up and down in lateral guides to ensure motion parallel to the upright cylinder. To each end of the cross-head *side-rods* were fixed, their bottom ends attached to one end of the two side-levers. These were pivoted about their mid-point, and at their other end were connected to each other by a *cross-tail*, to the centre of which was attached a *connecting-rod*, this leading up to a *crank-pin* on the *paddle-shaft*. As the connecting rod was comparatively long this allowed effective turning action without the rod having to move far from the vertical. Each of the two cylinders powered a different crank-pin, these being set at right angles to each other to provide an even turning of the shaft. At least two pumps, the *air-pump* and *feed-pump*, were also powered by the movement of the side-levers. The whole thing was set on a massive *foundation plate* which contained the *condenser* and *hot-well*.

The steam was produced by two rectangular *box boilers*, on the *Nemesis* made of wrought-iron rather than copper, these being cheaper but more liable to corrosion, their life expectancy being no more than three years compared with nine for copper. The flat plates were just riveted together for leaks were of little importance as they worked at

---

[1]   Engine details largely from Brown (1993), Griffiths (1997), McMurray (1972). The Science Museum, London, has a beautiful working model of the engines of the paddle-steamer Ruby, similar in size and vintage to the *Nemesis*.

very low pressures, only 4 pounds per square inch (4 psi) when all the furnaces were lit. Each had two *safely valves* of the deadweight type. The sea water in the boiler surrounded the *furnaces*, three in a single tier on the *Nemesis*, the *combustion chamber* and the *flues* which carried the hot gases to the *funnel*. The more efficient tubular boiler, in which the hot gases passed through small tubes rather than large-section flues, was not introduced until 1843.

Steam gathered in the space at the top of the boiler and was there led to the engine, power resulting not from steam pressure on the cylinder but rather the low pressure on the other side due to condensation. This condensation was brought about by a fine jet of sea-water sprayed into the *jet-condenser*, this drawn from the sea by the feed-pump, the rose of which could sometimes annoyingly become blocked by seaweed. The air-pump extracted air and water from the condenser and discharged it into the hot-well from where the salty water was returned to the boilers, excess being pumped overboard. 'Surface-condensers', which kept fresh boiler water and salt cooling water separate, were being trialled in the 1830s but were not yet reliable.

Side-lever engines were quite easy to operate but they were not easy to start. For this several engineers were needed, to activate the controls and valves in the correct sequence so that the wheels turned in the required direction, ahead or astern. Once steam was up, this usually taking about 1 hour 20 minutes from lighting the furnaces, the entire engine – cylinders, condenser, air-pump – was flooded with steam by opening the steam-supply valve, the cylinder-valve being moved by hand so that steam was present both above and below the piston. The side levers and connecting-rods were then positioned for correct direction of rotation, and water injected into the jet-condenser to create a vacuum in the condenser, the air-pump and one side of the piston; then atmospheric pressure acting on the opposite side produced the work. Speed was then regulated by the steam-supply valve, the regulation of cooling water to the condenser being of great importance. Then if speed was to be maintained the six furnaces had to be almost continuously fed, ash being raked from the front and cooled by bilge water. If the coal was of high quality each furnace had to be thoroughly cleaned once a day, but if of poor quality up to four times a day. And then the boilers needed frequent 'blow-down'; twice during each 4-hour watch the bottom layer of water, which had the highest salt concentration, was blown out to sea. And all this in cramped quarters and in raging heat.

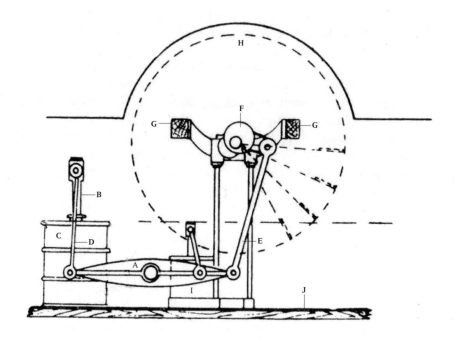

Diagram of side-lever engine

A Side-lever
B Piston
C Cylinder
D Side-rod
E Connecting-rod
F Paddle-shaft
G Paddle-beam
H Paddle wheel
I Air-pump/Feed-pump
J Foundation-plate

If side-lever engines were reliable and comparatively easy to maintain, they had two major drawbacks. Firstly, they were exceedingly inefficient, consuming huge quantities of fuel, perhaps a ton for every 12 miles travelled. This derived from the fact that massive weights were moved up and down, stopping and reversing at every stroke. The stresses thus created meant that the machines had to be extremely strong and thus very heavy, and this meant a great amount of power needed to move them. Secondly, they were very bulky, the whole machinery in the *Nemesis* – engines, boilers, bunkers – probably occupying all the space between the front of the paddle-boxes and the main mast, about 40 ft, a quarter of her length. So whilst perhaps adequate for powering regular packet services in calm waters, side-lever engines were of little use for merchant ships. Screw propulsion developed more thrust per unit of power applied to the shaft compared with paddles, and this efficiency in its turn allowed the development of the compound engine. This was both more economical and more compact, leaving more space for profitable goods and passengers, so not until these became commercially viable in the 1860s did steam come into its own for long commercial voyages.

NOTES

Chapter 1

1. Details of the maiden voyage and of the first three years of service are taken largely from Bernard (1844). The author was a friend of Captain Hall, sailed with him in 1842/43, and used Hall's notes in compiling his book. This sold well and a second edition was published the following year (Bernard 1845) and a significantly amended third edition the year after (Bernard 1846). Hall's personal diary (Hall, no date) also gives some relevant data, and where facts conflict this is preferred.
2. Greenhill & Giffard (1994) give an excellent account of the Royal Navy in the first half of the nineteenth century.
3. Throughout, data on all Royal Navy ships follows Lyon & Winfield (2004). This invaluable compendium gives details of all RN ships 1815–89.
4. Greenhill & Giffard (1994).
5. Walker (1938).
6. Ibid.
7. Hall's life largely from O'Byrne (1849), *Dictionary of National Biography*, and *Illustrated London News* (23 Dec. 1854, pages 641––2).
8. Both quotations from O'Byrne (1849).
9. Pool (1993).
10. Keppel (1899), Stuart (1967).
11. Cochrane (2005).
12. Lord Adolphus from *Dictionary of National Biography*.
13. IOR/L/PS.
14. Peacock/Barrow letters in IOR/L/PS.

15.   Creuze (1840).
16.   Bernard (1844).

Chapter 2

1.   Data on voyage to the East largely from Bernard (1844).
2.   Guest (1992), *Dictionary of National Biography*.
3.   Keay (1991) gives a thoroughly readable history of the HEIC.
4.   For a history of the spice trade see Keay (2005).
5.   IOR/L/PS and *Dictionary of National Biography*.
6.   IOR/L/MAR.
7.   This and subsequent Secret Committee quotations below from IOR/L/PS.
8.   Cammell Laird Archives in Wirral Archives, UK, for list of Laird ships
9.   IOR/L/PS.
10.   This and other letters below from IOR/L/PS.
11.   Gibson-Hill (1954) gives a valuable account of early steamers in Asian waters.

Chapter 3

1.   Hollett (1995).
2.   History of Lairds from Anon (1959), Hollett (1992, 1995).
3.   Guest (1992) gives a fine account of Colonel F. R. Chesney's Euphrates Expedition with these ships in 1835 - 1837.
4.   History of steamships largely from Gardiner & Greenhill (1993), Griffiths (1997), Rowland (1970); for steam warships Gardiner & Lambert (1992).
5.   Corlett (1975).
6.   Pool (1993).
7.   Railways from Bagwell (1974), Crump (2007), Flanders (2006), Wolmar (2007). Freeman (1999) beautifully illustrates the profound effects that railways had upon the culture of Victorian Britain.
8.   Gardiner & Greenhill (1993) give a good account of the development of paddle and screw power.
9.   Corlett (1975).

10. Pool (1993).
11. Hollett (1995).
12. Greenhill & Giffard (1994) and others.
13. Airy (1840).

Chapter 4

1. Reprinted in SFP, 5 November 1840.
2. Cammell Laird Archives, in Wirral Archives, UK.
3. Dimensions of *Nemesis* from Creuze (1840). Sutton (2000) gives an account of the construction of a similar wooden ship. Brown (1978) summarises knowledge of the *Nemesis* at that date, largely from Bernard (1844) and Creuze (1840).
4. Corlett (1975).
5. Ibid.
6. Logs in IOR/L/MAR.
7. Ibid.
8. Ibid.
9. Lyon & Winfield (2004).
10. Gardiner & Greenhill (1993).
11. IOR/L/MAR.
12. Bernard (1844).
13. Gardiner & Lambert (1992).
14. Anon (2003).
15. Winter (1990).
16. Mundy (1848).
17. IOR/L/MAR.
18. Lyon & Winfield (2004).
19. Corlett (1975).
20. Hollett (1995).
21. Roff in Gardiner & Greenhill (1993), Gardiner & Lambert (1992), Greenhill & Giffard (1994).

Chapter 5

1. Keay (1991).
2. Voyage very largely from Bernard (1844).

3.   Hollett (1995).
4.   Ibid.
5.   Mundy (1848)
6.   Jacobs (1991)
7.   IOR/L/PS

Chapter 6

1.   Data on crew numbers and pay from IOR/L/MAR. Bernard (1844) has a little additional data.
2.   Ranks and duties from Anon (2003), Fremont-Barnes (2005), Lavery (2007).
3.   Walker (1938).
4.   Flanders (2006), Pool (1993).
5.   Holmes (2005).
6.   Hall (no date).
7.   Mundy (1848).
8.   Earl (1837).
9.   Greenhill & Giffard (1972) give a fine account of life on board nineteenth-century passenger ships, Jacobs (1991) on VOC vessels. Further data from Greenhill & Giffard (1994), Pool (1993), Sutton (2000).
10. Walker (1938).
11. Hope (2001).

Chapter 7

1.   IOR/L/PS
2.   Voyage largely from Bernard (1844)
3.   IOR/L/PS
4.   Ibid.
5.   Wilson (2003)
6.   IOR/L/PS
7.   Bernard (1844)
8.   IOR/L/PS

Chapter 8

1. For the history of Singapore *see* Hall (1981), Makepeace et al. (1921).
2. Levien (1981). Surgeon Cree provides a fascinating and beautifully illustrated account of his naval career.
3. Cunynghame (1844)
4. Bernard (1844).
5. IOR/L/MAR.
6. Bernard (1844).
7. Brown (1993), Gardiner & Lambert (1992), Greenhill & Giffard (1994).
8. History of steam in the Royal Navy largely from Brown (1993), Gardiner & Lambert (1992). Data on individual ships from Lyon & Winfield (2004). Also Brown (1978).
9. Company marines from Low (1877), Sutton (2000).
10. Sutton (2000).
11. Data on ships in the east from Gibson-Hill (1954), also Roff in Gardiner & Greenhill (1993), Sutton (2000).
12. Details of *Enterprize* from Low (1877), Gibson-Hill (1954).
13. Sutton (2000).
14. Ibid.
15. Guest (1992).
16. Greenhill & Giffard (1994).
17. Cunynghame (1844).

Chapter 9

1. Much has been written on the first Opium War. For a general account I have relied particularly on the excellent work of Fay (1975). Gelber (2004) also proved most valuable, particularly as it concentrates upon what the British thought they were doing, and why. Beeching (1975) provides a very readable if less scholarly approach. Bernard (1844) descibes the actions of the *Nemesis*. Waley (1958) gives an invaluable insight into the Chinese perspective. Cunynghame (1844) and Ouchterlony (1844) provide contemporary views of events leading to the war, and interesting eyewitness accounts of the conflict. Other valuable references are Elleman (2001), Gregory (2003), Hanes & Sanello (2002), Wakeman (1966), and Wang (2003).

2. Moxham (2003).
3. Sutton (2000).
4. Gelber (2004).
5. Ibid.
6. Blake (1999).
7. Gelber (2004).
8. Beeching (1975).
9. Elleman (2001).
10. Blake (1960) provides a biography of Elliot.
11. Gelber (2004).
12. Hernon (2003).
13. Sun Tzu (1988).
14. Blake (1999).
15. Sutton (2000).
16. Waley (1958).

Chapter 10

1. Hanes & Sanello (2002).
2. *See* for example Low (1994).
3. SFP.
4. Ibid.
5. *United Services Journal* 1840, part 2, p. 109–11.
6. Gelber (2004) gives a fine account about the debates in London concerning China and opium.
7. Levien (1981). For further information on HMS *Rattlesnake* see Goodman (2005).
8. Fay (1975).
9. Hanes & Sanello (2002).
10. Gelber (2004).
11. References for war as for Chapter 10.
12. Ships' arrivals and departures in Singapore from SFP. For details of ships *see* Table 9
13. Earl (1837)
14. Earl (1837), introduction by C. M. Turnbull (1971)
15. SFP.
16. Levien (1981).
17. Ouchterlony (1844)
18. SFP.

19.   Holmes (2005).
20.   Ouchterlony (1844)
21.   Hernon (2003), Ouchterlony (1844)
22.   Hanes & Sanello (2002)

Chapter 11

1.   Bernard (1844).
2.   References for war as for Chapter 10. Details of this action, the first involving an iron warship, also from *Canton Register* 19 January 1841 from SFP 4 February 1841.
3.   Ouchterlony (1844).
4.   Galbraith (1841).
5.   Gelber (2004).
6.   Galbraith (1841).
7.   Ibid.
8.   Bernard (1844).
9.   SFP.
10.   Bernard (1844).
11.   Wakeman (1966).
12.   Levien (1981).
13.   Farwell (1973).
14.   Galbraith (1841)

Chapter 12

1.   SFP.
2.   References for war as for Chapter 10.
3.   Bernard (1844).
4.   Fay (1975).
5.   Bernard (1844).
6.   Ibid.
7.   Farwell (1985).
8.   Fay (1975).
9.   Ouchterlony (1844).
10.   Bernard (1844).
11.   Ibid.

12. From SFP.
13. Ibid.
14. Levien (1981).
15. David (2006), Holmes (2005).
16. David (2006), Farwell (1973).
17. Laurie (1853).
18. David (2006).
19. Ibid.
20. Fay (1975), Gelber (2004), Wakeman (1966).
21. Sun-Tzu (1988).
22. Cunynghame (1844).
23. Gelber (2004).
24. Wakeman (1966) gives full details of 'The Battle of San-yuan-li'.
     Low (1994) gives a version deemed suitable for Chinese readers as
     the return of Hong Kong to China in 1997 approached, the noble
     peasant vanquishing an army of a thousand men of 'the Aggressive
     Forces of Western Capitalism'.
25. Low (1877)
26. Levien (1981).
27. Ouchterlony (1844)
28. Wakeman (1966) provides a fascinating account of the origins of
     the Taiping Rebellion and of its leader Hong Xiuqan (Hung Hsiu-
     chüan).

Chapter 13

1.   Fay (1975).
2.   Levien (1981).
3.   Hope (2001).
4.   Gill (1995), Holmes (2005).
5.   Bernard (1844).
6.   Fay (1975) gives an excellent account of the typhoon. Data also
     from Bernard (1844), Blake (1960), SFP 30 Sep 1841
7.   Gelber (2004).
8.   Data on *Phlegethon* from IOR/L/PS, SFP.
9.   IOR/L/PS.
10. Ibid.
11. Bernard (1844).

12.   Fay (1975), Waley (1958).
13.   Fay (1975).
14.   Blake (1960).
15.   Hernon (2003).
16.   Bernard (1844).
17.   Gelber (2004), Hanes & Sanello (2002).

Chapter 14

1.   Chinese history largely from Gascoigne (2003), Haw (2005).
2.   Waley (1958).
3.   Ouchterlony (1844).
4.   Waley (1958).
5.   Bernard (1844).
6.   Farwell (1985).
7.   Farwell (1985).
8.   Fay (1975).
9.   Keppel (1899).
10.   Waley (1958).
11.   Fay (1975).
12.   Ibid.
13.   Gregory (2003).
14.   Fay (1975).
15.   Bernard (1844).
16.   Ouchterlony (1844).
17.   Bernard (1846).
18.   Loss of the *Madagascar* largely from Dicey (1842).
19.   Bernard (1844).
20.   Ouchterlony (1844).
21.   Levien (1981).
22.   Wakeman (1966).
23.   Cunynghame (1844).
24.   Fay (1975)
25.   Ouchterlony (1844)

Chapter 15

1. Waley (1958).
2. IOR/L/PS.
3. Bernard (1844).
4. Waley (1958).
5. Ouchterlony (1844).
6. Waley (1958).
7. IOR/L/PS.
8. Bernard (1846).

Chapter 16

1. Fay (1975).
2. Farwell (1973), Fay (1975), Holmes (2005).
3. Data from various sources, as Table 9.
4. Gardiner & Greenhill (1993), Greenhill & Giffard (1994).
5. IOR/L/PS, SFP.
6. Data on these voyages largely from SFP, IOR/L/MAR, Low (1877).
7. SFP.
8. Haw (2005).
9. Keppel (1899).
10. Stuart (1967).
11. Cunynghame (1844).
12. Keppel (1899).
13. Farwell (1985).
14. Keppel (1899).
15. Ouchterlony (1844).
16. Waley (1958).
17. Ouchterlony (1844).
18. Keppel (1899).
19. Bernard (1844).
20. Keppel (1899).
21. Ouchterlony (1844).
22. Cunynghame (1844).
23. Keppel (1899).
24. Levien (1981).
25. Bernard (1844).

26. Forbes (1848).
27. Ouchterlony (1844) gives a full account of that day's campaign.
28. Cunynghame (1844).
29. Levien (1981).
30. Waley (1958).
31. Bernard (1844).
32. Keppel (1899).
33. Bernard (1844).
34. Fay (1975).
35. Ouchterlony (1844).

Chapter 17

1. *See* for example Elleman (2001), Fay (1975).
2. Bernard (1844).
3. Gelber (2004), Gregory (2003), Haw (2005), Wakeman (1966), Wang (2003).
4. Waley (1958).
5. Fay (1975).
6. Cunynghame (1844).
7. Gelber (2004).
8. Fay (1975), Hanes & Sanello (2002).
9. Fay (1975).
10. Hanes & Sanello (2002).
11. Keppel (1899), Levien (1981).
12. Farwell (1973), Holmes (2005).
13. Cunynghame (1844).
14. Holmes (2005).
15. Story of the *Ann* largely from the *Chinese Repository* 12, no. 3 (March 1843):): 113–21, and no.5 (May 1843): 235–48. Also SFP, Ouchterlony (1844), Cunynghame (1844).
16. Bernard (1844).
17. Bernard (1844), Hall (no date), Keppel (1899).
18. Cunynghame (1844).
19. IOR/L/PS, IOR/L/MAR.
20. Bernard (1844).
21. See *Connoisseur* 175, no. 706 ((Dec 1970):): 245.
22. Cunynghame (1844).

23. Cunynghame (1844).
24. SFP.
25. Ibid.
26. Ibid.
27. Hall (no date).
28. Farwell (1985).
29. Bernard (1844).
30. Brown (1978), IOR/L/MAR.
31. SFP.
32. The *Great Britain* largely from Corlett (1975).

Chapter 18.

1. Duff (1968).
2. Grigsby (1953), Lyon & Winfield (2004).
3. Bernard (1846). National Archive censuses give data on Dr Pope but not on Afah.
4. Greenhill & Giffard (1994).
5. Kerr (1992) describes Victoria's second visit to Scotland.
6. Bernard (1846).
7. Details of Hall's life from Anon (1879), Clowes (1901) Vol. 6, *Dictionary of National Biography*, Hall (no date), *ILN* 23 Dec.1854, p. 641–2, O'Byrne (1849).
8. Keppel (1899).
9. Troubetzkoy (2006).
10. *The Sailors' Home Journal*, no. 2 (April 1853): 17.

Chapter 19

1. Dates from SFP and other sources.
2. David (2006) gives a fine account of the building of the Indian empire from Victoria's accession in 1837 to the death of Albert in 1861. Also Hernon (2003).
3. Dalrymple (2013).
4. Farwell (1973).
5. The only existing logs for the *Nemesis* are a few for 1843/44 in IOR/L/MAR.

6. IOR/L/MAR.
7. Ibid.
8. Dates from SFP.
9. IOR/L/MAR.

Chapter 20

1. Hall (1981) for general history, Keay (1991) for HEIC, Tarling (1963).
2. Much has been written about the Brookes of Sarawak. For a biography of James Brooke by one of his friends see St John (1879); for a recent account *see* Barley (2002); for a beautifully illustrated one *see* Reece (2004).
3. Earl (1837).
4. Keppel (1899).
5. Templer (1853).
6. Hall (1958).
7. ST 30 Jan. 1848.
8. Mundy (1848) contains Brooke's own account of his early days in Sarawak.
9. Mundy (1848).

Chapter 21

1. *See* for example Rutter (1930), Tarling (1963, 1993).
2. Trocki (2007).
3. Earl (1837).
4. Keppel (1846).
5. Congalton's life from SFP, Thomson (1864).
6. SFP.
7. St John (1879).
8. Keppel (1846).
9. Mundy (1848).
10. Templer (1853).
11. Keppel (1846).
12. Keppel (1853), Rutter (1930).
13. Belcher (1848), *Dictionary of National Biography*, SFP.
14. Payne (1960), Reece (2004), Runciman (1960).

15. Keppel (1899).
16. Mundy (1848).

Chapter 22

1. Roff (1954), SFP for dates and passengers.
2. Howarth & Howarth (1986) give a well-illustrated account of the history of the P & O, though there are some inaccuracies concerning the early years.
3. Cunynghame (1844).
4. Largely from Rutter (1930).
5. Levien (1981).
6. Ibid.
7. Tarling (1963).
8. Rutter (1930).
9. IOR/L/MAR.
10. Wakeman (1966).
11. Ibid.
12. David (2006), Hernon (2002).
13. Details from SFP.
14. Details from Mundy (1848), St John (1879), Templer (1853).
15. Mundy (1848).
16. Ibid.
17. Mundy (1848). For a history of Labuan as a colony *see* Hall (1958).
18. IOR/L/MAR, SFP.
19. IOR/L/MAR.
20. Rutter (1930).
21. Roff (1954).

Chapter 23

1. The story of the *General Wood* from ST and SFP January to May 1848.
2. Dates from SFP and ST. Visit of Brooke to England from Keppel (1853, 1899), St John (1879)
3. Rabson & O'Donoghue (1988).
4. Wills (2003).

5.   St John (1879).
6.   Keppel (1853).
7.   Data from advertisement for her sale, ST 29 April 1851, Vigors (1849).
8.   Hall (1958), SFP, ST.
9.   Keppel (1853).
10. Hall (1958) gives a readable, if dated and rather fanciful, account of the history of Labuan.
11. St John (1879).
12. IOR/L/MAR.Chapter 24.

Chapter 24

1.   Data from IOR/L/MAR, SFP, ST.
2.   From SFP.
3.   Ibid.
4.   From ST.
5.   Data from Baring-Gould & Bampfylde (1909), Barley (2002), Keppel (1853), Rutter (1930), SFP, ST, St John (1879).
6.   SFP.
7.   Data on the McDougalls largely from McDougall (1882), Saint (1985), Saunders (1992).
8.   McDougall (1882).
9.   SFP.
10. *Straits Times.*
11. Account of Sulu mission largely from SFP, 2 July 1849, and ST.

Chapter 25

1.   Details of Batang Maru from numerous sources including Barley (2002), Keppel (1853), Makepeace *et al* (1921), Runciman (1960), Rutter (1930), SFP, St John (1879), Walker (2002).
2.   Vigors (1849).
3.   Anon (1849).
4.   Vigors (1849).
5.   Rutter (1930). See also Tarling (1963).
6.   Roff (1954), Roff in Gardiner & Greenhill (1993).

7. Keppel (1853).
8. Ibid.
9. China operation from Helms (1882), SFP, ST.
10. Keppel (1853).
11. Particularly by Keppel (1853), but also in a number of books about James Brooke.
12. Keppel (1846, 1853).

Chapter 26

1. Thai history largely from Hall (1981), Manich Jumsai (1999, 2000), Runciman (1960), Tarling (1975).
2. Crawfurd (1828).
3. SFP.
4. Details of the mission largely from Frankfurter (1911), St John (1879), SFP and ST particularly 8 and 18 October 1850
5. Templer (1853).
6. Manich Jumsai (1999).
7. St John (1879).
8. Lyon & Whinfield (2004). Levien (1981) for crew.
9. SFP.
10. Helms (1882).
11. ST 13 April 1852.
12. Roff (1954), Roff in Gardiner & Greenhill (1993).

Chapter 27

1. Myint-U (2007) gives a very readable account of Burmese history from the earliest times to the 21st century. Data also from Hall (1981), Hernon (2003).
2. Hernon (2003).
3. Myint-U (2007).
4. Bird (1897) gives losses due to illness.
5. Laurie (1853).
6. General Campbell in 1828 from Blackburn (2000).
7. Hall (1981).

Chapter 28

1.   Trocki (2007).
2.   SFP.
3.   Data on ships' movements from IOR/L/MAR, SFP, ST.
4.   ST.
5.   Laurie (1853).
6.   Details of war largely from Hall (1981), Hernon (2003), Laurie (1853), dates from SFP, ST.
7.   Laurie (1853).
8.   Laurie (1853), Low (1877).
9.   Cecil (1978).
10.   Sutton (2000).
11.   Quotations from Laurie (1853).
12.   Low (1877).
13.   Ibid.
14.   *Rangoon Chronicle* 16 Feb 1853 in ST 29 March 1853.
15.   Low (1877).
16.   Details of Loch from Keppel (1899), SFP.
17.   Keppel (1899).
18.   ST.
19.   David (2006), Farwell (1985).
20.   Hall (1981).
21.   Myint-U (2007).

Chapter 29

1.   Brown (1993), Gardiner & Lambert (1992), Greenhill & Giffard (1994), Lyon & Winfield (2004).
2.   Troubetzkoy (2006).
3.   Data on ships from Lyon & Winfield (2004).
4.   Gardiner & Greenhill (1993).
5.   Addison & Matthews (1906), Brown (1993).
6.   Data from SFP, ST.
7.   Fogg (2002)
8.   Low (1877)
9.   IOR/L/MAR
10.   Rabson & O'Donoghue (1988).

11. SFP.
12. Data on the last years of the five largely from IOR L/MAR/8/15, the annual Reports of the Bengal Marine Service.
13. Low (1877).
14. ST.
15. SFP.

BIBLIOGRAPHY

Addison, A. C. and W. H. Matthews. *A Deathless Story: The "Birkenhead" and its Heroes*. London: Hutchinson & Co., 1906.

Airy, G. B. "On the Correction of the Compass in Iron-Built Ships." *United Service Journal*, no. 139, part 2 (June 1840): 239–43.

Allom, T, & G. N. Wright, *The Chinese Empire Illustrated*. London: Fisher, Son & Co. 1859.

Anon. *Builders of Great Ships*. Birkenhead: Cammel Laird & Co., 1959

———. "List of Royal Navy ships in commission 1st May 1840 with ratings, ages, yards built." *United Services Journal*, no. 139, part 2 (June 1840): 137–9.

———. "Pirates of the Indian Archipelago." *United Services Magazine*, part 3 (1849): 574–88.

———. "Obituary: Admiral Sir William Hutcheon Hall, F.R.S., K.C.B." *Proceedings of the Royal Geographical Society & Monthly Record of Geography* 1, no. 3 (March 1879): 214–16.

———. *Ships' Miscellany: A Guide to the Royal Navy of Jack Aubrey*. London: Michael O'Mara Books Ltd, 2003.

Bagwell, P. S. *The Transport Revolution from 1770*. London: Batsford, 1974.

Baring-Gould, S. and C. A. Bampfylde. *A History of Sarawak under Its Two White Rajahs 1839–1908*. London: Henry Southeran & Co., 1909. Reprint, Singapore: Oxford University Press, 1989.

Barley, N. *White Rajah*. London: Little Brown, 2002.

Beeching, Jack. *The Chinese Opium Wars*. London: Hutchinson, 1975.

Belcher, Capt Sir E. *Narrative of the Voyage of H.M.S. Samarang, during the years 1843–46*. London: 2 vols. Reprint, London: Dawsons, 1970

Bernard, W. D. *Narrative of the Voyages and Services of the Nemesis from 1840 to 1843; and of the Combined Naval and Military Operations in China: Comprising a Complete Account of the Colony of Hong Kong,* and *Remarks on the Character and Habits of the Chinese*. 2 vols. London: Henry Colburn, 1844.

Bernard, W. D. *Narrative of the Voyages and Services of the Nemesis from 1840 to 1843; and of the Combined Naval and Military Operations in China: Comprising a Complete Account of the Colony of Hong Kong, and Remarks on the Character and Habits of the Chinese*. 2nd ed. 1 vol, Henry Colburn, London, 1845.

————. *The Nemesis in China, Comprising a History of the Late War in that Country; with a Complete Account of the Colony of Hong Kong*. 3rd ed. 1 vol. London: Henry Colburn, 1846.

Bird, G. W. *Wanderings in Burma*. London: Bright & Simpkin, 1897 Reprint, Bangkok: White Lotus Press, 2001.

Blackburn, T. R. *The British Humiliation of Burma*. Bangkok: Orchid Press, 2000.

Blake, C. *Charles Elliot R.N., 1801–1875*. London: Cleaver-Hume Press, 1960.

Blake, R. *Jardine Matheson. Traders of the Far East*. London: Weidenfeld & Nicolson, 1999.

Brown, D. K. "Nemesis: The First Iron Warship." *Warship,* no. 8 (October 1978): 283–5.

————. *Paddle Warships: The Earliest Steam Powered Fighting Ships*. London: Conway Maritime Press, 1993.

Cecil, D. *A Portrait of Jane Austen*. London: Constable, 1978.

Clowes, W. L. *The Royal Navy: A History*. Vol. 6. London: Sampson Low, Marsten & Co., 1901.

Cochrane, Admiral Lord. *Memoirs of a Fighting Captain*. Edited by B. Vale. London: Folio Society, 2005.

Cook, C. *Britain in the Nineteenth Century 1815–1914*. London: Longman, 1999.

Corlett, E. *The Iron Ship*. Bradford-on-Avon: Moonraker Press, 1975.

Crawfurd, J. *Journal of an Embassy from the Governor-General of India to the Courts of Siam and Cochin China; Exhibiting a View of the Actual States of those Kingdoms*. London: Henry Colburn, 1828. Reprint, New Delhi: Asian Educational Services, 2000.

Creuze, A. F. B. "On the *Nemesis* Private Armed Steamer, and on the Comparative Efficiency of Iron-Built and Timber-Built Ships." *United Service Journal,* no. 138, part 2 (May 1840): 90–100.

Crump, T. *A Brief History of the Age of Steam*. London: Constable & Robinson, 2007.

Cunynghame, A. T. *An Aide-de-camp's Recollections of Service in China.* 2 vols. London: Saunders & Otley, 1844 Reprint, London: Elibron Classics, 2005

David, S. *Victoria's Wars: The Rise of Empire.* London: Penguin Books, 2006.

Dicey, J. M. "Letter to Admiral Sir William Parker dated 19 January 1842." *Chinese Repository* 11, no. 12 (Dec. 1842): 633–43.

Duff, D. *Victoria in the Highlands.* London: Frederick Muller, 1968.

Earl, G. W. *The Eastern Seas.* London: W. H. Allen & Co., 1837. Reprint, Singapore: Oxford University Press, 1971

Farwell, B. *Queen Victoria's Little Wars.* London: Allen Lane-Penguin, 1973.

———. *Eminent Victorian Soldiers: Seekers of Glory.* New York: W. W. Norton & Co., 1985.

Fay, P. W. *The Opium War, 1840–1842.* Chapel Hill: University of North Carolina Press, 1975 (paperback edition 1997).

Flanders, J. *Consuming Passions. Leisure and Pleasure in Victorian Britain.* London: Harper Perennial, 2006.

Fogg, N. *The Voyages of the Great Britain: Life at Sea in the World's First Liner.* London: Chatham Publishing, 2002.

Forbes, F. E. *Five Years in China, from 1842 to 1847, with an Account of the Occupation of the Islands of Labuan and Borneo by Her Majesty's Forces.* London: Richard Bentley, 1848.

Frankfurter, O. "Sir James Brooke in Siam (1850)." *Journal of the Siam Society* 8, no. 3 (1911). Reprinted in *Sarawak Museum Journal* 10, no. 17–18 (1961): 32–42.

Freeman, M. *Railways and the Victorian Imagination.* New Haven & London: Yale University Press, 1999.

Fremont-Barnes, G. *Nelson's Sailors.* Oxford: Osprey Publishing, 2005.

Galbraith, J. "Narrative of the Storming of the Chinese Forts." *United Services Journal,* no. 151 part 2 (1841): 239–45.

Gardiner, R. and B. Greenhill, ed. *The Advent of Steam: the Merchant Steamship Before 1900.* London: Conway Maritime Press, 1993.

Gardiner, R. and A. Lambert, ed. *Steam, Steel and Shellfire: The Steam Warship, 1815–1905.* London: Conway Maritime Press, 1992.

Gascoigne, B. *A Brief History of the Dynasties of China.* Rev. ed. London: Robinson, 2003.

Gelber, H. G. *Opium, Soldiers and Evangelicals: Britain's 1840–42 War with China, and its Aftermath.* Basingstoke: Palgrave Macmillan, 2004.

Gibson-Hill, C. A. "The Steamers Employed in Asian Waters, 1819–39." *Journal of the Malayan Branch of the Royal Asiatic Society* 27, part 1, (1954):120–62.

Gill, A. *Ruling Passions: Sex, Race and Empire*. London: BBC Books, 1995.

Goodman, J. *The Rattlesnake: A Voyage of Discovery to the Coral Sea*. London: Faber & Faber, 2005.

Greenhill, B. and A. Giffard. *Travelling by Sea in the Nineteenth Century: Interior Design in Victorian Passenger Ships*. London: A. & C. Black, 2005.

———. *Steam, Politics and Patronage: The Transformation of the Royal Navy 1815–1854*. London: Conway Maritime Press, 1994.

Gregory, J. S. *The West and China since 1500*. London: Palgrave Macmillan, 2003.

Griffiths, D. *Steam at Sea: Two Centuries of Steam-Powered Ships*. London: Conway Maritime Press, 1997.

Grigsby, J. E. *Annals of our Royal Yachts 1604–1953*. London: Adland Coles Ltd/G.G.Harrap & Co Ltd, 1953

Guest, J. S. *The Euphrates Expedition*. London & New York: Kegan Paul International, 1992.

Hall, B. *Account of a Voyage of Discovery to the West Coast of Corea & the Great Loo-Choo Island*. London: John Murray, 1818. Reprint, Uckfield: Rediscovery Books, 2006.

Hall, D. G. E. *A History of South-East Asia*. 4th ed. London:Palgrave Macmillan, 1981.

Hall, M. *Labuan Story*. Jesselton: Chung Nam Printing Company, 1958. Reprint Kuala Lumpur: Synergy Media, 2007.

Hall, W. H. Diary and assorted papers. Manuscript ref JOD/124. National Maritime Museum, London.

Hanes, W. T. and F. Sanello. *The Opium Wars*. Naperville: Sourcebooks, 2002.

Haw, S. G. *A Traveller's History of China*. 4th ed. London: Phoenix Paperbacks, 2005.

Helms, L.V. *Pioneering in the Far East*. London: W. H. Allen & Co., 1882.

Hernon, I. *Britain's Forgotten Wars: Colonial Campaigns of the 19th Century*. Stroud: Sutton Publishing, 2003.

Hollett, D. *Men of Iron: The Story of Cammel Laird Shipbuilders, 1828–1991*. Birkenhead: Countyvise Ltd. 1992.

———. *The Conquest of the Niger by Land and Sea*. Abergavenny: P. M. Heaton Publishing, 1995.

Holmes, R. *Sahib: The British Soldier in India, 1750–1914*. London: Harper Collins, 2005.

Hope, R. *Poor Jack: The Perilous History of the Merchant Seaman*. London: Chatham Publishing, 2001.

Howarth, D. and S. Howarth. *The Story of P & O*. London: Weidenfelt & Nicholson, 1986.

India Office Marine Records. Papers. IOR/L/MAR. British Library, London.

India Office Records. Private papers. IOR/L/PS. British Library, London.

Jacobs, E. M. *In Pursuit of Pepper and Tea: The Story of the Dutch East India Company*. Amsterdam: Netherlands Maritime Museum, 1991.

Keay, J. *The Honourable Company: A History of the English East India Company*. London: Harper Collins, 1991.

———. *India: A History*. London: Harper Perennial, 2000.

———. *The Spice Route*. London: John Murray, 2005.

Kemp, P., ed. *The Oxford Companion to Ships and the Sea*. Oxford: Oxford University Press, 1976.

Keppel, H. *The Expedition to Borneo of HMS Dido for the Suppression of Piracy: with Extracts from the Journal of James Brooke, Esq*. 2 vols. London: Chapman & Hall, 1846. Reprinted in one vol., Singapore: Oxford University Press, 1991.

———. *A Visit to the Indian Archipelago, in HM Ship Maeander with Portions of the Private Journal of Sir James Brooke, K.C.B*. 2 vols. London: Richard Bentley, 1853. Reprint, London: Elibron Classics, 2003.

———. *A Sailor's Life under Four Sovereigns*. 3 vols. London: Macmillan & Co., 1899.

Kerr, J. *Queen Victoria's Scottish Diaries...her Dream Days*. London: Brockhampton Press, 1992.

Laurie, W. F. B. *The Second Burmese War: a Narrative of Operations at Rangoon, in 1852*. London: Smith, Elder & Co., 1853. Reprint, Bangkok: Orchid Press, 2002.

Lavery, B. *Life in Nelson's Navy*. Stroud: Sutton Publishing, 2007.

Levien, M., ed. *The Cree Journals. The Voyages of Edward H. Cree, Surgeon R. N., as Related in his Private Journals, 1837–1856*. Exeter: Webb & Bower, 1981.

Low, C. C., ed. *The Opium War*. Singapore: Canfonian Pte Ltd, 1994.

Low, C. R. *History of the Indian Navy (1613–1863)*. 2 vols. London: Richard Bentley & Son, 1877. Reprint, Portsmouth: Royal Naval Museum, and 1990; London: London Stamp Exchange, 1990.

Lyon, D. and R. Winfield. *The Sail and Steam Navy List: All the Ships of the Royal Navy 1815–1889*. London: Chatham House Publishing, 2004.

Macartney, Lord. *An Embassy to China; Being the Journal kept by Lord Macartney during his Embassy to the Emperor Ch'ien-lung 1793–1794*. Edited by J. L. Cranmer-Byng. London: Folio Society, 2004.

Makepeace, W., G. E. Brooke and R. St J. Braddell. *One Hundred Years of Singapore*. London: John Murray, 1921. Reprint, Singapore: Oxford University Press, 1991.

Manich Jumsai, M. L. *King Mongkut of Thailand and the British*. 4th ed. Bangkok: Chalermnit, 1999.

———. *History of Anglo-Thai Relations*. 6th ed. Bangkok: Chalermnit, 2000.

McDougall, H. *Sketches of our Life at Sarawak*. London: SPCK, 1882. Reprint, Singapore: Oxford University Press, 1992.

McMurray, H. C. *Old Order, New Thing*. London: HMSO, 1972.

Moore, Joseph. *Eighteen Views Taken At Or Near Rangoon*. London: Thomas Clay, 1825.

Moxham, R. *Tea: Addiction, Exploitation and Empire*. London: Robinson, 2003.

Mundy, R. *Narrative of Events in Borneo and Celebes down to the Occupation of Labuan, from the Journals of James Brooke Esq., Rajah of Sarawak and Governor of Labuan, together with a Narrative of the Operations of HMS* Iris. 2 vols. London: John Murray, 1848.

Myint-U, Thant. *The River of Lost Footsteps: A Personal History of Burma*. London: Faber & Faber, 2007.

O'Byrne, W. R. *A Naval Biographical Dictionary*. London: John Murray, 1849. Third edition, Suffolk: J. B. Hayward & Son, 1990.

Ouchterlony, J. *The Chinese War: an Account of all the Operations of the British Forces from the Commencement to the Treaty of Nanking*. London: Saunders & Otley, 1844. Reprint, Uckfield:Naval & Military Press, 2004.

Payne, R. *The White Rajahs of Sarawak*. London: Robert Hale Ltd., 1960. Reprint, Oxford University Press, 1986.

Pool, D. *What Jane Austen Ate and Charles Dickens Knew*. New York: Touchstone, 1993.

Rabson, S. and K. O'Donoghue. *P & O: A Fleet History*. Kendal: World Ship Society, 1988.

Reece, B. *The White Rajahs of Sarawak: A Borneo Dynasty*. Singapore: Archipelago Press, 2004.

Roff, W. J. "Mr T. Wallace, Commanding H. C. Str. *Nemesis*." *Sarawak Museum Journal* 6, no. 4, 1–8.

Rowland, K. T. *Steam at Sea: A History of Steam Navigation*. Newton Abbot: David & Charles, 1970.

Runciman, S. *The White Rajahs*. Cambridge: Cambridge University Press, 1960.

Rutter, O. *The Pirate Wind: Tales of the Sea-Robbers of Malaya*. London: Hutchinson, 1930. Reprint, Singapore: Oxford University Press, 1986.

Saint, M. *Twenty Years in Sarawak 1848–68: A Flourish for the Bishop and Brooke's Friend Grant*. Devon: Merlin Books, 1985.

Saunders, G. *Bishops and Brookes: The Anglican Mission and the Brooke Raj in Sarawak 1848–1941*. Singapore: Oxford University Press, 1992.

SFP. *Singapore Free Press & Mercantile Advertiser*. Published in Singapore from 1 October 1835 to 1869. Edited by William Napier 1835–46, then by Abraham Logan until at least 1866.

Smith, E. C. *A Short History of Naval and Marine Engineering*. Cambridge: Babcock & Wilcox Ltd.; Cambridge University Press, 1937.

ST. *Straits Times*. Published in Singapore from 15 July 1845 to present day. Edited by Robert Carr Woods 1845–60.

St John, S. *The Life of Sir James Brooke, Rajah of Sarawak*. London: Blackwood, 1879. Reprint, Kuala Lumpur: Oxford University Press, 1994.

Stuart, V. *The Beloved Little Admiral: The Life and Times of Admiral of the Fleet the Hon. Sir Henry Keppel, G.C.B., O.M., D.C.L., 1809–1904*. London: Robert Hale, 1967.

Sun Tzu. *The Art of War*. Translated by T. Cleary. Boston: Shambhala Publishing, 1988.

Sutton, J. *Lords of the East: The East India Company and its Ships (1600–1874)*. Rev. ed. London: Conway Maritime Press, 2000.

Tarling, N. *Piracy and Politics in the Malay World*. Melbourne: F. W. Cheshire, 1963.

———.*Imperial Britain in South-East Asia*. Kuala Lumpur: Oxford University Press, 1975.

———.*The Fall of Imperial Britain in South-East Asia*. Singapore: Oxford University Press, 1993.

Tate, D. J. M. *Rajah Brooke's Borneo*. Hong Kong: John Nicholson Ltd., 1988.

Templer. J. C.,ed. *The Private Letters of Sir James Brooke K. C. B. Rajah of Sarawak, Narrating the Events of his Life from 1838 to the Present Time*. 3 vols. London: Richard Bentley, 1853. Reprinted vol. 1, Montana: Kessinger Publishing, 2007.

Thomson, J. T. *Glimpses into Life in Malayan Lands*. London: Richardson & Co., 1864. Reprint, Singapore: Oxford University Press, 1984.

Trocki, C. A. *Prince of Pirates: The Temenggongs and the Development of Johor and Singapore 1784–1885*. 2nd ed. Singapore: National University of Singapore Press, 2007.

Troubetzkoy. A. *A Brief History of the Crimean War*. London: Robinson, 2006.

Vigors, B. U. "Letter to the Editor". *Illustrated London News*, 10 November 1849. Reprinted in *Tate*, 1988.

Wakeman, F. *Strangers at the Gate: Social Disorder in South China, 1839–1861*. Berkeley: University of California Press, 1966.

Waley, A. *The Opium War through Chinese Eyes*. London: George Allen & Unwin, 1958.

Walker, C. F. *Young Gentlemen: The Story of Midshipmen from the 17th Century to the Present Day*. London: Longmans, Green & Co., 1938.

Walker, J. H. *Power and Prowess: The origins of Brooke Kingship in Sarawak*. Crows Nest: Allen & Unwin, 2002.

Wang Gungwu. *Anglo-Chinese Encounters since 1800: War, Trade, Science and Governance*. Cambridge: Cambridge University Press, 2003.

West, A. *Memoir of Sir Henry Keppel, GCB, Admiral of the Fleet*. London: Smith, Elder & Co., 1905.

Wills, C. *High Society: The Life and Art of Sir Francis Grant, 1803–1878*. Edinburgh: National Galleries of Scotland, 2003.

Wilson, D. *The Circumnavigators: a History*. Rev. ed. New York: Carroll & Graf Publishers, 2003.

Winter, F. H. *The First Golden Age of Rocketry*. Washington: Smithsonian Institution Press, 1990.

Wolmar, C. *Fire & Steam: A New History of the Railways in Britain*. London: Atlantic Books, 2007.

INDEX